D1368925

Scotch whisky distilleries, located by number on the map on the facing page,
followed in each case by the name of the owner/licensee, included in Chapter 9.
For Speyside and Glenlivet malt distilleries, see back end papers.

Eastern malt distilleries

1 North Port (Brechin) *Mitchell Bros Ltd*
2 Fettercairn *The Fettercairn Distillery Co. Ltd*
3 Glencadam *George Ballantine & Son Ltd*
4 Glenesk (formerly Hillside) *Wm Sanderson & Son Ltd*
5 Glen Garioch *Stanley P. Morrison Ltd*
6 Glenugie *Long John International Ltd*
7 Glenury-Royal *John Gillon & Co. Ltd*
8 Lochnagar *John Begg Ltd*
9 Lochside *Macnab Distilleries Ltd*

Northern malt distilleries

10 Balblair *Balblair Distillery Co. Ltd*
11 Ben Nevis *Ben Nevis Distillery (Fort William) Ltd*
12 Ben Wyvis *The Invergordon Distillers Ltd*
13 Brora *Ainslie & Heilbron (Distillers) Ltd*
14 Clynelish *Ainslie & Heilbron (Distillers) Ltd*
15 Dalmore *Mackenzie Brothers, Dalmore*
16 Dalwhinnie *James Buchanan & Co. Ltd*
17 Glen Albyn *Scottish Malt Distillers Ltd*
18 Glenlochy *Scottish Malt Distillers Ltd*
19 Glen Mhor *Scottish Malt Distillers Ltd*
20 Glenmorangie *The Glenmorangie Distillery Co.*
21 Millburn *Macleay, Duff (Distillers) Ltd*
22 Ord *John Dewar & Sons Ltd*
23 Pulteney *James & George Stodart Ltd*
24 Royal Brackla *John Bisset & Co. Ltd*
25 Teaninich *R.H. Thomson & Co. (Distillers) Ltd*
26 Tomatin *Tomatin Distillers PLC*

Perthshire malt distilleries

27 Aberfeldy *John Dewar & Sons Ltd*
28 Blair Athol *Arthur Bell & Sons PLC*
29 Deanston *Deanston Distillers Ltd*
30 Edradour *William Whiteley & Co.*
31 Glengoyne *Lang Brothers Ltd*
32 Glenturret *Glenturret Distillery Ltd*
33 Loch Lomond *Barton Distilling (Scotland) Ltd*
34 Tullibardine *Tullibardine Distillery Co. Ltd*

The Island malt distilleries

35 Highland Park *James Grant & Co. Ltd*
36 Isle of Jura *Isle of Jura Distillery Co. Ltd*
37 Oban *John Hopkins & Co. Ltd*
38 Scapa *Taylor & Ferguson Ltd*
39 Talisker *Scottish Malt Distillers Ltd*
40 Tobermory *Tobermory Distillers Ltd*

Lowland malt distilleries

41 Auchentoshan *The Eadie Cairns Group*
42 Bladnoch *Bladnoch Distillery Ltd*
43 Inverleven *Hiram Walker & Sons PLC*
44 Ladyburn *Wm Grant & Sons Ltd*
45 Littlemill *Barton Distilling (Scotland) Ltd*
46 Lomond *Hiram Walker & Sons PLC*
47 Moffat *Inver House Distillers Ltd*
48 Glenkinchie *John Haig & Co. Ltd*
49 Rosebank *The Distillers Agency Ltd*
50 St Magdalene *Wm Greer & Co.*

Islay malt distilleries

51 Ardbeg *Ardbeg Distillery Ltd*
52 Bowmore *Stanley P. Morrison Ltd*
53 Bruichladdich *Bruichladdich Distillery Co. Ltd*
54 Bunnahabhain *The Highland Distilleries Co. PLC*
55 Caol Ila *Bulloch Lade & Co. Ltd*
56 Lagavulin *White Horse Distilleries Ltd*
57 Laphroaig *D. Johnston & Co. Ltd*
58 Port Ellen *Low, Robertson & Co. Ltd*

Campbeltown malt distilleries

50 Glen Scotia *A. Gillies & Co. (Distillers) Ltd*
60 Springbank *J. & A. Mitchell & Co. Ltd*

Grain distilleries

61 Caledonian *Scottish Grain Distillers Ltd*
62 Cambus *Scottish Grain Distillers Ltd*
63 Cameron Bridge *Scottish Grain Distillers Ltd/ John Haig & Co. Ltd*
64 Carsebridge *Scottish Grain Distillers Ltd*
65 Dumbarton *Hiram Walker & Sons PLC*
66 Invergordon *The Invergordon Distillers Ltd*
67 North British *The North British Distillery Co. Ltd*
68 North of Scotland *North of Scotland Distilling Co. Ltd*
69 Port Dundas *Scottish Grain Distillers Ltd*
70 Strathclyde *Long John International Ltd*

THE Schweppes® GUIDE TO SCOTCH

Philip Morrice

Alphabooks

for Gillian

In an industry in which changes are always occurring, the accuracy of factual material constantly needs updating. The author and publishers of 'The Schweppes Guide to Scotch' would be grateful for information regarding changes for incorporation in future editions of this book.

This book was designed and produced by Alphabet and Image Ltd, Sherborne, Dorset, England

Line Drawings by Peter Haillay

First published in England in 1983 by Alphabooks, Sherborne, Dorset, England

ISBN 0 906670 11 X (hardback)

ISBN 0 906670 29 2 (paperback)

Filmset by Margaret Spooner Typesetting, Dorchester, Dorset, England
Printed and bound by Butler & Tanner Ltd, Frome, Somerset, England

Contents

Long John's Glenugie distillery

If a body can just find oot the exac' proper proportion and quantity that ought to be drunk every day and keep to that, I verily throw that he might leeve forever without dying at all, and that doctors and kirkyards would go oot o' fashion.

James Hogg

1 The cup that cheers

To ask for 'Scotch' in Scotland is to identify yourself as a stranger. Whisky means different things to different people in different places. Only in Scotland will the request for 'a whisky' guarantee that you are served with the native spirit, Scotch: the subject of this book. It is not about Irish whiskey (note the different spelling), although the book later describes the very real rivalry that once existed between Scotch and Irish. Nor is it concerned directly with the whiskies of North America, be they the straight Bourbon, Corn or Rye whiskies, or the many varieties of blended whiskies of the United States, or the excellent whiskies of Canada. However, the impact of whisky distilling on North America must be part of the story of Scotch, since a significant chunk of the Scottish industry has at various times been in American or Canadian hands, with the Canadians now enjoying control over an important segment of it. We are not concerned, either, with Japanese whisky, although we must remember the importance to the Scotch whisky industry of the large quantity of malt whisky sold in bulk to Japan in order to give character to the Japanese product. Likewise, malt whisky goes into the whisky production of a surprising number of other countries, as described in Chapter 8. First of all, however, we must define the true product in its three principal forms.

Malt whisky

Malt whisky is the separate and distinctive product of each of the 117 malt whisky distilleries established in Scotland at the time of writing. Some of these are currently out of production due to world economic factors, but this is hoped to be a temporary phenomenon. Each of the individual malt whiskies thus produced comprises unique characteristics which reflect the peculiar combination of geographical, physical and human factors which make up the production unit known as the distillery, and which have never been duplicated by any other distillery no matter how close in location, how alike in size or design or how similar in patterns of production. This is perhaps the greatest mystery attached to Scotch whisky, and contributes greatly to the romance surrounding the product.

The malt distilleries are concentrated in the Highlands, and above all in Speyside in the north-east of Scotland. The 'Highland Line' runs, very roughly, from just north of Glasgow diagonally north-eastwards across the country to just north of Dundee, and the products of all pot malt distilleries located on or above this line are called Highland malts. There are ninety-seven of these, and they can be grouped into Speysides, Glenlivets, Eastern Malts, Northern Malts, Perthshire Malts and Island Malts. The rest of the malt whiskies from elsewhere in Scotland fall into three clear categories: ten Lowland malts, eight Islay malts and two Campbeltown malts. The location of these distilleries is shown in the maps inside the front and back covers of this book, together with the owner or licensee of each distillery.

The term *single malt* refers to the bottling of the product of an individual malt whisky distillery, for sale in its unadulterated, unblended and original form after due time has been allowed for the whisky to mature. Although there are 117 malt whisky distilleries, there are not, alas, 117 bottled single malts, since some malt distilleries allocate their entire production for blending. Fortunately, the number of distillers bottling their malts at a suitable age is growing, and a few enterprising whisky merchants purchase mature malt whisky and bottle it themselves for retail purposes. Thus, there are over ninety single malts currently on the UK market, with rather fewer available overseas. A lucky chance may turn up rare bottles of other malt whiskies which have been bottled on a limited scale or for private purposes. The drinking of malt whisky, long restricted largely to Scotland, is now spreading as an increasing number of mature palates insist on what many would claim is the *only* true Scotch whisky. Part of the attraction is in the variety of whiskies available and the range of ages at which some single malts are bottled. Glenfarclas, for instance, can be bought at 8, 12, 15, 21 and 25 years old. Aberlour-Glenlivet has, to my knowledge, been available at different times as 8, 9, 10 and 12 years old. Some malt whiskies are sold at different strengths — 10 years old Macallan can be bought at both 70° and 100° proof.

Although total bottled malt whisky sales represent only about 2 per cent of the UK market for Scotch, and just over 1 per cent of the entire world market, demand is expected to grow, and in a few years the range of available brands, at least in Britain, has multiplied. The three top selling malts world-wide are Glenfiddich, The Glenlivet and Glen Grant, in that order. But increased sales as a result of growing popularity brings problems, not least because of limited production and the difficulty of meeting a demand for whisky of a particular age. Thus, Glenfiddich started off as a 10 years old, then became 8 years old and it sometimes carries no age description whatsoever. The popularity of the whisky, in spite of its modesty about its age, has caused no loss of confidence on the part of the consumer: this is, however, the risk a 'rare' malt could run if it becomes too widely available too quickly.

Mature malt whisky has three possible fates — some is drunk as a single malt as already described, the majority is blended with other malts to which are added varying quantities of grain whisky, and the rest is married with a selection of other malts only and bottled as a *vatted malt*. This is an available option when the entire production of an unspectacular malt has not been sold for blending, and the distiller is doubtful that it will hold its own against strong competition in the single malt field. Some vatted malts are very good indeed — Duncraggan, Glen Drummond, Glenleven, Mar Lodge, Pride of Strathspey, Royal Culross, Strathconon are some examples — and many others have a high reputation and are determined to keep it. But one should be quite clear what one is buying and this is rarely evident from the labels. Normally all that is known about a vatted malt from the label is that it contains only malt whisky, from a variety of distilleries. It will not say how many different whiskies have been used, but often it will say how old they are. This age means that *every* whisky which has been vatted (to make up what is, in effect, a blend of malts) must be at least as old as the label states. A good vatted malt has much to commend it, providing the marrying of the malts has been done with care and expertise, since an unhappy combination of single malts can produce an unsatisfactory result. Sometimes a particular single malt predominates, as in the case where the proprietor of the whisky distillery does not usually market his malt bottled in single form: an example is Glenforres, which is Edradour malt vatted with one other malt. The number of vatted malts is on the increase as malt whisky takes on a wider appeal, and new brands appear regularly. Those brands which are known to be vatted malts are indicated as such under the individual company entries in Chapter 9.

Grain whisky

Grain whisky is often characterised as a colourless, featureless neutral spirit whose contribution to Scotch whisky has been exclusively as a blending agent. Whilst this is largely correct it is not the whole truth, otherwise there would not be the small but devoted band of *aficionados* who choose it for preference. Given the entrenched position of the blended whiskies and the cult movement in favour of the malts, there is not much chance of a large swing towards grain whisky drinking, but even so, one brand of pure grain whisky is still bottled — John Haig's Choice Old Cameron Brig from their Cameron Bridge Distillery in Fife. Those involved in distilling insist that grain whiskies have characteristics all of their own, and I would not deny it. Some are more flavoursome than others, which is why, no doubt, at least one whisky merchant, George Strachan Ltd, goes to the trouble of occasionally bottling North of Scotland Grain.

By contrast with the malt distilleries, Scotland's grain distilleries are concentrated in the southern half of the country, with the notable exception of Invergordon. The output of a grain distillery is enormous compared with the average traditional malt distillery, and it is not surprising, therefore, that there are only fourteen. They do not have the same physical and environmental requirements of a malt whisky distillery, and their location and size are more matters of strictly commercial consideration.

Of the fourteen, three distilleries have potential for both malt and grain production: Ben Nevis and Lochside producing Highland malts, and Moffat being also a Lowland malt distillery.

The production of the grain distilleries is used for blending, but only after the whisky has been aged for the statutory three years minimum. Grain whiskies are sold to the blenders in the same way as the malts, and it is interesting that the bulk of grain whisky is produced by companies prominent in the blending side of the industry.

Blended whisky

This is the Scotch that most people know, with a bewildering range of brands and an almost infinite number of variations of blends. It is a marriage of a variety of malts with one or more grain whiskies. The division into standard and De Luxe or premium blends does not bear close examination, particularly with the appearance of sub-standard, i.e. lower strength, and Super De Luxe brands. The classification is somewhat arbitrary anyway, since it is made by the brand proprietors who sometimes employ their own descriptions such as 'fine', 'old' or 'rare', without defining them.

Those who promote De Luxe blends will argue that they contain a very high proportion of malt whisky to grain. Malt whisky is much more expensive than grain whisky because of a more complicated production process and because it usually requires longer maturation before it can be used to the blender's satisfaction. Moreover, one ton of maize used in grain whisky distilling is roughly half the price of one ton of malted barley used in pot-still malt distilling. The higher price demanded for De Luxe whiskies is, therefore, justified if there is an uncommonly high proportion of malts. Unfortunately, few blenders will say how much malt to grain there is in his product. It is worth checking when buying a De Luxe whisky to see if it has a minimum age on the bottle. Many De Luxe whiskies are marked 10, 12, 15, 21 or even 25 years old. One can then be sure that all of the whiskies in the blend, including the grain, are at least as old as the label states, and that the proportion of malt will be reasonably high: usually at least 50 per cent. Even this does not give a cast-iron guarantee of quality, since some malts are better 'marriers' than others, whilst some mature (and so become ready for blending) more quickly. Thus, there is no single rule which determines that a blend which contains a greater proportion of malts, or malts of a greater age, is better than a blend containing less or younger malts. But age is, nevertheless, some sort of guide.

Those so-called De Luxe whiskies which claim this accolade through little other than their own advertising may have nothing special to offer regarding the proportion of malts to grain or the age of the whiskies in the blend, and may not be worth the extra cost over and above the price of a standard blend. Indeed, such is the power of persuasive advertising and promotion that some of the standard blends have been able to inch up their prices so as to occupy the middle ground in price terms between the standard and the De Luxe blends. Some of these are very good whiskies indeed, and some are lucky to be so favoured.

The Super De Luxe brands stand apart on price alone, but they are usually very fine whiskies, often being of great age. Examples are Bell's Royal Reserve 20 years old, Chivas Royal Salute 21 years old and Johnnie Walker Swing.

Age is a much less important factor in standard blends, most of which are 4 years old, although some, such as Mackinlays, are 5 years old while others, rarely advertising the fact, are merely the statutory minimum of 3 years old. In the area of standard blends there is a constant battle amongst the producers to establish new loyalties among the members of the whisky-drinking public. So well entrenched are the market leaders that it is difficult for a new brand to make much impression. However, market shares vary considerably between Scotland, Britain as a whole, and the United States, as later chapters show.

The recent history of the everyday bottle of Scotch in Britain has not been entirely happy. Cut-throat competition, and a desire by many companies to get their brands on to the supermarket shelves, in a rather undignified rush, leads to tiny profit margins — as low as 1.5 per cent — and a certain debasing of this highly regarded product. Whilst slimmed-down profits mean a good price for the consumer, there is a serious danger of damage to the image of the product which has long reigned supreme as the most prestigious spirit in the world.

With an industry confronted by an ever deepening 'whisky loch' the temptation to move some of their 'liquid assets' has been too much for certain companies. They have challenged the smaller blenders, traditionally occupying the lower end of the market, by launching cheaper brands rather than allowing a downward floating in the price of their main brands. Thus, new brands such as Claymore, Glen Clova, King's Royal, C. & J. McDonald, and refurbished 'sleepers' such as Braemar and Old Mull, have appeared on the scene at cut-to-the-bone prices, often alongside the major label of the parent company. Whether the 'cheapies', as they are known, contain less mature whiskies or are in fact the same as the standard brands with a different label, could be an interesting exercise in consumer research but some of them, including those named, are certainly acceptable as everyday drinking whisky.

This is not an entirely new challenge for the distillers, as they have long faced a similar situation in the European market place against low-priced locally bottled Scotch whiskies, such as Label 5, one of the top selling Scotch whiskies in France, Double Q in Germany, and Francis and W5 in Italy, plus the array of hyper- and supermarket own-label whiskies.

Overseas the pattern varies from country to country, where brand leadership will often depend on the energy and success of the local agent. Worldwide, however, Johnnie Walker Red Label still claims to be the biggest selling Scotch, despite its withdrawal entirely from the British market owing to the need for the Distillers Company PLC (DCL) to comply with an EEC ruling, but more about that tale later.

There are more than 1000 brands currently available in the UK and export markets at the time of writing. Many are found in only a handful of countries and never in Britain; others have a worldwide reputation. There are far more standard blends of Scotch whisky than De Luxe blends. My reckoning is that the total number of registered brands, many of which are inactive or appear inter-mittently, approaches 2000, and these may be found in the index.

Whisky liqueurs

The whisky liqueurs are a mixture of malt whisky, honey and herbs, although the ingredients and the precise proportions vary from product to product and are a closely guarded secret of the proprietor. Those currently available are: Drambuie (owned by the Drambuie Liqueur Co. Ltd), Dunkeld Atholl Brose (Gordon & MacPhail), Glayva (Ronald Morrison & Co. Ltd), Glen Mist (Glen Mist Liqueur Co./Hallgarten), Lochan Ora (Chivas Bros Ltd), Loch Lomond (Barton Distilling (Scotland) Ltd) and Sconie (Sconie Liqueur Co./ADP PLC), and certainly more will follow.

When and how to drink it

Having shown that Scotch whisky offers a wealth of choice, it is worth considering how best to enjoy this drink which so many claim to be the cleanest and most reliable of all spirits.

A Scot will take his whisky at any hour of the day. However, it is particularly good just before lunch or dinner or in the late evening, and these are the traditional imbibing times in Scotland. Scotch can, in fact, be drunk with a meal, whether it be a humble sandwich or *haute cuisine*, since it will never spoil the taste of good food or be affected in its turn by strongly flavoured dishes. A good malt compares well in price with Cognac and is, some say, often superior as an after-dinner aid to digestion. If, however, single malts — and perhaps even the best of the De Luxe blends — are to become serious challenges to Cognac and liqueurs for after-dinner drinking, a special glass needs to be designed for straight sipping. Bowmore Islay Malt ran a competition to find the ideal-shaped malt whisky glass and did, in the end, come up with a rather pleasing design, but whether it will become widely adopted is another matter.

As an aperitif, Scotch whisky is extremely satisfying with a little pure spring water such as Malvern, whose recognition as a water of special quality is reckoned to go back to Roman times, and this, the purest water of all, has been flowing from the Malvern hillsides ever since. The purists add water because, as they will tell you at any distillery, it releases the oils in the dram and allows the bouquet to rise.

Even in the hot summer of 1976, when wells all over England were drying up, Schweppes' Malvern Water continued to flow. Still Malvern, in its traditional glass bottles and distinctive red caps, can be found in Britain wherever there is a range of whiskies on show — cocktail bars, restaurants, public houses, hotels, as well as off-licences and supermarkets. Thus the more particular amongst us can be sure of consistency in the water which we add to our favourite malt whiskies, and so it is certainly worth asking for Malvern Water wherever one is.

The purity of Malvern is epitomised in this little eighteen century rhyme: 'The Malvern Water, says Dr John Wall, is famed for containing just nothing at all.' Dr Wall, a highly reputable physician, was the first doctor to make scientific claims for the medicinal virtues of Malvern Water, just as many of his profession did in the latter half of the nineteenth and early part of this century for particular brands of Scotch Whisky. The only difference today is that medical men still testify as to the purity of Malvern Water, but will never now associate their names with specific whiskies.

Malvern is, of course, not a mineral water, but the purest plain water, and the standard against which others have come to be judged. Mineral waters have a flavour and that is what makes them attractive as straight drinks. Conversely, whisky drinkers choose Malvern because it has no flavour; it just helps to release the magic of the particular whisky. There is nothing wrong with plain tap water provided it is soft water, as hard water does not help the flavour. With a malt, however, there is no better addition than Malvern; to add anything but the best of waters kills the flavour, and to take a malt with anything other than water is considered heresy.

Serious tasting of single malts might involve taking the whisky neat, but then the samples should be correspondingly modest. Taking them with spring water allows greater flexibility in the number of malts to be tried, and should not dilute the taste unduly, but some argue that the bouquet should be fully appreciated before adding water. Always have on hand a plentiful supply of cheese — a good hard English one such as a medium Cheddar is ideal, and anything too sharp should be avoided. The function of the cheese is to clean the palate after each malt, in preparation for the next.

Taken thus, a bottle of malt should go quite a long way, and will give much pleasure to those whose first requirement is quality rather than quantity. Malts do not benefit from the addition of ice, either 'on the rocks' or with water.

The only regularly bottled grain whisky, Choice Old Cameron Brig, should not be drunk with anything other than water, or its rather peculiar medicinal flavour is completely lost.

A good De Luxe whisky made up of well-aged malts with not too high a proportion of grain should be treated much like a malt. It may not, however, rate the Cognac treatment and might better be taken with water.

Turning to blended whiskies, there is a wide range of mixers to suit most tastes. If a long refreshing drink is required, then a standard blend will suffice to act as a base. Scotch and soda is a traditional standby, having established itself in the late nineteenth century in the homes and clubs of London as a natural successor to brandy and soda, for so long the Englishman's traditional pre-dinner drink until phylloxera wiped out successive grape crops in France in the 1870s.

The most popular mixers with Scotch are Schweppes Original Dry Ginger Ale, which has a strong peppery taste, and the smoother American Ginger Ale: Schweppes, of course, sell more ginger ale than any other brand of ginger ale, which must say something for the quality. Their heritage, after all, does go back to 1783. The smoother American Ginger Ale is reported to have received a real boost at the time of Prohibition in the United States, when it was an ideal disguise for the rough imitation whiskies produced at the time. Whisky and 'American' appeals particularly to younger drinkers and those looking for a long whisky-cocktail style of drink.

It is an interesting phenomenon in Britain that the south of the country has a preference for dry drinks like Original Dry Ginger Ale. As one moves further north, however, the palate seems to prefer sweeter drinks; this applies to all drinks — not just mixers. So the consumption of lemonade is most noticeable in Scotland — to the extent that it is often offered in bars free, like water, a service from the publican. Whisky and lemonade is to some a very smooth drink, easy to sip and savour while, as the Scots say, 'discussing a drink'! It is certainly how many Scots have traditionally taken their whisky long. And for would-be slimmers who still want to enjoy their whisky, Schweppes produce American Ginger Ale and Lemonade in their 'Slimline', low-calorie range of mixers.

A surprisingly good drink on a hot day is blended Scotch and orange juice with plenty of ice cubes. It sounds an odd mixture, but is pleasantly refreshing. A fairly good measure of whisky is needed so that the flavour comes through the orange juice. The practice of mixing Scotch with cola drinks is still largely confined to certain countries in Latin America.

There are a number of proprietary brands which use Scotch whisky as a base and which might be best described as whisky-wine blends, such as Scotsmac, a mixture of whisky and British wine, produced by Saccone & Speed Ltd. Others are mentioned under the appropriate companies in Chapter 9.

When buying blended Scotch for occasions such as parties, where it may be knocked back without a second thought, it makes no economic sense to go for anything other than the cheapest super-market brands which sell at prices considerably below those of standard brands. A recent test carried out in Scotland by The Consumers' Association (published in the magazine *Which?*) revealed that the panel of ninety testers could not say whether they were drinking one of the three leading brands used in the test (Bells, Haigs, and Teachers) or one of the five cheaper brands (Augustus Barnett's Special Scotch, Claymore, Glenside, Robertson's Yellow Label or Sainsbury's). It would seem, therefore, that unless you are addicted to a special brand — and some people are, and can distinguish it from the others when it is out of the bottle — or are likely to be embarrassed by offering an unknown or supermarket brand, there is a small financial advantage in buying the whiskies marketed specifically for the supermarkets and chain off-licences. A much earlier test by *Which?* to compare standard with De Luxe blends produced a similar result: the panel did not consider any one particular whisky more outstanding than the rest. It certainly says a lot for packaging and promotion in that the individual's taste and preference is obviously dictated so much by what he sees and hears rather than by what he tastes and smells — The Consumers' Association's tests were conducted with the whisky already poured into glasses and with no visible distinguishing features. There have been prosecutions of licensees serving cheap 'unknown' blended whiskies under the guise of well known brands by refilling the bottles of the latter. Such cases might be extremely difficult to prove, since one standard blend might seem very much like the next, but chemists in Scotland have recently built up analytical profiles of a number of established blends which make them easily identifiable. The main element in any comparison between whiskies is the level and ratio of isobutyl and isoamyl alcohols. Since there are so many variations, no two whiskies can be exactly alike, and a particular whisky can now be 'fingerprinted'. The bald chemistry can take away some of the mystique, but it can also help to end fraud.

A word of encouragement for those who may have put the odd bottle of malt away for a rainy day: neither it nor any other bottled Scotch will be affected by the length of time you keep it. It should not suffer in any way by clouding nor should it change in colour or taste, so long as it is kept in the original sealed bottle.

The medicinal properties of Scotch whisky are perhaps less often acknowledged today than they once were. Certainly in the nineteenth century medical men were quick to put their names to highly questionable testimonials regarding the health benefits of one brand or another. Alcohol in moderation was, and still is, regarded in a positive way by the medical profession.

The industry today would not dare to claim the medical advantages of its product for fear of falling foul of the advertising code, as well as incurring the wrath of the anti-alcohol lobby. However, there is one sure-fire cure which whisky performs and to which even the most strident critic could take no exception, and that is a hot whisky toddy to combat a heavy cold. My own recipe is as follows:

2 ounces of any blend
juice of half a lemon
large teaspoonful of honey
Mix together with freshly boiled water in a glass and drink rapidly; then straight to bed.

This, incidentally, is a most enjoyable drink on a cold winter night, even without the excuse of illness. For those who find that their cold persists, the treatment can be repeated at pleasurable two-hourly intervals. It is said that when prolonged treatment is needed you should hang your hat at the foot of the bed; you will know that you are winning when a second hat appears.

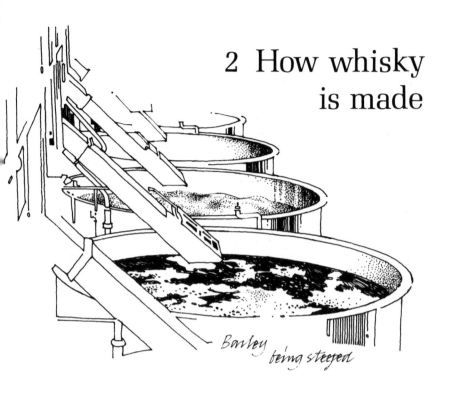

Barley being steeped

2 How whisky is made

The Scots, and most of the rest of the world with them, believe that their native land is uniquely endowed with those things essential for making the best whisky. The ingredients which go into Scotch whisky are not exotic: barley, peat and plenty of good, soft water for malt whisky, and for grain whisky, a steady supply of high quality unmalted cereals: most often maize but sometimes barley again, wheat, rye or oats.

Barley is as essential to malt whisky as the grape is to wine. It is the traditional crop of Scotland to the extent of once being the nation's staple, and it features in many old recipes. However, the barley for malting must be ripe, clean and dry and, sadly, Scotland has not for many years been able to produce enough of this raw material to meet the needs of the industry. Recent figures show that 42 per cent of the distiller's requirements were met by Scottish barley, 35 per cent by English and the rest was imported to fill the gap, mainly from Canada and Australia. Scotland does provide all the peat needed by the distilleries for heating the kilns and 'smoking' the whisky in order to influence the flavour. The water, of course, is entirely Scottish, and without its pure and sparkling characteristics Scotch whisky would be no more. Not surprisingly, some imaginative entrepreneurs from abroad have tried importing Highland spring water in order to produce a credible substitute for Scotch, but without success: they could not take the pure air or capture and transport the unique combination of elements in the Scottish atmosphere to go with the water. The magic is missing, as every Scotsman knew it would be.

Physical and human factors

It is not possible to pinpoint exactly which factors of geography and climate are so important in making Scotland the unique home of malt whisky. One can only look at the various elements and guess at which of them will have contributed most in the character-building of a particular whisky. Water is easy enough to test in terms of quality — it is either hard or soft, and there is little mystery about its chemical make-up. The Highlands boast water that has a marvellous softness, much influenced by the granite and the peat over which it often flows. The valley of the Spey — the fastest flowing river in the United Kingdom — and its tributaries support more distilleries than anywhere else in Scotland, although very few draw water from the Spey itself, but rather from nearby burns and wells. The coolness of the water is also important, for this can affect the ultimate flavour of the whisky. Thus some distilleries cease production during July and August, giving over this time to maintenance and other duties.

Scotland is also blessed with pure, clean air, and the location of most distilleries is far from the industrial belt of Strathclyde. The air of northern Scotland is also free of pollution, thanks to the direction of prevailing winds and the absence of any near neighbour from whom air-borne pollution might travel. The sea, too, exerts a strong influence on those whiskies whose distilleries are coastal or on the islands. Thus, malt whisky is not simply a wonderful drink, it is an expression of the nature of the land in which it is distilled.

This great and romantic industry has, despite its enormous through-put, no more than brushed against the land which has given it so much. It is a gentle industry: it does not choke the air, nor kill the rivers or sea. It is not a blight on the skyline and does not frighten its neighbours by shrillness or loud noise. Unfortunately, it is not labour intensive in a country which has long suffered from chronically high unemployment. Those who work the distilleries often do so for all their active lives; many are second or third generation not only in the industry but in the same distillery or even at the same trade. But to put this into perspective, one should also realise how thinly spread the Northern Scots are. For example, when the Tomintoul-Glenlivet

Distillery was opened in 1965 it had a work force of only fifteen, which increased to thirty after a period of expansion to double the distillery's capacity. Totally insignificant, one might say, but not so trivial when one considers the remoteness of Tomintoul and the fact that the village held no more than 300 people. The opening of the distillery was therefore an important event in economic and employment terms. But it is at the commercial end of the process where employment is concentrated, and the bottling halls and despatch warehouses for whisky tend to be built in areas of heavy population to the south, in and around Glasgow and Edinburgh. Quite a different scene and quite different people tend to be engaged in this part of the industry, where it starts to resemble other packaging and despatch processes.

In only a very few cases do distilleries operate independently. Most are owned by larger concerns whose main interests are in blending, and many are now in Canadian or foreign hands. The parent companies, no matter what their interest, generally keep their distance from the distilling, judging it better not to upset the delicate balance between man, machine and nature which must be present if a good whisky is to result.

Distilling is an ancient craft and something of its historical origins is explained in Chapter 3. In technical language, distillation involves the separation of the different elements in a liquid by volatilisation and condensation, whereby a liquid is vaporised and subsequently recovered in part through condensation. This is no more than the first-form physics exercise of heating a liquid so as to produce vapour and using a piece of cold glass or other instrument to condense the vapour back into liquid.

The liquid to be distilled has to have already undergone some process of fermentation, either naturally as in the case of wine, from which spirits such as grappa or grape brandy can be distilled, or induced by, for example, the addition of yeasts. The distillation process is thus applied to a liquid containing water and alcohol. The process itself involves separating the alcoholic beverage from the water. This is achieved by heating the liquid so that alcoholic vapour is given off and then returned to liquid form by means of cooling. Different processes of distilling apply to different kinds of alcoholic drinks and there are marked differences between the two classes of Scotch whisky — malt and grain. Each of the two basic processes is explained in detail later in this chapter, but the two kinds of whisky share some of the early stages before they go their different ways.

Malting

No distiller of malt whisky can contemplate a production programme without adequate supplies of barley, which must be dry before it is stored, or it will become mouldy. The barley is therefore dried in kilns or by a warm air process before being put into large storage bins.

The first major step in the production begins with the malting of the barley, during which it must germinate. The dry barley is cleansed of dust and any other impurities and then soaked in water in large tanks called steeps. Here the barley is steeped for two or three days while it soaks up enough water to cause germination. The residual water is drained off and the soggy barley spilled out on to the stone or tiled floor of a large airy building known as the malting house. It is spread to an even depth of up to about two feet by malt-men using large wooden shovels called skips.

Germination soon begins, with each grain of barley sprouting a tiny root. The process creates a natural heat, which is at its greatest closest to the floor, and so the barley has to be turned with skips to keep the temperature even, and to prevent the germinating seeds becoming a matted mass of roots. Large forks are also pulled

In the malting house

21

through the barley to help it 'breathe'. The barley thus begins to dry, and is progressively thinned out on the malting floor to a depth of only a few inches, and the thinning and spreading of the grain bring the growth of the rootlets to a stop. Throughout this germination process the temperature of the grain has been kept at around 16 °C (60 °F).

The process of turning and spreading is back-aching work, and labour intensive. There are now two main mechanical alternatives widely used. In one method the germinating barley is put in large revolving drums (nineteen to fifty tons capacity) into which air is blown to keep the temperature down. The Saladin box (named after the Frenchman who invented it in the late nineteenth century, although it was not widely used in the Scotch whisky industry until much later) is the other method, involving a long rectangular box in which revolving metal tongues move up and down, turning and airing the entire load of grain. Early users of this method were Glen Mhor, Tamdhu and Muir of Ord. Two other systems sometimes favoured by maltsters are the German Wanderhaufen (or 'moving heap'), a long box with a number of screw conveyors which move the barley slowly up the box, and the so-called Static Box, which is a more sophisticated piece of equipment capable of doing the steeping, germinating and kilning processes in sequence.

At the end of this germination period the product is known as 'green malt', although it still looks very much like the original pale yellow, ripe barley. If it has undergone the traditional process, it will have taken from eight to fourteen days, but if one of the more modern techniques has been used, it can be complete in only seven days, since closer control of temperature and humidity allows quicker germination.

The final stage in malting is to dry the green malt thoroughly, and for this it is transferred to a kiln. It is this process which gives the typical malt distillery its best known feature: the pagoda-style roof, which will immediately identify an otherwise unremarkable collection of commercial buildings. But the kiln does much more than simply dry the green malt; it is at this stage that the distinctive peaty flavour is introduced, later to contribute to the character of the particular whisky of that distillery. The green malt is spread on the perforated metal floor of the kiln to a depth of one to three feet ready to be exposed, in the traditional method, to the warming and flavouring influences of the peat smoke rising from the fires below. The kiln is ventilated by the opening in the pagoda roof.

At one time all the distilleries in the Highlands relied exclusively

Stoking the kiln

on peat for drying the green malt. Now more efficient fuels are used, principally coal and anthracite, although peat will always have its part to play as the agent through which malt whisky acquires its distinctive flavour. Even in the most technically advanced distilleries, where the malt is dried more quickly by fans, the warm air which is wafted across the malt is heavy with the familiar peaty aroma which it imparts to the malt. The importance of the peat should never be overlooked, since the 'smokiness' and the amount of body of the final product will have been directly influenced by the quantity and quality of peat used. However, once the peat has served its purpose, other fuels are used in order to speed the drying of the malt. The malt is turned on the kiln floor during drying to ensure an even degree of peating, and the temperature in the kiln kept below 70°C (158°F). The time taken for kilning and peating varies between distilleries, but it can be completed in less than twenty-four hours if the hot-air blasting method is used.

The malting process is long and arduous, and much of it is now done by specialist firms of maltsters, who deliver the malt by bulk carrier to the distillery. Some of the individuality of the product of the distillery is inevitably lost in this case, but maltsters supplying a variety of distilleries will often try to ensure that the mix destined for a particular client will have certain distinctive characteristics, rather than simply supply to a standard formula. In Islay, where the industry has stuck to tradition more than in any other part of Scotland, there are as many distilleries doing their own floor malting as in the whole of the rest of Scotland.

A recent innovation has been the construction of a malting plant at Roseisle in Morayshire by The Distillers Company in which germination and kilning take place in the same vessel. This permits very large batches (320 tonnes) to be handled at one time. The process, to some extent, is like that of the Saladin Box, whereby an arm carrying the screws travels radially on a central pivot whilst conditioned air for germination and hot air for kilning enters through a perforated floor and blows through the barley.

During malting the natural enzymes in the barley have been breaking down the stored starch into a soluble sugar known as maltose. Once this stage has been reached, the growing process of the seed is stopped by the heat of the kiln so that the maltose can be used later for fermentation. Up to now, therefore, the entire procedure has been designed simply to hasten what is in effect a natural process. From the kiln the dried malt, containing no more than 3 per cent moisture, is stored in bins until the next stage.

Mashing

The dried malt is put through dressing machines so as to remove the tail-ends of the now dead rootlets and any other superfluous matter. The dressed malt is then coarsely milled (malt which is too finely milled is thought to have an adverse effect on the flavour of the whisky) and the resulting grist from the mill is put in vast circular mash tuns, holding between 1000 and 5000 gallons,* or more, depending on the size of the distillery. Starting at 60-68°C (140-155°F), water at increasingly high temperatures is added to the grist, which is thoroughly stirred by revolving paddles in the tuns. Only the first and second 'extraction' waters (carrying the soluble substances from the grist) go on to the fermentation stage, the liquid being drained off through the bottom of the tuns into large storage tanks called underbacks. The liquid here is now known as wort or worts. The third, and where appropriate, fourth extractions are kept

* 1 imperial gallon = 1.2 US gallons
= 4.546 litres

as the 'sparge', which is much weaker than the worts and is returned to the hot tanks for use again when the next batch of malt grist is put in the mash tun. The hot wort in the underbacks is passed through a heat exchanger where it is cooled to about 21-27°C (70-80°F) to prevent decomposition of the maltose and destruction of the highly sensitive yeast which is to be added in the next stage. The wort is a sweet, sticky, semi-transparent liquid and is still a long way from resembling anything like the end product. Its production from the malt will have taken between eight and ten hours.

The residual soggy barley, known as draff, is disposed of at this point, to be later used for cattle food.

Fermentation

The transformation of grain into spirit now changes pace as the wort moves into the fermentation stage. The warm sweet liquid is pumped into the washbacks, more large-scale vats ranging in capacity from 1000 to as much as 13,000 gallons, traditionally made of wood such as larch or pine, but nowadays more often made of steel. When the tanks are three-quarters filled a carefully measured

A mash tun

25

amount of fresh yeast selected specifically for the purpose is added and fermentation begins. The mixture of wort and yeast is called wash, and in this the yeast multiplies at a phenomenal rate, creating such activity and heat that overhead paddles are used to control the froth which is generated. The process of the yeast attacking the sugar produces alcohol, which in turn inhibits the activity of the yeast until the frothy, bubbling liquid becomes a gentle low-strength alcoholic brew, ready for the next transformation. It is pumped into the 'wash charger' for storage before distilling. This process has taken between thirty-six and forty-eight hours, and has involved the production of sugary dextrose from the maltose, and the conversion of dextrose to alcohol and carbon dioxide by the yeast. It is the most dramatic step in the entire cycle of malt whisky production, and it is no coincidence that the brewer who oversees this part of the operation is the most important link in the chain. Moreover, it is at this stage that the excise officer first appears, since there is now an alcoholic content to the product and he is able, in consultation with the distiller, to calculate the amount of spirit which should eventually be drawn from it.

Checking the alcohol content of the wash

Malt whisky distilling

If the pagoda roof is the most familiar external feature of a malt whisky distillery, the pear-shaped, gleaming copper still, with its Loch Ness monster neck, is easily the most memorable internal feature. These pot-stills have not changed in basic design in over two centuries. They are of two sorts and each distillery will have at least one of each. The larger one is the wash still and it is in this that the wash is given its first distillation to produce the 'low wines'. These pass on to the 'spirit' or 'low wines' still for the second distillation, and it is after this subsequent treatment that whisky is produced.

The wash is heated in the wash still and the vapour thus formed goes up the narrow neck of the still and then down the wall of the still house to a coiled copper pipe known as the worm, which lies in a cold water tank. The vapour condenses in the cold worm and the distilled liquid now flows into the low wines charger for short-term storage. From there it goes to the second still where it is again heated, and the vapour collected after condensation goes to the spirit safe. Here the stillman can gauge the strength of the liquid by testing its specific gravity, and its purity by adding distilled water, which causes impure spirit to cloud. The spirit safe is so called since it is a sealed, glass-sided, brass-bound box, looking rather like a heavy-duty aquarium. Access during distillation is given by way of large locks to which only the resident excise officer has the key. The purpose of the spirit safe is to allow the stillman to test and control the spirit, so as to ensure that what passes on to the next stage will result in acceptable whisky. Inside the spirit safe there are a number of jars which can be filled by the stillman by remote control, using external taps which direct the spirit to the appropriate jar, where its specific gravity can be measured by means of a hydrometer, or into which distilled water can be poured. It is at this point that the stillman must use his judgement and experience to make sure that he gets the right 'middle cut', i.e. that part of the distillation which will be retained as whisky. By the turn of a tap he can direct the contents of the spirit safe on to the spirit receiver or back to the low wines charger. The stillman first sees that the distillate to be sent to the receiver does not contain appreciable quantities of foreshots (those lighter alcohols and other elements which detract from the pure ethyl alcohol needed for whisky): these are returned to the low wines charger and eventually distilled again. Towards the end of a distillation cycle the heavier elements in the low wines will also vaporise and reappear in the safe as 'feints', such as fusel oil. As soon as the stillman detects feints in any quantity he will stop the flow to the receiver and redirect

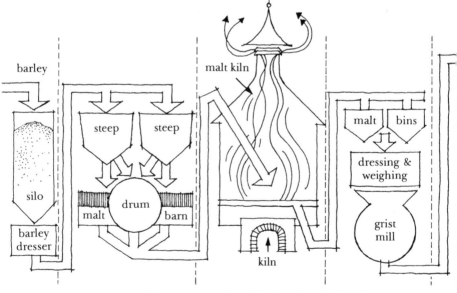

The sequence of production of malt whisky

the feints back again to the charger. Both foreshots and feints do, however, have an important contribution to make to the final product since it is these impurities which combine with the somewhat characterless pure spirit to give the particular whisky in question its credentials as an individual malt whisky, and which make each one different from all the others.

It is at this final stage that the exciseman confirms his earlier calculations as to the amount of excisable spirit to be produced from a given quantity of wash. He, and everyone else engaged in the distilling process, are aided by a colour code used in the distilleries to identify the liquids in the masses of pipes — red is for wash, blue is for low wines, feints or foreshots, and black is for clear spirit.

Needless to say, the heating of the stills is a matter of considerable sensitivity. Some are heated externally by coal, gas or oil, but the disadvantage with this method is that the heavier parts of the wash drift to the bottom of the still where the heat causes them to burn and stick to the inner surface. This is countered to some extent by a mechanical device called a rummager, which scrapes the bottom of the pot with a copper chain attached to four rotating arms. An increasingly popular alternative is to heat the still by means of an internal steam coil.

Whatever is left in the still after all required vaporisation has taken place is poured off as 'pot ale' or 'burnt ale', and can be used later as

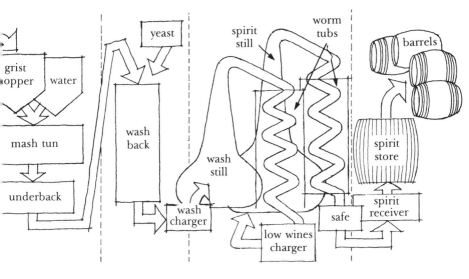

animal food or fertiliser. The residue in the low wines still is, on the other hand, little more than water and is flushed away as waste, as its name, 'spent lees', might suggest.

As a final act, the spirit receiver gives up its precious, usually colourless, liquid to the spirit store where the fiery raw commodity is reduced in strength from about 115-120° proof to about 110° proof by the addition of distilled water.

Though perhaps three weeks away from the barley grains, the spirit so far has been a relatively short time in the making compared with the long period of hibernation about to start before it can appear as mature Scotch whisky.

Grain whisky distilling

The events which led to the appearance of grain whisky in the early part of the nineteenth century are described in Chapter 4, since it is important to put this development, which was to change the entire face of the whisky industry in Scotland, into its proper historical context.

There are two essential differences which distinguish grain from malt whisky distilling. The first is that grain distilling is a continuous process whereas malt, as described, is not, in that each complete round of distillation is separate from the next, hence the skill required of the distiller in maintaining the established standards and patterns peculiar to his distillery. At the time of the great whisky depression, in the first ten years of this century, a few malt distilleries went over in part to continuous distillation with the aim of producing better returns. The product was vastly inferior to the normal pot-still whisky, and found few buyers, and the experiment was short-lived.

Secondly, the grain whisky distillery is, in most instances, operating on a totally different scale from that of the malt. The fourteen grain distilleries in Scotland produced in 1980 a total of 238 million litres of pure alcohol, whereas 117 malt distilleries produced 178 million litres. Production by both was considerably down in 1981 and 1982, and many units, particularly malt whisky distilleries, have been closed for lengthy periods, and both have had their production drastically cut back. In some years, grain whisky production has been more than double that of malt. Moreover, the spirit from a grain whisky distillery can, with simple adaptation, be used in the production of gin or vodka.

Much of the preparation for the distilling of grain whisky is similar

Long John Grain - Strathclyde

to that for malt whisky. However, when the cereal used for grain whisky is delivered to the distillery, only a small proportion will be barley. This is malted much as described earlier in the chapter, and it goes through the same germination, drying and storage processes. Some distilleries, however, no longer dry the malt but simply use the green malt as it is. But the bulk of the starch used in grain whisky distilling comes from maize. It is not malted but ground fine and then cooked to a high temperature in order to expose every last particle of starch to the later action of the malt enzyme (diastase) which will convert the starch into sugar. The barley malt is mixed with the much larger quantity of maize (one part malt to nine parts maize), and hot water added. This mashing process is very like that which produces malt whisky, with the wort being drained off to the underbacks and then cooled before going on to the washbacks, where yeast is added to induce fermentation. After two days of this, the wash is conveyed via the wash chargers to the stills.

Apart from the scale of the operation, the process so far has been very similar to that in malt distilling, but now matters take quite a

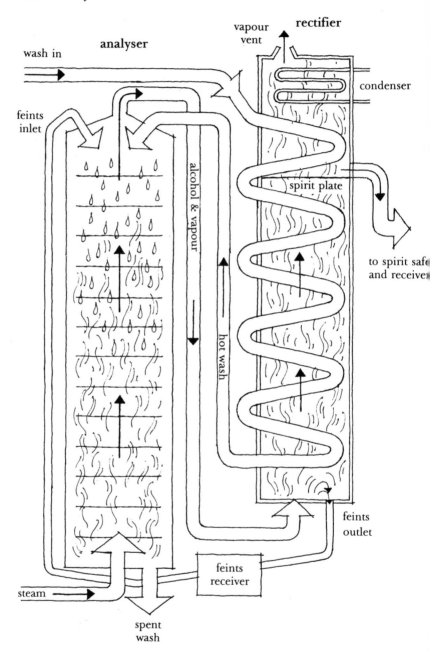

The Coffey still

different course. The usual equipment for grain distilling is the Coffey still, or some near adaptation of it, consisting of two columns. The first column is a rectifier column made up of a series of heavy wooden frames through which a continuous convoluted copper pipe, the worm, passes from top to bottom. There is a perforated copper plate within each of the frames, with a drip pipe leading to the frame below. The wash flows from top to bottom of the column via the copper pipe and is then carried to the top of the second, analyser, column. This also consists of a number of wooden frames divided by perforated copper plates, but minus the worm. The wash flows from top to bottom of the second column, but its progress is impeded by steam rising from the boilers at the base of the column. This forces the wash to find a passage by flowing backwards and forwards across the perforated plates and through the traps at alternate corners of the plates until eventually reaching the bottom of the analyser column. The purpose of this bewildering process is to separate, by means of the steam, the alcohols and more volatile liquids which vaporise, rise to the top of the column, and then pass back to the bottom of the rectifier, going inside the frames but outside the worm. The wash which reaches the bottom of the analyser is nothing more than spent wash, although it still carries some fine grain sediment known as dreg. It is flushed away to cool and settle in the dreg ponds, where the liquid is drained off and the sediment eventually transformed into animal food. The vapour, on reaching the bottom of the rectifier, begins to rise and condense on the coil running up and down the rectifier, which is carrying wash from the washbacks. This is cold when it enters the top of the column but gets warm as it makes its downward journey. At a certain point on the rectifier column a plate is inserted with the purpose of directing away to the spirit still the alcoholic vapour which has condensed and which will become the grain whisky, whilst the more volatile vapours — the foreshots — carry on up the column to be dispersed out of harm's way. The feints, in the meantime, have condensed further down the column and are directed back to the analyser for further distillation.

The whisky which has been produced passes through a spirit pipe which is immersed in water in the worm tub. This further cools the whisky before it reaches the spirit receiver. Since the spirit is now stronger than is required for the grain whisky which is later to be used in blending, it is piped to large vats in the spirit store where water is added to bring down the strength by a suitable margin, usually to about 11° over proof. This process, so difficult to describe and comprehend, is the route which produces the less interesting of the two strands of Scotch.

But let us not conclude that all grain whisky is necessarily a whisky entirely devoid of character. The North of Scotland Distillery, for instance, keeps a higher than normal content of foreshots and feints (congeners) when distilling its whisky in order to give it more character, so that it can be recognised as North of Scotland grain. The distillery also maintains that grain whisky improves with age, and their associated companies use it at 6 years old in their own blends.

Maturation

It is laid down by law in the United Kingdom that no whisky may be bottled or otherwise disposed of for consumption until it has reached a minimum age of three years in wooden casks from the time of distillation. This measure was brought in many years ago to counter the practice of selling unmatured, raw whisky to the unsuspecting public, and it is discussed in Chapter 5. Although this requirement applies equally to malts and grains, it is in the malts that ageing plays a particularly significant role. Once grain whisky has met the minimum legal requirements it can be used for blending, and the company concerned can realise some of the enormous capital which it inevitably has tied up in maturing whisky stocks. A malt whisky, on the other hand, will gain much from longer maturation and may in fact alter in character as each year is added to its age. A five year old malt will be more palatable than the same whisky at the minimum legal age of three years. Double the period and you will have a whisky of some stature. Add another five years and you should have a whisky of such maturity and body as to be equal of the finest Cognac. Whether much will be gained by ageing further is debatable, and, for many, twelve years is regarded as the optimum age. Indeed, beyond this age problems of consistency as between different casks of the same whisky of the same age can arise and, thus, the marketing of older whiskies can run certain risks. It should be remembered that ageing only takes place in the cask and, unlike wine, never in the bottle. But, while it ages no further, a good malt may improve in character, when it is said to 'brandify', if left undisturbed in the bottle.

Whilst on the subject of the age of a whisky as shown on the label, the year of distillation, which is sometimes shown on a bottle of malt, tells you nothing at all if it does not also give the year of bottling. You cannot assume that a malt which is shown as being distilled in 1959 is, in 1983, twenty-four years old, since it may be old stock on the shelf, and bottled years previously. If it was bottled in 1971 it would, of course, be only twelve years old. What is important is the number of years the whisky has been *in cask* before bottling, and this is precisely what is meant when the label states that it is, say, fifteen years old. One of the most informative labels of any single malt is that of Knockando, which shows the season in which the whisky was distilled (1970) and the year in which it was bottled (1982), a true twelve year old. If a single malt does not state any age, you are fairly safe in assuming that it is probably no more than six years old. Those who have preferences for Lowland malts will claim that they do not improve much beyond five years old and are best bottled then.

But what makes maturation so important in the creation of a fine, mellow whisky? Again there is no easy answer, since it is probably a combination of a number of factors. The influence of the casks in which it is stored is certainly important, but so are the chemical interactions which occur during maturation, and which must remain largely a mystery. During maturation there is a significant reduction in the quantity and strength of the whisky from the 120° (or 68.5 per cent of alcohol by volume) at which the law requires newly distilled spirit to be filled in casks. This is due to evaporation and the loss of alcoholic vapour through the porous wooden casks, this lost whisky being known as 'the angel's share'. Add to these processes the interplay between water, the ethyl alcohol and the various congeners within the casks, the physical — sometimes extremely remote — location of the warehouse and the effects of the Scottish climate which inevitably penetrate to the casks, a combination of much cold and damp during the long winters with short breaks of brilliant dry warmth during the relatively short summers, and you have some idea of what may contribute to giving malt whisky its fabled uniqueness.

Cooperage

The importance of the size and nature of the casks in which the whisky is matured really cannot be overstated. The size of cask determines the period for which the whisky is to be matured. The names of the casks and the quantities they represent are as follows:

butt	108 gallons/491 litres
hogshead	55 gallons/250 litres
American barrel	38-42 gallons/173-91 litres
quarter	28 gallons/127 litres
octave	14 gallons/63.5 litres

The bigger the cask, the longer maturation will take. However, this is balanced to some extent by the fact that the owner of the whisky in cask — usually the blender — will pay proportionately higher storage fees for the smaller sizes of cask. The traditional barrel in which malt whisky is matured is the used sherry cask. It is ideal in size (about 500 litres) and shape and the sherry-stained wood colours the whisky naturally over a long period. Alas, as whisky production expanded, demand outstripped supply and the sherry cask is almost a thing of the past, although Macallan Distillery still uses nothing else. Where they are available they are used over and over again, and when their life is at an end they are broken up and serviceable staves are used with new wood to make up further casks. This process of breaking and remaking casks is a continuous one undertaken by the coopers, amongst the last traditional craftsmen still in widespread employment in Scotland today. Many distilleries employ their own cooper, who is as much a part of the scene as the maltman or distillery manager himself.

The increasing scarcity of casks led to the invention by William Lowrie in 1890 of the wine-treated cask. Into new oak casks was introduced dark sweet sherry which was allowed to soak and stain the wood before the whisky was put in. Today, a brown syrupy substance called 'pajarete', which is used in Jerez as a colouring and sweetening agent for certain sherries, is employed. It is made from grape juice and is reduced by heating to between one-third and one-fifth of its original volume. Diluted pajarete is swilled round the barrel prior to its being filled with new whisky. The preferred wood is still American white oak. Another innovation by Lowrie & Co. was the importation of used American whisky barrels in collapsed form for rebuilding at the cooperage in Scotland. Lowrie's Glasgow cooperage, now owned by Scottish Grain Distillers Ltd, is today the largest in the world and meets many of the requirements of the huge Distillers Company group, including Lowrie's parent company, James Buchanan & Co. Ltd.

The cooper, equipped with his basic tools of the hammer, the adze and the saw, examines, dismantles, repairs and rebuilds every cask before it is declared fit for filling. Thereafter he is responsible for regular inspection of the filled casks to ensure that there is no seepage or damage to them as a result of stacking when they are placed in the warehouse for their long 'sleep'. He is also on hand, for obvious reasons, at that delicate moment when the distiller and the excise officer together agree on the strength of a particular batch of whisky before it is filled. It is only at this point that the distiller can tell if he has produced good — and profitable — new whisky and has successfully run the gauntlet of the many minor hazards presented by such a non-standard, unmechanical process as pot malt whisky distilling, a process which can mar or ruin the precious liquid at the end of it.

Blending

'Distilling is a science and blending is an art', said the late Samuel Bronfman, founder of The Seagram Co. Ltd, now the biggest distilling company in the world. There is something to be said for his view, for whilst distilling does have its romance and mystery, there is a certain formula and routine which has to be followed with the same exactitude and repetition as in any other manufacturing process. However, when it comes to the blending stage, much more is left to the discretion of the human senses, and it is they rather than physical considerations which are the arbiter in the making of a blended whisky.

One of the best descriptions of blending, by the managing director of Macdonald Martin Distilleries PLC, states that it is 'the art of combining meticulously selected, mature, high-quality whiskies, each with its own flavour and other characteristics, with such skill that the whole is better than the sum of its parts, so that each makes its own contribution to the finished blend without any one pre-dominating.'

The first commercially marketed blend is generally accepted to have been Usher's O.V.G. (Old Vatted Glenlivet), which was introduced in 1853. Blending had certainly been going on before then, since whisky merchants and innkeepers had no doubt found it profitable to add grain whisky to malt whisky in order to produce a cheap mixture with a wide appeal to those (the majority in the Lowlands and in England) who found the undiluted Highland malts too heavy on the palate and the pocket. There were also earlier 'blends' which were the vattings of whiskies of different ages from the same distillery. As will be seen in Chapter 4, the impact of blending was rapidly to change the face of the industry, and for nearly a century now the vast bulk of the whisky produced in Scotland has been consumed in blended form.

The success of many blends is, according to their owners, due to sticking to a well established formula (a closely guarded company secret, and only changed in order to accommodate occasional variations in the availability of the ingredient single whiskies). A blend may require anything from fifteen to forty different single malts, to which will be added a proportion of one or more of the various grain whiskies. Certain whiskies will not go successfully with others, and keeping the incompatible apart is all in the blender's art. The malts and the grain in a blend must be orchestrated in such a way as to complement and enhance their respective characteristics, and without this objective, blending becomes no more than the dilution of rich malts with cheaper grain whisky. For instance, the creation of a 'light' whisky of the kind much appreciated in North America, such as J & B Rare or Cutty Sark, is not achieved by simply adding more grain whisky, but rather by the skilful use of lighter malts, such as those of the Lowlands, in preference to the flavoursome Islays and heavier Highland varieties. The lightness of the blend will be emphasised by only the most modest addition of colouring.

Since colour can be an important attribute, at least in the eye of the consumer, it is appropriate to state here that new whisky as it leaves the still is either colourless or a very pale yellow, and becomes even paler when natural local water is added to reduce the proof strength to that decreed by law. Such colouring as the whisky may collect when maturing in cask will depend on the type of cask used, but the colour will almost certainly still need to be enhanced, usually by a minute quantity of caramel essence or a small amount of sherry. Consistency of colour is seen by the blender as an important part of maintaining the quality and outward appearance of his product, and so established has this become that those loyal to a particular brand will treat with the greatest suspicion any bottle that is the tiniest shade off its usual colour.

Colour apart, the blender's main aim is to produce a whisky which is different from others and therefore recognisable. Thereafter he must recreate that whisky to the same standard and with the same features which his customers have come to expect of it, otherwise he is failing in his task. Selection of the single whiskies is therefore of enormous concern to him. He must decide at what age they will best suit his needs, and for this he will need an extensive library of whiskies: the library of Seagram's at Paisley runs to well over 600 types and ages of malt and grain whisky. He will also need to take into account the variations which occur in a particular single whisky, and the type of cask and the warehouse in which it is stored.

Once the blender has selected his single whiskies they are sent from the warehouse where they have been maturing to the blender's premises, and here, after checking, they are put in the blending vat and mixed together, the precise method of bringing together the

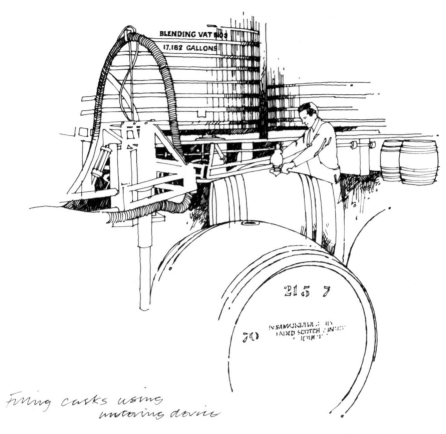

BLENDING VAT NO. 3
17,182 GALLONS

Filling casks using
motoring device

different whiskies varying between establishments. At this point colouring is added as necessary. After thorough mixing the blended whisky is stored in casks for a further period, usually of no more than eight months, to 'marry' before bottling. Sometimes the single malts are vatted together and the grain whiskies kept separate, and mixed only at the bottling stage. Macdonald & Muir Ltd claim that this process produces a smoother blend. Needless to say, the proportion of malt to grain whisky is kept secret by the blenders, although some will claim that their whisky contains over 50 per cent malt. Certainly most blends will have a minimum grain content of 60 per cent and the cheapest of them could be well over 90 per cent. It is doubtful that anyone would market a blend with less than 5 per cent malt whisky, although there is nothing legally to prevent him from doing so. But it is not simply a question of the proportion of malt to grain, but also the quality of the malts used. For blending purposes, these are graded into different classes, the very best being known as 'crackerjacks'.

Nosing

From this description one can see that, like all arts, blending does not follow a rigid set of rules but is rather the individual's adaptation of certain basic principles in order to produce his own particular finished piece of work. It might be said that master blenders, like great poets, are born, but unlike poets the faculty on which they rely is that of smell. Nosing the whisky is the most important of the blender's tasks, for it is through this that he discerns which whiskies will combine to give satisfaction. At the first nosing the blender simply wants to verify that the whisky fresh from the stills is up to standard. If it passes the test, it is consigned to the store for the stipulated period of maturation and the blender may not encounter it again until years later, when it reappears for blending. Each cask of whisky is given another nosing before the blending process and is sniffed again on being reduced to the strength required for bottling. For all this, the blender's equipment is extremely simple — a tulip-shaped glass and fresh water to add to the whisky, but only to aid with the nosing, since he rarely drinks the samples.

Whilst companies protect the recipes for their various blends, it is a fairly logical deduction that those who both distil and blend will tend to use a high proportion of whisky from their own distilleries in their house blends. But every distiller-blender, no matter how great his resources, will need to rely on other malt whisky distilleries beyond his control, so great is the fragmentation of the industry and the diversity of single whiskies which go into a blend. And it cannot be denied that some blenders are less fastidious than others in maintaining the consistency of their blends, and will sometimes instead work according to the whiskies which are currently available.

Bottling and distribution

In some cases, bottling and blending are located at the same place, in others the bottling has been centralised for a number of distilleries or blenders. In either case, the procedure is much the same. After its successful marriage, the blended whisky is emptied from the casks into glass-lined tanks and water added to reduce it to the appropriate proof strength. The whisky is then filtered and refrigerated to remove those congeners (or impurities) which might cause the whisky to cloud if it were exposed to low temperatures in bottle. It is then pumped into the bottles, which are capped and labelled in the same process. The bottled whisky is inspected once more before sealing, and then packed in cartons for despatch to agent or wholesaler, or, in the case of export consignments, into large containers for the markets of the world.

A number of distillers and blenders do considerable business supplying blends for resale under the buyers' own labels, such as those of the large supermarket chains. Invergordon Distillers (Holdings) Ltd is one such company although, like other suppliers, they will rarely identify their customers since quite often the customer's cheaper brand is on the shelf beside the supplier's own, more expensive, brand.

A number of distillers and blenders, large and small, rely almost entirely on the services of specialist bonding companies for the blending, bottling and distribution of their whiskies. One of the largest of these is Strathleven Bonded Warehouses Ltd, which is almost entirely concerned with the blending, bottling and despatching of International Distillers & Vintners' J & B Rare. In order to hold their bonded warehouse certificate, they are required to make the facilities available to the trade generally, but the handling of the vast export orders for J & B occupies about 90 per cent of Strathleven's throughput of ten million proof gallons per annum. Yet Strathleven have maintained their independence and are probably the biggest independent bottling company in the world — they certainly are in Europe.

In contrast with the large, single-storey functional warehouse estate which comprises the Strathleven complex at Dumbarton, the premises of William Muir (Bond 9) Ltd are pleasingly quaint, though the bottling output is almost three million cases annually, and a blending service is provided in separate premises at Cumbernauld. Both are concerned exclusively with Scotch whisky, thus avoiding any danger of picking up the malign influences of other spirits in the blending or bottling processes. The benefit of the economies of scale which Bond 9 can offer the small blender or exporter are manifest, and some twenty-five companies regularly use the services, as do some of the larger distillers when their in-house bottling halls cannot cope with demand.

By-products

Like any other industry, that of Scotch whisky has had increasingly to pay attention to costs and seek ways of raising extra income. The most fruitful area has been in the production of animal feed. The discarded barley rootlets left over at the end of the malting stage were traditionally sold off as cattle food, and now the solids, left behind after the wort is run off at the end of the mashing process, are sold for winter cattle feed. This has become an important side-line in distilling, and in 1974 Chivas Bros Ltd and Glenlivet Distillers Ltd — then quite separate companies — became joint partners as pioneers in a new process by which distillery waste products are transformed into dried cubes known as dark grains. By this method the unused protein content of the barley and maize is recovered and sold to farmers in an easily stored and relatively inexpensive form.

Innovation has led to other waste products being turned to good use. Littlemill and Loch Lomond, for example, were amongst the first distilleries to put to use the large quantities of carbon dioxide which are given off in the fermenting vats. Ingenious methods of saving energy or employing waste heat have been developed too. Glengarioch Distillery has been applying it to glass-house use for the cultivation of tomatoes and even tropical fruits — and this in chilly Aberdeenshire. Yet another distillery experimented in using its surplus water and heating to run an eel farm.

Important as the economic aspects might be, saleable by-products also mean less waste matter to be disposed of. The more that is processed through effluent disposal plants the better, since the increase in the size of distilleries has meant that the rivers and streams are not always capable of absorbing the liquid waste. Nor is it at all certain that the sea is able to cope, for there are on record complaints that coastal distillery effluent was destroying sea life. But on the whole the industry's record is good and imaginative in terms of environmental responsibility, and the instances of serious pollution few and far between.

Research

Pentlands Scotch Whisky Research Ltd (PSWR) was set up in the 1970s by a group of seven independent Scotch whisky distillers and blenders on the initiative of the Chairman of The Highland Distilleries Co. PLC as a non-profit research organisation. Apart from undertaking specific research projects on behalf of their members, PSWR hold symposia and have tackled such subjects as by-products and flavour language. The research workers cover all aspects of the industry — distilling, blending, maturing, bottling and packaging — although they do contract work out, for example to universities, as required. PSWR collaborates in particular with the Distillers Company's much larger Research Station and Technical Centre at Glenochil in Clackmannanshire, which has a much longer history of developing new techniques and solving technical and quality problems for the group.

Imperial distillery

3   In the beginning

The aura and respect which have made Scotch whisky such a prestigious drink today owe much to the mist-covered hills and glens, tales of hidden stills and tumbling waters and other such features, which combine to create an impression of Scotland, the home of 'uisgebaugh'. This strange word is Gaelic for 'water of life', translated from the Latin *aqua vitae*. There is variety in the way it is spelt, but whatever the variations, the corruption of 'uisge' into 'usky' finally gave us the generic term 'whisky'.

There are many arguments as to the date from which Scotland can call itself a nation. Unity was scarcely a national characteristic, and not until the early fourteenth century did the country of Scotland really exist in a coherent form. Even then it was a nation of many parts, owing both to geographical and ethnological factors, and later to religion and economics. Even today, Scotland still falls into naturally separate domains, and this is reflected to some extent in the make-up of the complex whisky industry. The Highlands, where it all began, is the production base for malt whisky, whereas the Lowlands is the location of most of the grain whisky distilleries. It is also in and around Glasgow and Edinburgh that most of the blending is done and from where the commercial end of the operation is run, although the headquarters of many companies lie in London or even further afield.

The origins of distilling are somewhat obscure, but it is generally accepted as having been first attempted in Asia as long ago as 800BC, and to have found its way to Europe via Egypt. There are rival claims as to whether its practice in the British Isles originated in Wales, Ireland or Scotland. Although distilling is mentioned by the sixth-century Welsh poet Taliesin in his 'Mead Song', St Patrick is held to have introduced distilling to Ireland from Scotland in the fifth century, rather than vice versa. Whichever is true, it is clear that distilling was a Celtic craft, and was not to be known to other Britons for many centuries.

The first recorded mention of distilling in Scotland was as late as 1494, when an entry in the Exchequer Rolls lists 'Eight bolls of malt to Friar John wherewith to make aqua vitae'. It is interesting that this first reference should involve a man of religion, but it reflects the role of the church, and particularly the abbeys, in the development of distilling, which was regarded as an off-shoot of agriculture. Distilling, as well as the making of ale and wine, was carefully developed in the abbeys and monasteries of both Scotland and England, and a combination of monastic discipline and rural location provided a suitable environment for the patient perfection of these crafts in their different forms. The climatic and geographical differences were to account for the diversity of their products: aqua vitae in the north, wine in the south, and ale throughout. The term aqua vitae was for a long time to be applied to any distilled alcoholic liquid and it was to be centuries before anything resembling what we know as whisky today was to emerge.

The sixteenth and seventeenth centuries

During the sixteenth century distilling made considerable advances throughout Europe. The dissolution of the monasteries contributed to this in Scotland and England, since many of the monks who had been driven from their sanctum had no choice but to put their skills to use, and so knowledge of distilling was quickly spread to others. How widespread it became in Scotland is evident from an Act of the Scottish Parliament of 1579 which prohibited the distilling of aqua vitae, save for lords and 'gentlemen' who could do so for their own use. The reason for this measure, the first specifically related to aqua vitae, was the detrimental effect of a high level of distilling not on the sobriety of the labouring classes but on grain supplies which were needed for food. Although the stills then in use bear little resemblance to their modern counterparts, the basic principles of the process had already been established. The only method of quality control was the distiller's own senses of taste and smell, and it would have been evident to him even then that a twice or thrice distilled spirit was of better quality than the product of the first distillation — a well established axiom of the Scotch whisky industry, even though triple distillation has now all but disappeared. There are references to four times distilled aqua vitae during the seventeenth century.

By this time, patterns of distilling in Scotland and England had developed along quite separate paths. In England, the practice was concerned almost exclusively with distilling wine into a form of brandy, whilst the Scots turned their attentions increasingly to distilling malt wash. Although the Scots appear to have stuck firmly to various grains in their distilling, there were increasing signs of dubious raw materials being used by English distillers, with detrimental effects on the health and eyesight of their customers. The charter granted to the Worshipful Company of Distillers in 1636 by Charles I contained regulations banning the use of 'many harmful or unwholesome ingredients', and reflected the malpractices of the trade. The superiority of the Scottish product was already established, and although the Company of Distillers tried to impose standards on their members the gap between the two widened, and the industry in England was to deteriorate into the excesses of mass spirit production which were to do so much harm during the 'Gin Era' in the first half of the eighteenth century. The removal of the already limited powers of the Company of Distillers by the government of the day did not improve matters.

The formal relationship between the distiller and government was struck by the introduction of the first excise tax by Charles I in 1644, and this inspired the Scottish Parliament to impose a duty on aqua vitae produced in the country. Since distilling was essentially for private purposes the units were small, although a few larger distilleries were beginning to appear in the latter part of the seventeenth century and, in defiance of the old Scottish Act of 1579, were openly selling their product. The most famous of these was Ferintosh at Dingwall. The owner, Duncan Forbes of Culloden, had (as a reward for loyalty to the Crown) been granted in 1689 the privilege of distilling aqua vitae free of duty. There were two minor conditions: only grain grown on the Ferintosh estate could be used, and a modest annual payment was to be made in return. This special arrangement persisted for nearly a century. During that time, Ferintosh whisky became famous throughout Scotland, but the final loss of its duty-free status caused Forbes's descendents to withdraw from distilling and Ferintosh disappeared, a fact much lamented at the time by Robert Burns.

Legal and illegal whisky

The eighteenth century witnessed a bitter struggle between Highland distiller and smuggler on the one hand, and Lowland commercial interests and London authority on the other. The frustrations and intensity of the struggle can be traced by the attempts of government to enforce ever more swingeing fiscal measures throughout the century. A few years after the Act of Union in 1707, Parliament sought to bring Scotland into line with England by imposing a malt tax which would have greatly affected the price of ale, the main beverage then in both countries. The reaction was predictable and the move came to nought, but it did not deter those in the South who believed that Scotland (which had been relatively under-taxed) was getting off too lightly. A further attempt to introduce the malt tax in 1725 at half the English rate led to serious riots in Glasgow and Edinburgh which spread as far as the Orkneys. However, the tax became law and ale gradually lost its place to whisky produced either by the licensed Lowland distilleries, which began to dilute the malted barley with unmalted grain, or the illicit Highland distilleries which produced a better quality whisky from malted barley, on which no tax had been levied.

The Highland distilleries had, therefore, benefited from the malt tax at the expense of the drinking public. They also enjoyed a certain fiscal advantage over the English distillers until 1751. Private distilling was eventually banned and further pressure led to the Wash Act of 1784, designed to arrest the southward flow of cheap spirits produced almost exclusively by relatively new Lowland distilleries. A distinction was drawn between Highland and Lowland distilleries, in that the former were taxed much less severely than the latter. This distinction may have been partly political and partly a reflection of the belief that the Highlander faced greater economic and physical disadvantages than his Lowland competitor. The difference was substantial. The Highlander paid an annual licence fee of £1 per gallon, based on the still's capacity, whilst the Lowlander was levied five pennies per gallon of wash, on the same basis as the English distiller. But the authors of the legislation had overlooked the fact that a gallon of wash from an English distillery produced a greater quantity of gin than the same gallon of wash would produce in a whisky distillery, and two years later the Act was amended. As a result, the Lowland distillers also paid the yearly licence fee, which was raised to £1.10s. per gallon of estimated still content, and an extra two shillings per gallon duty was imposed on Scotch whisky 'imported' into England. This duty of course encouraged smuggling, and the licence fee made the ingenious Scots distiller improve methods so as to increase production far beyond the capacity of the old still on which the exciseman's estimates were based.

The flow of spirits from north to south swelled, and a nonplussed government increased the duty and doubled the licence fee. The

47

large scale Lowland distillers became unable to hold the all-important London market against the restrictive legislation and fierce competition from English distillers, and many collapsed. The licence rose to £9 in 1793, to help finance a new war with France, then doubled and then trebled to £54 in 1797, to be doubled again in 1800, and in 1803 it reached an impossible £162. The situation was out of hand. Smuggling was widespread and the authority of government openly flouted. Far more whisky was being distilled illegally than was processed through licensed stills, and the oft quoted figure of 400 illicit stills to eight licensed ones in Edinburgh alone, in the year 1777, shows who was then winning. The much harassed industry came under added pressure when distilling was totally banned from time to time because of grain shortages, when near-famine conditions were not unknown.

Local dignitaries and sometimes even the excise officers were often involved in the illicit distilling and smuggling, so the government in London decided in 1814 to try a new approach. The old system based on still capacity was dropped and a standard charge of £10 per still introduced, plus a duty on wash. Stills of less than 500 gallons capacity were not allowed to operate above the Highland Line and Highland distillers were prohibited from selling their whisky below it. The minimum still capacity in the Lowlands was 2000 gallons, and Lowland distillers were still compelled to register for trading on the English market. But the government failed to appreciate that for the Highlander, at least, distilling was more than a commercial activity, it was an essential part of his way of life. It helped him eke out a bearable existence in an otherwise harsh and ungenerous environment, and it provided him with the means of offering hospitality to family, friends or passing strangers. His whisky was as much part of his wealth as his crops and animals, if he were lucky enough to possess any of the latter. He was not likely to give it up lightly. The 1814 Act did nothing, therefore, to diminish the illegal distilling and smuggling, and by 1815 the Glenlivet area alone was said to boast 200 stills, every one of them totally outside the law.

The exciseman's lot was not a happy one. He was working against a highly motivated, hostile and sometimes desperate section of the population, whose activities were either supported or connived at by a majority of the rest. He was often working in unfamiliar territory and was obliged to do so to a rule-book, whereas his adversary had none. Like all tax collectors in history, he had no natural allies, save the government of the day which left him to execute its unpopular policies. In fact and fiction he was portrayed as heavy-handed, humourless, dim-witted and not always honest. Rewards were offered for information on illegal stills, but very often the system was abused, as the 'uncovered still' would actually be one recently abandoned as worn out through excessive use. The exciseman (or gauger) was not always sufficiently expert to recognise this, and often thankful in any case to be able to report a 'captured' still. As he was required to destroy it there and then, the evidence was thus obliterated. Very often the person who had made the 'discovery' and had led the gaugers to the illegal still was its former owner, who would then use the reward money for capital investment and be back in business with a new still in a different and well hidden location!

The other side of the story, that of the exciseman's, should not be forgotten. He was expected to make his living from the proceeds of the take which he shared with the exchequer, and from which he had to meet all his expenses, including sometimes costly legal fees. Often his adversaries were as well armed and determined as he was himself, and contemporary annals abound with tales of bloody clashes. Small wonder, then, that some gaugers found it easier to co-operate with the smugglers, ensuring for themselves a steadier income and fewer broken bones. On the other hand, there were many honest excise officers, some of whom became noted writers on life in eighteenth and nineteenth century Scotland, the most celebrated of them all being Robert Burns.

The difficult life of the exciseman was made no easier by the utter indifference of the population at large to smuggling, and when the highest in the land were openly partaking of illicit whisky it was obvious that events had taken a turn towards the absurd. These were crowned by the visit to Edinburgh in 1822 of King George IV, who adopted Highland dress and called for Glenlivet, claiming that he drank nothing else. The Glenlivet served then was, of course, illicit. George IV's love of whisky is reported on an earlier occasion, on his passage across the Irish Sea the year before, when the Duke of Buckingham and Chandos recorded in his memoirs that 'the passage to Dublin was occupied in eating goose-pie and drinking whiskey [old spelling] in which His Majesty took most abundantly, singing many joyous songs, and being in a state, on his arrival, to double in number even the numbers of his gracious subjects assembled on the pier to receive him.' However, there is no guarantee that the whisky on this occasion was Glenlivet; given King George IV's keen sense of occasion, it may well have been Irish whiskey, but clearly the monarch's taste for the fruit of the still was well established, whether the whisky was legal or smuggled.

Things had to change. The Duke of Gordon had in 1820 made a statesmanlike speech in the House of Lords in favour of more realistic treatment of the Highland distiller. In return for reasonable legislation he undertook, along with other great Scottish landowners, to cut out the illicit stills and ensure that his tenants took out licences. A Commission was set up and reported in time for Parliament to pass the Act to Eliminate Illicit Distilling in 1823. The minimum still size had been reduced to forty gallons in 1816 and remained at this more sensible level; the licence fee of £10 was retained and a duty of 2s. 3d. (11p) per gallon of proof spirits charged. (The imperial gallon was introduced in 1825 under the Consolidation Act, and this was applied as a standard measure for all distilling purposes.)

The Duke of Gordon and his fellow landowners were most anxious to demonstrate support for the government's reasonableness, and pressed their tenants to 'go straight'. The response was negative and often surly. Any tax or licence was deemed an interference in the Highlander's freedom to distil, and it was to be many years before this attitude was to disappear. Nevertheless, by 1824 George Smith of Glenlivet had successfully applied for the first licence to distil under the patronage of his landlord, the Duke of Gordon. Local residents were hostile, as the story of George Smith and his famous Glenlivet Distillery in Chapter 9 (see George & J.G. Smith Ltd) reveals, but there was a growing wish on all sides to see matters regulated and others eventually followed suit, but with great caution at first, since illegal distilling was still prevalent and profitable.

The Act of 1823 thus not only cleared the air, but effectively gave new and enlightened guidelines along which distillers and merchants could work, and it says much for its compilers that it remains today the foundation stone on which all subsequent distillery law was based. It marked the end of an intriguing period in Scottish history, one followed by the struggle between pot-still distiller and patent-still distiller and the eventual compromise which was to form the foundations of the modern Scotch whisky industry.

4 Whisky comes of age

From the 14,000 cases of illicit distilling awaiting trial before the Act of 1823, the level of prosecutions fell dramatically to 392 in 1830, to 73 in 1854, to a mere handful in 1874. There were occasional bursts of renewed enthusiasm and activity by the smugglers — something which has continued even to the present day, and inevitably coinciding with particularly fearsome jumps in the rate of duty. By 1855 the tax had reached 8s. (40p) — the same as that imposed on English distillers — and by the turn of the century it stood at 11s. (55p). The effects of legislation were gradually being felt. The consumption of legal whisky, i.e. whisky on which tax had been paid, had fallen to two million gallons in 1823, but within two years of the Act it had jumped to nearly six million gallons.

Non-stop whisky

The face of the industry, still very much a cottage one in most respects, was certainly changing, and its rapid commercialisation helped to hasten the demise of the illicit stills. A major step towards expansion took place in 1826 with Robert Stein's invention of the patent or continuous still, which differed from the traditional pot-still in that the distilling was a single continuous process rather than the double, or sometimes triple, distillation which the pot-still involved. Stein was from a prominent Lowland distilling family who had intermarried with the Haigs, and it was John Haig who was to put the patent still to full commercial use at his distillery at Cameron Bridge in Fife, rather than at Robert Stein's own distillery at Kilbagie. For some time a number of distillers had regarded the pot-still as too slow and too variable in its end product for their commercial needs. They wanted something more exact, from which standards could be set and maintained, and Robert Stein was the first to come up with a satisfactory answer. His still, in the opinion of the excise officers who examined it, produced a whisky more stable and far freer of impurities than any pot-still malt whisky. Its success was assured, and the last Stein still in Scotland, at Cameron Bridge, remained in active production until 1928.

Stein's invention was soon to be improved on and overtaken by Aeneas Coffey, Inspector General of Excise in Ireland, who produced in 1830 a more sophisticated, efficient and reliable version of the patent still, using twin columns. The principles established then are very much the ones followed today in modern grain distilleries in Scotland, as described in Chapter 2. Although Coffey's idea had been met with scepticism in Ireland, the Scots gave him a much better reception when he arrived to sell his invention. His still was patented in 1832, and there soon followed a rush of new distilleries churning out large quantities of the cheap 'patent', or grain, whisky. The distillers were encouraged in their enterprise by the fact that, for some inexplicable reason, these stills did not come under excise control, an anomaly which was not rectified until 1838. The effect on the malt whisky distillers was predictable: illicit distilling increased in the Highlands and consumption of duty-paid whisky fell dramatically to about one-eighth the amount consumed before the 1823 Act.

The Highland malt distiller was at open war with his Lowland competitor, whose production far outstripped that of the typical pot still, and who was enjoying freedom, albeit temporarily, from any excise or fiscal control over patent stills. Also, the Highland distillers' bitterness was deepened by the knowledge that certain Lowland grain distillers were clandestinely mixing cheap grain whisky with malt, which they then sold in the Highland area at prices well below that with which the Highlander could compete. The parliamentary Commission of Sir Henry Parnell (1833-1836) exposed some of the unfairness and inconsistencies, but it was deficient in follow-up, and the rivalry and distrust between Highland and Lowland distillers was to simmer on for decades.

The first of the big blenders

The grain whisky spilling out of the Lowland distilleries was either consumed locally, more or less in its raw state, or was sent to England where it would reappear as gin, still then the popular comfort of the masses. The grain whisky was a neutral, characterless spirit and it soon occurred to some merchants that it would be more acceptable and sell better if it were mixed with the more robust, vivacious malt whiskies of the north. At the same time, certain innkeepers found the undiluted, highly flavoured Highland malts too much for some of their customers, and produced a more palatable and cheaper drink by adding grain whisky. The blending of malt and grain whisky began, therefore, almost naturally. The somewhat primitive methods used in the pot-stills worked against a consistently high quality, and the blending or vatting of different production batches had been officially approved by the Excise, in order to try and improve quality. Andrew Usher is credited with first exploiting the practice of blending whiskies (in this case vatting malts) on a fairly large commercial scale, when he began selling his Usher's Old Vatted Glenlivet in 1853. It was some time later, in 1865, before blending of grain and malt whiskies from different distilleries was given official blessing, in the form of the Blending Act.

The success of blended whisky encouraged grain production and ever-fiercer competition. This caused the six leading Lowland grain whisky distillers to form a 'Trade Arrangement' in 1856, and a second one was concluded in 1865. Their purpose was to allocate the available trade in agreed proportions, and to remove the worst elements of cut-throat pricing competition, and the Arrangements were moderately successful, the partners in the second Arrangements ultimately forming the nucleus of the Distillers Company (DCL), which was to grow rapidly into the single biggest force in the industry.

Beginnings of the 'boom'

About this time, a totally unconnected event in France was unwittingly helping to cement the foundations of the burgeoning whisky industry. French wine growers had for long been importing American vines with which to renew and strengthen their traditional vineyards. The rugged American species was immune to the ravages of a vine louse known as *Phylloxera vastatrix*, but it did carry the disease to French vines. The disease first struck France about 1860 and spread like wildfire. It had probably not appeared earlier as the bug would not have survived the lengthy Atlantic crossing. But with the advent of steam and a briefer journey its arrival in Europe was assured, and it soon set to work on the delicate French vine roots. By 1865 it was firmly established and by the early 1880s reached the Cognac district. The results were catastrophic, and within a few years brandy, the traditional mainstay of the British middle classes, had virtually disappeared from their cellars. The French industry was to recover, but only after many years, by which time Scotch had taken the place of brandy as the spirit to which the Englishman added soda to make his pre-dinner drink. Some argue that Scotch whisky was, in any case, destined to dominate the British spirits market given the rapid development of the industry that was taking place, and that the role of the 'bug' is over-stated. Nevertheless, it was a happy coincidence for Scotland's distillers and the growing band of blenders and whisky salesmen.

The Scotch whisky industry was beginning to boom. The widespread use of the Coffey still had quite changed the pattern of production, with grain whisky outstripping malt whisky by the mid-1860s, a trend that was never to be reversed. Indeed, such were the opportunities seen in the new demand for whisky in the 1880s that distilleries in England began producing spirit for shipping to Scotland and Ireland for blending with the mature product. Four such distilleries were Bank Hall and Vauxhall in Liverpool, Lea Valley in London, and Bristol Distillery. They all employed the Coffey patent still for producing either gin or patent still whisky. Bank Hall and Lea Valley also had pot-stills and produced malt whisky. There was even a Welsh whisky distillery at Bala in North Wales, which was recorded in 1893 as being in production. The blending of grain and malt whiskies was firmly established by now, and the distiller was slipping into the background, the blender and merchant predominating as the industry became increasingly commercialised and market-orientated.

Unlike the few Highland malts which had established reputations arising from their distinctive flavours, blended whisky had at first no external distinguishing feature, as it was sold in bulk for the grocer or innkeeper to dispense from the keg. It was many years before the law was altered to allow Scottish merchants to send whisky in bottle for sale in England, and it was this development which allowed the new breed of whisky merchant to promote his particular blend, and in so doing to develop the concept of brands. Although it was the quality of the blend which won customers, it was its availability under a recognised name which ensured it continued in demand. The way to ultimate success was no longer in Scotland, but in London and elsewhere in England. Enterprising young Scotsmen came forward to meet the commercial challenge, and the few who succeeded were to enjoy great wealth and high national honours. Those entrepreneurs who made the greatest impact were James Buchanan of the firm of that name, Tommy Dewar, the younger Dewar son of John Dewar & Son, Peter Mackie of White Horse Distillers Ltd (the name adopted by the company after his death), and James Stevenson of Johnnie

Walker fame. Each was distinguished in his own right and made his own particular contribution to the modernisation of the industry, and the wider appreciation of Scotch whisky. Buchanan, with great panache and self-confidence, no capital and little knowledge of the industry to back it, captured London's imagination with his Buchanan Blend, the first widely accepted brand name. Dewar, by sheer force of personality and self-advertisement, demonstrated that a brand of whisky could be sold if attention was attracted to it by sufficiently spectacular publicity. Peter Mackie was obsessed with maintaining standards and hounding out of business the less scrupulous merchants who traded in immature whisky. Stevenson carried on the work of Alec Walker and through administrative skill and business acumen secured Johnnie Walker's place as the largest-selling Scotch whisky in the world.

To complete the 'Big Five' it is necessary to add John Haig & Co. Ltd. This was an enterprise already well established before the whisky boom of the late nineteenth century, and one more concerned, at least at first, with distilling than blending. Of the other four entrepreneurs, only Peter Mackie had inherited distilling interests. The rest were merely merchants who had made good, and Buchanan had started virtually from scratch. The company of Haig quickly followed the new pattern of trade established by the other four and, most noteworthy of all, was to precede all of them into DCL.

As slick salesmen filled their order books, so businessmen in the north moved in to make a killing. Distilleries had their production capacity enhanced, new distilleries were constructed and new companies popped up to offer ever better whiskies to a thirsty public. Whilst many succeeded, others failed, and once more survival of the fittest seemed to be as axiomatic as ever, until the dramatic collapse of the Pattison brothers, large-scale blenders whose financial security never seemed to be in doubt, and whose whisky was widely advertised and consumed.

The original Leith grocery partnership of the brothers Robert and Walter, trading as Pattison Elder & Co., had become Pattisons Ltd so that fresh capital could be raised to allow expansion. Extravagance in both private and business life-style followed, but this was based largely on borrowed money. A euphoric investing public swelled the coffers and whisky production was soon well ahead of demand. A feeling of unease began to replace the previous air of confidence, and doubts were cast as to Pattisons' viability. The share value plummeted and by December 1898 Pattisons' was finished, with both brothers ending up in prison on charges of fraud. A major name in the new industry had foundered and disappeared almost overnight, taking with it many smaller companies with doubtful credentials.

The proceedings connected with the Pattisons' case revealed, moreover, that Pattisons' whisky was almost entirely cheap, unmatured grain spirit to which were added tiny quantities of malt whisky. Some of the old doubts about Scotch whisky were returning to the minds of the English consumer, who was the mainstay of the industry, and the Scotch whisky houses must have worried more than a little about a possible resurgence in Irish distilling and a fresh challenge from across the Irish sea. Irish whiskey had been popular in England during the period 1866-75 and, indeed, had dominated the market. The capture of the English market by the Scots was due largely to the efforts of the great whisky salesmen such as Buchanan and Dewar, rather than any inherent preference for the Scottish product over the Irish, although the blended Scotch whiskies were considered less of an acquired taste than their Irish pot-still rivals. As the following figures of English imports (in million proof gallons) show, the Irish challenge persisted for many years:

	from Scotland	*from Ireland*
1880	1.8	1.6
1888	2.2	1.5
1900	7.1	4.2
1910	4.4	1.8

Having lost the battle for the English market, Irish whiskey was eventually to find itself a poor second to Scotch in every other market. It is worth recalling that a century ago Irish whiskey enjoyed greater sales in the United States than did Scotch. Today its presence is almost insignificant, and sales of all Irish whiskey brands taken together are less than any single one of the major Scotch whisky brands. Perhaps the Irish just had less foresight and imagination than their Scottish competitors. Aeneas Coffey had certainly found this, and his move from Ireland to Scotland with his patent still was an event of great significance for the latter. Moreover, it is only in very recent years that the Irish have broken with tradition and produced a blended whisky combining pot-still whisky with grain.

Apart from the Irish competition, the merchants also had to fight against the growing strength of the Temperance Movement, who campaigned vigorously for total abstinence. Since its start in 1826 much zealous proselytising had gone on, but with more success in England than in Scotland. The campaign evoked much support and could not be ignored by politicians.

Scotch whisky was also having to overcome the social prejudices arrayed against it. For many years it had been considered by the upper classes as being suitable only as sustenance against the elements when shooting or fishing on their Highland estates. Even as late as 1880 it was still considered, outside Scotland, to be a very inferior kind of spirit, and if it were found in the homes of the well-to-do, it would invariably be below stairs where the servants were often of Scottish origin. Upstairs in the drawing room, the drinks then were more likely to be brandy or Dutch gin, or occasionally rum.

It was against all such prejudice and opposition that the Buchanans, Dewars and Mackies worked in order to establish the respectability of their native drink in the latter part of the nineteenth century and into the next one.

5 To conquer the world: the twentieth century

Whilst Scotch whisky continued its upward path, bitterness and rivalry between the pot still malt distillers and the blenders simmered on. But one could scarcely do without the other. The malt distillers found that an increasing proportion of their production was being bought by the blenders, who were in turn dependent on their Highland colleagues if they were to promote a credible blended whisky. It was the activities of certain unscrupulous blenders and patent still grain distillers which were undermining what should have been a natural, co-operative arrangement. The poor malt distillers saw themselves as the defenders of the true Scotch whisky craft against the tricksters and fast-talking salesmen who had sprung up overnight and who threatened to destroy the very heart of the industry. The malt distiller could not compete with the patent still grain distillery since the very nature of malt whisky distilling was more expensive in materials and time, and necessarily involved an operation on a much smaller scale. Moreover, the dreadful truth was that the mass of the drinking public preferred a lighter, less flavoursome blended whisky to the heavily peated Highland malts. The writing was already on the wall for malt whisky as a drink, but the malt distillers were not easily quietened. They turned to political and legal means to advance their cause, taking as the main target of their attack those blenders who passed off their product as 'Highland Malt', although it invariably contained a much higher proportion of grain whisky than malt.

Politics and the law

A select committee of the House of Commons was set up under Sir Lyon Playfair in 1890 as a result of pressure from local MPs. It was required to look into the question of whether spirits should be compulsorily held in bond for a certain minimum period before being released for consumption, and to enquire into the system of blending, and whether the Sale of Food and Drugs Act and the Merchandise Marks Act should apply to spirits. The committee did not define whisky (which is what the Highland malt distillers had wanted) and in effect gave their blessing to the blenders. Perhaps they were too conscious of the amount of trade by then involved in blended whisky, and this may also have caused them to hold their hand on the imposition of a minimum age under which spirits could not be sold for domestic consumption, which would have amounted to compulsory bonding. They concluded that such a measure 'would harass the trade' and thought the matter should be left in the hands of the public, who showed 'a marked preference for old spirits'.

With a clean bill of health, whisky distilling continued to flourish. By the end of the nineteenth century there were 161 distilleries producing thirty-six million gallons of spirit. Unfortunately for the Highland malt distillers, the greater proportion was coming from the patent stills, and although both distillers and blenders were enjoying a boom, the Highlanders remained largely unplaced in their fury that the chief beneficiaries of the boom were the Lowland grain distillers and the blenders.

The next attempt to strike a blow for the malt distillers was the Sale of Whisky Bill tabled in Parliament in 1904, with the object of distinguishing to the consuming public between whisky made from malted barley alone and that containing only, or partly, unmalted grain. It got no further than the first reading. A further Bill the following year seeking compulsory bonding for a minimum of three years together with clearly defined descriptions for malt, grain and blended whiskies met the same fate, but was a further indication of the growing unease over some of the worst anomalies of the industry. Cases were quoted of large quantities of English spirit being mixed with a small proportion of unmatured grain spirit, of concoctions being sold as Scotch whisky which owed their origins to imported German spirit or, worse still, to such unlikely substances as rice, molasses or even sulphuric acid.

The atmosphere was right for a dramatic prosecution, which was held not in Scotland but, of all places, in the London borough of Islington, the venue of the famous 'What is whisky?' case. The local council, flushed with an earlier success against fraudulent brandy producers, charged a number of local retailers under the Merchandise Marks Act with selling as whisky 'articles not of the nature, substance and quality demanded'.

The North London Police Court was the field on which the patent still distillers joined battle with the pot still distillers, each side providing technical witnesses in order to damn the other's case (and the former undertaking to defray the costs of the police court action). On 26 February 1906 the magistrate, Mr Fordham, found in favour of the council and the defendants were fined. The judgement shocked DCL and the grain distillers generally, and notice of appeal was lodged immediately. The case went to Clerkenwell Quarter Sessions some three months later. Within a month, involving seven sittings, it was evident that the bench of lay magistrates could not come to a decision, and so the original judgement stood.

Jubilant though the malt distillers were, many people in the industry — including some of the less intransigent Highland distillers — were concerned that the doubts hanging over Scotch whisky would be harmful to the industry as a whole. In particular, they feared that it would allow further exploitation by foreigners who were already taking advantage of the increasing popularity of Scotch whisky abroad to mix good Highland malt with cheap local spirit, and sell it as the genuine article. Moreover, the considerable infrastructure which had been developed by the blenders and grain distillers in southern Scotland was aimed not only at meeting native demand but at supplying the entire United Kingdom, including the vital London market, as well as the growing demand from overseas. If that were to collapse, the malt distillers would be worse off than ever, since they lacked both the capital and commercial knowledge to replace it. Also, there remained the unspoken but nagging doubts as to the acceptability of the pungent unblended malts by the wider public in Britain and abroad. The malt distillers had won on principle, but risked bringing the entire edifice down around them.

Peace and compromise were obviously vital to the industry, and representatives of both sides eventually put their case to the government. The upshot was the appointment in February 1908 of a Royal Commission which was charged with (a) considering whether restrictions should be applied to the materials or processes used in the production of Scotch or Irish whisky or any other spirit to which the term whisky might be applied, and (b) looking into the merits of having a minimum period during which whisky should be matured in bond.

The malt distillers had modified their stand considerably and were now pushing for the definition: 'Patent still spirit is not Scotch whisky except when made in Scotland and blended or mixed with 50 per cent of Scotch malt whisky.' The grain distillers were largely basing their case on what the general public wanted, and DCL had already demonstrated that there was a public demand even for unblended patent still whisky by introducing, largely for public relations reasons, a bottled grain whisky called Cambus.

Various undesirable practices came to light as a result of the Commission, such as a London-produced 'whisky' which consisted of unmatured patent still spirit to which had been added a tiny proportion of malt whisky, and known as N.S.S. One of the witnesses to the Commission revealed that the letters stood for 'Never Saw Scotland'.

After nearly eighteen months of deliberation the Commission concluded that whisky was a 'spirit obtained by distillation from a mash of cereal grains saccharified by the diastase of malt', and that 'Scotch whisky is whisky as above defined, distilled in Scotland'. A similar definition applied to Irish whiskey. But they did not find in favour of having a minimum period during which whisky should be matured in bond. Eventually this was to be changed by the Immature Spirits Act of 1915 which specified two years compulsory bonding, extended to three years by an amendment the following year, as described later in the chapter.

The Royal Commission of 1908 was a triumph for the grain distillers and did nothing to heal the breach between them and the malt distillers. A temporary pact emerged very soon, however, when the entire industry turned its fury on the Chancellor of the Liberal government, Lloyd George (a confirmed temperance man), who introduced a swingeing increase in duty from 11s. (55p) to 14s. 9d. (74p) — 39 per cent — in the 1909 budget, and changed the licensing system whereby the flat rate of ten guineas was dropped in favour of a sliding scale dependent on quantity produced. There were objections from both sides of the industry, including a plea from Peter Mackie, who had both blending and distilling interests, that the increased duty be applied in such a way as to be less onerous the older the whisky. This was clearly designed to comfort the pot still malt distillers, whose product required longer maturation than that of the patent still distiller before it was acceptable to most consumers. Lloyd George was unmoved, and the Finance Bill, unaltered in terms of the provisions for whisky, was duly passed by the Commons, but when it reached the House of Lords it was rejected. This precipitated a parliamentary crisis, and was seen as a direct challenge to the representatives of the people by the Upper Chamber. A resolution condemning the action was passed by a large majority in the Commons, Parliament was dissolved and an election held. The Liberals fared badly, losing 100 seats, although remaining by one seat the party with the most members in Parliament. Their only hope of getting their Finance Bill through was an alliance with the Irish Nationalists, who had been strongly opposed to it because of its effects on Irish whiskey. They were, however, prepared to support the new government, but at a price involving the introduction of bills to weaken the Anti-Home Rule for Ireland lobby. The net result was that the teetotaler Lloyd George got his way on the whisky taxes and delivered a hefty blow to the Scotch whisky industry. Demand fell, production slackened and stocks began to build up ominously. The effects were to be far-reaching and were to underline the growing importance of exports.

The Distillers Company

On that note, it is perhaps appropriate to consider the vital role played by the Distillers Company Limited (DCL) in the development of the Scotch whisky industry. Although the history and structure of each of the constituent DCL companies is examined in detail in Chapter 9, so central has the group been to the shaping of the industry as we know it today that it requires to be looked at in the context of what was happening to Scotch whisky at about the time of the First World War. However, we first need to slip back in time in order to see how the company came about.

DCL's date of birth is taken as 24 April 1877, on which date the company was registered in Edinburgh. The company, in fact, grew out of the First Trade Arrangement entered into in 1856 by six Lowland grain distillers, with the aim of protecting the individual and collective interests of the participants. The parties to the Arrangement and the share of the trade allocated to each was as follows: Menzies, Barnard & Craig, 41.5 per cent; John Bald & Co., 15 per cent; John Haig & Co., 13.5 per cent; McNab Bros & Co., 11.5 per cent; Robert Moubray, 10.5 per cent; John Crabbie & Co., 8 per cent.

There was, not surprisingly, a certain dissatisfaction amongst the members, and a new Arrangement was concluded in 1865 with D. Macfarlane & Co. replacing John Crabbie & Co. An agreement was reached with English and Irish grain distillers which was highly satisfactory to the Scottish group; but then nothing further was achieved until Robert Stewart, a grain distiller who had remained outside the grouping, made a proposal to form a limited liability company into which all their resources would be pooled. After several months of negotiation and reflection, the plan went ahead on

John Bald's Carsebridge distillery

a nominal capital of two million pounds. Five of the six members of the Second Trade Arrangement came in, Menzies, Barnard & Craig opting not to, and were joined by Stewart & Co. Of the six, only John Haig & Co. still exists as a company, but three of the six distilleries (each member company owning one distillery) are still operating, although probably bearing little resemblance now to the originals. They are: Cambus at Alloa (Robert Moubray), Cameron Bridge in Fife (John Haig & Co.), and Port Dundas near Glasgow (H. Macfarlane & Co.). Two have disappeared, namely Glenochil (McNab Bros & Co.), Kirkliston (Stewart & Co.), and Carsebridge (John Bald & Co.) closed in 1983.

Although the new structure was a move forward and a binding one, it was to be some years before the different elements settled down to work together in total harmony. In referring to the different partners in a speech made shortly after the company's formation, a local lawyer spoke of 'the determined Haig, the politic Bald, the impetuous Macfarlane, the subtle Moubray, the anxious Stewart, the cautious McNab and the bold Menzies.' Although the Menzies partnership had got cold feet at the last moment over joining, they had, in fact, entered into a working arrangement with DCL on formation of the company and eventually came back to the fold with their Caledonian Distillery in 1883.

Canny expansion was the order of the day and the company looked round for other worthwhile properties. One of the first to catch its eye was Chapelizod Distillery in Dublin, which was renamed Phoenix Park. This was the beginning of DCL's less-than-happy connections with Ireland. Of greater significance, however, was the decision to build new facilities at South Queensferry as the centre of the group's blending and exporting activities, something which was to help DCL eventually gain such a commanding position in both these areas.

A date of particular note for DCL was 1889. William H. Ross became Company Secretary and Accountant and launched an impressive programme of both malt and grain distillery construction and acquisition. Examples were the building in 1894 of Knockdhu Highland Malt Distillery and the acquisition in 1902 of Ardgowan and Loch Katrine distilleries, as well as the entire share capital of J. & R. Harvey & Co. Ltd, who owned Dundashill Distillery. The Pattison disaster in 1898 helped DCL grow in an unexpected way, since the rush out of whisky meant the company was able to purchase properties at much reduced prices. Soon after the turn of the century DCL took a policy decision to involve itself in related activities such as the manufacture of yeast for bread-making, and the acquisition of patent still distilleries in England and a further distillery in Ireland (Dundalk, Co. Down), but the main interest remained over-whelmingly Scotch whisky.

The next major event in DCL's development was the formation of Scottish Malt Distillers Ltd, combining the five Lowland malt distilleries of Rosebank, Glenkinchie, St Magdalene, Grange and Clydesdale (the first two are still in operation under Distillers Company ownership, St Magdalene now being generally known as Linlithgow). Saucel Distillery at Paisley was added in 1915, but for use as a bonded warehouse. The following year the well known blending houses of John Hopkins & Co. Ltd and John Begg Ltd became DCL possessions.

During the war DCL enjoyed a certain privilege inasmuch as they were allowed to go on distilling, when most other distillers were not, in recognition of their vital role as principal supplier of yeast to the nation's bakers when imports of foreign yeast were halted. By the end of the war further acquisitions had been made in the form of J. & G. Stewart Ltd and Andrew Usher & Co., both ancient Edinburgh blenders and whisky merchants. The other branch of the Haig family, John Haig & Co. Ltd of Markinch, followed in 1919. Expansion also took place in industrial spirits with the purchase of Bristol Distillery and Bank Hall Distillery in Liverpool. However, this programme of expansion was not engineered for the sake of sheer grandiosity; rationalisation of the company's resources was going on all the time. Thus, Yoker and Camlachie Distilleries were bought for use as bonded warehouses and Phoenix Park and Dundalk closed down for good.

An important infusion of both material and knowledge followed the merger with James Calder & Co. Ltd in 1921. This gave DCL Bo'ness and Gartloch (both long since defunct) and put Sir James C. Calder on the board. A new venture in Ireland involved purchase of the entire ordinary share capital of The Distillers Finance Corporation Ltd of Belfast and its various subsidiaries, including the United Distilleries Ltd. The move was partly designed to thwart the ambitions of the American Fleischmann Co. Included in the deal was Tanqueray, Gordon & Co. Ltd, London gin distillers. As if bitten by the gin bug, DCL then went ahead in 1924 and bought the gin houses of Sutton, Carden & Co. Ltd, Boord & Son Ltd and Sir Robert Burnett & Co. Ltd. That same year, the Distillers Agency was set up and Peter Dawson Ltd, the blenders, acquired.

These events were a mere prelude to the single most important event in DCL's later history, its amalgamation in 1925 with the major blending and distilling houses of John Walker & Sons, Buchanan and Dewar, the latter two having previously merged to form Buchanan-Dewar Ltd. This was the crowning achievement of Mr William H. Ross, who became chairman and managing director of the enlarged company. DCL's ascendancy was now unassailable, which was just as well since foreign interests were soon to be casting covetous eyes at Scotland's considerable whisky assets.

Further, less spectacular moves followed almost immediately in the industrial spirit field and by acquisition of the balance of the shares in Scottish Malt Distillers Ltd, as well as the remaining assets of Sir James Calder's company, Macdonald, Greenlees & Williams Ltd, and some sundry works. Overseas companies were formed in Australia and Canada to promote the company's interests there.

To conquer the world: the twentieth century

The remaining member of the 'Big Five', Mackie's White Horse Distillers Ltd, was netted in 1927, when the shareholders accepted DCL's offer for the whole of the ordinary capital. Ross had achieved his objective and DCL had more or less reached its optimum size in relation to the rest of the industry. Although further rationalisation and take-overs in whisky followed, they were of a more modest nature, for DCL was by now conscious of the need to avoid appearing too monolithic or monopolist. The last thing they wanted was a one-company industry, and so their attentions were in later years turned more to areas other than Scotch whisky.

Just as the First World War had uniquely helped DCL, Prohibition was another event harmful to the industry as a whole but beneficial to Scotland's whisky giant. It spelled ruin for many of the smaller distillers, but DCL was now big enough to ride out the storm and pick up some useful properties for a song. Two such acquisitions were that of Bulloch Lade & Co. Ltd and Wright & Greig Ltd in 1927, with their well established brands and, in the case of Bulloch Lade, substantial stocks of mature whisky. The following year the Glasgow blenders Benmore Distilleries Ltd joined the DCL clan, and in 1932 Banff distillery was bought from the Mile End Distillery Co. Ltd which in turn was owned by Taylor, Walker & Co. Ltd. Teaninich and Linkwood distilleries were bought in 1933 at prices of £285,000 and £80,000 respectively, and the Glasgow blenders, Macleay, Duff & Co. Ltd, for £325,000. The purchase of Baird-Taylor Ltd, the Glasgow firm of whisky wholesalers, and the disposal of Connswater grain distillery in Belfast both took place in 1935. The following year Donald Fisher Ltd became a wholly owned subsidiary, and Cambus distillery, which had earlier been destroyed by fire, was rebuilt. The old established Leith blenders of D. & J. McCallum went to DCL in 1937 after going into liquidation. In the same year DCL purchased the important gin company, Booth's Distilleries Ltd, which brought with it the substantial whisky business of Wm Sanderson & Son Ltd, of VAT 69 fame, and a range of smaller firms — Low, Robertson & Co. Ltd, John Bisset & Co. Ltd, and John McEwan & Co. Ltd. The next whisky purchase was not until 1944, when the Leith merchants, A. & A. Crawford Ltd entered the DCL fold, as did the now defunct Gilmour, Thomson & Co. Ltd and the still active J. & W. Hardie Ltd, both whisky merchants, in 1947. A further minor take-over was the whisky-broking enterprise of J.B. Barclay & Co. Ltd in 1948.

And so it went on: amalgamation, rationalisation, absorption, diversification. But through it all DCL maintained — at least as regards its Scotch whisky activities — the principle of competition as between the constituent companies, and avoided the image of a single, mass produced DCL whisky flooding the market and washing away all their external competitors. The very size of the group has given rise to hostile comment, much of it based on fear or envy, but without DCL it is hard to see how Scotch whisky would have survived two World Wars and Prohibition in the United States, all in the space of thirty years.

With that summary of the Distillers Company's birth and growth, we can return to the effect of events from 1914 onwards on the whisky industry as a whole.

Two World Wars

The outbreak of war is always a signal for the introduction of restriction and control affecting every facet of human intercourse. The Scotch whisky industry was no exception, and suffered considerably in both World Wars. Indeed, with their old enemy Lloyd George as Prime Minister they could look forward to the maximum of inconvenience throughout the First World War. The first step was the Intoxicating Liquor (Temporary Restrictions) Act, which greatly curtailed the licensing hours. This was followed in 1915 by the Immature Spirits Act, laying down a minimum of two years in bond for all spirits, extended the following year to three years. The Central Liquor Control Board was set up to oversee matters affecting all aspects of the alcoholic drink industry. Although this fell far short of Lloyd George's dream of nationalising the industry, the Board nonetheless had considerable powers and did, in fact, nationalise all of the industry's activities in an area of fifty square miles around Carlisle, in what is now Cumbria, and established the Carlisle and District State Management Board to carry out the day-to-day running of them. A similar arrangement was made for an area around Invergordon. These extraordinary measures were taken because of the large munitions works in the areas and the threat which it was felt that uncontrolled drinking would pose to safety and productivity. The Board also decreed that whisky could be sold at an alcoholic strength of 35° below proof (37.2 per cent alcohol by volume). By May 1916 the Board had prohibited all distilling except in those few cases where distilleries had a licence from the Ministry of Munitions for the production of industrial alcohol. The industry reacted clamorously, and a compromise was reached whereby the pot stills were allowed to continue in production at a level of 70 per cent of that over the previous five years. However, a total ban on pot still malt distilling was eventually imposed in June 1917 (not to resume until 1919), whilst grain whisky distilling continued at a severely reduced level. The strength at which whisky could be sold was a matter of continuing controversy, but the final outcome was that from 1 February 1917 spirits had to be sold within an upper limit of 30° under proof (40 per cent alcohol by volume) and a lower limit of 50° under proof (28.6 per cent alcohol) anywhere in Britain engaged in the munitions industry (this qualification in fact embraced wherever there was a sizable population). Thereafter sales of whisky on the home market were reduced to 50 per cent of what they had been the previous year.

The problems at home were matched by difficulties abroad, due in large measure to the hazards facing sea transport, but made worse by the banning of whisky imports in 1917 by Canada and the United States. The final blow came with the 1918 budget which doubled the duty on whisky and imposed fixed prices, thus causing the distillers and blenders to absorb some of the increase. Consumption fell drastically; Lloyd George was happy and the malt distillers wondered whether they had any future. The grain distillers were in a slightly better position, supplying a commodity much needed in the war effort. Although they saw their output fall, and the amount of grain whisky distilled almost cut in half, the emphasis was put on industrial alcohol and baker's yeast, the latter being a natural by-product of the process.

The end of the war did not bring immediate relief, and it was a full year before distilling was freed of restrictions, although the fixed price remained in force, and the Central Control Board with it, until November 1921. The next twenty years of peace represented a period of mixed fortunes for Scotch whisky, and included the closing, in many cases permanently, of a large number of distilleries, the disappearance or absorption of many companies, greater concentration in fewer hands and the arrival of the North Americans on the whisky scene. Survival had become the byword of the industry, and much of the rivalry between pot still and patent still was suppressed in favour of a united front, in view of the shared fear of government's intentions towards them.

With the Second World War, new restrictions were introduced. There was total prohibition on grain whisky distilling, although the malt distillers, being less dependent on imported raw materials, were allowed to carry on until 1941. A complete ban was then imposed on all distilling until 1944. As the end of the war brought no sign of relief the distillers resorted to old-fashioned political lobbying in order to advance their case. They had the sympathetic ear of the Prime Minister, Winston Churchill, whose own tastes in such matters were not restricted — as popular biographers would have us believe — to brandy. Churchill saw the enormous importance of the Scotch whisky industry and gave instructions accordingly: 'On no account reduce the barley for whisky. This takes years to mature, and is an invaluable export and dollar producer. Having regard to all our other difficulties about exports, it would be most improvident not to preserve this characteristic British element of ascendancy.' Any benefits from his attitude were short-lived, with the coming to power of the Labour government in July 1945. Their view — not surprising in a country racked by shortages and still under strict rationing — was that cereals, including barley, must be allocated first and foremost to meet essential food requirements. Supplies to the distillers had to be controlled, and in 1945 were only 43 per cent of the amount available to them just before the war. It was not until 1949 that distilling on the pre-war scale was permitted, and the distillers had to wait until 1953 before the rationing of grain supplies was lifted and 1954 for the removal of all the war-time restrictions.

Prohibition

Far too much has already been written on this bizarre period of American history from 1920 to 1933 for anything new to be said about it here. It led to many violent deaths, corruption on an unprecedented scale, divided families, divided cities and a divided nation. It was a well-meant policy being imposed on a society which had neither the will nor the means to carry it out. Its effects on Scotch whisky were profound.

After the privations of the First World War, Scotch whisky enjoyed a modest boom, but it proved short-lived as the effects of the Depression began to bite. Any hopes of expanding exports to the United States appeared dashed by Prohibition, and exports standing at over seven million gallons in 1920 dropped by a million gallons the following year. But, by a loop-hole in the American legislation, some Scotch whisky was legitimately imported into the United States for 'medicinal purposes'. The quantities so imported were far in excess of the needs of the American sick, but went nowhere to meeting the demands of the American drinking public. Nevertheless, the genuine article was to be found, albeit in restricted quantities, which only served to increase the lust for it. Counterfeit Scotch was being brewed in every available bath and bucket the liquor racket could lay hands on, and unscrupulous German spirit manufacturers added many thousands of cases of their own diabolical concoction, which was so well dressed up in bottle and label as to appear to be genuine Scotch whisky. Their activities suffered a serious setback when Peter Mackie, of White Horse fame, successfully prosecuted one firm for exporting German spirit under the label of Black and White Horse Scotch Whisky.

Apart from the whisky which was imported under the medical loop-hole, the Scotch whisky houses could not legally export to the United States, and most were not prepared to take any direct measures to infringe American laws. Yet, by standing idly by they feared they would witness the decline and eventual destruction of Scotch whisky's place in the market of greatest potential, once the tiresome Prohibition laws were repealed. If they did not act to meet the covert demand for Scotch whisky, they knew the American public would either turn to alternatives or have their health and taste for Scotch whisky permanently ruined by the imposters.

Whilst there may be no evidence that a conscious, positive decision was taken in the matter, records do show that exports of Scotch whisky to Canada, the then British West Indies, the French Atlantic islands of St Pierre and Miquelon — indeed to anywhere within striking distance of the United States — simply mushroomed overnight. The number of vessels engaged in 'rum running', i.e. carrying wines and spirits to offshore destinations outside United States territorial waters, was phenomenal. It was not an enterprise entirely without chance, but the dangers seemed small when compared with the risks run by the bootleggers, who were responsible for landing the illicit goods on United States territory and ensuring their safe delivery.

Scotch prospered under these conditions, particularly as the official distilling of American domestic whiskies had ceased. However, in addition to the counterfeit substitutes, the practice of cutting (diluting the genuine Scotch with water, wood alcohol or some other additive) was a further threat, and one which was most successfully tackled by Francis Berry of Berry Bros, whose blended whiskies were well established in the United States. Whilst enjoying increased sales, he was very anxious to avoid adulteration of his whisky. Yet there seemed to be no easy answer. That is, until he met one Captain Bill McCoy at Nassau in the Bahamas, then a very popular entrepôt for the suppliers of Rum Row (the alley in the high seas just outside American limits and stretching 150 miles from Montauk Point on

Long Island to Atlantic City in New Jersey). This highly respectable firm of London wine and whisky merchants then launched a new brand of Scotch, the first of the 'light' whiskies, exclusively for export. For the pulsating Bahamas market, which was the back door into Prohibition America, Francis Berry saw obvious advantages in working with Captain McCoy, whose reputation for dealing only in genuine goods had led to the coining of the phrase 'It's the real McCoy'. On this basis the new Cutty Sark established a formidable reputation in the United States which was to hold it in good stead when Prohibition was repealed and far beyond.

Other companies shared in the spoils of Prohibition, and the period is the source of many a good tale. Chivas Bros, the Aberdeen whisky merchants, were said to be working all the hours of every day to blend and bottle their whisky, which was then packed in waterproof boxes and dropped outside US territorial limits for collection by their 'customers'. Similarly, Teacher's were supplying the bootleg trade with Highland Cream in cases sewn up in hessian. William Manera Bergius of Teacher's justified it in the following terms: 'We are letting the Americans have good Scotch whisky to drink in place of their own somewhat poisonous distillations, and we are bringing good American money into this impoverished country.' During Prohibition, the company shipped 137,927 cases of Scotch via its own particular 'rum run' to Antwerp, then on the vessel *Littlehorn* to San Francisco Bay. Joseph Hobbs, who owned the *Littlehorn*, was the principal go-between for Teacher's and he was subsequently to become prominent in his own right in the Scotch whisky industry. Although Scottish by birth, Hobbs spent a great deal of time in Canada, including a period as agent for DCL. He returned to Scotland in 1931 when it seemed that Prohibition's days were numbered and, in preparation for the great boom in the United States market, he entered into association with National Distillers of America to acquire and run a number of malt distilleries, through the Glasgow firm of Train & McIntyre, blenders and merchants. The distilleries bought in this way were Bruichladdich, Glenury Royal, North Esk (now Glenesk), Fettercairn, Glenlochy, Benromach and the now defunct Strathdee Distillery. Management was put in the hands of a separate subsidiary, Associated Scottish Distilleries Ltd. The venture enjoyed mixed fortunes, and National Distillers of America withdrew from Scotland in 1954 when they sold Train & McIntyre and four of their distilleries to DCL. The others were sold to separate purchasers.

On balance, Prohibition was far from being a bad thing for the

Scotch whisky industry, which not only used the time to consolidate its reputation in the United States but also managed to ward off attempts by dispossessed American distillery concerns to establish themselves in Scotland at this time. But there were also victims. Campbeltown whisky is said to have enjoyed a boom during American Prohibition, but the period was in fact the cause of the old whisky capital's fall from glory. Excess demand led to a reduction in quality which in turn gave Campbeltown a bad name. During the 1920s all but one of the twenty distilleries in and around the town were closed, the exception being Rieclachan, which struggled on until 1934. Only two were ever to return to active life: Glen Scotia and Springbank.

Repeal in 1933 saw a scramble by American companies for the exclusive agencies for the better known brands of Scotch. The smarter operators had already established themselves in this respect when they detected that Prohibition was bound to join the league of lost causes. Amongst these was Joseph Kennedy, the Boston politician of Irish origin who was to become the United States' most prominent father. In anticipation of Repeal he secured for himself the New England agency for Dewar's and Haig (as well as Gordon's gin) and had busied himself importing stocks under special licence for 'medicinal' purposes to be ready for the expected boom. It was thanks to the efforts of the best of the import agencies that Scotch was able to take a significant share of the US spirits market, facing as it did something like 20,000 different liquor brands flooding the country on Repeal.

The burden of duty

Perhaps the heaviest weight of all which the industry had to bear throughout the first half of this century was that of taxation. The upward trend in the nineteenth century was continued and indeed accelerated in the twentieth century. Standing at 11s. (55p) per proof gallon in 1900 it jumped to 14s. 9d. (74p) in 1909, putting the price of a standard blend up from 2s. 6d. (12½p) to 4s. 6d. (22½p). In 1918 it was raised to 30s. per proof gallon and the year after to 50s. Scarcely another year had gone by when there was another massive increase to 72s. 6d. per proof gallon, making the retail price 12s. 6d. (62½p) per bottle. The public were outraged; the price had almost trebled in less than twelve years. Will Fyfe, the great contemporary Scottish entertainer, caught the mood of the nation and reached new levels of popularity with a song written by David Mackenzie decrying the iniquitous event. He sang it in one of Britain's first talking films, 'Elstree Calling'.

Verse: It's really high time that something was done
To alter the way that the country is run,
They're not doing things in the way that they
should
Och! Just take for instance the price of food.

Chorus: It's twelve and a tanner a bottle,
That's what they're asking today,
It's twelve and a tanner a bottle,
It takes all the pleasure away.
Before you can get a wee drappie
You have to spend all that you've got,
Och! How can a fellow be happy
When happiness costs such a lot?

Verse: There's taxes on this, taxes on that,
While we're getting lean the officials get fat,
You must admit it's a bit underhand,
Putting a tax on the breath of the land.

Chorus: Repeat

Verse: Now I used to meet with some old pals of mine
When whisky was cheap and went doon like
wine,
Now I never meet them I'm sorry to tell,
I dodge roo'nd the corner and drink by m'sel.

Chorus: Repeat

Will Fyfe apparently had the desired effect, for no further increases in duty were attempted until 1939 when, against the background of war declared, a slightly nervous Chancellor added 10s. (50p) per gallon. Thereafter increases came almost annually, until by April 1948 duty stood at 210s.10d per gallon (over £10). By then, the retail price of a bottle of Scotch had risen to 33s. 4d. (£1.67p) of which over three-quarters represented duty.

The trend was established and there was no doubt in anyone's mind that the Exchequer had developed a bad habit which it would never be able to kick. But by now exports had firmly taken over as the main source of income. Volume sales were greater and the profit much more handsome than in the cut-throat home trade. Scotch whisky had long been established in the old Empire, and the countries of the Commonwealth offered good prospects for the future. However, the main hope was in the United States, and the efforts made during Prohibition to preserve Scotch whisky's good name had paid handsome dividends. Other markets were also opening up as the world put itself to rights again after the ravages of a Second World War. Ironically, both Germany and Japan were to become important customers of the Scotch whisky industry and in due course one of them, in some eyes, a considerable menace.

The last three decades

The fifties and sixties were decades of expansion, with disused distilleries refurbished and brought back into production after many years of idleness, existing distilleries greatly expanded and modernised, and totally new units constructed. The thrust towards growth came from DCL and the two Canadian giants, Seagram's and Hiram Walker, mainly in malt whisky, but smaller companies also took the plunge and new faces joined the traditional grain spirit distillers, with mixed results.

Despite a marked setback in 1968 the industry continued on its path of growth for the first half of the 1970s, with new malt distilleries appearing and old ones being enlarged and improved. There was also considerable reorganisation of company ownership, and this, together with progress in production capacity at individual distilleries, is detailed under the company entries in Chapter 9. The industry was booming and the product riding high (or so it seemed at the time) and almost immune to outside influences — even to the effect of the oil crisis of the winter 1973-74. But the continuing prosperity through most of the seventies was rudely shaken by the realisation that, once more, the Scotch whisky industry had no way of avoiding the general economic trends in Britain and, more importantly than in the past, in the world at large. Nor could the industry offset its depressed traditional markets with increased opportunities in the fast-growing new economies of the OPEC countries, as certain other manufacturers had done, since in most cases religious restrictions were to mitigate against Scotch becoming a mass-market consumer product for their populations. The distiller, blender and exporter alike were about to face a period as challenging and testing as any in the turbulent history of their industry.

Before we consider how these factors have affected the industry and what the future holds, it would be helpful to explain how its constituent parts inter-relate in presenting and promoting Scotch whisky throughout the world.

6 A diversity of interests

The great majority of the companies which distil, blend and deal in Scotch whisky today can trace their origins to small family beginnings, modest partnerships or one-man ventures. Many of these thrived for no more than the duration of the commercially active life of the person behind the business. Others folded quietly and almost as quickly as they were set up, and a few crashed with such reverberations as to threaten the very structure of the industry. Many others were absorbed by rivals or joined up with like-minded concerns in order to secure survival in an increasingly competitive world, whilst others provided the vehicle with which foreign interests were to secure a foothold in what was increasingly regarded as an attractive investment industry. The result of these many changes and rationalisations is that very few companies of any significance today have remained unchanged since their inception in terms of their corporate structure, ownership and range of activities. The Scotch whisky industry is no different from any other industry, except that despite all the amalgamations and the emergence of a few giants, it is still a fascinatingly diverse sector of industrial life in Britain in which the links with the past are deliberately retained and often emphasised.

Attempts at short-hand description of the complex industry lead to over-simplifications and glaring omissions. Here I shall try to unravel the tangle, but leave to Chapter 9 the task of describing in detail the genesis of individual companies and their relationship to each other.

The distillers

Distilling is the start of it all. The total number of established distilleries — including the few that distil grain *and* malt whisky, or are located together and therefore count as both grain and malt — is 131. Of these, a considerable number has been closed down over the last few years for indeterminate periods, but for present purposes the established figure of 131 is appropriate. In terms of ownership these may be broken down as follows: the giant Distillers Company owns fifty, the two Canadian distilling companies have nineteen (ten owned by Hiram Walker and Sons and nine by Seagram Distillers), other foreign interests have eight, and the remaining fifty-four are owned by companies within the control of United Kingdom nationals. The importance of Distillers Company at the primary production stage is immediately apparent. The Canadian and foreign-owned distilleries are part of a wider enterprise and have invariably been acquired to meet the objectives of an overseas parent company. Of the fifty-four non-DCL distilleries in UK hands, the majority belong to groups with other interests as well as whisky. The most diverse of these is perhaps the Scottish and Universal Investment Trust, which has a wide range of activities and, through the Whyte & Mackay group of companies, owns three distilleries. The large brewers are also represented: Scottish and Newcastle Breweries Ltd have two distilleries operated by their subsidiary Waverley Group Ltd, as does Allied Breweries Ltd through William Teacher & Sons Ltd; Whitbread & Co. PLC boast six distilleries, of which four were inherited when they acquired Long John International Ltd, plus the currently silent Ben Nevis grain and malt distilleries acquired in 1981. International Distillers and Vintners Ltd (who are tied up with another large brewing concern, Watney & Mann Ltd, since both are subsidiaries of the Grand Metropolitan Group) has four distilleries. The six distilleries of The Invergordon Distillers are a useful asset for Carlton Industries. Amalgamated Distilled Products, now with three units, is a rapidly growing concern, having in 1982 added two malt distilleries to its original Glen Scotia Distillery when it bought the American owned company of Barton Distilling (Scotland) Ltd. Of the remainder, the medium-sized independent companies concerned purely with distilling and selling Scotch whisky are: Highland Distilleries which, along with its associate companies, owns six; William Grant & Sons and Arthur Bell & Sons which have respectively four and five units. This leaves Macdonald & Muir and Stanley P. Morrison, which each have two and can still legitimately claim to be truly family firms, as can William Grant & Sons. There is one other company which counts as a two-distillery operator: the rather complex partnership which owns the North of Scotland Distilling Co. Ltd (whose distillery at Cambus is nowhere near the North of Scotland) and Speyside Distillery Co. Ltd (whose Highland malt distillery really is located where its name implies).

The remaining seven distilleries are each owned by individual

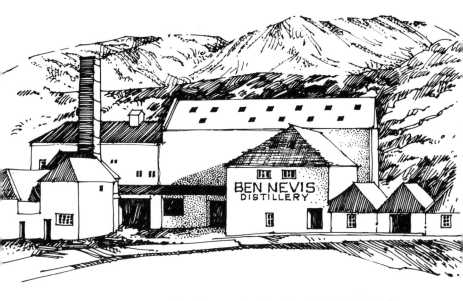

firms having a variety of backgrounds. The North British Distillery Co. (owning the North British distillery) is a large commercial concern in its own right; Macallan-Glenlivet (Macallan), Tomatin Distillers (Tomatin) and Eadie Cairns (Auchentoshan) have all had their original family interest diluted to varying degrees, and Tobermory Distillers (Tobermory), which represents a variety of interests. This leaves perhaps only two distilleries which can truly claim to be run on a private or family basis — J. & A. Mitchell & Co. (Springbank) and J. & G. Grant (Glenfarclas).

In grain whisky production the two big operators are Distillers Company, with five distilleries, and the North British Distillery Co. whose extensive plant in Edinburgh is the source of grain whisky for many companies who do not have a grain distillery of their own. Of the other large operators only Seagram's is without its own distillery.

Of the 117 malt whisky distilleries under consideration, forty-five are owned by Distillers Company, twenty-four by Canadian and foreign companies, thirty-eight by large or medium sized native companies, and ten by smaller local firms, giving a total of twenty-seven separate companies engaged in malt whisky distilling, or twenty-eight in all distilling if the company engaged exclusively in grain distilling is added. This compares with ninety-seven malt distilleries owned by thirty-nine companies in 1960, and 109 distilleries owned by forty companies in 1970. The growth in the number of distilleries which took place in the sixties and seventies is accounted for by completely new constructions and the reopening of abandoned units. At the same time, there is a trend towards concentration of ownership in fewer hands, partly because of the general move in industry towards larger trading units, but more particularly because only substantial organisations have had the resources to establish new distilleries. Since blenders are reluctant to purchase new fillings (whisky to be used for blending) from a completely new distillery until the product is known, the owner of the new distillery usually has to be able to use the whisky in *his* own blends.

The number of companies involved seems sufficiently large to ensure against dominance of any particular sector, but there is a growing fear that the cream of the malt whiskies — the Speysides and Glenlivets — are being concentrated in increasingly fewer hands. Of the fifty-seven in these categories, no fewer than thirty-five are owned by just three companies — Distillers Company (twenty-two), Seagram's (nine) and International Distillers & Vintners (four). Seagram's strengthened their position enormously by the take-over of The Glenlivet and Glen Grant Distilleries Ltd. An attempt by Hiram Walker & Sons to capture some additional real estate in Speyside by making a bid for Highland Distilleries, which would have given them an additional pair of Speyside distilleries plus four other Highland malt distilleries, was rejected by the Monopolies and Mergers Commission on the grounds that it was not in the public interest, since it would mean a further concentration in distillery ownership, which would limit competition in the market for malt whisky fillings. It may well be that after the unsuccessful courting of Highland Distilleries the industry will settle down to the present structure of the traditional Distillers Company giant, two major Canadian companies, a dozen or so large to medium-sized companies and a balance of small single- or two-distillery operations.

The number of distilleries owned is not, of course, a precise reflection of the size or importance of the company concerned, since the production capacity of the individual distillery varies enormously — from tiny Edradour with 50,000 proof gallons* per annum, to Tomatin with the largest malt whisky capacity of any distillery at five

---

* 1 Imperial proof gallon	= 2.59 litres of pure alcohol
	or = 1.36 US proof gallons
1 litre of pure alcohol (LPA)	= 0.386 Imperial proof gallon
	or = 0.528 US proof gallon
1 US proof gallon	= 1.893 litres of pure alcohol

The Imperial proof gallon, the traditional measure for alcohol in the U.K., is equal to 0.57 Imperial gallon of pure alcohol at 51°F, which is equal to 2.59 litres of pure alcohol at 10.6°C.

million proof gallons. Variations in capacity at the grain distilleries are less marked.

For the 117 *malt whisky* distilleries under consideration, one can estimate — since no precise figure is available — a total capacity in the region of 250 million litres. From this basic figure the seriousness of the over-capacity situation now confronting the industry compared with ten years ago can be quickly discerned:

year	amount distilled (in '000 LPA)	as a percentage of estimated capacity
1973	199,112	79.6
1974	214,669	85.9
1975	178,926	71.6
1976	167,411	67.0
1977	171,457	68.6
1978	209,279	83.7
1979	203,871	81.5
1980	177,913	71.2
1981	110,083	44.0
1982	96,649	38.6

With practically all distilleries operating well below capacity and many in fact closed for indeterminate periods, it is impossible to give an accurate production league table at this time. Taking the ten year period in question, a reasonable estimate would be as follows:

position	company	percentage of total malt production	number of distilleries	
1	Distillers Company	35	45	
2	Seagram's/Glenlivet	9.2	9	
3	Highland Distilleries	7	5	(does not include Glengoyne Distillery, owned by an associate company)
4	William Grant	5.5	3	
5	Hiram Walker	5.5	9	
6	Arthur Bell	3.7	5	(does not include Bladnoch Distillery acquired in 1983)

The great difference in production throughput can be seen from these figures. William Grant & Sons had, for example, 5.5 per cent of the total with only three distilleries, whilst Hiram Walker & Sons had the same share but with nine distilleries. The seventy-six distilleries referred to above accounted for two-thirds of production, yet it took the remaining forty-one to make up the rest.

A comparable league table for *grain whisky* production would be:

position	company	percentage of total grain production	number of distilleries
1	Distillers Company	42	5
2	North British	13	1
3	William Grant	12	1
4	Invergordon	7	1
5	Hiram Walker	6.5	1
	Others	19.5	5

Here again there are some notable differences, with Distillers five distilleries producing forty-two per cent of total production, whilst the five distilleries not classified by ownership were responsible for well under half the Distillers Company total.

The blenders

It is to the blenders that Scotch whisky owes its latter-day commercial success, for without them distilling would have remained a cottage industry, little more than a native craft for the production of the national drink. Scotch would probably have enjoyed no wider international appeal than Swedish schnapps or Peruvian pisco. The rise of the great blending houses is described in Chapter 4. Suffice it to say that their importance today is undiminished and that by and large the successful pioneering companies have survived in one form or another.

At first the link between distilling and blending was a tenuous one, the distillers preferring not to get involved in the large-scale marketing that was needed to promote a new brand, and the blender wishing to be free to buy his whiskies as best suited his needs. However, common interests gradually drew the two together, the distillers seeing the advantage of having secure outlets which they could control and which would soak up their vast and expensive stocks of maturing whisky, and the blender wishing to protect his line of supply. Today most of the principal companies engaged in distilling are also blenders on a large scale. This applies to both malt and grain distillers, with the notable exception of The North British Distillery Co. Ltd, which does not compete in any way with the blenders to which it supplies its grain whisky. Other distillery companies have outlets for part of their production through associated or subsidiary companies, which blend and market whisky as a means of using up a guaranteed proportion of their distillery's production. But there are exceptions: Macallan-Glenlivet and Glenturret distilleries have no current active blending interests, contenting themselves with supplying their whisky to other firms for blending, and bottling a proportion of their production for sale as a single malt.

The importance of the relationship between distiller and blender is borne out by estimated world sales of branded whiskies for the following companies, all of which have substantial distilling and blending interests:

position	company	percentage of world sales
1	Distillers Company	42
2	Arthur Bell's	10
3	International Distillers & Vintners	9
4	Highland/Cutty Sark	8
5	Seagram's	7
6	Hiram Walker	6

This leaves an awful lot of companies scrambling for the remaining 18 per cent of world sales. All of the big six above are, of course, integrated distilling/blending operations, although a rather complicated relationship exists between Highland Distilleries, Robertson & Baxter, the Glasgow blenders, and Berry Bros & Rudd who own and market the highly successful Cutty Sark brand. Nowhere is there a front-line blending company which is independent of the distilling companies. The last important company to lose that independence was probably Stewart & Son of Dundee, which had never owned a distillery but whose parent company, Allied Breweries, acquired Wm Teacher & Sons in 1976 and with it two good Highland malt distilleries. There are, of course, many smaller blending companies which are independent of the distillers, but most of the longer-established ones have been bought up by the larger groups in order to trade on their good name or to acquire a particularly well established brand. Those blenders who still survive independently are probably engaged mainly in specific export markets which they will have successfully cultivated for their particular brands.

The brokers

A broker in any commodity is a middle-man who deals in shortages and surpluses. Whisky broking is essentially filling in deficiencies in

supplies to meet the specific requirements of the blenders who, by
tradition, used never to deal with each other directly over matters of
buying or exchanging whisky stocks. Brokers hold stocks either in
their own bond or at the distilleries, where they will usually pay a
storage fee to the distillery company.

The number of accounts which a broker will now hold has shrunk
considerably, but the parcels of whisky in which he deals are
correspondingly much larger, thus reflecting the change in the face
of the industry. Consequently the number of broking firms has
diminished. Quite a few blenders and merchants still dabble in
broking, and the larger groups will often have a broking subsidiary,
but the number of genuinely independent whisky brokers still
dealing is small. Lundie & Co., Stanley P. Morrison, Peter J. Russell
& Co. and Andrew R. Wilson are amongst the better known names,
although Morrison's distillery and blending activities have tended to
overshadow its original broking role, and Peter J. Russell markets its
own brands. Although the role of the broker may have altered in
detail, and his impact on the industry is now less crucial, he
nevertheless has a future as long as the profusion of companies
engaged in blending continues. No matter how hard the accountants
and marketing men might try, it is beyond them to forecast with any
steady accuracy what the requirements for matured whisky will be in
the future. The broker, therefore, fills and holds until maturity up to
the full range of grain and malt whiskies, and may also supply
blended whiskies. He will relieve the blender of whisky surplus to
requirements, and let him have his precise needs by type and age.

Surprisingly, a formal or official classification of malt whiskies
does not exist. When trading whiskies, blenders and brokers refer to
first and second class whiskies and then 'the rest', although there is
some movement on the borders between these informal classifications.
Only thirty-three distilleries are generally considered to produce
'class whiskies. Of these nearly half are of Distillers Company ownership, representing one-third of the company's malt distillery portfolio. Others are Macallan-Glenlivet, Glenfarclas, Glenmorangie,
Ardmore and Glendronach (both Teacher's), Balvenie and Glenfiddich
(both Wm Grant & Sons Ltd), The Glenlivet, Glen Grant, Benriach-
Glenlivet, Longmorn-Glenlivet and Glen Keith-Glenlivet (Seagram's),
plus three distilleries belonging to The Highland Distilleries, two in
the Hiram Walker collection and one of Arthur Bell's.

The whisky merchants

Whilst there is today a decreasing number of firms trading exclusively in Scotch whisky either at the wholesale or retail level, there are many who trade in whisky as part of their general role as wine and spirit merchants. Many such firms have their own brands of whisky, some of them well known locally, or in certain export markets where a merchant may have been particularly successful on his own account, or thanks to a particularly diligent agent.

While the merchant's position in the total industry is today a modest one, it is worth recalling that many of the big names in Scotch whisky, such as Bell's, Buchanan's, Dewar's, Johnnie Walker and Teacher's, began life as whisky or wine and spirit merchants. As they prospered, so the nature of their business activities changed, and all too often the retail or even the wholesale side of the business was allowed to wither as their blending and, later, distilling interests became the focal point of the firm. Nevertheless, some of the major companies have, for reasons of public relations as much as anything, retained their connections with their past by maintaining old established retail outlets: Seagram's subsidiary Chivas Bros Ltd still has its highly successful wine, spirit and grocery shop with restaurant above in Union Street, Aberdeen; and Justerini & Brooks (of J & B fame and a subsidiary of International Distillers & Vintners) still have their original wine and spirit merchants' premises in St James's Street in the most fashionable part of London. Each such company has its own brands of whisky, and in the case of Chivas and J & B these were quite obscure until the trading companies who owned them were snapped up by bigger fish who were able successfully to promote the brands far and wide.

There has, alas, been a drift away from the long-established practice whereby practically every wine and spirit merchant had his own brands of whisky, and this is also true of some of the larger companies. John Harvey & Sons, of Bristol sherry fame, had an interesting range of whiskies with attractive names — Tent Peg, Gold Blend and Westward Ho! — but the marketing of them died out, perhaps with the passing from Harvey's control of the blenders Stewart & Son of Dundee to Allied Breweries. The House of Sandeman, notable port and sherry shippers, had for many years their own brands of whisky which were well established in the United Kingdom. They had come by these as the result of an agreement drawn up in 1939 between themselves and their name-sakes in Edinburgh, Sandeman & Sons Ltd, whereby the latter's whiskies — Sandeman VVO, Red Funnel, Baronet and

Sandeman (King of Whiskies) — were marketed by Geo G. Sandeman Sons & Co. Ltd in the south of England, and the Edinburgh Sandemans became exclusive agents in Scotland for the ports and sherries of their London cousins. There was in fact a long-standing family connection between the two companies, and the amalgamation which took place in 1963 was perhaps logical, if not inevitable. The Edinburgh Sandemans, who had sold their whiskies so well in Scotland, had a pedigree stretching back to 1760 through their forerunners Laidlaw and Sandeman, and it must be a matter of regret that the Sandeman labels disappeared so abruptly on amalgamation. Greens Ltd, the City wine merchants, have also recently given up their house blend, Queen's, after many years. Until 1976 it had been their practice to break down and bottle this specially made-up blend at their duty paid cellars in Shoreditch, from whence it was sold in modest quantities — never more than 100 dozen bottles in a year — in the City of London and in Greater London. Through a subsidiary they were also selling a De Luxe blended whisky under the name S.H. Day & Co. Rare Old Scotch Whisky, again in small quantities, but this too ceased in 1974.

Another highly regarded London merchant to have once had its own whiskies is Hatch, Mansfield & Co. Ltd, but in this case they were exclusively for export and the trade ceased shortly after the Second World War. These whiskies were very popular with the Establishment in India, and the 1923 price list of the agent there, Spencer & Co. Ltd, shows an impressive list of leading customers and range of whiskies supplied by the two firms and by the wine and spirit merchants Cockburn & Campbell Ltd. The Hatch Mansfield whiskies included Vat E.F.G.H. Matchless, Royal Sovereign and Strathspey. Even Pimm's Ltd, who produce that magnificent aperitif Pimms No. 1 Cup, used to have their own brand of Scotch whisky known as Grand Fleet, but that too has been in abeyance for some time, and the Warrington distillers and wine merchants of vodka fame, C. & J. Greenall Ltd, had a fair range of whiskies — Glenisla, Glen Sloy, Grand Old Highland, Rare No. 10 and VSOB — until they decided to concentrate on white spirits about twelve years ago.

Whilst many such companies have for reasons of economy opted out of own-brand whisky, others carry on. El Vino Co. Ltd, the well known Fleet Street wine merchants, have been selling their main brand, Connoisseur's Blend, through their own outlets since shortly after the company was founded in 1879, and a subsidiary's brand, Burncastle, for a rather shorter period and more intermittently. Some of the provincial wine and spirit merchants also have their own whiskies. For example, Killingley & Co Ltd of Nottingham have Olde Smithy, which they claim contains 45 per cent malt whiskies — perhaps this is why they sell 3000 cases per annum. McMullen & Sons Ltd of Hertford have equal success with their brand Gairloch. They are brewers as well as wine and spirit merchants, and sales are almost entirely through their own tied outlets. Some of the independent Scottish merchants have enjoyed considerable success in marketing both their own brands of whisky as well as leading blends and single malts. Peter Thomson (Perth) Ltd is one such firm, and their Beneagles is very familiar locally and in certain overseas countries. Another Perth firm operates in a like manner with its blends of Moorland and Ghillie and its agency for the single malts produced by the Invergordon Distillers. While many such companies are concerned with trade in a wide variety of wines and spirits, the Elgin wholesale merchants Gordon & MacPhail put the emphasis much more on whisky and only whisky. Apart from their own blends, they have an impressive range of malt whiskies for the home trade and export. They are as near to the complete, old-style whisky merchant as will be found anywhere.

Fringe operators

Freed of the burden of financing maturing stocks and maintaining the quality of a particular blend, and, most of all, of advertising it, some smaller companies cause much irritation to the big distillers and blenders by undercutting the heavily promoted main-line brands. These secondary or single-market brands are often put together from whatever source the proprietor can find mature whisky, and the actual process of blending, bottling and transporting is often done on a sub-contracted basis. Quite a different picture from that conjured up by the more traditional companies.

Foreign interests

Canadian and foreign penetration of the distilling section of the industry is substantial, accounting for twenty-seven distilleries (twenty-four malt and three grain), and about 30 per cent of total capacity, including about 21 per cent of malt capacity. The reason for the intrusion of North American interests was probably a combination of under-valued distillery properties in Scotland during the Depression years, and a determination by Canadian and American firms to step back into the United States market with ample stocks of Scotch whisky behind them just as soon as Prohibition ended. The enthusiasm and optimism of the North Americans was in marked contrast to the gloomy predictions of the domestic industry leaders, and between their arrival on the scene in 1930 and the outbreak of the Second World War, Hiram Walker & Sons, for instance acquired a Highland malt distillery, built a Lowland malt distillery (as well as their own grain distillery) and purchased a bonding company and a firm of blenders. Conditions immediately after the war continued to favour outside investment, since the devaluation of sterling made the purchase of distillery property even more attractive. Hiram Walker, for example, continued to pursue their expansionist policies, and bought three further Highland malt distilleries in the fifties.

Hiram Walker & Sons were the main overseas company in Scotch whisky until Seagram's acquired the much cherished Glenlivet Distillers group. This increased their distilling holding to nine, and they moved into first place in terms of malt whisky production by overseas companies, and second only to Distillers Company in the malt production league. The acquisition of Glenlivet Distillers wiped out the substantial minority shareholding by the Japanese giant, Suntory, in Glenlivet, which reflected Suntory's heavy dependence on bulk imports of malt whisky for admixing in Japan to produce good quality Japanese blended whisky. Wisely, perhaps, Japanese companies have kept a low profile as far as ownership and shareholding in Scottish companies are concerned, but their agents have long been busy purchasing large parcels of malt whisky for use in the concoction of Japanese whiskies, of which more will be said in Chapter 8.

Currently, the only United States owned company is Inver House Distillers Ltd, an off-shoot of Publicker Inc. of Philadelphia, which now only owns the Moffat dual-purpose grain and Lowland malt distillery, having recently sold Bladnoch Distillery to Arthur Bell & Sons. William Whiteley & Co. was, along with a myriad of subsidiary and associated companies, owned for over forty years by private American interests but was sold to S. Campbell & Son (a Pernod Ricard subsidiary) in 1982. Two fairly important parts of the Scotch whisky industry were recovered from the Americans when, firstly, Schenley were required under United States monopolies legislation to divest themselves of certain interests, allowing Whitbread & Co. PLC to bring Long John International back into British ownership and, secondly, when Amalgamated Distilled Products acquired the Chicago-based Barton Brands Inc. including its subsidiary, Barton Distilling (Scotland) Ltd, who have the Littlemill and Loch Lomond distilleries. An earlier reversion to native hands from American control was the break-up in 1954 of the grouping of seven distilleries run through local subsidiaries by National Distillers.

Glenturret distillery

As for other foreign interests, these are represented by companies already prominent in some other aspect of distilling. Aberlour-Glenlivet and its local parent, S. Campbell & Son Ltd, were bought in 1974 by the Pernod Ricard group of France, which subsequently acquired William Whiteley & Co., including Edradour Distillery. Martini Rossi of Italy own William Lawson Ltd and their Highland malt distillery at Macduff. In both cases such an arrangement has enabled fairly obscure distilleries to find enhanced outlets for their production via the already established Continental distribution networks of their European parents. The French took a further slice of the cake when Cointreau S.A. quietly moved in on Glenturret Distillery Ltd in 1981. Growing interest in the industry by French distillers no doubt reflects the increasing importance of Scotch whisky in that country.

Lochside Distillery, which is both grain and Highland malt, belongs to the biggest distillers in Spain, DYC, and Tobermory Distillery also used to have a Spanish principal, Domecq the sherry producers, but is now back in native hands. In these cases the overseas interest may have been less benign, although it is not possible even to guess at how much of the distillery's production is shipped to Spain in bulk form for mixing with local spirit in order to produce 'national' whiskies, which then offer unwelcome competition to imported Scotch in the bottle. DYC, on the other hand, would argue that they have helped to promote consumption of whisky of all kinds in Spain and are therefore supporting Scotch whisky too.

There are also American and other foreign interests in some of the blending and exporting companies, but even in total these do not amount to a significant proportion of the industry. What is impossible to discern is what proportion of the industry is still Scottish as opposed to British. Certainly, Scottish interests have long since ceased to have over-all control.

Foreign participation in an industry as close to the Scotsman's heart as whisky and distilling has caused more than a few ripples from time to time. The Canadian presence is now well established and was probably treated from the start with considerable tolerance. After all, had not Scots been responsible to a great extent for populating large parts of Canada, and had their forefathers not in fact given birth to the Canadian distilling industry by taking their skills with them when they emigrated? Perhaps there was even a small measure of secret pride at how well the offspring had done, and perhaps it was natural they should return to the old country to invest some of their profits. But whether or not this sentiment existed it would not be automatically extended to any other foreign adventurer who might seek to buy into existing companies, or set up new enterprises. Whilst no one can deny that the injection of foreign capital was a vital shot in the arm to the industry at crucial moments in the recent past, the reaction to any further major incursions following the Seagram purchase of the Glenlivet Distillers group is likely to be hostile.

The face of the industry today

This summary, read with Chapter 9, should give a clear, if still complex, picture of the commercial structure of the industry. Although many companies have disappeared altogether, at least as independent entities, a large number still exist and new ones start from time to time. The fact that the really large battalions prefer generally to keep their operations at least superficially fragmented helps them to avoid a monolithic image which they might otherwise have, and adds to the intriguing personality of this multi-faceted industry. Thus, The Distillers Company, for instance, continues to trade through a staggering range of companies which are invariably in competition with each other. Many of the other large companies also appear to break up their operations by using subsidiaries, many of them of the non-trading variety, and often deliberately distance themselves from a brand which is succeeding under the aegis of a company which they own, but may not wish to associate with too openly. It would not be too rash to conclude that there are probably many more companies active in the industry than it can reasonably support in terms of modern economies of scale. Further rationalisation seems inevitable, but distillers and whisky men generally have a certain tenacity, and probably the shake-out will take some time. Certainly any substantial permanent reduction in the number of distilleries, or in the range of operating companies, will rob Scotch whisky of much of its charm and attraction. It is to be hoped that the majority, if not all, of the closures which have taken place in the last year or so will be temporary, but it is perhaps too much to expect that others will not be added to the casualty list before the situation shows signs of improvement. The single biggest blow was undoubtedly Distillers Company's decision to close, from 31 May 1983, eleven malt distilleries, thus reducing the group's malt distilling capacity by an estimated 12 per cent. This came only two months after they shut down Carsebridge grain distillery.

Changes in the structure of the industry are bound to have implications for employment, but these will be softened by the fact that distilling is in no way labour intensive. A medium size distillery such as the North of Scotland, which makes about 7.5 million LPA of grain whisky per annum, employs a total staff of only seventeen including the manager, the chemist and engineer, with, in times of normal production, three shifts per day, three men to each shift. The total number employed in all branches of the industry in 1978 was estimated to be 25,316, although by 1982 these numbers had been reduced to about 21,000, i.e. a fall of 17 per cent.

No matter how much the Scots believe in their native drink, it is the rest of the world who will judge whether it should continue to enjoy the international acclaim and following it has had for nearly a hundred years. The industry's duty clearly lies in maintaining the standards by which others judge it. One traditional distiller (David Macdonald of Macdonald & Muir) put it most aptly: 'Personally, I feel that only by continuing to maintain such high standards will our whiskies, and indeed Scotch whisky as a whole, continue to maintain a position as the world's most prestigious and companionable drink.'

It was with a view to keeping standards up as well as defending the interests of the industry that two associations were formed — the Malt Distillers Association of Scotland, and the Scotch Whisky Association.

The Malt Distillers Association of Scotland

This association originated in a meeting at the Gordon Arms Hotel in Elgin on 20 January 1874, when a group of distillers met with a view to improving communication amongst themselves to their mutual benefit and to taking a common line on issues where their interests were at risk. Most of the distillers there were already members of The Elgin Distillers' Association which represented distilleries coming under the control of the Elgin-based Excise Office. Membership of the new association was extended to distilleries 'north of the Grampians'. The Campbeltown and Islay distilleries were not included since they already had their own organisations, as did the Lowland distillers who were also, obviously, excluded. The members were therefore largely from the 'Golden Triangle' of Highland malt whisky distilling, plus a few from further afield — Talisker on the Isle of Skye and Highland Park in the Orkneys. The name adopted was the North of Scotland Malt Distillers' Association (NSMDA) with a membership of thirty-six out of the forty-nine within the Association's recruiting area. The Association's stated objects were:

> To increase the friendly interchange of ideas amongst themselves, the removal of all obstructions to the proper carrying on of their business not only as regards improvement in the Excise Laws but also for the making of new arrangements as to the customs of sales which would put both buyer and seller on a more equitable footing and ensure a uniformity of practice.

This banding together of traditional distillers was necessary because of the threat both to the excellence of their product and to their own very existence during the rapid expansion that was taking place in the Scotch whisky industry as a whole in the second half of the nineteenth century, as described in Chapter 4. The fledgling Association was soon to find itself facing new challenges apart from those arising from changes within the industry itself. The first and most persistent of these was against increases in excise duty, afflicting malt and grain distillers and blenders alike, something which of course continues in the present day. Another challenge was the campaign of the Temperance Movement, which was to become a powerful political force and whose compelling appeal had to be countered with clever propaganda and skilful use of the industry's political allies.

More positively, the Association voluntarily tackled the problem of water pollution from the effluent of the distilleries, which was for those days an amazingly enlightened approach, and reflected the distillers' grasp of the vital importance of the environment to the industry.

The turn of the century brought problems in the form of over-production, and some spectacular financial collapses on the blending side of the industry. The distillers themselves did not escape unscathed, and some which could not finance excessive stocks ended in bankruptcy. But the problems facing the distillers in the North were not unknown in the rest of Scotland, and after the bitterness and rivalry arising from the 'What is Whisky?' enquiry had abated, all malt distilleries throughout the country sought co-operation, and in 1925 the Association was enlarged, with increased territorial limits and a new name: The Pot Still Malt Distillers' Association of Scotland. There had also been a very real fear on the part of the NSMDA that the voluntary restraint in production by their members with the re-appearance of the spectre of overproduction in the 1920s would be exploited by the Campbeltown and Islay distillers. After a period of informal negotiation and mutal confidence-building, agreement was reached for all to reduce distilling by 25 per cent. This breakthrough resulted in the wider body being set up.

The restructured association emerged to face the deepening bite of recession, and a new struggle with local farmers who were incensed at the switch that was taking place away from Scottish barley (which the distillers claimed was often too moist and unevenly graded for their purposes) to imported barley. This became a case of 'free trade versus protectionism' and the latter struck its first blow with the imposition in 1932 of a 10 per cent *ad valorum* duty on foreign barley. The controversy over home-produced against imported barley raged against a background of utter despair on the part of the malt distillers for the future of their industry. Sixty distilleries had gone out of business between 1900 and 1925, and complete cessation of distilling had been agreed for the 1932-33 season, following several years of heavy cutbacks in production. The guiding hand of DCL had led the Association to adopt these policies, and changes in the pattern of distillery ownership led to changes in attitudes within the Association.

The barley problem was solved — and a new one of shortage put in its place — by the outbreak of the Second World War, at which time definite signs of improvement in the industry were visible. The total number of distilleries of all kinds at work had increased to ninety-two in 1939 from sixty-four in 1934. The war brought the controls already described and a fresh batch of problems for the Association, and by the time it was ended the industry had its eye on markets across the Atlantic and elsewhere overseas. It was not until 1954 that the malt distillers had finally shaken off the last of the war-time restrictions. But then the Association faced a new hurdle in the form of measures taken by the government against restrictive trading practices, considerably reducing the Association's traditional role in recommending prices to its members in order to avoid the ravages of cut-throat competition. The heavy weight of these controls and restrictions had a debilitating effect on the Association, but by the mid-sixties it was beginning to find new roles for itself, not least in tackling an old problem which the long years of depression had put aside: that of pollution and waste disposal. Changes in the management of industrial relations in Britain required the Association to register as an employers' association, and to adopt, for the first time, a written constitution. It took the opportunity of registration to change its name to The Malt Distillers' Association of Scotland and to give itself simple objectives: to protect and promote the interests of the Pot Still Malt Whisky Industry of Scotland both at home and abroad.

The new association has become increasingly a pressure group for the industry, as well as a source of advice to its members on administrative questions and employment matters. Today membership embraces all of the malt distilleries with the exception of the Campbeltown distillery of Springbank.

The Scotch Whisky Association

The SWA also embraces most of the distilling companies, as well as a high proportion of the blending houses. Total membership hovers at around 130 but many companies are, through their subsidiaries, members several times over and practically all of Distillers Company subsidiaries enjoy individual membership. On the other hand, some of the smaller blenders and exporters eschew membership either because they find the dues, based on a percentage of turnover, excessive or because their interests and those of the Association do not necessarily completely coincide.

In view of its wider membership — grain distilleries as well as malt distillers and firms engaged only in blending — it is not surprising that the SWA's origins are more recent. Its forerunner, The Whisky Association, was formed on 1 January 1917 as a breakaway organisation of Scottish and Irish distilling interests from the Wine and Spirits Brands Association. This Association, however, was concerned only with the home market and paid no attention to the growing prospects for export. The restrictions introduced by a wartime government caused the Association to identify itself more closely with its membership, i.e. the distillers and blenders of Scotland and Ireland, and so a change in title was introduced in 1917 to The Whisky Association, with the aim of 'creating a strong, centralised, homogenous body . . . which will be capable of adequately voicing the opinions and defending the interests of all Scotch and Irish whisky distillers, blenders and exporters.' The exclusive link with the proprietary brand owners was broken, such had been the expansion of the organisation's responsibilities. The Whisky Exporters Association, which had been set up under the umbrella of the Wine and Spirits Brands Association, was absorbed by the new body to become its Export Section. The community of interests between the Scottish and Irish distillers was perhaps more imagined than real and a Scottish branch of the Whisky Association emerged in 1918. The upheavals in Ireland and the formation of the Irish Free State made the single body an anachronism, and by the time the Whisky Association was dissolved in 1942 most of the Irish distillers had either become victims of the slump between the wars or had ceased to be active members. In any case, the old Association's constitution was out-moded and contained no provision for alteration. Its successor, the Scotch Whisky Association, adopted its objectives as follows:

> To protect and promote the interests of the Scotch Whisky trade generally both at home and abroad and to do all such things and to take all such measures as may be conducive or incidental to the attainment of such objects.

> To protect the interests of owners of proprietary brands of Scotch Whisky by taking such steps as the Association may think fit to regulate prices, both wholesale and retail, and to prevent such proprietary brands being sold either wholesale or retail at prices above those fixed by the Association.

With the introduction of legislation to protect the consumer against price fixing, the second of the Association's objects was to prove to be totally invalid at least as far as the United Kingdom market was concerned. However, the Association's interests had all along been concerned with influencing and correcting conditions in overseas markets and to reflect the rapid growth in importance of these compared with the British market. The sterling work done in the all-important USA market, both before and after Prohibition, was good groundwork for the task of representing the industry's interests to the government in connection with British entry into the European Community. Its responsibilities in this sphere and in the protection of Scotch whisky worldwide continue, and are mentioned again in the next chapter.

7 Name your poison...

The wording or marking of goods as proof of origin, ownership or authenticity has only become widespread relatively recently, but has been carried out for many centuries in limited areas, such as the hall-marking of gold and silver and the branding of livestock. The practice of branding goods with the proprietor's name or mark spread during the nineteenth century, partly in order to promote the goods in question but more probably as protection against shoddy imitators. The use of labels and trade marks enabled a manufacturer or trader to identify and distinguish his product from others, and the introduction of legislation covering trade marks and trade descriptions made it illegal to copy or imitate the names and descriptions of a particular brand.

As Chapter 4 relates, the arrival on the scene of blended whisky in the mid nineteenth century soon led to the introduction of brand names and the concept of the proprietary brand, whereby a particular blend of whisky sold in bottle bore the name of the blender or a particular trade name assigned to it, a name unique to that whisky and, as such, protected by law.

Many of the early whisky barons were more than content to see their product grow in popularity with nothing other than their own name on the label. Thus we had Johnnie Walker and Dewar's, Haig and Mackie's. The first three have persisted in the use of the family name whilst Mackie's has given way to White Horse, although the original name is retained by the associate company of White Horse Distillers Ltd as a secondary brand. Curiously enough, the highly egotistical James Buchanan was quite happy to see his original Buchanan Blend become the world famous Black and White, which was purely a reflection of the colour of the original label and bottle. He would no doubt be pleased and amused to see his name and likeness on the current Buchanan Blend following its recent reintroduction as an additional Distillers Company brand in the UK market.

There are many other respectable blended whiskies which have always been marketed under the name of the company's founder: Peter Dawson's, John Begg, William Lawson's, Mackinlay's, Teacher's, Ballantine's, Hankey Bannister, Lang's, Sandy Macdonald, Johnny Wright's, to name but a few. Some of these actually have much longer titles, such as Peter Dawson's Special and Teacher's Highland Cream, but the descriptive words in the brand name were dropped after a time, or at least printed in much smaller lettering than the proprietor's names. Some company names cannot in fairness be separated from the rest of the trade name. Thus we have *Stewart's* Cream of the Barley, *Crawford's* Three Star, *McCallum's* Perfection, the Real *Mackenzie* and *Munro's* Square Bottle. Less common are the instances where a partnership led to both names being employed, such as Whyte & Mackay's and Justerini & Brooks, although the latter has long since been abbreviated to J & B for marketing purposes. One of the most egotistical examples of a whisky brand reflecting the proprietor's name was the long-since defunct blend belonging to Hatch, Mansfield & Col. Ltd called Vat E.F.G.H. Matchless, the initials being those of one of the original partners, Ernest Frederick George Hatch.

What's in a name?

The use of the company or proprietor's name has diminished in importance as the range of brands on the market has increased, and some imaginative thinking has had to be done in order to avoid repetition of an existing name. Many obviously have a Scottish connotation — Braemar, Highland Clan, Highland Tower, Flying Scot, Ghillie, White Heather, Scots Aristocrat, Sma' Still, Cream of Scotland, Dew of Ben Nevis, and so on. Just as popular are titles with a royal flavour — Highland Queen, Prince of Scots, King George IV, King William IV, Royal Edinburgh, King of Kings, King's Royal, The

Queen's Seal, Royal Ages, and many others. Where such names as Grey Hen, Black Colonel, Dad's Favourite and the rather preposterous Pig's Nose and Sheep Dip came from, and why, requires a little more imagination.

As complete a list of Scotch whisky brands as I have been able to put together will be found in the index. It will never be possible to have a list which is not in some way defective, since new brands appear and existing ones lapse all the time. Many are not always available and will lie dormant for years only to be revived by the owner to meet a particular market opportunity, and those which are thought not to be currently available are indicated as such in the company descriptions in Chapter 9. Many brands are exclusively for export and will never be seen in Britain. Indeed, they may only be found in one or two specialised overseas markets, never to be encountered anywhere else, but nonetheless of perfectly respectable origins.

The situation becomes more complicated in countries where blended whisky is imported in bulk for bottling locally. Unless a specific agreement has been reached between the supplier and the importer to sell the whisky under a proprietary label as the locally bottled version of a particular well known Scotch, it will be sold under a brand name belonging to the importer. It is, of course, Scotch whisky except that it lacks the right to claim the magical 'bottled in Scotland' cachet for its label. I have not consciously tried in this book to encompass such local brands, but the following is a list of some of the better known US-bottled brands of Scotch whisky, supposedly available exclusively in that market but no doubt with some finding its way to third countries:

Andy MacDuff	Glen Coull
Bellows	Hamilton
British Sterling	Hathaway
Churchill	Highland Piper
Clan Macgregor	Hudson Bay Co.
XII Clans	Inverness Gold
Coventry	John Drew
Custom House	John Hardy
Devonshire	J.W. Dant
Duggan's Dew	Kennedy's
Dunscot	Kennedy's Regal Selection
Fleischmann's Golden Glen	King Charles Special Reserve
Forty Drummers	Legacy (Sazerac)

Lord & Lord	Scots Lion
MacClay	Sir Malcolm
McIntosh	Stonehouse
Park & Tilford Special Selection	Sutton Grumpy
Parliament Royal	Thomas Morton
Royal Treasure	Whiteside
Savory & Jones 8 years old	White Tavern
Scoresby Rare	

Even greater confusion arises over the policy of most whisky companies whereby they market a range of brands (often at different price levels) but sell their less well known labels through a variety of subsidiary companies. Very often the parent company's purpose is the perfectly reasonable one of wishing to protect the market position of their principal brands, whilst at the same time competing at the lower end of the market with secondary brands which cannot be directly linked with their prestige product. Whether they are, in fact, the same whiskies under different labels is doubtful, since the range of single whiskies available to a blender is such as to permit many variations between blends for the same company. A picture of who owns what emerges from Chapter 9, although I cannot but suspect that the true parentage has not been acknowledged in the case of every down-market whisky company known to be trading in the world market for Scotch.

Some whiskies are known by different names in different countries. Haig's De Luxe whisky, Dimple, is known as Pinch in the United States, whilst Haig is known there as Haig & Haig after the family off-shoot which established itself in the United States many years ago to market Scotch whisky. Similarly, North Americans may be surprised to find that their Dewar's (pronounced Doo-ers, as their advertisements say) is better known in its native land as White Label.

The stories behind certain brand names make interesting reading. Highland Queen, for example, was taken by Macdonald & Muir Ltd of Leith as their principal brand because Mary, Queen of Scots, when she travelled from France to Scotland to take up her title, had landed at a spot not very far from where the company's original premises were later to be established in the Kirkgate. The image or silhouette of the young Queen on horseback is used to this day as Macdonald & Muir's trade mark and is, along with the brand name, registered throughout the world. The origin of the name VAT 69 can be found under the entry for Wm Sanderson & Son in Chapter 9.

Brand names can occasionally lead to quite unforeseen results.

97

Hill, Thomson & Co. Ltd market their St Leger (named after the famous annual horse race) as a light blend. It has been particularly successful in the French-speaking Quebec province of Canada where it occupies second place in the market, and where the French meaning of the brand name unintentionally underlines the whisky's 'lightness' — to its obvious success. A De Luxe whisky recently introduced into the United Kingdom market is Eadie Cairns's National Choice, the label depicting Red Rum, the famous three-time Grand National winner. Here the whisky distiller and blender is hoping to benefit from the popularity of a particular personality.

Owners will, of course, go to great lengths to protect their brands and whisky names, as did George Smith over a hundred years ago in order to preserve his exclusive rights to The Glenlivet. More recently, William Grant and Sons Ltd successfully took legal action against an Aberdeen firm of wine and spirit merchants who had bottled a small quantity of whisky distilled at Glenfiddich, for sale under their own label but with 'Glenfiddich' prominently displayed.

There are, of course, many blends of whisky made up especially for a particular customer — perhaps a club, hotel, exclusive retail outlet or regimental mess. Such London stores as Harrods, Fortnum and Mason and the Army and Navy Stores all have their own whiskies, to say nothing of more distinguished institutions like the House of Commons. James Turnbull, the Hawick whisky merchants, have dealt in special label blends, an example being their Southern Mist, the club label of the Royal Southern Yacht Club. Diner's Club has its own exclusive brand of De Luxe whisky which it supplies only to its members, and even ships have had their own whiskies. Lowrie's used to produce QE2 for that famous liner and, in an earlier age, Hill Thomson made a special blend, Very Rare 11 years old, for the ships of the White Star Line. Whiskies can also be made up for special occasions. The Elgin merchants and exporters Gordon & MacPhail successfully promoted a range of bottled 25 year old malts in 1977 to mark the Queen's Silver Jubilee, as well as a specially labelled blend on the bicentenary of the founding of the nearby town of Fochabers. Companies wishing to promote an international brand image have found it useful to have their own whisky, and Dunhill and JPS (John Player Special) are already on the market, to be joined shortly by Gucci.

The power of the package

What often sells whisky is, regrettably, the label or the shape of the bottle rather than its contents. Some bottles have very distinctive shapes indeed, such as Graham's Black Bottle and Tomintoul-Glenlivet and, of course, Dimple Haig, once much sought after for the old sixpences and silver three-penny bits. Alas, a change in caps in 1973 meant a narrower bottle neck and the end of the Dimple piggy-bank. The dumpy bottle introduced many years ago by Haig has been copied so extensively as to be commonplace. Similarly, the Johnnie Walker rectangular bottle has many imitators, but, on the occasions where the labelling has got unfairly close to the original Red or Black, the company has usually succeeded in obtaining a Court ruling forbidding the sale of whisky in such containers. In some markets, empty bottles from well known brands have a resale value, since unscrupulous dealers can refill them with a cheap and sometimes harmful substitute, much to the detriment of the distiller's reputation. This has been countered to a large extent by the invention of the non-refillable bottle, which has a special fitment at the mouth which allows only one-way pouring. Even so, the more determined counterfeiters have been known to bore holes in the base of the bottles, refill them and then reseal them by heating. The give-away is the tiny bubble of glass which tells where the resealing has taken place.

Bottle sizes vary considerably, especially from country to country, and this can lead to confusion and problems for the consumer. The standard bottle of Scotch in Britain has for long contained 26¾ fluid ounces, or 75 centilitres. This size also appears in many export markets, but one has to take care both at home and abroad that an attractively priced whisky is not in fact in a smaller bottle — 70 cl or even 65 cl. It is not easy for the naked eye to spot the difference in size, and the labels, whilst legally bound to be specific on the matter, sometimes employ the smallest possible print. The half, quarter, and gill bottles are probably better known in the home market than anywhere else. Their existence reflects the ubiquitous use of Scotch whisky as a highly convenient aid to celebration and as a stimulant in inclement weather, as well as the high price of the product as a result of taxes.

Many brands are bottled in miniatures, and these are widely known, especially to the international traveller. The collection of these miniatures has become a popular pastime, but one which seems to me to be quite pointless unless you allow yourself to taste the contents — and thus render worthless the prized collector's piece. One firm, Whisky Galore of Newtonmore, Inverness-shire, has a list of over two hundred such tiny bottles.

At the other end of the scale, some of the better known brands come in litre size (popular with the duty-free trade), imperial quart (40 fluid ounces, or 1.136 litres), magnums (1.5 litres), tregnums (2.25 litres) — first introduced by Long John — and giant size (3.75 litres).

When it comes to retail sales, some companies stick to the old-fashioned standard whisky bottle and nothing else, while many others have seen fit to add expensive corrugated packaging and brightly coloured cartons with attractive designs. The expense of elaborate gift packaging, which contributes little to the security or handling of the whisky, does of course add to the retail price, but this is absorbed without too much difficulty since Scotch is sold in many markets as a high-cost luxury item. Compared with many other consumer items, however, Scotch whisky is somewhat conservative in its approach to packaging. Aberlour 12 years old VOHM (Very Old Highland Malt) has tried a bold and successful experiment in this area: the bottle and label layout used are very similar to those employed for Remy Martin VSOP Cognac. The purpose is clearly to convey an image of quality for a comparatively little-known whisky. It is unlikely that many people have actually purchased Aberlour by mistake for Remy Martin, but it is interesting to speculate as to whether any Cognac drinkers have been won over to drinking single malt whisky through this clever device. What cannot be denied is that Aberlour VOHM has made impressive progress in the Far East where the Chinese have a strong preference for Cognac.

Some whisky companies have had imitation whisky jugs or old-style flagons made up for their older whiskies to be sold in the exclusive end of the market. Ye Whisky of Ye Monks was an early example of this, but there are many others. Govancroft Potteries Ltd of Glasgow are leading manufacturers of leadless, handmade stoneware flagons for this purpose, and the beautiful whisky-filled ceramics of Peter Thomson (Perth) Ltd are perhaps better known than their Beneagles whisky which goes into them. Whyte & Mackay have a ceramic reproduction of a pot still by Wade in 22 carat gold finish and filled with a litre of Whyte & Mackay De Luxe 12 years old whisky.

But it is the label rather than the bottle which provides the information the consumer needs to know. Unfortunately, such words as Special, Old, Matured, Extra, Ancient, Reserve, Finest, Supreme, Cream, and the like mean very little and are simply employed to give the brand a particular ring of authenticity or quality. They are invariably applied to standard blends, although De Luxe can usually now be taken to indicate a better quality blend

a

WHYTE & MACKAY
SPECIAL
SCOTCH WHISKY

100%
SCOTCH WHISKY

DOUBLE LION BRAND

PRODUCT
OF SCOTLAND

b

Sole Proprietors

Whyte & Mackay
DISTILLERS LIMITED

ESTABLISHED 1844 GLASGOW, SCOTLAND

d

c

75cl.   40% Vol.   70°PROOF

e

DISTILLED, BLENDED AND BOTTLED IN SCOTLAND.

What to look for on the label of a Scotch whisky blend
a it must say Scotch   *d alcoholic strength*
b that it is a product of Scotland *e it should say distilled, blended*
c quantity   *and bottled in Scotland*

containing a higher than usual amount of well-aged malts in the mix. If the age is added to the label, usually 8 years or older, this underscores the quality nature of the particular whisky, since all of the whiskies in the blend, including the grain, must be at least as old as is claimed on the bottle. In other words, if only one of the single whiskies making up the blend is 8 years old, whilst all the others are much older, the blend nevertheless can claim only to be 8 years, the age of the youngest whisky in the blend.

The use of the description 'Liqueur Scotch Whisky' has largely been dropped at the insistence of The Scotch Whisky Association, since it gave the impression that the drink in question was more a liqueur containing Scotch whisky, like Drambuie or Glayva, than a straightforward blended whisky.

Less than honest labelling occurs too with bottled malts — perhaps only to be expected in view of the profitability of that

One of the most informative labels of a single malt is that of Knockando, showing the season the whisky was distilled, the year and month bottled and the consequent age, plus the distillery address, fluid contents and proof strength, but it does not say distilled and bottled in Scotland.

particular sector in recent years. The range of single malts on the market, bottled by the malt distillery or an associated company, has expanded considerably in recent years, and these are listed under the appropriate entry in Chapter 9. Certain others are bottled by independent whisky merchants, although some distillers are now objecting to this as they wish to bottle their product in exclusivity themselves. The term vatted malt is explained in Chapter 1, and quite a number have been around for some time, for example Mar Lodge, Strathconon, Royal Culross and Duncraggan, to list but a few. Many new ones have come on the market recently but have been labelled in such a way as to blur the distinction between single and vatted malts. The Duart Castle label states that it is 'finest single malt Scotch whisky' with Isle of Mull under the name. Tobermory Distillery is the only distillery on the Isle of Mull but there is no obvious connection between it and Duart Castle, which certainly is not a distillery.

The enthusiast has to be on his guard when purchasing expensive bottled malts, as this is an area where careful guidance is needed. Few wine and spirit merchants stock much more than a handful of the many malts now available, and even then in limited quantities. Good sources of supply are some of the top class London stores, such as Harrod's and Fortnum and Mason's, and the Edinburgh wine and spirit merchants Lambert Bros. Most good wine and spirit merchants elsewhere in Scotland will stock a reasonable range of bottled malts, but the situation in other parts of Britain is totally inadequate. When it comes to world availability, the only single malt whisky to enjoy anything like an international reputation is Glenfiddich, which has been an outstanding success in marketing terms. Thereafter, Macdonald & Muir's Glenmorangie is second favourite in Britain, and has a strong following in Scotland, Glen Grant and The Glenlivet are all fairly widely advertised and do well at home and abroad. But, these apart, the quantities involved in the sales of other single malts are really very modest.

The young pretenders

Whilst misleading descriptions constitute one problem, the existence of rogue brands purporting to be Scotch whisky is another, and more serious one. Their appearance in Britain is probably now fully safeguarded against by the existence of legislation and a vigilant Customs and Excise and the Scotch Whisky Association. The industry's worries on this score lie mainly abroad, and legion are the cases pursued by or on behalf of the Scotch Whisky Association and its members in many parts of the world. Particular vigilance is required against the admixers, i.e. those unscrupulous companies which use imports of bulk malt whisky for giving flavour and some character to the local neutral spirit, the sum of the two being passed off as Scotch. Examples of actions taken involved the Athens Court of First Instance, which issued injunctions refraining Distillery Dumont from selling its concoctions under the labels of Royal Band and Royal Castle. The complaints were about the firm's use of English brand names, labels and packaging in such a way as to give the impression that the products were entirely Scotch whisky. Further injunctions against the same Greek company were issued in respect of their Country Club and Nordren brands. Another Greek company to fall foul of the Courts on similar grounds had a cheery range of anglophone labels — Captain Jock, Old Guard, Grand Monarch, Crown, The King of Whiskies and Three Fives. A more blatant example in the Netherlands involved the admixed brand called Three Towers, whose label included a thistle and a map of Great Britain. One Italian admixture called Guardian's Whisky depicted a strip of tartan on the label and described itself in English as 'fine blended whisky distilled and aged with the methods and traditions of the old Scotch distillers'. This was held by the Milan Court to be deceptive, as was Loch Ness 'Scotch Whisky'. The admixers even resort to registering name-plate companies in the UK, often in Scotland, so that the names can be used on the labels to help give authenticity to their products.

However, the 'baddies' are not by any means always from outside Scotland. The Scotch Whisky Association has been quick to take legal action in Britain against companies suspected of assisting the admixing trade by supplying bulk malt without proper safeguards against its misuse, to the detriment of Scotch whisky, or by allowing improper use of their Scotch whisky labels.

To get a better picture of the extent of the problem it is perhaps worth noting some of the whisky brand names used in a variety of countries and which have given cause for concern. The following is only a random sample:

Argentina	Maltwhisky	Walter Scott
	Whiskymalt	
Brazil	Duck Scot	Queen Rose
	Good Mark	Whiskent
Colombia	Whisky Mark Royal	
Cyprus	Royal Bruce	
Denmark	Queensberry	
Ecuador	Old Boy	
Germany, West	Kelt	Old Tay
	Gaylord	Queen's Club
Italy	Barklay's	Old Moor De Luxe
	Black Swan	Old Windjammer
	Gilman	O & M
	Governor's Cellar	Red Piper
	Knight of the Moor	Scotch Rill
	Lloyd Logan	Silver Queen
	Old Choice	Union Jack
	Old Highland	Whitman
Malawi	Camerone Cream of the Glen	

Mauritius	McCoy Glenrosa	Glenside
Nicaragua	Queen Victoria	
Panama	Howard Maclaren	
South Africa	Auld Lang Syne Drummond's	Highland Mist
Spain	Five years Highland Star Kilt Morrison Bros	Queen Bess Royal 77 Wiskat
USA	Bond Street	Loch-A-Moor
Venezuela	Black Watch	

Admixtures usually comprise blends of very young malt whisky and local spirit made from wheat, rye or oats to which a British-sounding name is given in the hope that it will be taken for the real thing. This is downright misleading, but not quite as bad as counterfeit brands of similar admixtures which actually claim to be Scotch. Some of the rogue brand names which have turned up from time to time verge on the ridiculous, such as King Victoria in Japan. My favourite, however, is Auld Piss from Ecuador. Perhaps the local blender had asked an expatriate or visitor from Britain to suggest a suitable Scottish-sounding name to give it authenticity and ensure instant sales!

The labels are all important, and these range from the austere to the richly embossed, from the garish to the artistic. Some labels have scarcely changed since they were first introduced. A & A Crawford's Three Star, for instance, has remained unaltered since 1900. The Mackinlay's label has changed subtly at different times over the long period of that brand's life, and has recently been changed back to an earlier, more pleasing design. Others have varied greatly over the years.

Winning them over

Whilst the label is important at the point of sale for identification purposes, it is the advertising and the promotional campaign which has gone before which actually rings up the sales. The importance of advertising was quickly grasped by the most successful of the nineteenth century whisky blenders, and a good advertising programme has remained an essential part of any whisky company's sales campaign. This has resulted in most of the principal brands having a long-established and easily recognisable motif or theme. Everyone knows the striding, smiling figure of Johnnie Walker as well as they know the black and white terriers which together symbolise Buchanan's Black and White. Nor does the famous White Horse need much explanation, although Dewar's pipe major is perhaps less well known. Both Bell's and Glen Grant have employed famous cartoonists to draw attention to their products in a very sophisticated way, and the Glen Grant Highlanders are now firmly part of the Scotch whisky scene. The 'Afore Ye Go' cartoon advertisements are equally successful. Other whiskies, such as Cutty Sark and Dewar's, adopt a more sober or artistic approach to their advertising, which is no less pleasing in its effect.

In Britain, although the budgets allocated to advertising and promotional activities are huge, they are kept down by a mutual agreement not to use television, and advertising is a fairly straightforward affair.

In those countries which have not succeeded in keeping Scotch out of the market through fiscal measures or trade restrictions, political pressures from local distilling interests can lead to interference with the freedom to advertise. It is often left to the discretion of the local agent as to how to promote a particular brand in overseas markets, and a cash allowance is made to the wholesale price of the whisky in order to enable him to meet the cost of advertising.

The cost of large-scale advertising is prohibitive, and only the really big companies undertake it in any systematic way, either at home or abroad, but it is essential if they are to keep up volume sales. Smaller companies have a more selective approach, either aimed at particular areas or sectors of the population, or relying on point of sale advertising. The range of gimmicks can be quite staggering, and Teacher's was one of the first companies to use this promotional method. The items included drip mats, knives, corkscrews, cigarette cases, propelling pencils, comb sets, scissors, hussifs and even a bath sponge. The very small companies with established outlets and no thought to expansion probably do not need, or cannot afford, to advertise beyond sending the annual Christmas card to their agents.

Amounts spent on the promotion and advertising of Scotch whisky are colossal, and much of this is accounted for by competition between brands rather than the promotion of Scotch against other spirits or other forms of drink. However, Scotch is becoming

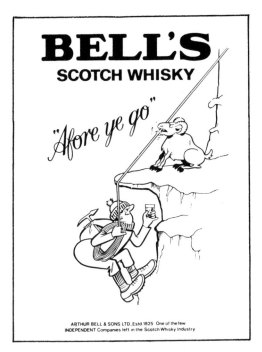

increasingly the target of the ad-man responsible for publicising other whiskies, particularly in the United States, where attacks against 'expensive imports' have become more and more common as domestic whiskies slip in popularity. And the Irish have recently taken on the Scots — even on their home territory — in a bid to give their product more appeal beyond the native bog by emphasising the difference between Irish whiskey and Scotch and pointing out that the former is triple distilled whilst Scotch is only twice distilled (conveniently ignoring the fact that triple distillation still takes place at Auchentoshan).

There is no certainty that advertising itself actually helps to widen the appeal of Scotch in new territories. In France the advertising of Scotch was banned in 1957, and in that year the country imported a mere 157,000 proof gallons. But by 1982, France had become Scotch whisky's third most important market. Advertising played no role whatsoever in this phenomenal development (other than the advertising by association through the much-loved products of Hollywood, where Scotch has long been the preferred drink of the big screen's hero and villain alike). On the other hand, the outstanding success of Chivas Regal as a top-price quality Scotch in the United States, where it sold over a million cases in 1980 (compared with 135,000 in 1962), is often attributed to the ingenious advertising campaigns which took a witty approach to snob appeal and made it pay off.

107

Great events have long been considered a most effective way of promoting Scotch whisky. Some of the early antics of the big blenders were rather crude or amateurish, such as the employment by Dewar's of Highland pipers at the Brewers' Exhibition and the singing of songs in praise of a particular whisky at the music halls. Today more sophisticated methods apply through what is known as sponsorship, whereby a company promotes its image by providing the financial backing or prize money for a particular public event. Cutty Sark are now closely associated with the International Tall Ships Race, including the award of a £5000 trophy, which is a silver model of the famous tea clipper. Haig is well known for its activities in County cricket, and Seagram's are currently involved in cycling and, perhaps most unexpected of all for a Scotch whisky company, give support to the alcoholics' association, Accept.

Other examples of sponsorship are the (William) Grant's Whisky Piping Championships and the much coveted Balvenie Trophy, Whyte & Mackay's Army Rugby Union Challenge Cup Competition, and The Glenlivet Haggis Hunt. Such activities are equally popular in the United States, where there are, for example, J & B's famous Gold Putter Award for golfing, the Black and White backgammon championships and Teacher's Annual Ski Championship.

If a promotion can be linked to a brand name, so much the better. An instance of this was J. & W. Hardie's 'The Antiquary Challenge', in which competitors were invited to telephone a given number and listen to BBC Television's Arthur Negus describe in detail a piece selected from the antique collection at Scone Palace. The challenge was to estimate the value of the antique; the prize a cheque to the value of the piece itself. The 'phone-in' was linked to a poster display in all major Scottish towns, and ran over four months with a different challenge and a different prize each month.

With so many established brands on the market and little apparent room for growth it is surprising that new major brands come forward as frequently as they do. The sophisticated launch of John Buckmaster's Glorious 12th at the opening of the 1980 grouse season is a case in point, involving as it did lavish entertainment for selected representatives of the trade and journalists in the beautiful setting of Leeds Castle in Kent. The show involved the delivery by helicopter of the first grouse of the season, shot (presumably that day) in Scotland and flown down for the occasion. Perhaps this sort of treatment is appropriate when launching a new and expensive De Luxe brand.

The Glenfiddich story

Although the tales of great commercial successes and ingenious promotional wheezes belong to the famous blenders, there is one outstanding example of brilliant marketing which has done more for malt whisky than perhaps anything else. This is the growth of Glenfiddich Highland Malt, which occupies a much envied position as the best-selling single malt in the world. This is not to say it is the best malt whisky in Scotland. But it is certainly the most widely available and must take much of the credit for capturing a place in the consumer spotlight for single malt whisky, a product which had previously been the preserve of the connoisseur and the privileged, and almost exclusively in Scotland.

As recounted elsewhere, the dominance of blended Scotch whisky, indeed the expansion and very survival of the industry itself, had been based on the assumption that Highland pot-still malt whisky was too strong in flavour and body to be welcome to the palates of the educated masses. But worldwide the market for Scotch whisky grew to be an enormous challenge to the distillers and blenders of Scotland, and it was members of the Grant family at William Grant & Sons Ltd who realised that even if a tiny proportion of that market could be turned back to the original Scotch, the rewards would be considerable.

Glenfiddich had been bottled off and on as a single malt throughout the distillery's unbroken history, but from 1920, when Grant's blended whisky activities first overshadowed the malt whisky side of the business, until the 1960s it had never amounted to more than a sideline to Grant's considerable volume business in blended whisky. By the late 1950s deliveries scarcely amounted to 500 cases per annum. But already a new marketing plan had been drawn up and by 1964 allocations had increased eight-fold with sights set on new pastures in the south of Scotland and England. For the first time, a single malt whisky was being advertised nationally throughout Britain. Nor did the people at Grant's overlook the United States, the most prized market for every distiller and blender; but there the approach was highly selective and aimed at opinion-formers and the moulders of consumer trends. By 1963 2000 cases of Glenfiddich were being exported, by 1966 8000 cases.

Grant's next turned to Sweden, a hard nut to crack in view of the protective role played by the State alcohol-importing monopoly. But careful cultivation and preparation culminated in the Swedish Government allowing malt whisky to be imported for the first time in

May 1967. Footholds were also established in Canada, Australia, France and Italy; indeed in Western Europe generally. Glenfiddich had been successfully launched and phase one of the operation completed.

The next phase, to sell Glenfiddich in volume, began in 1969. The tools to achieve this were the creation of the Glenfiddich Sales Division within the company and under the control of the founder's great grandson, David Grant, and a switch in packaging, all adding up to a much more robust marketing approach. The Glenfiddich experiment was paying off handsomely, and the company soon faced the problem of demand outstripping supply. The difficulty could not be remedied by merely increasing current production, since the single Glenfiddich being bottled had on average to be 8 to 10 years old. The answer was the careful allocation of supplies so as to keep key markets satisfied, combined with a programme of buying back mature Glenfiddich — at much higher prices than those paid for the new whisky — from the blenders who prized it as an ingredient in their blends. Glenfiddich received the Queen's Award for Export Achievement in 1974, when 119,500 cases were exported. In 1982 total sales of Glenfiddich were estimated to have climbed to over 360,000 cases.

The advance of Glenfiddich owed a great deal to inspired and well orchestrated promotion campaigns. However, Grant ingenuity was sorely tested in France where the advertising of imported spirits, including whisky, was forbidden by law. To circumvent this Grant's set up the Academy of Pure Malt Scotch Whisky, with headquarters in Scotland and a branch in France. Distinguished Scots were invited to become governors of the Academy, although its activities were designed to propagate knowledge and appreciation of malt whisky abroad rather than in the United Kingdom. The first President of the French branch was Robert Courtine, a well known *journaliste-gastronome*, and a number of prominent Frenchmen in these and other fields were appointed academicians, after the style of the Academie Française. Given French law, the Academy has to be circumspect in its activities — which are more closely related to the art of good living in its wider sense than the mere indulgence in one branch of it. It organises an annual luncheon prepared by one of France's outstanding chefs, as well as various meetings and educational visits. There are two annual prizes: le Prix de L'Academie for the person who has done most to promote good living, and the Glenfiddich Award for the writer who has contributed most by his work to the same end. The Academy awards diplomas to those who have attended a whisky nosing and have thus taken an important step towards understanding the mysteries of Scotland's great gift to the world.

An American branch of the Academy was set up in 1974 where Fellows, as they are known, are able to take part in various promotional activities directly related to Glenfiddich.

Although the Academy of the Pure Malt Scotch Whisky was no doubt launched as something of a tongue-in-cheek operation, and is only thinly disguised as a means of promoting Glenfiddich, the people at Grant's are to be awarded full marks for having opened up entirely new markets for single malt whisky, to say nothing of having enriched the lives of those who were previously ignorant of the product.

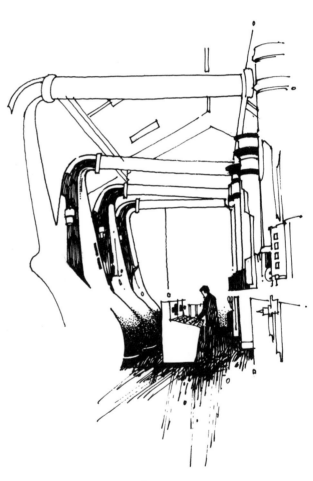

The stillhouse at Tormore

8

The world's cup: today and tomorrow

At the time this book went to press, the Scotch whisky industry was only one of many suffering the effects of the economic recession in Britain and abroad. A spate of distillery closures could be taken as an indication of more difficulties to come, but it is necessary to look at such events in the light of trends and figures over the last decade or so, starting with the recent production figures for malt and grain whisky.

Table 1: Production in thousands of litres pure alcohol (LPA)

cal. year	malt	grain	total	% change
1972	176,245	258,776	435,021	
1973	199,112	271,987	471,099	+ 8.3
1974	214,669	261,726	476,395	+ 1.1
1975	178,926	215,338	394,264	−17.2
1976	167,411	194,854	362,265	− 8.1
1977	171,457	221,101	393,558	+ 8.6
1978	209,279	250,020	459,299	+16.7
1979	203,871	255,138	459,009	− 0.06
1980	177,913	237,957	415,870	− 9.4
1981	110,083	157,898	267,981	−35.6
1982	96,649	151,021	247,670	− 7.6

As can be seen, total Scotch whisky production reached its peak in 1974 then fell away rapidly until it made a sharp recovery in 1978, only to plunge drastically in 1981 and 1982 to production levels of fifteen years previously and down 48 per cent on the peak year of 1974.

It is worth comparing the 1982 figure with the total production figures for earlier periods.

Table 2: total production in million proof gallons

year	production	related world events
1901	30.0	Queen Victoria died
1913	24.0	
1914	28.0	outbreak of World War I
1918	14.8	war ends, malt whisky distilling still banned
1919	13.2	tax increased by 150%
1920	22.5	Prohibition
1921	29.3	
1927	16.0	
1930	20.0	slump
1932	9.0	Prohibition repealed
1938	36.3	
1939	37.8	outbreak of World War II
1941	3.2	limited malt distilling only
1943-4	nil	total ban on distilling
1946	14.3	restricted distilling
1950	29.1	
1955	38.6	
1960	66.9	3 new distilleries start
1963	90.8	
1965	126.5	2 distilleries rebuilt after 60 years of silence
1968	113.6	two increases in taxation
1978	177.3	
1981	103.5	
1982	95.6	

Although different twelve month periods have been used at different times — calendar year, fiscal year (1 April-31 March) and distilling year (1 October-30 September) — the variation is not of any direct relevance for comparison purposes. What is clear is that whisky production has been extremely volatile and stability only entered the trade to any satisfactory degree in the 1950s. If the figures for the longer random period from 1900 were broken down as between malt and grain whisky production, similar patterns would emerge, with slightly more volatility in the grain whisky figures than in those for malt whisky. The reasons for the fluctuations during the first half of the present century are recorded in Chapter 5. While production varied enormously during this period, so did the number of distilleries in operation: there were 156 in 1901, 127 in 1913, 134 in 1921 and only 84 in 1927, dwindling to 15 in the disaster year of 1932-33. Today there are 131 established distilleries, about the same as in 1921. Although all 131 are covered in this book, many of these have either been temporarily closed for most of 1983, or have been shut for a considerably longer period. In 1978 these were producing six times as much whisky, either from modern distilleries built to replace those permanently abandoned during the locust years, or from ancient distilleries where output has since been greatly enhanced by modern techniques; in 1982, however, they produced only about three and a half times as much as in 1921.

The 1982 figures — in many ways disastrous — are not altogether surprising in the wake of the severest peace-time economic recession the world has known since the days of the Great Depression. Table 2 suggests that, historically, Scotch whisky follows the general economic trend and is able to climb back again in times of recovery, and I come back to this at the end of the chapter.

But making Scotch whisky is, as explained in Chapter 2, much more than simply adjusting production to meet projected needs for the next twelve months. The statutory requirement whereby Scotch whisky must be warehoused for three years, and the general trend towards using whisky matured well beyond the minimum legal age in order to improve the mix of a particular blend, means that enormous quantities of whisky, far in excess of annual production, are warehoused. Table 3 shows the quantities of stocks in bonded warehouses in Scotland, England and Wales during the ten year period 1971 to 1980, the most recent figures available.

Table 3: warehoused whisky stocks in millions of litres

1971	2,124.27
1972	2,249.61
1973	2,484.45
1974	2,637.56
1975	2,777.17
1976	2,814.28
1977	2,824.92
1978	2,860.21
1979	2,958.04
1980	3,048.40

Whilst throughout the 1950s and 1960s the ratio of new whisky to maturing whisky was roughly between 1:4 and 1:5.5, this has shot up in recent years to a ratio in excess of 1:7. The amount of capital tied up in Scotch whisky is truly formidable and no accurate figure can be placed on it, but an estimate in 1979 put it at just over £1,010 millions, since when it has certainly increased both in money and real terms.

A question which intrigues many is the proportion of malt whisky produced to grain whisky. For the period covered by Table 1, malt as a percentage of total production varied from 39 per cent in 1982 to 46.2 per cent in 1976. It has certainly been below 40 per cent in earlier years and was as low as 30 per cent in 1965. Apart from the freak war years, it has never been above 50 per cent during this century. Allowing for the malt whisky which is bottled 'single' (about 1.5 per cent) and that which is exported in bulk (9 per cent), one can say that over the last few years approximately 30 per cent of total whisky production is represented by the malt content of blended whisky — a not altogether unsatisfactory figure when one is trying to guess at the average percentage of malt in a blend. For the De Luxe brands it will probably be higher and for the standard brands lower, and in some cases a lot lower.

For the various categories of Scotch whisky the world percentage market share in 1981 was approximately as follows:

bottled blend	73.5
bulk blend	17.5
bottled malt	1.4
bulk malt	7.2
bottled grain	negligible
bulk grain	0.4

Employment and productivity

Despite its importance to the Scottish economy, Scotch whisky is a less significant source of employment than might be expected, although much of that employment is found in scattered communities where even a small number of jobs is of great importance. In 1978, the total number employed in Scotland was estimated at 25,316, and by 1983 this had dropped to approximately 21,000. The 1978 figure breaks down by activity as follows:

maltings	500
distilling	5089
warehousing	1375
blending	2921
bottling and packaging	12,000
by-products	359
management, sales and administration	3072

Those employed in malt distilling numbered 3,068 and those in grain distilling 2,021, thus reflecting the greater automation in grain whisky distilling. This is underlined by the following figures for 1978:

3,068 employees produced 80.6 million proof gallons of malt, or 26,286.5 gallons per employee.

2,021 employees produced 96.3 million proof gallons of grain, or 47,673 gallons per employee.

In other words, a grain distillery employee produces almost twice as much as his malt distillery colleague. An interesting fact, but one that is of little significance when the production time, methods of production and materials used are brought into the equation. But it is little wonder that the Lowland entrepreneur was so anxious to put his money into patent-still distilleries during the second half of the last century.

It is possible to approach the question of employment from a different angle, i.e. based on a whisky output figure which is made up of withdrawals from stocks. A report by J.K. Thomson for the Scottish Council gave the average annual output per employee on the basis of grain output of 85.15 million gallons and malt output of 39.27 million gallons (i.e. a total of 124.42 million gallons) as follows:

	proof gallons
malt distilling	12,800
grain distilling	42,133
warehousing	90,487
blending	38,744
bottling	7,732
administration	45,501

None of these figures contains any surprises other than to emphasise even more the high output per capita of grain whisky distilling compared with that of malt whisky. In this case the grain employee is credited with producing well over three times that of his malt colleague. The labour-intensiveness of bottling and despatch is brought out here, where almost half the total work force in the industry is deployed, and practically all of that is in the southern part of Scotland. The division between Highlands and Lowlands remains, and the distribution of the work-force underlines the victory conceded many years ago now to the patent-still distiller and blender by the pot-still distiller. Of the total employed in the industry, something approaching 75 per cent will be found in the Lowlands.

There have been attempts to tilt the balance of the industry more in favour of the Highlands, such as by the establishment of the extensive grain distillery and related installations at Invergordon, but apart from Arthur Bell & Sons PLC at Perth, no major company has its headquarters in the north and the decision-making is done in Glasgow, Edinburgh and London.

United Kingdom market

The first 'exports' of Scotch whisky were to England. At first they were of no great importance either to Scotland or England, and the taste for the pungent, strongly flavoured Highland malts was very limited in the latter. However, as we have seen, this changed dramatically in the second half of the nineteenth century with the introduction of blended whisky, and the English market became the key to success for such adventurers as Buchanan, the Dewars and Walker. The difference in approach to the English market has persisted to this day, and although companies generally gross up their sales throughout the kingdom in order to arrive at total home trade, Scotland is still looked upon as a separate market from that of England and Wales. Certainly many companies will have a different agent in Scotland from the one handling its whisky in the rest of the country. Distillers Company subsidiaries, for example, deal mainly with wholesalers and the brewery groups in England and Wales, but in Scotland they find it necessary to cultivate and supply the individual licensed retail outlets.

Competition is even keener in Scotland than it is elsewhere in Britain, and a fair share of the Scottish market is probably regarded as a prerequisite to success in the United Kingdom, as well as a good selling point abroad. Curiously, however, the traditional leader in the Scottish stakes, Bell's, have only recently used this to promote themselves in the rest of Britain and abroad, but have done so with marked success. Second place in the Scottish league goes to the Famous Grouse, known usually as simply Grouse. An old established brand with a devoted following in Scotland, it has been heavily promoted by Highland Distilleries with phenomenal success, to the extent that it often sells at a price which is slightly above that of most standard blends. Such is the impact of a good promotional campaign. Third place is currently claimed by Whyte & Mackay for their Whyte & Mackay Special brand, which also has a significant share of the total UK market.

The situation in the UK market was upset considerably following a ruling of the EEC Commission in December 1977. This forbade a system of dual pricing by the subsidiaries of the Distillers Company. Under that system a UK trade customer was charged a higher in-bond price (about £13 per case then) if he bought their brands for resale within other EEC countries than if he bought them for ultimate UK consumption (about £8 per case). The difference was intended to reflect the higher marketing costs necessarily borne by the appointed sole distributors of those brands in the continental EEC if they were to compete successfully with traditional local (and often tax-favoured) spirits. In the absence of this price difference UK trade customers would have been able, without themselves making any contribution to the vital marketing expenditure, to take advantage of the effort and expenditure of the continental EEC sole distributors and thus establish very profitable 'parallel exports' on the basis of the lower prices at which they could obtain supplies originally intended for the UK market. In Distillers' view this would have destroyed the ability and incentive of the sole distributors to promote the brands effectively and, in the longer run, would have undermined its export business both within and outside the EEC. Distillers clearly believed that the dual pricing system would put parallel exports on an equal footing of competition — but fair competition — with exports established via the sole distributor route.

Following the Commission's adverse ruling, the Distillers Group promptly withdrew from the UK market Johnnie Walker Red Label (its biggest seller in that market and in fact the world brand leader) together with Haig Dimple (since restored to the UK market). The Group also increased the UK prices of other brands like VAT 69 and Black & White so as to render them unattractive for parallel export. In view of the price-sensitive nature of the UK market these increases amounted to a conscious decision to price the brands out of that market, in the interests of preserving the larger potential for sales of these brands in export markets.

The Distillers Group sought to fill the gaps with increased sales from Haig Gold Label and White Horse, whose UK prices had not been increased, and from two new brands, John Barr and The Buchanan Blend, from the stables of John Walker and James Buchanan respectively. In the lower price sector of the UK market help was derived from The Claymore whose origin, in fact, owed nothing to the Commission's 1977 decision.

Nevertheless the situation regarding the over-all British league table for blended Scotch whisky is now somewhat confusing. DCL brands together were estimated to be down to about 25 per cent of the UK market in 1982, compared with 50 per cent in 1973, with Haig and The Famous Grouse disputing third place at about 8 per cent each. Teacher's is the best selling brewer's whisky (Allied Breweries) with 15 per cent of the market, but pride of place goes to Bell's which, with over 24 per cent of the UK market, successfully transformed its position as Scotland's No. 1 whisky into Britain's No. 1 whisky, and is now selling nearly as much as all the DCL brands put together.

Statistics can be interpreted in many ways, but after the first four positions on the UK whisky chart — Bell's, Teacher's, Haig and Famous Grouse — the order for large-selling brands and their claimed percentage of the UK market in 1982 is reckoned to be:

Claymore (DCL)	7%
Grant's	6%
Whyte & Mackay	5%
White Horse (DCL)	4%
Long John	3%
Highland Queen	2%
Mackinlay's	2%

Thus eleven brands take an estimated 86 per cent of the market, which does not leave a great deal of room for the many other brands trying to find a niche for themselves in Britain's pubs and off-licences, where the total consumption in 1982 was 46 million LPA, a reduction of 4 per cent from 1981.

Nor is distribution uniform. A whisky which sells well in one part of the country can be a complete flop somewhere else, or just unobtainable. This is not entirely explained by the different marketing approaches as between Scotland and the rest of the country. Of recent origin, John Barr does well in the Midlands and north-west of England, whilst Teacher's does better south of the border than it does in its native Scotland. Highland Queen, popular in Scotland, has taken the road south and is making headway in Wales and Berkshire. Mackinlay's is successful in the south and south-east of England, whilst Long John traditionally does well in London and the north-east. Similarly, Whyte & Mackay do better in the north of England than they do in the south. But these are transitory matters, and the success or otherwise of a particular whisky owes more to the distiller's advertising agent and marketing organisation than it does to the intrinsic merit of the contents of the bottle under promotion.

United States market

Nowhere is the effect of good promotion more amply displayed than in the vital American market, where league positions are studied with the enthusiasm — nay desperation — of any baseball or football league. In 1981 and 1982 the top six brands in order of sales were reckoned to be (in thousands of cases):

	1982	1981	percentage change
J & B Rare	2,850	2,350	+21
Dewar's (DCL)	2,300	2,200	+ 4.5
Cutty Sark	2,000	1,700	+17
Johnnie Walker Red Label (DCL)	1,500	1,570	− 4.5

The other six brands selling in excess of 500,000 cases were, in alphabetical order:

> Chivas Regal
> Inver House
> Johnnie Walker Black Label (DCL)
> Old Smuggler
> Passport (bottled in Scotland)
> Passport (bottled in USA)

In the United States it seems that once a brand starts losing popularity nothing can stop it following a downward spiral. Bell's, Black & White, Haig & Haig, Teacher's and VAT 69 have at some point in their history experienced the slip and then the slide from favour in the eyes of the American consumer, never, so far, to return to their former sales pinnacle despite changes in management, agent or advertising, although Bell's are currently engaged in a dogged campaign to re-establish themselves in a reasonable position in the market. It will be interesting to see whether Cutty Sark, which has fallen from first to third place in the US market in just a handful of years , can correct its decline and break the historical trend. Once a brand has achieved a certain class image it is very difficult to change. When Continental Airlines started serving Chivas Regal to coach-class passengers, and Johnnie Walker Black Label to first-class passengers, many of the latter felt strongly miffed that the lower fare paying passengers were getting better treatment, at least in terms of the Scotch being offered. The airline had no choice but to make Chivas Regal available in both classes whilst leaving Black Label as an option for first-class imbibers.

What is interesting is that none of the leading brands in the US enjoys an important share of the UK market. Indeed, two of the top three US brands, J & B Rare and Cutty Sark, were until comparatively recently almost unknown in Britain. Dewar's has had a certain following in Scotland as White Label, but its success is as an export whisky. The owners of J & B Rare, International Distillers and Vintners Ltd, only put their whisky on the UK market because they were worried by reports of Americans visiting Britain and being unable to find their favourite brand. Some of the most successful export brands, therefore, had to introduce a British or Scottish dimension to their marketing for fear of undermining the international acceptability of their whisky. Nevertheless, it is the American market — which is considerably larger than the UK market itself — which has been the principal outlet for Scotch whisky internationally.

In world sales terms the leading brands are reckoned to be as follows:

1. Johnnie Walker Red Label (Distillers Company)
2. J & B Rare
3. Dewar's (Distillers)
4. Cutty Sark
5. Ballantine's
6. Johnnie Walker Black Label (Distillers)
7. Black & White (Distillers)
8. Chivas Regal
   Haig (Distillers)
10. VAT 69 (Distillers)
11. Bell's
    Passport
    Teacher's

All of the above, except Passport, are known to varying degrees in Britain, although Johnnie Walker Red Label has been withdrawn by DCL. Nevertheless, few of the leading UK brands are near the top of the international league. Bell's is a comfortable first in Britain but only eleventh equal with Passport and Teacher's over all, the latter being second in the British pecking order. Grouse does not feature at all in the big export league and the only other brand which is relatively important in both markets is White Horse.

These are how matters stand, but experience shows that it takes a great deal of luck and enormous expenditure to launch a new brand successfully on either the British or overseas markets. Whilst the greater part of the market is carved up between a comparatively small number of companies and brands, an enormous range of brands and smaller companies compete for what is left of it. Many of them are content to nurse a particularly narrow sector of the home market, especially if whisky represents only a modest part of their total business, whilst others are happy to maintain their share of a specific overseas market where they might have an energetic agent. One thing is clear, however, which is that exports are more important in both turnover and volume terms for most companies, and by 1982 represented, in volume terms, 85 per cent of all Scotch whisky sales.

Exports started to show an appreciable contribution to firms' order books during the second half of the last century, destinations being mainly those countries where Scots had settled or had followed the flag in the service of the Crown or in business. By the turn of the century exports totalled five million gallons. The more troubled the home market became, the more the blenders looked overseas. Exports were not without their ups and downs, as wars intervened and governments took measures to prevent or reduce the import of foreign spirits in order to protect domestic industries. Prohibition in the United States, as we have seen, was a mixed blessing. Nevertheless, the Scotch whisky industry had discovered the world and the ever-upward trend in exports was established, and by 1939 it had well and truly overtaken domestic consumption, by 9.4 million gallons to 6.9 million gallons. After the war, domestic consumption was held back by rationing until 1959, by which time the ratio of home to overseas consumption was 1:3. Swingeing taxes at home and active promotion abroad have raised that to more than 1:5.5, or 1:4 if only exports in bottle are considered.

The all-important American market is also the most competitive, and many of the smaller export companies have either opted out of it altogether or have specialised in it to the exclusion of all others. Unhappily, there are currently signs that it is no longer the golden goose that it was and a new flippancy in consumer tastes has seen a discernible drift away from 'brown liquors' to white or clear spirits such as vodka, tequila and white rum, as well as to wine. All whiskies, Canadian and American as well as Scotch, have taken an un-comfortable tumble. Nevertheless, a plateau appears to have been reached in whisky drinking of all kinds, with American and imported whiskies combined failing to take their accustomed 50 per cent plus of the spirits market, being down to 48.5 per cent in 1980 compared with 65 per cent ten years earlier, and showing no signs of recovering. During that period, Scotch's share of the US spirits market has remained fairly static whilst demand for domestic whiskies has fallen heavily. Conversely, Canadian whisky has done rather better than Scotch and now holds about the same share of the US market, having been well behind its elder and better a decade earlier. At the same time the United States has diminished in its importance to the industry over all since, in 1982, it took only about 31 per cent of total exports compared with 50 per cent in 1970.

As the producer of any commodity knows only too well, the antics of governments and the activities of competitors are merely temporary diversions compared with the disaster which the frailty of consumer taste can spell for him. This is as volatile in the United States as anywhere and no amount of advertising can reverse a downward trend once the consumer has been turned off a particular product. And it is in this that Scotch whisky can take some comfort as regards its American fortunes. In 1969 its market share of all spirits sold in the United States was 12 per cent. Since then it has scarcely advanced and, indeed, may have declined slightly in most recent years. But in the same period bourbons have declined from 24 per cent to 14 per cent, and American blended whiskies from 21.3 per cent to 9 per cent. Most of the slack has, however, been taken up by white spirits.

The rest of the world

Australia was, until the outbreak of the Second World War, the most important overseas market for Scotch whisky. But both this traditional market, and that of New Zealand, have declined in relative importance over the years due to a succession of fiscal measures taken by their governments against Scotch whisky, in order to encourage consumption of domestic drinks, including national whiskies such as the Corio range, Four Seasons, Glencar and Bond 7 in Australia, and 45 South and Wilson in New Zealand. As a result of import duties and transport costs, the price difference between whisky bottled in Scotland and that bottled in Australia can be as much as 50 per cent.

Another distant market of great importance, but one which needs a cautious watch kept on it, as explained later, is that of Japan. Japan has, of course, its own domestic whisky industry and Suntory is believed now to be the largest selling whisky of any kind in the world. Many are the apocryphal tales of Japanese whisky, both in the raw materials used and in the attempts at duplicating the conditions in

Scotland which are necessary for the production of a decent whisky. They used to give rise to much mirth, but the laughter now sounds rather hollow when viewed against the prospect of Japanese whisky being produced not only to satisfy the national thirst but also for export to markets where Scotch has traditionally been the dominant spirit. The improvement in flavour and thus the wider acceptance of Japanese whisky probably owes more to the imported malt whisky mixed with the local neutral spirit than anything else, and, as will be seen when we discuss the knotty problem of bulk exports, it is this which represents the greater part of Scotch whisky exports to Japan. Japan is nevertheless important in its own right as a market for bottled Scotch, particularly of the De Luxe variety, and the situation has greatly eased there with the lowering of the crippling tariffs which were levied against Scotch whisky. However, it did take a sustained diplomatic effort and Prime Ministerial intervention before the Japanese would budge.

Many of the top brands in the US market occupy lead positions in the Japanese market, except that White Horse has clearly been in the number one slot in Japan for many years. In 1982 the order, in terms of volume, was as follows:

1. White Horse (Distillers)
2. Cutty Sark
3. Johnnie Walker Red Label (Distillers)
4. J & B Rare
5. Johnnie Walker Black Label (Distillers)*
6. Haig (Distillers)
7. Ballantine's
8. Old Parr (Distillers)*
9. Dewar's White Label (Distillers)
10. Chivas Regal*
11. Bell's
12. Passport

(*De Luxe whiskies)

Occupying six out of the nine top brands, it is, perhaps, not surprising that the Distillers Company has taken such a firm line against the export of bulk malt whisky, especially to Japan. Japanese taste for Scotch whisky, rather than their simply valuing it as just another prestigious import, is underscored by the fact that virtually all imported whisky consumed in Japan is Scotch. The next most sought after imported spirit is Cognac, but the margin between the two is in the region of 4:1 in favour of Scotch. Nevertheless, Japan has been a market in decline and one that has suffered more than most from parallel exports which have sorely undermined the prestige image of the product in general, and of certain brands in particular.

The countries of the European Community can conveniently be taken as a group for export purposes and it is to them that many companies look in their search for expanding markets. Taken together, they are second only to the United States, and in 1982 France, Italy and West Germany individually occupied third, fourth and fifth places in the export league. Much of the market potential which these countries offer arises from the fact that the discrimination practised against Scotch whisky in certain member states — France, Italy and Greece — should be removed under the provisions of the Treaty of Rome. There are some signs that this may happen, following successful action over fiscal discrimination in Ireland against imported spirits. But it may be a long, slow struggle. The breakdown of fiscal barriers will be particularly important in France, which is a growth market for Scotch but where it originally faced a tax barrier of 49 per cent more than the tax on brandy, and 106 per cent more than that on rum. However, the process of equalisation of the rates of tax on all spirits is under way as a result of pressure applied through the EEC Commission. Another piece of blatant French discrimination is the advertising code which forbids the advertising of Scotch whisky, but allows virtually unrestricted advertising of Cognac, rum and other domestic alcoholic beverages. French concern over the national level of alcoholic intake may lead to restrictions on the advertising of other spirits as well as Scotch, but some importers of Scotch began advertising in France in 1981, following the EEC Court of Justice's judgement in July 1980, confirmed by the Court in December 1982, condemning the French practice and stipulating that products from other Member States must be allowed to advertise under the same conditions as similar domestic products. This may do nothing positive for Scotch, but it should at least even up the competition in what is currently the most important market in Europe and third after the United States and Japan. However, France's rapid rise in the export league is not due entirely to a change in Gallic tastes, since a good proportion of the whisky is re-exported to third countries, such as Japan. Similar trends are developing in the Netherlands and West Germany.

France has therefore become one of the most important overseas markets for Scotch whisky, and this despite no long tradition of whisky drinking in that otherwise most civilised of countries, and the many attempts by the French government to impede its progress. Some French sages on the subject of wines and spirits have been scathing in their attacks on Scotch whisky, seeing its dominance in international drinking as being due to the spread of American habits around the world. (The Americans are also blamed for the widespread use of English.) Such was the annoyance which Scotch whisky's success caused in official French circles that President de Gaulle stopped it being served at official receptions at the Elysée Palace. But as a contemporary French commentator remarked, 'The more the government shows that it does not like the Anglo-Saxons, the more the French drink, eat and dress British.' Indeed, the circle has been completed, since many of the old wine importers in Scotland became whisky blenders and eventually exporters, and now send their product to the country from which once they imported most of their wines. Like the United States, France has also become an important destination for bulk blended whisky and for brands aimed exclusively at that particular country. Whilst the range of these brands is not as great as in the United States, it is growing. Two recent additions are 320 Ligger's and Abernathy Malt, the latter presumably being of the vatted variety. Some of these French brands inevitably find their way into third markets.

Apart from the handful of countries which formally ban its importation, there is scarcely a country or territory in the world to which Scotch whisky is not exported, but its significance is greater in some places than others. For example, Venezuela has a population of thirteen million, but it was the fifth biggest market in the world in 1982 in *value* terms, because Scotch exports to Venezuela have a higher value per litre of pure alcohol than to any other major market in the world, as almost all of the whiskies sold there are high-priced De Luxe blends such as Johnnie Walker Black Label, Buchanan's De Luxe, Haig Dimple and Chivas Regal. Thus the Venezuelan figure is out of line with the average for the world as a whole by almost 100 per cent, since the price of whisky exported to Venezuela was on average £7 per LPA, whilst the world export average price was £3.46. The fact that Venezuelans invariably drink their Scotch with large measures of Pepsi Cola or Coca Cola should not upset the traditionalists in view of the contribution made to Britain's export earnings!

The leading export markets over the last ten years have been fairly stable. Remembering that the United Kingdom is a good second to the United States in over-all consumption, the order of the first ten export markets in 1982 was, in *volume* terms, as follows:

127

		percentage of export market
1.	USA	31.34
2.	Japan	10.25
3.	France	8.18
4.	Italy	4.41
5.	West Germany	3.31
6.	Australia	3.16
7.	Spain	2.63
8.	South Africa	2.60
9.	Belgium/Luxembourg	2.31
10.	Venezuela	2.21

Whilst the principal markets remain steady and most, except the United States, show encouraging growth potential, there are some very wild fluctuations from time to time. The twenty-fold increase in exports to Syria in 1979, for example, seems inexplicable. On the other hand, the dramatic drop in supplies to Ayatollah Khomeni's Iran is less surprising, perhaps, compared with earlier years under the Shah.

The extent to which politics can affect the distillers' interests abroad has been brought home most recently in Latin America where, following the South Atlantic war, there was an inevitable and dramatic drop in exports to Argentina, which was directly involved in the conflict and which introduced a trade embargo on British imports, and to Guatemala and Venezuela which were amongst Argentina's strongest supporters, and which also have territorial claims for which they hold Britain responsible. Quantitatively exports were, for the three countries, down respectively by 62 per cent, 73 per cent and 32 per cent in 1982 compared with 1980 (1981 figures not being available). Other factors may, coincidentally, have affected the recent poor performance in these countries, especially in Venezuela, which had long been a rich market for Scotch but one in which a deteriorating economic situation has led to the government there taking increasingly stringent fiscal measures against imported and luxury goods. But exports of Scotch whisky in 1982 were down generally throughout Latin America with the exception of Bolivia and Peru, both of which strongly supported the Argentine line, and, surprisingly, Cuba and Nicaragua.

Scotch whisky, like most other so-called luxury goods, faces an amazing array of customs duties and taxes around the world aimed, ostensibly, at keeping down the level of alcoholic intake, but designed in fact to protect domestic distilling industries or, more likely, simply to raise revenue. This leads to a tremendous variation in world prices for a bottle of the 'Auld Kirk'. However, the difference in prices cannot simply be attributed to the varying levels of taxation from country to country, since similar price gaps as between the same bottle of whisky are found in duty-free outlets around the world. Like anything else, Scotch whisky prices reflect what the particular market will bear.

The market for malt

So specialised is this that it requires separate consideration, although the consumption of single and vatted bottled malts must not be exaggerated since it is still, by industry standards, of very modest proportions and of interest only to certain companies.

The bottled malt whisky market accounted in 1982 for about 1.4 per cent of the total world market for Scotch (2 per cent of the UK share and 1 per cent of exports). This compares with 0.9 per cent in 1978, and there must be still considerable potential for further advance, although it would be unrealistic to expect this ever to amount to more than 5 per cent of total Scotch whisky sales. These figures include both single and vatted malts, although no major vatted malt brand has yet made its mark in the market place. Limitations on growth are increasing consumer preference for a whisky to which a mixer can be added, for which malts are entirely unsuited, the high cost of promoting new cult whiskies over a protracted period and problems of wide-scale distribution of a product still largely unknown. Against this, there is the attraction of very healthy profit margins of as much as 15 times that on a standard blended whisky.

The development of Glenfiddich is gone into in some detail in Chapter 7 because it shows that a single malt can make a major market entry, as a result of which Glenfiddich is the biggest selling bottled single malt both domestically and overseas and, as such, is far ahead of its nearest rivals Glen Grant and The Glenlivet. But these are both mainly export whiskies. On home territory, the only real rival to Glenfiddich is Glenmorangie. Two malts which have done surprisingly well abroad, mainly in France, are Glen Deveron and Aberlour-Glenlivet, both of which come from distilleries owned by foreign companies, respectively Martini & Rossi and Pernod-Ricard. The outlook is generally bright, although the price-cutting which has been the scourge of high-profile blended whisky brands in some foreign markets is also affecting single malts in such places as Italy, which is by far the biggest importer of them. This could back-fire on certain malt whisky distillers who may over-commit themselves on supplying aged whiskies at heavily discounted prices now, only to find that they are unable to meet their obligations later against rising prices.

The main overseas markets for bottled malt are, in order of volume, Italy, France, United States, West Germany, Japan, Canada, Netherlands, Spain, Australia and Belgium/Luxembourg, with Italy by far the most important destination.

The following single malts can be said to have made some sort of impact already, either in the home market or abroad and, in some cases, in both:

Glenfiddich	Laphroaig
Glen Grant	Knockando
The Glenlivet	Cardhu
Glenmorangie	Isle of Jura
The Macallan	Tomatin
Dufftown-Glenlivet	Tormore
Glen Deveron	Highland Park
Aberlour-Glenlivet	Bruichladdich
Glenfarclas	

The high cost of promotion and advertising and the limited public which is likely to be won over to malt whisky may mean that different approaches to marketing are called for, especially as widespread distribution of the lesser known malts is difficult to achieve unless distillers and wholesalers are prepared to waive the usual minimum supply requirements. Direct selling to the public is another approach, and this is already possible by ordering by post from certain merchants who specialise in malt whiskies.

Another angle is that of the mail-order club, which is precisely what The Highlands and Islands Malt Whisky Club is. It developed along the lines of wine by mail order, in which a number of merchants specialise, and was launched in order to generate more enthusiasm for, and knowledge of, the single malts of Scotland. After some research, the Club organisers launched their venture with a selection of six malts designed to cover almost the full spectrum of flavours. Their selection was The Macallan, Tobermory, Glengoyne, Dalmore, Tormore and Bowmore. Three of these are now fairly widely marketed, whilst the other three are difficult to find. In addition, the Club has a regular newsletter to help educate its members in matters malt, organises competitions and generally promotes the wider appreciation of single malt whiskies. With 2000 members, the Club is looking at the possibility of setting up a United States branch. The address is Mathiot House, St Thomas Street, London SE1 9TG .

In 1983 work began to convert the 800 year old wine vaults at Leith, one of the world's great whisky ports on the outskirts of Edinburgh, into the Scottish National Whisky Museum. A huge project, likely to become a major tourist attraction, which has the support of public as well as private bodies, the museum will put on a permanent display of the romantic as well as the industrial history of Scotch whisky. Associated with the museum project is the Scotch Malt Whisky Society (The Vaults, Leith, Edinburgh), a consortium of connoisseurs whose chief aim is to encourage the consumption and appreciation of choice malt whisky which has not been chill-filtered in the normal commercial bottling process. The Society's bottled product, having gone through only a coarse filter to remove impurities, is the nearest thing to drinking a dram straight from the sherry-wood cask in which it has matured for so long. A different malt is offered to members every month, and distribution was launched at the Edinburgh Festival of 1983. Eventually the Society hopes to represent all the malt whisky distilleries in Scotland.

Agent and friend

Scotch whisky's success during this century in the markets of the world owes a great deal to the agents in various countries who took on the product, nursed it through those difficult early years of establishment in the market place, and then worked hard to keep it there. The importance of these sales agents and distributors in contributing to the success of Scotch whisky worldwide cannot be over-emphasised. It is largely to them that certain brands owe their pre-eminence, particularly in the United States. They vary considerably in their structure, from small family concerns who know their domestic market intimately, to large conglomerates with nationwide, and sometimes international, distribution networks. In size and nature they are as varied as the companies within the Scotch whisky industry itself and, like it, they have their problems, not least that of parallel trading. Under this system, unscrupulous middlemen buy up consignments of a well-known brand at discounted prices in one market, then ship it to a high price market where the brand sells at a premium price, where they dump it, thus undermining the marketing strategy of the local agent who relies on a reasonable margin to cover his investment in promotion of the brand and building up a distribution system. Some distillers, however, have found it necessary to have their own outlets in certain export markets where they have either set up their own offices or acquired a local company for the purpose. This, in fact, was a more usual step when Scotch whisky enjoyed its first export boom at the turn of the century, since good agents just did not exist in some countries, which led to the distillers and blenders opening overseas branches, sometimes to be run by a member of the family. However, these were, by and large, replaced over the years by the exclusive agent, and his future prosperity is of enormous importance to the continuing success of Scotch whisky overseas.

Bottle versus bulk

Probably the most vexing question facing the industry, and one which has caused considerable divisions within it, is the opposing attitudes towards the bulk export of both blended and malt whisky. Historically, whisky has been exported in bulk ever since the early consignments of Highland malts in cask to England and, thereafter, to the far-flung colonies. However, exporting overseas on a large scale followed the introduction of bottling as the principal form of packaging. This not only increased greatly the employment opportunities in Scotland but also created a medium through which the quality and nature of the whisky being sold could be readily identified, assuming that the label bore no false or misleading information. As the fame of Scotch spread, so the importance of the packaging, i.e. the bottle, grew as being the only way in which the purchaser could quickly ascertain what he was buying. Whisky bottled in Scotland is, therefore, seen immediately as being exactly what it is, and in overseas markets this has almost the same cachet as chateau-bottled French wines. In many countries there is nothing other than bottled-in-Scotland whisky available. However, in some important markets, such as the United States, Australia and New Zealand, a good deal of blended Scotch is imported in bulk for re-bottling locally. In 1982 the American market took 41.76 million LPA of bottled blended whisky and four-fifths that amount, 36.1 million LPA, in bulk blend. However, the bulk blend was worth a much smaller proportion of the value of the bottled exports, such is the premium which the latter commands over Scotch bottled in the United States, practically all of which is destined for the shelves of supermarkets and cut-price liquor stores. Although locally bottled

Scotch sells at a markedly lower price than whisky bottled in Scotland, the difference is not sufficient to tilt the balance of demand away from the up-market, more appealing, Scotland-bottled product on which, incidentally, practically all of the industry's US advertising budget is expended. Perhaps the situation is a throwback to the 'Real McCoy' days of Prohibition, when Scotch bottled in Scotland was treated with respect, if not reverence, as the one reliable product in a sea of hooch and poisonous concoctions of every description. In the United States there was a small swing away from imports of bulk blend to imports of bottled Scotch, following repeal of the Wine Gallon Assessment Act which discriminated against imported bottled spirits by a differential of 20 per cent. However, the advantage was not sufficient to have any long-term effect on the balance between bottled-in-Scotland and locally bottled Scotch.

In the Antipodes the snob appeal of drinking the real thing has not been of sufficient weight to counter-balance the effects of particularly heavy taxes on bottled spirits, to which must be added a consideration for the saving in transport costs of bulk over bottled whisky. In Australia only about 10 per cent of the Scotch sold is bottled in Scotland. In New Zealand it is more like 12 per cent. Other countries which import bulk blended whisky are West Germany (about 40 per cent of all blended Scotch), France (15 per cent), Belgium and Luxembourg (13 per cent), Brazil (35 per cent) and South Africa (7 per cent). In every case, the earnings from bulk blend are far less, proportionately, than those from bottled exports.

Although it would be as well to suspect that the adulteration of bulk blended Scotch with immature spirit does happen in some distant warehouse or down some foreign back street, it is unlikely to be on a large scale since practically all of the exports of bulk blend are to respectable destinations and the profits to be gained from diluting blended whisky would only justify the trouble in a few countries. Exports of bulk blend are much more directed at slipping under tariff barriers and, in the distant markets, at savings on transport costs, especially as the whisky can be shipped in containers at 110° proof and diluted at destination to 70° proof with local soft water. The real problem is that it is usually competing with bottled imports which it can undercut in price.

Much more worrying is the practice of exporting malt whisky in bulk, since this is seen as a threat to the very fabric of the industry. It is a subject on which the industry stands divided. It is also a subject on which those who benefit from it, i.e. by actively exporting in bulk part of the output of their malt distilleries, are usually reticent, whilst those who eschew the practice are loud in their protests. It probably has its origins in the 1920s, when Scotch whisky distillers were eager to supply their product to Canada and Australia for blending with grain spirit to produce local whiskies which were being increasingly protected by discriminatory taxes on imported bottled Scotch. Indeed, the raison d'etre behind the setting up of the Distillers Company of Canada Ltd by the DCL parent company was to import malt whiskies from Scotland for blending with Canadian grain whisky so as to produce a Scotch-style Canadian whisky for the local market.

In 1982 the export of 22,682,475 LPA of bulk malt whisky represented a little over 9 per cent of all Scotch whisky exports. By far the most important market is Japan, which took 16,927,000 LPA of bulk malt in 1982, representing two-thirds of its total imports of Scotch whisky. Other significant markets for bulk malt are as follows:

Imports of bulk malt in 1982

	litres pure alcohol	percentage of total imports of Scotch
France	864,734	4.2
Spain	851,131	12.9
Argentina	759,562	73.4
Brazil	494,860	43.1
USA	415,447	.5
Uruguay	380,527	47.2

Small quantities go to a variety of countries, no doubt for admixing with local spirits in order to be passed off as Scotch whisky or sold legitimately as national whiskies.

Although bulk malt exports developed partly in order to get round tariff barriers, there has never, except in Italy, been a tradition in any overseas country of drinking unblended single malt whiskies. The exports of bottled malt represents about 1 per cent of all Scotch whisky exports. The undeclared but indisputable facts are that virtually all the bulk malt is destined to be blended either with local 'whisky' or neutral spirit. Some of the end product will masquerade as Scotch whisky, and some of the nonsenses which the admixers get up to have been discussed in the previous chapter. The main purpose of the bulk malt is to give character, body and colour to the otherwise insipid local product. The end result ranges from the awful to the highly acceptable, in the case of the well-aged, better Japanese blends. Thanks largely to the efforts of the Scotch Whisky

Association, the deplorable practice of some Japanese whiskies trying to pass themselves off as Scotch has largely ended, although it still goes on in less sophisticated countries. On the other hand, the adding of malt whisky to a Japanese blend has given the latter something that it would not otherwise have had, and must play some part in the improving position of Japanese whisky sales not only in Japan but — admittedly to a limited extent as yet — in certain third markets. Certainly, Japanese diplomats feel sufficiently confident of the best Japanese whiskies to proffer them as gifts, even to their British colleagues! In Japan itself, local whiskies have steadily improved their market share, largely at the expense of the bottled-in-Scotland brands of Scotch whisky. Other countries may have had less successful results but they have nevertheless achieved a locally acceptable product made reasonably palatable by the addition of bulk malt whisky, which drives down the sales of bottled Scotch already encumbered by heavy import duties.

Since no company will reveal commercially confidential information it is impossible to be precise when trying to apportion responsibility for bulk malt exports. However, few would contest that much of this trade is in the hands of the foreign-owned companies. One Highland malt distillery — Lochside — is owned by Spanish distilling interests, and until recently Suntory had a 12 per cent holding in Glenlivet Distillers Ltd, until the latter was acquired in 1978 by Seagram Distillers Ltd. This company exports bulk malt for blending with local spirit to produce national whiskies under the Seagram label in such places as Japan, Venezuela, Brazil and Argentina. Another bulk exporter is Hiram Walker, which has local distilling interests in Spain and Latin America but which has recently limited bulk exports to Japan. An obvious worry for the indigenous interests in the industry is that foreign owners will use the malt whisky distilleries as a source of raw material for their distilling and blending interests in their country of origin, or wherever else they have local distilling interests, to the detriment of the Scottish industry and the international standing of Scotch whisky. Moreover, as the trend continues, so other countries feel encouraged to enter the trade and establish their own distilleries so as to produce local substitutes for Scotch whisky. Not only does this increase employment opportunities, but it also saves the country in question foreign exchange, as local consumers are directed by means of tariff and quota away from the imported bottled Scotch and on to the national whisky.

As in many an argument, the case either way is not clear cut. The amount earned in 1982 by exports of bulk blend, bulk malt and bulk grain together was £113.45 million, compared with £27.42 million in 1978. Tidy sums, but insignificant when compared with total Scotch whisky export earnings in those years of, respectively, £871.60 million and £661 million. What is of concern is that in 1978 bulk exports of all kinds represented just over 4 per cent of earnings. By 1982 they accounted for 13 per cent. In value terms one LPA of bulk Scotch earned £1.49, whilst one LPA of bottled Scotch was worth £4.32. No wonder prominent Scotch whisky brands are being left on the supermarket shelves of the world, where their relatively high prices cannot compete with the cheaper locally bottled blends and the bogus Scotch or 'local' whiskies which sit by their side. Nevertheless, the companies engaged in the trade argue that it is a useful export earner which would be lost if bulk malt exports were withheld by voluntary agreement within the industry. The proponents also argue that the spread of whisky distilling around the world actually helps Scotch by boosting worldwide whisky consumption. This is a plausible argument, but it hardly holds water in the case of Japan. There, exports of bottled Scotch increased fivefold between 1970 and 1978. A most satisfactory state of affairs, until one considers that bulk malt exports increased ten times over the same period.

The issue is at its most emotional when the question of employment and the effects on it of bulk exports of both blended and malt whisky arises. A recent analysis of the problem (*Should Scotland Export Bulk Whisky?* by J.K. Thomson, Scottish Council) came to the conclusion that if bulk *blended* exports ceased, there would be an over-all increase of 2,337 employed in the industry, but a decline in the numbers engaged in distilling and blending. This would represent a net gain in jobs of almost 9 per cent to the industry as a whole. The ceasing of bulk *malt* exports would result in a net loss in over-all employment of 272 with the extra jobs arising in grain distilleries, blending and bottling being more than offset by the loss of jobs in the malt distilleries. Taking into account the effects on related industries of halting all bulk exports, the report estimates that employment in Scotland would increase by 5,843 as a result of ending bulk blend exports and decrease by 680 by ending bulk malt exports.

The old Highland versus Lowland argument looms up again in this debate, since the employment gain of ending bulk exports would be largely in the Strathclyde industrial belt, while the losses would be sustained by the malt distilleries, the vast majority of which are located in the traditionally neglected Scottish Highlands.

The amount of grain whisky exported in bulk is of little importance, and most of it goes to Brazil where it is diluted and blended with imported bulk malt to be sold as Scotch. If this was to become a common practice the image and quality of Scotch whisky would be bound to suffer, for foreign commercial undertakings can hardly be expected to take the same traditional pride and care in the preparation of the end product as the Scotch whisky industry itself. Nor would they be necessarily subject to the same rigorous controls under which the British industry works, which earns it the right to claim on the label that the contents have been 'bottled under British Government supervision'. However, for the time being, the grain distillers' hands are fairly clean in this matter, and it is interesting that it is they and some of the large blenders who see themselves defending Scotland's precious assets whilst the malt distillers — or at least those actively engaged in bulk exports — are presented as endangering the very future of Scotch whisky.

Not a great deal can be done at governmental level to interfere with bulk exports because this could raise problems in terms of the rules governing international trade. That aside, there has so far been no agreement within the industry itself to limit or withhold bulk exports, as too many firms have a vested interest in one or other form of the trade and are unwilling to sacrifice their own immediate earnings for the eventual greater good of the industry. With government and industry either unable or unwilling to act, it may be the trade unions who will take up the cudgels, and certainly it is from them that most of the pressure comes. A recent report by the Scotch Whisky Combine, representing the eight unions with members employed in the industry, states that 30 per cent of all Scotch whisky exports in 1980 were in bulk and estimates that one-third of the jobs in the industry could be lost over the next ten years unless governmental action is taken. Since then about 2000 jobs, i.e. 8.5 per cent of the 1980 total, have been lost and the volume of bulk exports continues unabated. Two of the measures called for in the report are restriction of the term 'Scotch whisky' to whisky distilled, blended and *bottled* in Scotland, and a minimum malt content of 25 per cent and a maximum of 60 per cent in blended whisky.

The role of government

There is little doubt that close government involvement in every step of the whisky-making process has helped Scotch whisky's image, although the keen interest taken by HM Customs and Excise has not always been universally welcomed by distillers. The role of the excise officer is well defined and grew up as distilling in Scotland gradually organised itself. The system of excise control today is largely based on the recommendations of a committee set up in 1798 to look into the problems of illicit distilling in Scotland. Although we should not assume too readily that illicit distilling is now entirely a thing of the past, nowadays illegal stills are more likely to be found in a garden shed, garage or cellar in the suburbs than in the hills and glens. In the distilleries themselves, the distillery officers (for that is what they are called) will be on the look-out for illegal pipes tapping the system, and an important part of their job is to familiarise themselves with the plant and be alive to any alterations for just such a purpose. But the greater part of their duties is ensuring that all of the alcoholic spirit is fully accounted for, and that the State eventually gets its due share in the form of revenue when the whisky is finally delivered from bond. HM Customs and Excise is invested with the authority to prepare, interpret and apply the legislation governing the good order of the industry. It is sometimes instrumental in ensuring that misleading information does not appear on labels (although prime responsibility for labelling falls to the Ministry of Agriculture, Fisheries and Food), and generally acts as watchdog and arbiter to the industry in matters affecting correct production and ware-housing procedures, to the extent that these are required to comply with the law.

The excise officer's close involvement in the distilling process is not only to ensure that everything is done legally and above board, but also to make thorough readings of the quantity and strength of the spirit. The distillery officer's first priority is to take readings and measurements in order to calculate the attenuation charge and spirits charge on which the duty chargeable may be assessed. As for the calculation of allowances made for evaporation, a basic 2 per cent per annum is allowed and either a further 2 per cent for whisky in butts (108 gallons/490 litres) or 3 per cent for whisky held in hogsheads (55 gallons/254 litres). These allowances from duty were first introduced by Mr Gladstone for the loss in bulk and strength of those spirits stored in bonded warehouses. Gladstone is still described as the best political friend the industry ever had.

The assessment of duty has for long been based on alcoholic strength, and the accurate measuring of this has always been an obsession of the exciseman. As from 1 January, 1980, the OIML (International Organisation of Legal Metrology) system was adopted

Customs man watching new
whisky being racked into sherry casks.

throughout the European Community for measuring the alcoholic
strength of spirits. In the United Kingdom, proof gallons were
replaced by litres of pure alcohol (LPA*). The Sikes hydrometer
accordingly gave way to another kind of alcohol hydrometer, used
for taking readings in conjunction with a Celsius thermometer and a
special book of tables. At the same time as this changeover the old
imperial measurements were abandoned in favour of metric units.

Under the OIML system the strength of spirits is expressed in
terms of percentage volume of alcohol at 20°C, shown as '% vol'. This
represents the ratio of the volume of ethyl alcohol, measured at
20°C, contained in the mixture of ethyl alcohol and water to the total
volume of the mixture measured at the same temperature.

In practice this method of ascertaining the strength of spirits is
very similar to that which was employed under the Sikes system,
which had its origins in the Hydrometer Act of 1818, whereby the
hydrometer invented by Bartholomew Sikes (an excise officer who
had died in 1803) was finally adopted as the instrument for
measuring alcoholic strength, replacing a rather inaccurate earlier

* 1 litre of pure alcohol (LPA)	=	0.386	Imperial proof gallon
	or =	0.528	US proof gallon
1 Imperial proof gallon	=	2.59	litres of pure alcohol
	or =	1.36	US proof gallons
1 US Proof gallon	=	1.89	litres of pure alcohol

instrument called the Clarke hydrometer. Proof was the standard of strength of distilled alcoholic spirit. Spirits of proof strength were defined in the Customs and Excise Act of 1952, wherein proof spirit means that at a temperature of 11.5°C (51°F) the spirit weighs precisely twelve-thirteenths of a volume of distilled water equal to the volume of the spirit. Proof spirit is 57.1 per cent alcohol and 42.9 per cent water. Until the introduction of the OIML system proof strength was measured in degrees, starting with proof itself at 100°. Scotch whisky has usually been sold in Britain at 30° under proof, i.e. 70° proof, but it is sometimes found at 75° and 100° proof. The rate of duty for spirits in the United Kingdom is currently £15.19 per litre of alcohol. The amount of duty actually payable per bottle of Scotch depends on the percentage of alcohol by volume. It is a sad fact, but the United Kingdom taxes Scotch whisky higher than the governments of any of the major export markets. The industry has for long seen itself disadvantaged in fiscal terms compared with the treatment of other sectors of the alcoholic drinks market, pointing out that the present tax regime claims about 80 per cent of the current price of a standard blend, compared with 38 per cent of the price of a pint of beer and just under 50 per cent of the cost of a bottle of imported table wine. The increase in wine drinking in Britain and the fall in the consumption of spirits is quickly taken by the industry as proof that the public, in times of economic difficulty, will move to less heavily taxed drinks. This takes no account of changes in taste and the fact that the main wine-producing countries have undertaken sustained promotional campaigns in the United Kingdom, which they see as a large market with enormous growth potential.

In certain overseas markets Scotch whisky is supplied at strengths different from those standard in Britain. In the United States proof whisky is reduced to standard American strengths which differ from the British. The scale of equivalents is as follows:

British (Sikes)	American	OIML
100°	114.2°	57.1°
87.7°	100°	50°
75°	86°	43°
70°	80°	40°

This represents more than a modest difference, and can lead to confusion on either side of the Atlantic, as whisky specifically for export to, or bottled in, the United States inevitably has an American proof strength on the bottle. Further confusion had arisen because of the variety of methods of measuring alcoholic strength employed in Europe. France and Belgium used Gay-Lussac; Austria, Italy and Russia used Tralles; Germany had its own Windisch scale, and the Spaniards the Cartier system. There is a move within the European Community to adopt a common system.

For the excise officer to do his job it is necessary for the distiller to maintain a complete history of every cask of whisky in his possession from the moment it enters the bonded warehouse. This is done by means of the bond book which records a great deal of detailed information, which will vary according to the type of warehouse, but which may be summarised as follows:

1. The date of warehousing of the cask of new whisky, and age if different.
2. The number assigned to the cask by Excise, and its capacity.
3. The temperature, hydrometer indication and percentage of alcohol.
4. The quantity in litres of alcohol.
5. The kind of cask and current location in the warehouse.
6. The owner's name.

On its eventual removal from the warehouse, the distiller writes it off by recording date of despatch and destination. Subsidiary information may, however, need to be entered in the bond book should there be any loss from a cask because of leakage or when the whisky in a damaged cask has to be transferred to a new one. Details of any samples drawn off are also recorded, since any reduction in quantity will affect the amount of duty eventually paid.

At the end of 1982 there were in the United Kingdom approximately 600 bonded warehouses under the supervision of HM Customs and Excise, including one at each of Scotland's distilleries. Scotch whisky usually passes from distiller to blender to wholesaler under bond, which means that no excise duty has been paid. The people concerned in the transaction have literally given their bond or guarantee to HM Customs and Excise against the duty chargeable to deliver the whisky from one Crown warehouse to another. This applies to all dutiable wines and spirits, hence the network of bonded warehouses covering the entire country.

Once the whisky leaves the merchant's bonded warehouse for the retailer duty is paid unless, of course, it is destined for export. In this case the whisky in question will probably face another barrage of regulations and controls at its destination, since foreign governments have learned well from successive British governments that Scotch whisky is a highly prized commodity which lends itself all too easily to being taxed, restricted and generally used for swelling Treasury coffers.

Given the long history of illicit whisky-making and illegal trading in whisky that went on in Scotland, it is not surprising, perhaps, that following the 'pacification' of the Highlands in the eighteenth and nineteenth centuries the degree of control over distilling, blending and distribution was exceedingly tight and, indeed, was applied throughout the wine and spirits industry in Britain. However, by 1981 moves were afoot to liberalise the system of control, helped to a great extent by the wider use of computerisation by HM Customs and Excise. Apart from simplification of accounting procedures, much of the responsibility and accountability at the distilleries and warehouses would be shifted from officials to the traders themselves. Thus, the system of Crown locks on stills would be replaced by distillers' locks or seals, of a type approved by Customs and Excise, and the account of spirits produced would be kept by the distiller instead of the Officer of Customs and Excise. It is expected that implementation of the various changes will be largely effected by 1984, following the necessary legislative steps. The hope is that effectiveness of revenue control will be maintained with less direct personal supervision, but with the industry enjoying greater freedom to run its own affairs. Against this, the penalties for transgression will be greater.

Despite the vigilance of HM Customs and Excise, fraud is not unknown, as in the case of the Edinburgh Liquor Company whose owner was jailed in 1981 for two years for having substituted 1000 gallons of coloured water for whisky, thus defrauding the revenue of £60,000 in uncollected duty. The ruse was simple. The cases of real whisky were smuggled out of bonded warehouse without payment of duty and replaced with identical cases containing bottles of suitably coloured water. Discovery was made when some of the cases were moved from one warehouse to another. A case was accidently dropped, the bottles smashed and the fraud revealed. Presumably, under the new system, there will not be so many excise officers around to witness such accidents.

And what of the future?

If the vine bug had not devastated France and the Irish had been quicker off the mark — after all, Coffey was an Irishman and first applied his patent still in his native land but could raise no support for it — then Scotch whisky would probably never have enjoyed anything like the success it has. Apart from local and world economic factors, could the Scottish industry itself not be endangered by some unforeseen natural catastrophe? Perhaps a barley blight is the only serious possibility. Even so, stocks of whisky are such as to enable the industry to meet its obligations for a fairly lengthy period, and to organise itself so as to protect its image and plan for a rapid recovery. And, of course, science has advanced so much since the scourge which attacked the French vineyards more than a hundred years ago that a visitation of this sort could be more readily countered and overcome.

A much more real threat to Scotch whisky is the fickleness of human taste. Although the loyalty of the devotee will allow him to admit no alternative, the fact is that there are many other spirits and, indeed, many whiskies which are nothing to do with Scotland and which are widely drunk. The world can live without Scotch whisky; it would be a poorer, drabber place, but alternatives would soon fill, albeit inadequately, its place on our bar shelves and in our cocktail cabinets. There are already worrying signs of a shift away from the 'brown' spirits in the drinking habits of Americans. That market is

143

still of such importance to the industry that any major setback in the United States would have far-reaching repercussions in Scotland. The American swing to white spirits and wine may be temporary or may not run deep. The various market surveys purport to show that it is a trend amongst younger people. In this the Scotch whisky industry can take heart since theirs is a product which more mature people turn to — and having once made the commitment, rarely abandon it.

The threat from other spirits and drinks may not, therefore, be all that serious if the life-long commitment of mature Scotch drinkers can be relied on. There is every chance that it can be, providing Scotch whisky's highly respectable image can be kept up, and it is here that the really difficult questions arise. The threat lies in two directions and there is no easy answer to either. The first is from other whiskies and the second is from spirits containing quantities of malt whisky which purport to be Scotch.

As a reference point, let us take world percentage sales of all whiskies as being very roughly as follows:

Scotch	American	Canadian	Japanese	all others
35	26	15	14	10

American and Canadian whiskies are sold by and large in North America and, apart from the odd exception, do not compete seriously with Scotch in third countries. In the United States all three compete on fairly equal terms, or at least on terms with which they are all familiar and reasonably comfortable. The large Japanese share represents, for the moment, mainly domestic sales. Exports there are, but of no great importance. With the exception of Irish whiskey, which is exported, the rest are all national whiskies aimed at the respective domestic markets, although some exports on a regional basis do take place. A high proportion of the Japanese and national whiskies contain small quantities of malt whisky from Scotland. Together they represent 24 per cent of the world market for whisky of all kinds.

The question which follows logically is whether the Scotch share of the world market would be 59 per cent instead of 35 per cent if bulk malt were not exported for use in local whiskies. American, Canadian and Irish whiskies are all palatable, wholesome drinks requiring no contribution from Scotland. Why should Japan and other countries not be able to produce whiskies of similar calibre from their own resources? The short answer is that they have tried and failed. They are new to the game. The Scots and Irish have been at it for centuries, the Americans and Canadians for generations, their forefathers having taken the knowledge with them from the British Isles. Moreover, some of the physical conditions required in whisky making may be natural to all four but not found elsewhere. In any case, they are four quite distinctive products involving different raw materials and production methods. The so-called national whiskies are pale imitations of Scotch. They may have encouraged the wider drinking of whisky, but it is doubtful whether they have actually been instrumental in more Scotch being consumed in these markets, which are effectively protected by tariff barriers in order to nurture the national product.

To what extent Scotch would be enjoying a bigger share of the world market today, had bulk malt exports been banned, is hard to say, but it is a fair guess that if they continue to grow, the position of Scotch must surely be undermined. There are countless cases where UK finished products have been undermined by cheaper foreign competition in third countries. It is impossible for Scotch whisky to compete with national whiskies on price, since the latter invariably enjoy preferential duty treatment on their home territory and are unburdened by the statutory requirements on maturation laid down for bottled Scotch whisky, which adds greatly to its cost. If the national whiskies were robbed of any flavour or character — and we must assume that this is why Scotch malt is added — their sales performance might be quite different at home, and any attempt to enter third markets in direct competition with Scotch would be nicely nipped in the bud. Will the lesson be learned and the sacrifice made by those parts of the industry for which bulk exports are not only profitable, but essential in terms of their survival?

The second threat, from the admixers who pass off their concocted brews as genuine Scotch, must be pursued relentlessly, not only because they are undercutting Scotch but, more seriously, because they do a great deal of harm to its worldwide reputation. Greater vigilance and a determination to act against the miscreants will help, particularly if given government backing. More pressure on the supplying companies would contribute, but again they would no doubt plead financial necessity. Perhaps more vigorous advertising in which non-authentic Scotch is attacked as an inferior substitute is the answer, if a divided industry cannot do something on a voluntary basis to curb bulk exports.

In 1982 about 9 per cent of our total whisky exports by volume was bulk malt. Yet this represented only 4 per cent of the total earnings from exports of Scotch whisky. 9 per cent by volume equal to 4 per cent by value makes little long-term economic sense.

Another direct threat, although a less serious one than that outlined above, comes from political initiatives abroad. These may be straightforward acts of protection which have been introduced for domestic political reasons, usually to protect a fledgling industry or a depressed area. But Scotch whisky can also suffer from wider political developments. It was a favourite whipping boy of the Temperance Movement right up to and including the First World War both in Britain and the United States. Any resurgence in prohibition would be bound to have an adverse effect, just as the Islamic Revolution has bitten into Scotch exports to certain Muslim countries, especially in the Middle East. Scotch whisky is bound to feel the effects of any such movements which ban the consumption of alcohol as part of their creed.

Nor will whisky escape the general damage caused by economic recession. If people take to drink in greater quantities because of a depression they will, for financial reasons, probably have to move down market, which is unlikely to benefit Scotch. Distilling, blending and marketing of Scotch, like any other major industry, has suffered serious setbacks, with falling demand and rising stocks leading to a massive reduction in production in 1981 and 1982. There have been redundancies and lengthy shut-down periods for the distilleries during the past few years, and some of the weaker companies in the industry have either gone out of business or been absorbed by bigger companies.

With depressed demand at home and abroad, the Scotch whisky 'loch' had by 1981 reached the alarming proportions of something in excess of 3000 million litres of pure alcohol maturing in approximately twenty-two million casks. However, at least one body of distinguished economic forecasters — the London Business School — were then predicting fairly promising prospects for the latter part of the decade, with consumption in the UK increasing by 4 per cent per annum, and 6 per cent per annum in export markets. Given certain difficulties in older stock, and allowing for evaporation, they estimated that the surplus will have been worked off during the consumption year of 1987, or at the latest in 1988, with full productive capacity being utilised in the intervening years. Demand thereafter would be in excess of current capacity.

An action plan for the future

Facing up to the problem of bulk exports is not the only way of securing the future of this noble drink in a world of change and inconsistency. Other matters such as advertising, promotion and packaging, to say nothing of better protection for Scotch whisky also need to be tackled with greater vigour.

A possible outline action plan for the industry might include all or some of the following elements under the broad headings of definition, promotion, presentation, protection and innovation.

Definition

In formal terms, Scotch whisky is defined within Schedule 7 to the Finance Act, 1969, in the following way:

a. the expression 'whisky' shall mean spirits which have been distilled from a mash of cereals which has been:
   (i) saccharified by the diastase of malt contained therein with or without other natural diastases approved for the purpose by the Commissioners; and
   (ii) fermented by the action of yeast; and
   (iii) distilled at less than 166.4 degrees proof in such a way that the distillate has an aroma and flavour derived from the materials used, and which have been matured in wooden casks in warehouse for a period of at least three years;
b. the expression 'Scotch whisky' shall mean whisky which has been distilled in Scotland;
c. the expression 'blended whisky' or 'blended Scotch whisky' shall mean a blend of a number of distillates each of which separately is entitled to the description whisky or Scotch whisky as the case may be;
d. the period for which any blended whisky or blended Scotch whisky shall be treated as having been matured as mentioned in sub-paragraph (a) of this paragraph shall be taken to be that applicable in the case of the most recently distilled of the spirits contained in the blend.

In layman's language this means that: the whisky should be distilled from cereals; the distillation should be such that flavour is derived from raw materials; the distillate should be matured in wooden casks for a lengthy period and the distilling process must take place in Scotland.

There is an urgent need to find a new legal definition for Scotch whisky which would add to the present criteria regarding contents, process of distillation, maturation and geographical limitation, by laying down minimum alcoholic strength (say 40 per cent alcohol by volume) and a minimum malt content (say 20 per cent). At present, some whiskies are of a strength as low as 32 per cent with as little as 5 per cent malt content.

Labelling should be tightened up, and the industry should introduce its own product definitions along the following lines:

a. Standard blends bottled in Scotland should state: 'Bottled in Scotland under British Government Supervision', and show the alcoholic strength and the volume of the contents.

b. Bulk blend bottled overseas should state: 'Product of Scotland, bottled in . . .' This should be made a condition of supply and brand names used for bottled-in-Scotland whisky should not be employed.

c. De Luxe blends should only carry this description if they contain whiskies which are all a minimum of six years old. The age of the youngest whisky in the blend should be stated on the label. All De Luxe whiskies should be bottled exclusively in Scotland.

d. Single malt whiskies should be the product of one distillery and either bear the name of the distillery as the brand name or, if not, indicate at which distillery the whisky was made. The label should show the year of distillation, the year of bottling, and the consequent age of the whisky, which should be bottled only in Scotland.

e. All other bottled malts should state either that they are a blend of several malt whiskies or the vatting of a selection of malt whiskies. Geographical limitation may be included, e.g., 'A vatting of Speyside and Islay malts', or 'A blend of Highland malts'. They should be bottled in Scotland and show their age.

Promotion

The generic campaigns being undertaken by The Scotch Whisky Association in the United States and Japan should be extended to other key or growing markets such as France, Italy, West Germany, Spain and South Africa. Local consumers' associations should be contacted to help expose fraudulent admixes posing as Scotch and to help explain to their members what the different categories of Scotch are and what to be on guard against. Associations of Scotch whisky importers should be set up wherever possible to form local pressure groups and to help in the education of the general public.

Tastings or 'nosings', especially of De Luxe and malt whiskies, should be organised in conjunction with local gourmet clubs.

Presentation

More imaginative advertising both at home and abroad is sorely needed if Scotch whisky is to break out of its middle class/middle age image. There are exceptions, but most advertising still centres on the bottle and the glass rather than concentrating on who is holding the latter and where. Similarly, the packaging needs a face-lift away from the dreary, undescriptive labels and stock bottle shapes. It is significant that no award was made in the Scotch whisky category in the 'Wine & Spirit' Design Awards for 1983.

Protection

Active prosecution of admixers passing their product off as Scotch should be maintained, with as much publicity as possible given to the cases. Importers' associations should be urged to apply pressure on supermarket chains not to stock such products and to discriminate in their shelf arrangements as between local whiskies and Scotch so as to avoid confusing the consumer, against threat of withdrawal of supplies. Industry agreement to be secured for the rapid phasing out, say over a period of five years, of all bulk malt exports, with a larger term objective for phasing out bulk blends except in clearly defined markets where this would be impracticable.

Innovation

Scotch whisky is a diverse drink and this needs to be demonstrated. At the cheap end, it can be mixed with just about anything and in the luxury category, i.e., fine old single malts, it is sipped straight as an after-dinner reward. But practically everyone promotes his particular whisky as if it were to be treated with only reverence and water. Its use as a long, mixed drink has yet to be fully exploited, to say nothing of its compatability with certain fruit juices. There may be further possibilities for using malt whisky as a liqueur base and the phenomenal success of the Irish in promoting Irish whiskey-based cream liqueurs is worth close study.

The good news

Scotch whisky has retained its traditional 50 per cent of the UK spirits market, which has admittedly shrunk over all. Selling prices have improved, thus allowing firms to maintain profitability. In addition, material costs have flattened and interest rates are down. The

149

downward movement of sterling against the dollar helps in the United States and other dollar related markets. Despite distillery and other plant closures, few firms have actually left the industry.

Despite the pitfalls, therefore, I have a good deal of faith in the ability of Scotch whisky to adapt to a given situation, and for the industry to survive more or less at its present size, although some trimming will no doubt take place from time to time through force of economic circumstance. This hope, however, will only be realised if everything possible is done to protect the product's international reputation and adapt to the demands of the consumer.

9 The companies

The Scotch whisky industry today is a conglomeration of companies ranging from the giant Distillers Company to small one-man wholesaling operations. The picture is far from clear. In this chapter I attempt to show how companies relate to each other, and who owns which distilleries and which brands. It has been a major task unravelling the web that has been spun, willy nilly, over the decades. Distillers, blenders, brokers, exporters and merchants are covered, and wine and spirit merchants and regional brewers which have their own brands are also mentioned.

Although it is a long-established industry, Scotch whisky is a constantly shifting scene. This must therefore be taken as a snap-shot of the situation as captured at the time this book went to press. The period immediately before has been one of considerable change, and who is to say that the years that immediately follow will not also see even greater upheavals.

Companies are listed in alphabetical order, regardless of size, age or importance. Where substantial subsidiaries with a personality worth recording exist, these are shown separately from the parent company but are cross-referenced and indicated in the text with an asterisk. Brands believed to be not currently marketed are indicated by a dagger symbol after the name. To find out about a particular distillery, it is necessary to check against the lists of distilleries in association with the maps at the front and back of the book. The name of the owner or the licensee is given for each distillery and a description of the distillery will be found under the appropriate company entry in this chapter. Membership of the Scotch Whisky Association (SWA) is indicated where appropriate. As mentioned in Chapter 6, all malt distilleries except Springbank are members of the Malt Distillers Association of Scotland.

Aberlour-Glenlivet Distillery Company Limited

The House of Campbell, West Byrehill, Kilwinning, Ayrshire
KA13 6NL

Distillers   *A subsidiary of S. Campbell & Son Ltd**

As I have said elsewhere in this book, the whisky industry is relatively young. This does not, however, inhibit the more imaginative distilling companies from associating themselves with the rich history of their locale. Such is the case with the Aberlour-Glenlivet distillery situated by the Lour Burn. With that acute sense of history which characterises the Scotch whisky trade, the proprietors will point out to the visitor that St Dunstan (or Drostan as he was known in Scotland), Archbishop of Canterbury in AD 960, carried out his early baptismal ceremonies in a spring of pure mountain water which today is used by the Aberlour-Glenlivet distillery.

Long before he became primate of all England, St Dunstan, Abbot of Glastonbury, travelled to Scotland as a Christian missionary, assisted by three loyal friends Colm, Medan and Fergus. At Skirdustan on the banks of the river Spey they established a religious cell in the proximity of a spring of pure mountain water, which they used for baptisms. The parish of Skirdustan later became the parish of Aberlour, and the Well of Drostan continued to flow and was in fact the prime reason for the Aberlour-Glenlivet distillery being established at that spot. The ready supply of water power had earlier led to the establishment of a meal mill and a sawmill, but the precise date of the introduction of distilling on any scale is unknown.

The present distillery was founded in 1879 on the site of an earlier distillery built in 1826 by James Gordon. It stands in a fold of the land, well shielded from the road by conifers, thus leaving totally undisturbed the beautiful countryside which surrounds it. The original owner, a local banker called James Fleming, sold out in 1892 to R. Thorne & Sons Ltd, who did much to improve and expand the original structure which had been seriously damaged earlier by a fire. Ownership subsequently passed to W.H. Holt & Sons Ltd, and then to S. Campbell & Son Ltd in 1945, who were in turn taken over by the Pernod Ricard Group in 1974.

Since its foundation the distillery has been extensively modernised, and it can now produce one and a quarter million gallons of whisky annually. Adjacent to the distillery itself is a complex of specially designed warehouses which have been built over the years for storage of the distillery production. Aberlour Malt Whisky is, of course, known to connoisseurs as a bottled single malt, and is available at 12 years old. As a good all-round Highland malt with a classic bouquet, it has earned the wider recognition it now enjoys.

152

It is selling in twenty-three countries, marketed by Campbell's Distillery Ltd. It has previously been sold in bottle at 8, 9 and 10 years old.

Aberlour-Glenlivet also forms the basis of the House of Campbell's White Heather and Clan Campbell blends which are widely exported.

Brand   Aberlour-Glenlivet 12 years old Highland Malt

Acredyke Whisky Limited

35 Robertson Street, Glasgow G2
Blenders and exporters

Set up in 1960, this firm of export blenders is owned by the Rum Co. Ltd of Basle, where it has its European sales office. Along with its associated companies, it offers a fascinating range of labels, almost exclusively for the export market.

Brands

(Acredyke Whisky Ltd)

Acredyke's Scotch No. 10	Golden Scot
Flame of Scotland	Old Inn
Flying Scot	Red Crown

(Dalgarloch Whisky Co. Ltd)

Glendamore	King's Court
Highland Flock	Royal Court
Highland Grand	

(Findoch Whisky Co. Ltd)
Sir Patrick

(Garthamloch Ltd)

Club Star	Scotland's Honour
Golden Ribbon	Scotland's Prestige
Highland Gold	Scotland's Pride
Old Century	

(Inchrachan Ltd)

King's Club	Queen Size
King Size	

(Kinbirnie Whisky Co. Ltd)

(Kintocher Whisky Co. Ltd)

Ascot House	Club Crown
City Club	Club 99
Clan House	Glen's Eagle
Club	

153

(*Merkbrae Whisky Co. Ltd*)
Scotland's Glory

(*Rum Co. Ltd, Basle*)
Guard's Club   Mount Royal
King of Clubs

Markets Export, mainly Western Europe.

Ainslie & Heilbron (Distillers) Limited

5 Oswald Street, Glasgow G1 4QU   *Member of SWA*
Distillers, blenders and bottlers   *A subsidiary of Distillers Company PLC* *

The firm traces its origins back through the Ainslie line to 1868, when James Ainslie & Co. came into being as wine and spirit merchants. They prospered and eventually became distillers when they took over Clynelish Distillery in 1896, completely rebuilding it in 1898. It is located about a mile from Brora on the eastern coast of Sutherland. The distillery has a long history going back to 1819 and the product is of high repute. The original establishment was known as Brora Distillery, which was eventually incorporated into Clynelish Distillery. It was built by the first Duke of Sutherland — then the Marquis of Stafford — to utilise the grain of the local farmers who had moved to more cultivated land on the coast as a result of the Highland clearances. It was thought to be an ideal site because of its proximity to the Brora coalfield, but the coal turned out to be of poor quality and not much use as a source of power. James Ainslie & Co., along with many other whisky firms sucked into the turn-of-the-century crisis, suffered a severe change in fortune shortly after buying Clynelish, but managed to avoid bankruptcy until 1912. The distillery then became the joint property of Mr John Risk (who had previously owned the now silent Bankier Lowland malt distillery) and DCL, and they together formed the Clynelish Distillery Co. Ltd. Risk was bought out by DCL in 1925, John Walker & Sons Ltd* having become a shareholder in Clynelish in the meantime. Clynelish's coastal location ensures a strongly flavoured whisky, not unlike an Islay. A new malt distillery was built alongside Clynelish and the name Brora revived. Like Clynelish, it is licensed to Ainslie & Heilbron (Distillers) Ltd, but is at present closed.

In 1913 James Ainslie & Co. amalgamated with Walter Baillie & Sons, Robertson Brothers and John Gillon & Co.* to form Ainslie, Baillie & Co. Ltd of Leith. This new company, however, was liquidated in 1921 on the retirement of Robert Ainslie, son of the original James Ainslie, and passed into the hands of Sir James

154

Calder, who had acquired another firm of whisky merchants of an even more ancient lineage, David Heilbron & Son, dating back to 1827. These two companies were merged with Colville Greenlees & Co. Ltd, distillers, of Campbeltown, and owners for many years previously of the now defunct Argyll Distillery, to become Ainslie & Heilbron (Distillers) Ltd, and in 1922 they moved to Glasgow from where they have traded ever since. The company became part of the DCL empire when in 1926 the latter purchased from Sir James Calder the firm of Macdonald, Greenlees and Williams (Distillers) Ltd, of which Ainslie & Heilbron had become part.

Although it is not one of the major DCL subsidiaries, Ainslie & Heilbron nonetheless enjoys considerable success in a wide range of export markets, and Ainslie's Royal Edinburgh is one of the leading brands in Belgium. Ainslie's Royal Edinburgh is exported in bulk to Australia where it is bottled at Distillers Group warehouses.

Brands

Ainslie's King's Legend
Ainslie's Royal Edinburgh
Ainslie's Specially Selected
  De Luxe

Clynelish Finest Highland
  Malt
The Real McTavish

Markets Home and export.

Alexander Blending Company Limited

33-34 Alfred Place, London WC1E 7DP
Merchants, brokers and exporters

Established originally as H. Alexander & Co. Ltd in 1956, the company adopted its present title in 1957. Alexander Blending, with its subsidiary and associate companies, trades under a wide variety of labels, also dealing in bulk Scotch whisky. However, the company suspended trading in 1981.

Brands

(Alexander Blending Co. Ltd)

Black Scot†
Golden Rare†
Golden Rare No. 1†
Grand National†
Kinsman†

Kinsman Club†
Kinsman 12†
The Last Hole†
Par Excellence†
Scottish Hunter†

(Bonnie Blenders Scotch Whisky)

Bonnie's 1745 De Luxe†

Bonnie's 1745 Extra Special†

155

(*Duncannon Scotch Whisky Co. Ltd*)

Black Line†

Black Rose†

Duncannon†

Duncan's Choice†

Royal Mail†

Royal Mail Malt (vatted)†

James G. Allan & Sons

2 West Maitland Street, Edinburgh EH 12 5DS

Blenders and exporters

This is the trading company of Allans Ltd, whose founder, James Gill Allan, set up as a wine and spirit merchant in Edinburgh in 1836 and soon had three retail and wholesale outlets in the city. The firm's whisky interests were gradually developed and the current brands show considerable originality in their names. Clannalbhains Choice translates from the Gaelic as 'the People of Scotland's Choice'. Captain Paul recalls John Paul Jones, a famous Scot who is generally regarded as being the founder of the United States Navy, and Three Fingers is, of course, the popular informal measure for whisky used particularly in North America and South Africa.

Brands

Captain Paul 12 years old

Clannalbhain's Choice

Glen Allan 12 years old

Three Fingers De Luxe

Upstairs†

White Elephant†

Amalgamated Distilled Products PLC

26-28 Sackville Street, London W.1.

Distillers and blenders

Of fairly recent origin, ADP has expanded rapidly in the wine and spirit trade and especially in Scotch whisky. Following the establishment of a sound base with the acquisition in 1970 of A. Gillies and Co. (Distillers) Ltd,* ADP concentrated on building up a wide range of export brands through a network of subsidiaries and now supplies its whiskies, in bottle and in bulk, to over eighty overseas markets. A subsidiary, Grangemouth Bonding Co. Ltd, operates the group's blending and bottling plant at Grangemouth, which has storage capacity for over two million gallons of maturing whisky and a bottling capacity of one million cases a year. Against this background, the group set up a joint marketing company in the United States collaborating with Medley Distilling, and then set out on a take-over campaign. In 1981, George Morton Ltd* and

156

Northwest Vintners (including Foregate Liquor Co. Ltd) were acquired to be followed in 1982 by the acquisition of Barton Distilling (Scotland) Ltd* as part of their purchase of the American distilling concern, Barton Brands Inc. This added two distilleries — Littlemill and Loch Lomond — to ADP's single production unit, Glen Scotia.

Brands

(*Distillers Exporters Ltd*)
Noble Ryder†
Royal Escort

Royal Escort 12 years old

(*Glen Nevis Distillery Ltd*)
Glen Nevis
Glen Nevis 12 years old

Glen Nevis 8 years old
Pure Malt (vatted)†
Glen Ronald†

(*Harvey, Mackay & Co. Ltd*)
Harvey, Mackay's

(*Howard, Maclaren & Co.*)
Howard Maclaren Special

Howard Maclaren Special
12 years old

(*Kingsburn Blenders Ltd*)
Clan Kennedy
Gold Label
Kingsburn

Royal Club
Scottish Peer†

(*Fraser McDonald Distillery Co. Ltd*)
Glen Gyle 8 years old
   Highland Malt (vatted)
King's Rider

McDonald's
McDonald's 12 years old

(*MacGregor, Scott & Co. Ltd*)
Black Stallion†
Double Crest†

Glencoe†

(*Donald MacKenzie Distillery Ltd*)
Biltmore†

(*J. Ramsay & Co. (Distillers)*)
Glen Adam Malt (vatted)

(*Regent Bonding Co. Ltd*)
Regent De Luxe

(*The Sconie Liqueur Co. Ltd*)
Sconie Liqueur

(*Thomas Shaw (Export) Ltd*)
Shaw's Light†

(*Speymhor Distilling Co.*)
Speymhor

Peat cutters — Islay

Anderson & Shaw Limited

137 Shawbridge Street, Glasgow G43 1QH

Blenders   *A subsidiary of J. Deans & Co. Ltd*

Anderson & Shaw opened for business in 1869 in West Campbell
Street in Glasgow and immediately took as the trade mark for their
blended whisky Sir Edwin Landseer's famous painting 'The
Challenge', showing a Scottish red deer stag ready for battle. This
was a wise move, since Landseer was extremely popular with the
general public and Queen Victoria's favourite artist to boot.
Anderson & Shaw, by means of an early promotional gimmick,
enjoyed immediate success with their whisky. But there was more
to The Challenge than good advertising, as was proved by the
results of the London International Exhibition at Crystal Palace in
1884, when the judges awarded the only gold medal for excellence
to that brand of whisky. Helped by this, it went on to win success in
overseas markets in the Americas, Africa, Europe and Australia. By
contrast, Duncraggan is a recent introduction and, rather unusually,
is made up of two malts vatted together. Its acquisition by J. Deans
and Co. Ltd, themselves established in 1876, brought Anderson &
Shaw into the Scotcros group of companies in 1973. This trades in
packaging and transport equipment as well as food and drink.

Brands   Duncraggan Pure Malt (vatted)   The Challenge

Market   United Kingdom.

158

Ardbeg Distillery Limited

Ardbeg Distillery, by Port Ellen, Islay   *Member of SWA*

Distillers   *A subsidiary of Hiram Walker & Sons (Scotland) PLC**

Built in 1815, Ardbeg Distillery is situated on the south-east coast of Islay on a site originally used by smugglers. Ardbeg has until recently been privately owned, although DCL and Hiram Walker had minority interests in it until the latter acquired the entire shareholding in 1979. The founders were the MacDougalls, an old island family, and the company used to be known as Alex. MacDougall and Co. Ltd, bearing the name of the last surviving member of the family. Ardbeg, like most of the Islay distilleries, had small beginnings and in its early years capacity was a mere 600 gallons per week. However, growing demand for it by blenders for use in the higher class brands led inevitably to expansion, and production now stands at about 300,000 proof gallons per year, mostly for selling to the trade for blending purposes. But it is still very much a self-sufficient operation on a fairly small scale, using their own malt which is dried on locally cut peat-fired kilns. The local peat contributes considerably to the distinctive Ardbeg flavour. Another important factor is the water drawn from lochs Arinambeast and Uigeadale, situated three miles above the distillery in the heather covered Islay hills. This water runs over rocks and peat mosses, rendering it soft and beautifully adapted for distillery purposes.

Brand   Ardbeg 10 years old Islay Single Malt

Markets Once difficult to come by (it used only to be available to shareholders and one or two local hotels), Ardbeg has very recently been introduced to the UK market, and individual export orders can be arranged.

The Army and Navy Stores

101 Victoria Street, London SW1E 6QX

Wine and spirit merchants   *A division of the House of Fraser PLC*

This famous store — part of the House of Fraser since 1973 — requires little introduction, although few may realise that when it first opened for business in 1871 its purpose was to supply a wide range of goods and services exclusively to members of the Army and Navy Co-operative Society Ltd, rather than to the general public. Membership was restricted to Army and Navy officers and senior other ranks, plus many sectors of the Victorian establishment,

159

including Peers and senior Foreign Office officials. Over the years, however, it has developed into a chain of department stores catering for the needs of the public at large.

Given its military connections, wine and spirits naturally played an important part in the overall turnover of the society. For example, in 1888 they supplied 209,850 bottles of whisky (including no doubt a little of the Irish variety). They did much of their own bottling, receiving the whisky in bulk at their extensive cellars below the principal Army and Navy premises in Victoria Street. The catalogue for 1913 makes interesting reading and includes the following delights:

1. Special Vat of fine Highland Malt makes, 13 years old.
2. Coronation Whisky, a special blend of fine malt makes, over 13 years old.
3. Fine Old Vatted Highland Malt from Glenlossie Glenlivert Distillery, 10 years old.
4. Ben Nevis 1880.

These and others were available per dozen bottles, or per gallon and in 4, 7 and 14 gallon casks. Only malt whiskies were supplied.

Various blended whiskies were introduced later. A subsidiary store, Barker's of Kensington, also had an extensive range of its own whiskies, but none of these survive, although the main company still has its own blends and stocks a good range of whiskies, including single malts.

The traditional arrangements for handling Scotch whisky changed with the take-over in 1973, and The Army and Navy ceased bottling.

Brands

Fine Old Blended	Scotch Malt Whisky Mark
Fine Old Vatted Highland	IV†
Malt No. 7†	Vat B†
Finest Old Blended De Luxe	
(John Barker & Co. Ltd)	
B.O.H.†	Craigdoon†

Avery's of Bristol Limited

7 Park Street, Bristol BS1 5NG

Wine and spirit merchants

This is an example of the provincial wine and spirit merchant who has traditionally had his own blends of whisky for both his own retail trade and for supplying on a wholesale basis. The firm was established in 1793.

Brands Bristol VAT   Highland Blend   Queen Elizabeth

Baird-Taylor Limited

Trafalgar House, 75 Hope St, Glasgow G2 6AN

Whisky merchants   *A subsidiary of Distillers Company PLC**

One of the smaller members of the DCL family, this Glasgow firm of whisky merchants was set up in 1838. It was purchased for the sum of £225,000 by DCL in 1935 but allowed to carry on trading much as before, although it is now regarded as dormant for trading purposes.

Brands

Baird's	It
Baird-Taylor's Selected	Red Tape
Baird-Taylor's Superior	

Balblair Distillery Company Limited

3 High Street, Dumbarton

Distillers   *A subsidiary of Hiram Walker & Sons (Scotland) PLC**

Balblair is amongst that generous group of distilleries which throw their doors open to visitors, although many of the intending latter will be daunted by its distant location near the village of Edderton, at Tain in Ross-shire. For those who do make the journey, a warm welcome, an interesting insight into distilling, and possibly a dram at the end of the tour await them.

Balblair Distillery is the second oldest distillery in Scotland, dating back to 1790 or, as some would have it, to 1749. Whichever it is, the original site was somewhat removed from the present one, which was considerably enlarged in 1872 by its then owners, Andrew Ross & Son. Balblair has been blessed by ample local supplies of both water and peat, which no doubt accounts for the fact that the area was once badly infested by whisky smugglers.

Edderton is known as the 'parish of peat', but the peat here is light and crumbly and Balblair may well owe something of its characteristics — light in body and aromatic to the nose — to this fact. The little that is saved from the blenders is highly appreciated in either its 8 or 10 years form. Balblair came into the Hiram Walker fold in 1969. It is bottled by Gordon & MacPhail.

Brands

Balblair 8 years old	Balblair 10 years old
Highland Malt	Highland Malt

George Ballantine & Son Limited

3 High Street, Dumbarton G82 1ND *Member of SWA*

Distillers, blenders and exporters *A subsidiary of Hiram Walker & Sons (Scotland) PLC**

It was the Glasgow branch of this prominent family firm of wine and spirit merchants which helped Hiram Walker, the Canadian distilling company, to establish themselves in Scotland in the thirties.

Ballantine's reputation as whisky blenders was already well established by the latter part of the nineteenth century, but by that time the family had split up between the Edinburgh Ballantines and those who had gone into business in Glasgow. The story begins in 1827 when George Ballantine arrived in Edinburgh from his family farm in Peebleshire. He started out at the age of twenty-five as a grocer in Cowgate, and through a series of subsequent moves gradually developed a commercial interest in wines and spirits. His business developed along satisfactory lines until he apparently sold up in 1850 and departed Edinburgh, only to return some seventeen years later to set up in business again as George Ballantine & Son. Prosperity smiled on them even more benignly than before, and the business was transferred to Princes Street, the most prestigious commercial address in Edinburgh. This was in 1895, four years after the firm's founder had died, and there it remained until it finally faded away in 1938.

However, it is with the Glasgow Ballantines that we are principally concerned, since the business established there by George Ballantine junior in 1872 traces its succession to the present day firm of that name, which has contributed so handsomely to the Hiram Walker operations in Scotland today. The younger George made great strides forward as a wine, whisky and cigar merchant and was soon engaged in exporting. His nephew joined the business after a thorough grounding in wines gained during a period spent in France, but he, too, took the whisky side of the business seriously and continued the promotion of their Old Glenlivet brand. Ballantine's also entered into an arrangement with Talisker distillery to sell their product in the bottle which was labelled Talisker Fine Malt.

In 1919 the Ballantines of Glasgow sold their business to Messrs Barclay and McKinlay, who immediately set about expanding the whisky trade, with a particular eye to exports. This led to Ballantine's being adopted as the brand name in place of Talisker. In 1936 Barclay and McKinlay sold out to Hiram Walker-Gooderham & Worts Ltd, into whose hands passed the entire share capital of George Ballantine & Son Ltd. Shortly thereafter its share capital was transferred to Hiram Walker & Sons (Scotland) Ltd, which had been created to act as the holding company for all Hiram Walker's Scotch whisky interests. The company was retained as a wholly owned subsidiary, but the retail and wholesaling activities were phased out.

Indeed, the Ballantine name was to become known much more widely, especially in North America, due to the new owners' promotional efforts, and the company entered, at least in name, a new area of activity by becoming the operator of two of the Walker distilleries. The first of these was Miltonduff-Glenlivet Distillery, situated about three miles from Elgin, in true whisky country. The distillery was built in 1824, the year from which legal distilleries date their legitimate origins. It was almost certainly constructed on the site of an alleged illegal still and probably incorporated many of the features and equipment of its outlawed forerunner. The founders were Messrs Pearey and Bain. Later owners were William Stuart and Thomas Yool who introduced a number of important changes in the mid 1890s, and by 1896 annual production ran to over 300,000 proof gallons. But Miltonduff was to suffer, like so many other Highland malt distilleries, from the whisky crash in 1898 which left its mark for years to come. Yool sold the distillery to Hiram Walker-Gooderham & Worts Ltd in 1936, and they in turn licensed it to Ballantines. Then modernisation visited Miltonduff with a vengeance, and capacity was gradually increased over the years until it now stands at two million proof gallons per annum. However, when the

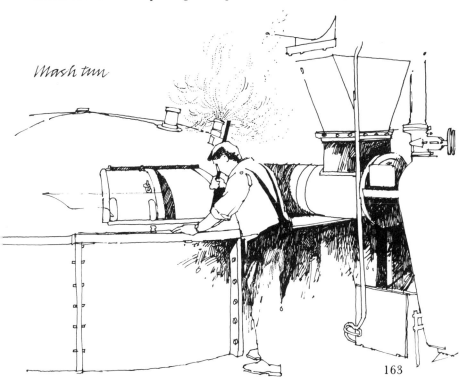

Mash tun

163

stills installed in 1896 were replaced and augmented in subsequent years, the new equipment was identical in shape and size to its predecessors, so well had they served the distiller's purposes. As a bottled single malt, Miltonduff-Glenlivet is a pleasant combination of lightness and maturity.

The other Ballantine distillery is Glencadam at Brechin, one of Scotland's oldest cities. Its history is not dissimilar to that of Miltonduff, having been founded one year later in 1825. After a number of changes in ownership it was bought in 1891 by the now defunct Gilmour Thomson & Co. Ltd, who used Glencadam in their blended whiskies both for export and home consumption. Hiram Walker bought Glencadam in 1954, and Ballantine's fell heir to it two years later. Expansion and modernisation followed naturally, lifting annual production to its present day level of 500,000 proof gallons.

Brands

(George Ballantine & Son Ltd)

Ballantine's	Ballantine's 30 years old
Ballantine's Gold Seal†	Miltonduff-Glenlivet
Ballantine's 12 years old	Highland Malt 5 years old
Ballantine's 17 years old	Miltonduff-Glenlivet
	Highland Malt 12 years old

(The Glencadam Distillery Co. Ltd)

Auld Glen	Glencadam Malt

Markets World-wide, with particularly strong representation in USA, Canada, Italy, West Germany, France, Spain, Netherlands, Switzerland, Greece, Japan and Colombia.

Balls Brothers Limited

313 Cambridge Heath Road, London E2 9LQ
Blenders and merchants

Established in 1854, this firm of wine and spirit merchants has for long marketed its own brand of blended whisky called Auld Sandy. It used to have an Irish equivalent in Ould Paddy. There are two subsidiaries, Gow's Restaurant and Wickham & Co. Ltd.

Brand Auld Sandy

Augustus Barnett & Son Limited

North Woolwich Road, Silvertown, London E16 2BN

Wine and spirit merchants

Although dating only from 1963, this well known firm of chain off-licence stores has 250 branches.

Brand   Augustus Barnett's Special

John Barnett & Company (London) Limited

521-531 Hackney Road, Cambridge Heath, London E2 9EF

Wine and spirit merchants   *A member of the Merchant Vintners Co. Ltd*

Brands   Strathlevent†   Wat Tyler†

Bartels, Rawlings International Limited

32-34 Borough High Street, London SE1 1XU

Blenders, brokers and exporters

The company became incorporated as a limited company in 1976 to acquire, as a parent company, the old established wine and spirit companies of Bartels Rawlings, Seven Pillars, Southwark Distillers and other companies now within the group, all of which have traded under the family control of Eric Joiner since the end of the Second World War. Bartels Rawlings International Ltd still remains one of the few independent family controlled companies in the Scotch whisky trade.

Within the group, Southwark Distillers Ltd owns a gin distillation plant, and also distils vodka, and apart from the internationally known brands of Scotch that this group exports throughout the world, they are proprietors of Rawlings London Dry Gin, Town Hall Gin, Barbers London Dry Gin, Cruiser Gin, Viatka Vodka, Southwark Gin and the celebrated Barvok Vodka.

Brands

(Bartels Rawlings Export Ltd)

His Excellency

His Excellency 12 years old Special Blend

His Excellency 21 years old De Luxe Blend (in ceramic jars)

His Excellency Pure Malt 5 years old (vatted)

His Excellency Pure Malt 12 years old (vatted)

165

(John McGeary & Co. Ltd)
John McGeary's Special No. 1   Export Blend

(Seven Pillars Co. Ltd)
Highland Laird   Highland Lassie

(Southwark Distillers Ltd)
Bartels Scotch Whisky   Jamie's Scotch Whisky

Barton Distilling (Scotland) Limited

Lomond Industrial Estate, Alexandria, Dunbartonshire

Distillers, blenders and bottlers   *A subsidiary of Amalgamated Distilled*
Products PLC*

This became a wholly owned subsidiary of Amalgamated Distilled Products PLC in 1982, when the latter acquired the American distillers Barton Brands Inc of Chicago, which had assumed control of Littlemill Distillery Co. Ltd and its associated companies, in 1971. Although Littlemill had been incorporated only in 1935, the distillery itself has a long and distinguished history and is generally looked on as one of Scotland's oldest. Local distilling was certainly in full swing by 1820, and before then the site at Bowling in Dunbartonshire had been that of a brewery. It is believed that a George Buchanan, a Glasgow maltster, bought the Auchterlonie estate in which Littlemill was situated in 1750, and in 1772 accommodation was put up for excise officers. It is not known when the changeover from brewing to distilling took place, or whether the two activities were carried on side by side for a time. A bewildering succession of owners ran Littlemill during the nineteenth century and some of them undertook extensive rebuilding. The American entrepreneur, Duncan G. Thomas, bought it in 1931 and operated it as Littlemill Distillery Co. Ltd. Barton Brands were invited to take an interest in Littlemill which they did in 1959, taking over completely in 1971 when Barton Distilling (Scotland) Ltd was incorporated and D.G. Thomas bought out.

Littlemill produces a Lowland malt but uses Highland peat and water from the Kilpatrick Hills. Production has stood at 400,000 proof gallons per annum since 1965. Littlemill had by then reached its maximum capacity, which caused its new American owners to build a totally new distillery at Alexandria on the banks of the River Leven, to which they gave the highly evocative name of Loch Lomond Distillery. This opened in September 1966 along with adjacent warehousing, bottling facilities and cooperage, and had an annual capacity of 500,000 proof gallons. It is a by-word in quality control and advanced methods within Scotland's whisky industry.

166

The product is classified as Highland Malt but only just, since it is actually located bang on the Highland Line on the site of an old printing and bleach works. The output of both distilleries is reciprocated throughout the industry and therefore appears in most major brands. Littlemill is also becoming well known as a single malt.

Brands

(Barton Distilling (Scotland) Ltd)

Crown of Scotland	Royal Award
Loch Lomond Liqueur	

(Dunglass Whisky Co. Ltd)
Dunglass Pure Malt (vatted)

(House of Stuart Bonding Co. Ltd)

House of Stuart	House of Stuart Royal 8
House of Stuart 12	years old
years old	

(Littlemill Distillery Co. Ltd)

Highland Mist	Littlemill Pure Malt 5 years
Highland Mist 8 years old	old
Highland Mist 12 years old	Littlemill Pure Malt 8 years
	old

(Peter Prime Ltd)
Peter Prime

Markets UK, USA, and many overseas markets.

John Bateson & Company Limited

232 Walton Summit Centre, Bamber Bridge, Preston, Lancs PR5 8AL
Wine and spirit merchants

A subsidiary of the Guinness brewing concern.

Brand Old Highland

Thomas Baty & Sons Limited

37-41 North John Street, Liverpool L2 6SN
Wine and spirit merchants

This well known Liverpool firm, established in 1827, had, like many older wine and spirit merchants, a range of Scotch whisky brands, but have phased out the bottling of whisky under their own labels.

One of their subsidiaries, Bushell, Maples and Co., was similarly engaged in the whisky trade but their brands are now dormant. The only two labels still used are Glencastle and Glendearg which are bottled for Baty by Hall & Bramley Ltd.* They are said to be extremely good quality standard blends and are in the main supplied to longstanding private customers in the home market.

Brands

(*Thomas Baty & Sons Ltd*)

Donacha Dhu†	Hamilton Murdoch†
Glencastle	Lochroy†
Glendearg	The Brothers†

(*Bushell, Maples & Co. Ltd*)

Bushell's Highland Queen†	Bushell's Three Star†

John Begg Limited

Trafalgar House, 75 Hope St, Glasgow G2 6AN   *Member of SWA*

Distillers and blenders   *A subsidiary of Distillers Company PLC**

'Take a peg of John Begg' is one of the oldest slogans associated with Scotch whisky. John Begg was one of the early legal distillers, building the Lochnagar Distillery in 1845. On 12 September 1848 Queen Victoria, Prince Albert and the Royal Family visited the distillery — which is a mere mile from Balmoral — and were shown round by Begg. Shortly afterwards he was rewarded by being appointed distiller to the Queen by royal warrant. For a time it was known as Royal Lochnagar Distillery, but has now reverted to its 'commoner' name. The company, which retains the licence for Lochnagar, became part of DCL in 1916, the giant being attracted no doubt by John Begg's export outlets and ownership of Lochnagar.

Begg had in fact built up a highly successful business with extensive warehousing both at the distillery and in Aberdeen. Spurred on by the popularity of his Lochnagar whisky, Begg got seriously involved in blending and set up a worldwide export business from a base in Glasgow. Henry Begg succeeded his father on the latter's death in 1880, but continued to trade as John Begg.

Lochnagar has recently become available in bottle as a single malt at 12 years old. A pleasant, friendly whisky it comes from the only distillery in Deeside, and to that extent is different. There is a hint of sweetness in the aftertaste which adds to its attraction for post-prandial imbibing.

Brands	John Begg's Blue Cap	John Begg's De Luxe
	John Begg's Gold Cap†	Lochnagar 12 years old
		Highland Malt

Beinn Bhuidhe Holdings Limited

Argyll Estates Office, Inveraray, Argyll PA32 8XE *Member of SWA*
Blenders and exporters

The company was formed in 1976, just prior to the 1977 International Gathering of the Clans in Scotland, one of the principal events on the Scottish calendar. The Duke of Argyll, as Chief of Clan Campbell, invited his kinsmen to the family seat at Inveraray Castle. A special whisky was blended for the occasion and it was so well received that the Duke and his associates decided to market it under his signature. The brand is available as a blend and as a single malt, including special presentation packages, at 12, 15 and 17 years old. The first two are in fact from Tamnavulin-Glenlivet distillery, and the 17 years old is from Tullibardine distillery, but sold under the Argyll label.

Brands

Argyll Highland Blend 12 years old

Argyll Highland Malt 12 years old

Argyll Highland Malt 15 years old (in Pot Still Decanter)

Argyll Highland Malt 17 years old

Argyll Special Blend

Arthur Bell & Sons PLC

Cherrybank, Perth *Member of SWA*
Distillers and blenders

Bell's is perhaps today the pride of the independents, and although it has traditionally been associated with the domestic market in Scotland, which it has dominated for many years, its recent phenomenal growth has been via the export trade. Two-thirds of its business in 1980 was in the UK, where it has about 25 per cent of the market; Bell's is hence strongly placed to claim to be a truly domestic tipple. Certainly Bell's has been the top selling Scotch in Scotland over a period of years. Inevitably such an obvious selling point has enabled Bell's to make inroads into overseas markets, including those where other brands are better known, and the signs are that Bell's will make strenuous efforts to capture a bigger share of overseas business. It may not, therefore, be too long before Bell's is as well known in some other countries as it is in its native Scotland, and over the last six years it claims to be the fastest growing brand of Scotch whisky in export markets generally. In fact, it is significant to note that Bell's was the only Scotch whisky distiller to receive the Queen's Award for Export Achievement in 1983, with export sales having risen from £3 million to £36 million in the last decade.

Bell's connection with Perth is a long one, starting as it did when Arthur Bell joined the wine and spirit merchants of Thomas Sandeman in about 1840, the latter having set up shop in 1825. By 1851, Arthur Bell found himself as one of two partners and the name of the company became Roy and Bell. As the firm made progress, Arthur Bell cast his net wider and began experimenting in the blending of grain and malt whiskies. For a brief spell, the Sandemans came back into the business when Bell's partner James Roy retired, and Arthur Bell, who had already brought his nephew T.R. Sandeman into the firm as a salesman, invited him to enter into partnership. The relationship was not a happy one and ended on a sour note. Despite this set-back, Bell found fresh capital and set himself new goals. He was a strong believer in educating his fellow Britons south of the border and he is believed to have appointed, in 1862, the first ever regular Scotch whisky agent in London.

As his business flourished, so Bell addressed himself to the problems of the trade as a whole. To take an example, he successfully campaigned for the introduction of standard bottle sizes for spirits throughout the UK. He also looked for opportunities abroad and by 1895 was selling whisky to Australia, New Zealand, India, Ceylon, Italy and France. Progress was steady rather than spectacular and this was due in some measure to Arthur Bell's abhorrence of advertising and the use of brand names. He preferred to rely on the quality of his whisky as its main selling point.

When Arthur Bell died in 1900 ownership of the company passed to his two sons Arthur K. and Robin Bell. They had a few years previously managed to persuade their father to use brand names, and the first to be registered by the Bells was Scotch Fir. They also had Colleen Brand for the Irish whiskey which they imported. Another brand to be adopted was Skerryvore, but the name of the company only appeared on labels for the first time in 1904 with the introduction of the Curler blend. They also turned to advertising, with impressive results in terms of increase in turnover. Expansion led to the acquisition of bonded warehouses in Leith which remained the company's main bottling facility until 1967.

But Bell's coming of age as an all-round whisky operation was in 1933 with the acquisition of P. Mackenzie & Co., Distillers Ltd of Edinburgh, which owned the Blair Athol and Dufftown-Glenlivet Distilleries. Blair Athol's true date of origin is contested but it is generally reckoned to go back to at least 1825. Its early years of operation were in the hands of Alexander Connacher & Co., but various others were involved subsequently until it was taken over and enlarged by P. Mackenzie & Co. After a lengthy period of closure, Bell's rebuilt Blair Athol in 1949 and doubled the number of stills from two to four in 1973. It draws its water from the mountain springs of Ben Vrackie via the Kinnaird Burn, and occupies an

170

attractive position in the Highland whisky town of Pitlochry. Production is on a small scale and is used both in the famous Bell's and as a straight 8 years old malt. It is a light, fresh whisky with just the right hint of smokiness. Of later origins, the second of the Mackenzie distilleries was established in 1896 just south of Dufftown in the Dullan Glen. Water is drawn from Jock's Well which has a high reputation locally for producing perfectly clear water, ideal for distilling purposes. Again, the end product is used in blending, and as an 8 years old single malt makes a good impression with a full fruity flavour. In 1936 A.K. Bell extended his distilling interests with the acquisition of Inchgower Highland Malt Distillery from Buckie Town Council. It dates back to 1871 in its present shape, but had a forerunner in the form of Tochineal Distillery which was built in 1824 by John Wilson but suspended by Alexander Wilson & Co. some forty years later in favour of Inchgower. The move took place in order to ensure a steady supply of suitable water. Its period of municipal ownership is uncertain, but the distillery is still closely associated with the town. Inchgower comes nicely from the bottle at 12 years old with lots of bouquet, well rounded and slightly sweet.

The family link at Bell's ended in 1942 with the death of the two Bell brothers, and the reins were passed to W.G. Farquharson. Under him, Bell's became a public company in 1949, reflecting its further expansion. He held the post of managing director from 1942 to 1968, continuing as chairman of the board until his death in 1973, giving him a total of fifty years service, having entered the company in 1923. He handed over the running of the company in 1968 to Raymond Miquel, who also succeeded him in the chair in 1973. This latter period saw enormous expansion at Bell's: between 1970 and 1980, distillery output increased from 4.75 to 13.44 millions of litres pure alcohol. Bottling output similarly increased three-fold in the same period. Distillery output was helped considerably by the opening of a completely new distillery, Pittyvaich-Glenlivet, in 1974, in the vicinity of the much older and more traditional Dufftown-Glenlivet. However, the stills in the new plant are faithful replicas of those at Dufftown-Glenlivet. Production capacity stands at an annual one million gallons. To keep pace with production growth, Bell's have been careful to provide matching storage, blending and bottling facilities and have branched out into other parts of the industry, notably bottle making. There are several subsidiary companies acquired or set up for marketing purposes. In 1983 Arthur Bell & Sons acquired Bladnoch Distillery Ltd from Inver House Distillers Ltd.

Brands

(Arthur Bell & Sons Ltd)
Bell's De Luxe 12 years old   Blair Athol 8 years old Highland Malt

Bell's Extra Special
Bell's Pure Malt 5 years old
Bell's Royal Reserve 20 years
old
Bell's Specially Selected

Dufftown Glenlivet 8 years
old malt
Inchgower 12 years old
Highland Malt
Royal Vat

(*Burn Brae (Blenders) Ltd*)
Burn Brae
King Select
MacMillan

Match
Queen Elizabeth

(*Forbes, Farquharson & Co. Ltd*)
Reliance
Scotch Broom

Scotch Pillar

(*C. & J. McDonald Ltd*)
Heathwood
McDonald's Special Blend
C. & J. McDonald

Queen's Choice
Scotch Fir

(*P. Mackenzie & Co., Distillers Ltd*)
The Real Mackenzie
The Real Mackenzie 8 years
old

The Real Mackenzie 12 years
old
The Real Mackenzie 20 years
old

Markets Principally UK. Main overseas markets: South Africa, United
States, Sweden, France, Spain, Italy, Japan, Canada, Greece, Norway.

James Bell & Company Limited

St Mary's Way, Sunderland

Wine and spirit merchants

This ancient firm of wine and spirit merchants first opened its doors
for business in Edinburgh in 1782. It has a long history of marketing
its Beltane Special brand of whisky, more recently as a subsidiary of
Lorimer's Breweries Ltd of Edinburgh which in turn is part of Vaux
Breweries PLC.

Brands

Beltane Special

Highland Command

Markets United Kingdom.

Dallas Dhu

Benmore Distilleries Limited

75 Hope Street, Glasgow G2 6AN   *Member of SWA*
Distillers and blenders   *A subsidiary of Distillers Company PLC**

This Glasgow firm was acquired in its entirety by DCL in January 1929 and, through it, Dallas Dhu Distillery entered the DCL fold. The distillery was one of a series built by Alexander Edward of Sanquhar and took its name from the Gaelic Dalais Dubh, which means black water valley. Constructed in 1899, it was for a time one of the most advanced in the Highlands. The distillery's water supply comes from the Scourie Burn which rises at the Witch's Hill and passes through the Skirypool Mosses and Altyre Estate. One can speculate that the Witch's Hill may have some connection with Macbeth's three witches, since the opening scene of the play is set at nearby Forres.

Dallas Dhu had several early owners; Alexander Edward sold it to Wright & Greig Ltd of Glasgow who in turn were succeeded in 1919 by J.P. O'Brien & Co. Ltd. But two years later they sold it to Benmore Distilleries Ltd, which had three other distilleries at the time, but which now only retains the licence for Dallas Dhu. The distillery, like so many others, was shut down for much of the inter-War period, and none of Benmore's three other distilleries — Benmore and

173

Lochhead at Campbeltown and Lochindaal on Islay — has survived. They were acquired in 1920-21 but fell silent on or shortly before the DCL take-over.

The present structure of Dallas Dhu — small and neat — is very much as it was originally, although malting of the barley on the premises has long since ceased. The twin stills have an annual production of about 300,000 proof gallons between them. Some of the whisky has been bottled as a single malt and sold as Dallas Mhor. The distillery is at present closed.

Brands

(*Benmore Distilleries Ltd*)

Bendaal†	Benmore Special Reserve
Benmore Pure Malt (vatted)	Dallas Mhor Highland Malt†
Benmore Selected	Gaelic Prince

Ben Nevis Distillery (Fort William) Limited

Lochy Bridge, Fort William, Inverness-shire PH33 6TJ

Distillers   *A subsidiary of Long John International Ltd**

The Ben Nevis Distillery was founded in 1825 by Long John Macdonald whose name is now associated with one of the more prominent groups in the industry, Long John International Ltd, which, until 1981, had no connection with the present distillery. The founder bottled his Highland malt and sold it as Long John's Dew of Ben Nevis, since he had built his distillery within the shadow of Britain's highest mountain. His descendants were subsequently compelled for financial reasons to sell the brand name Long John to the forerunners of Long John International Ltd, but, as D.P. Macdonald Ltd, continued to market Dew of Ben Nevis, eventually as a blended whisky, and enjoyed some modest success with it in Europe and Egypt.

The distillery was for long in the private ownership of Mr Joseph Hobbs, who had also owned the Lochside Distillery of Macnab Distilleries Ltd.* They shared the common distinction of being the only distilleries in Scotland at which both Highland malt and grain whiskies were produced under the same roof. Lochside no longer distils grain whisky and Ben Nevis has been silent for a considerable period. When it returns to distilling it is almost certain to be solely as a malt distillery. Sadly, it is many years since its malt whisky was bottled for general sale. However, a determined visitor to the area might be fortunate enough to sample Ben Nevis since it used to be made available in limited quantities to Inverlochy Castle Hotel, which is in the vicinity. Recent output at the distillery was in the region of 750,000 gallons per year, before production was suspended. However, with its purchase by Long John in 1981 some work should soon be started in order to repair and upgrade the fabric and appearance of the distillery to bring it up to the high standards of the other Long John distilleries. Immediate use is, on the other hand, being made of the warehouses.

Brand Dew of Ben Nevis 12 years old

Markets Western Europe and the United States. Limited amounts in the UK.

Berry Brothers & Rudd Limited

3 St James's Street, London SW1A 1EG   *Member of SWA*

Blenders and merchants

London boasts many fine wine and spirit merchants, but few can claim a longer continuous history than this well known St James's firm whose origins can be traced to the latter part of the seventeenth century. The founders set up shop as 'Italian warehousemen', importing the exotic products of the period such as tea, coffee and spices. They gradually added wines to their range and over the years these steadily became the predominant commodity in their trade, until by the 1880s business was exclusively in wines and spirits which the company supplied to a traditional clientele of individual private customers.

Berry Bros & Rudd remains essentially a family affair. It was a partnership until 1943 and is still an independent private company, almost entirely controlled by the two families of Berry and Rudd. The present chairman, Anthony A. Berry, is a direct descendant of William Pickering who owned the business in the early part of the eighteenth century and was responsible for rebuilding the firm's existing premises at 3 St James's Street in 1731. The Rudds appeared on the scene at the end of the First World War when Hugh R. Rudd became a partner.

The company has strong traditional links with the United States predating the First World War, when private customers there were supplied with fine wines from the cellar of Berry Bros. Exports of Scotch whisky began in 1923 with the introduction of the firm's now celebrated Cutty Sark brand. The prominence which Cutty Sark was to enjoy during Prohibition, thanks to the efforts of both Francis Berry and the legendary Captain McCoy, is already related in Chapter 5. Suffice it to say here that on the basis of its impeccable reputation, sales of Cutty Sark surged forward following Repeal in 1933. Further development was arrested by the intervention of the

Second World War, but was taken up in 1945 and followed a steadily rising curve until, in 1961, Cutty Sark had become the number one selling Scotch whisky in the United States. Since then it has remained one of the leading brands in that market and has been promoted in many others, and is today one of the largest selling Scotch whiskies in the world.

This is quite an achievement when it is considered that the brand owners possess no distilleries and do not even make up their own principal blend, a task undertaken for them by Robertson & Baxter Ltd* of Glasgow. Berry Bros & Rudd, however, make up certain other blends and remain responsible for bottling, packaging, shipping and marketing Cutty Sark abroad, and share with the blenders an interest in the brand through joint ownership of Cutty Sark (Scotch Whisky UK) Ltd* which markets the brand in the United Kingdom only.

The use of Cutty Sark as the brand name is evocative in two respects. Firstly, it recalls Robert Burns's famous poem 'Tam O'Shanter' in which the hero inadvertently calls out to the prettiest of the dancing witches 'Well done, Cutty Sark', referring to the chemise which she was wearing, thus drawing attention to his presence and leading to the devilish chase which is the high-spot in the poem. But for many more, it is a reminder of British sea-borne mercantile prowess, for Cutty Sark was the name given to a tea clipper launched from Dumbarton in 1869. She was later to hold the record for the fastest passage from Australia to London for many years, regularly completing the return journey in under 100 days. The image of speed and lightness of touch was no doubt considered appropriate for a whisky which was to become the first of the 'light' Scotches, a development of great importance in the American market. The Scottish artist James McBey was commissioned to produce a suitable label, and the attractive result is used entirely unchanged today, including the unusual designation of 'Scots' rather than Scotch whisky.

Brands

All Malt (vatted malt)	Blue Hanger (De Luxe)
Berry's Best (De Luxe)	Choicest Liqueur (De Luxe)
Berry's Highland Malt (vatted malt)†	Cutty Sark
	Cutty 12 (De Luxe)
Berry's Pot Still Liqueur (vatted malt)†	St James's (De Luxe)
Berry's Pure Malt	

Markets Worldwide in 150 separate countries and territories.

John Bertram & Company Limited

10 Links Place, Leith, Edinburgh EH6 7HA

Exporters   *A subsidiary of Distillers Company PLC**

Within DCL this firm continues to market some minor brands.

Brands   Dormy†   Ramshead
            Glenburn   Viscount
            Gloamin†

John Bisset & Company Limited

10 Links Place, Leith, Edinburgh EH6 7HA

Distillers and blenders   *A subsidiary of Distillers Company PLC**

Established in 1828, the Company has been the proprietor of the Royal Brackla Distillery at Cawdor near Nairn since 1926. The distillery was founded by Captain William Fraser in 1812, and obtained the 'Royal' prefix from William IV in 1835 as a mark of his appreciation of the distillery's product. There had been a number of subsequent owners before John Bisset & Co. Ltd, and in 1898 the Brackla Distillery Co. Ltd took over the tenants' rights in the lease and acquired additional adjoining ground from the Earl of Cawdor. In 1919 the Company made over their rights in the lease of the distillery to John Mitchell and James Leith, wholesale wine merchants in Aberdeen. They passed the lease to John Bisset & Co. Ltd in 1926, and DCL took over the latter in 1943. John Bisset & Co. Ltd originally set up business in Aberdeen but subsequently transferred offices to Leith. In 1965 a new malting was constructed and the distillery can be visited by special arrangement. The stills are of 5,000 gallon capacity and steam fired. Practically all of its current production is used for blending.

Brands   Bisset's Finest Old   Glenlogie
            Bisset's Gold Label

Markets USA and most countries in Europe.

Bladnoch Distillery Limited

Cherrybank, Perth and Bladnoch, Wigtown

Distillers   *A subsidiary of Arthur Bell & Sons PLC**

Bladnoch's immediate distinction is that it is the most southerly distillery in Scotland, and as such one of a handful which produce

Lowland malt. It has had a somewhat chequered history, including a period of eighteen years total closure when all the original distilling equipment was sent to Sweden, re-opening only in 1956. The founders were two brothers, Thomas and Andrew McClelland, who got Bladnoch Distillery under way in 1818. It was probably set up originally as a part-time distillery during the fallow months of September to March, the brothers occupying themselves with farming for the rest of the year, and it remained in the family for some time, passing to their nephew Charles McClelland. On his death, Dunville and Co. Ltd of Belfast assumed ownership and ran it through a subsidiary company, T. & A. McClelland Ltd,* now a subsidiary of Stanley P. Morrison Ltd.* There were several changes in ownership thereafter from A.B. Grant & Co. Ltd to Ian B. Fisher of McGown and Cameron Ltd, the now defunct firm of Glasgow whisky blenders, to a London financial concern, then to Inver House Distillers Ltd in 1973. In 1983 it was bought by Arthur Bell & Sons.

The distillery is situated a mile from Wigtown on the banks of the river from which it takes both its name and its water. It has had three periods of expansion, in 1878, in 1957 shortly after re-opening, and in 1965. Today it has a production capacity of 650,000 gallons. Its location in choice farming territory provides the distillery with a ready outlet for the valuable by-product of light grains used in cattle feed. Storage capacity is estimated at over two million proof gallons.

The distillery has suffered a recent temporary shut-down. The product is available from time to time as a single malt.

Brands   Bladnoch Lowland Malt

Markets Mostly Galloway region of Scotland.

Boddington's Breweries PLC

PO Box No 331, Strangeways Brewery, Manchester M60 3EL

Brewers and bottlers

The oldest of Manchester's breweries, dating from 1778, Boddington's Breweries Ltd was incorporated as a public company in 1888 when it succeeded Henry Boddington & Co., until then a private company. Ballantrae has been the firm's registered brand for over ninety years and is sold mainly through the company's own outlets where it accounts for over 60 per cent of Scotch whisky sales. The malt content is usually five to six years old when blended.

Brand   Ballantrae

Markets Manchester area and North-west.

W. Brown & Sons (Scotch Whisky Blenders & Bottlers) Limited

33 Townsend Street, Glasgow G4 0LA

Blenders and exporters

In addition to its own brands, W. Brown & Sons export old malt whiskies. Sennachie is the brand name used for 30 years old bottlings of single malts coming from Glenlivet distilleries, the exact provenance of which varies from time to time.

Brands

Ancient Privilege 5 years old
Black Stag 5 years old
Cairndew Mist 5 years old
Diplomatic Privilege 5 years old
Glen Stuart 5 years old
Glen Stuart 8 years old

Glen Stuart 8 years old
Glen Stuart Pure Malt (vatted)
Highland Privilege 5 years old
Sennachie 30 years old single Malt
Seven Earls 20 years old

Bruichladdich Distillery Company Limited

Bruichladdich, Isle of Islay

Distillers   *A subsidiary of The Invergordon Distillers Ltd**

This is the oldest distillery in the Invergordon group, dating back to 1881. It was built by a well known distilling family, the Harveys (now John and Robert Harvey Ltd*), who already owned the now defunct Dundashill and Yoker Distilleries. From 1886 they operated their new Islay venture as the Bruichladdich Distillery Co. (Islay) Ltd and so it remained until 1938, whereafter, following a period of closure, it had a more chequered history. In that year it was acquired by a partnership which enjoyed the support of National Distillers of America. The latter soon took control through their subsidiary, Train & McIntyre, and Bruichladdich became part of the latter's distilling organisation, Associated Scottish Distillers Ltd. 1952 saw the disposal of Bruichladdich to Ross and Coulter, a firm of Glasgow whisky brokers who have since passed from the scene. In 1960 it became the property of A.B. Grant and Co. Ltd, becoming part of Invergordon in 1968. Although expansion and improvement had been initiated under these earlier owners, Invergordon themselves added two new stills and enlarged the mash-house and tun-room, bringing capacity at Bruichladdich to 800,000 proof gallons.

It is sited near Port Charlotte on the western shore of Loch Indaal on the island of Islay, and as such is the most westerly located distillery in Scotland. Its product is highly regarded both for blending and as a bottled single malt. The distillery buildings are attractively finished in whitewash and run along the water's edge. Bruichladdich is growing in popularity and availability. Plenty of body with a nutty taste and more than a hint of peat.

Brand   Bruichladdich 10 years old Islay Malt

Markets UK and overseas.

John Buccleugh & Company Limited

20 Beatrice Street, Warrington, Cheshire
Wine and spirit merchants

Established in 1937.

Brand   Tartan Vat   Tartan Royal

James Buchanan & Company Limited

Buchanan House, 3 St James's Square, London SW1Y 4JU

Distillers and blenders   *A subsidiary of Distillers Company PLC**
Member of SWA

The black Scottish terrier and the West Highland white terrier together have for so long been one of the most familiar emblems of Scotch whisky throughout the world, that it is sad that the brand which they represent, Black & White, is, due to EEC complications, no longer readily available in Britain. However, the company's reversion to The Buchanan Blend as their principal product on the domestic market is a fitting tribute to their founder, since it was under this label that the enterprising James Buchanan first marketed his famous whisky in 1884.

Lord Woolavington, as he was to become, was Canadian by birth, but of Scottish parents who were to retrace their steps no more than a year after James Buchanan was born in 1849. But their stay in Scotland was also brief and the young Buchanan in fact grew up in Northern Ireland. His education was a short one, and at fifteen he had secured himself the post of office-boy in a Glasgow shipping firm with which he had family connections. This unambitious start to life was matched by the ten years of steady experience which he was later to gain in his brother's grain business. Whether the indirect links between grain and Scotch whisky were the motivation, or sheer intuition, is unknown, but whatever it was, James Buchanan gave up the security of his Glasgow employment to go to London in 1879 as agent for Charles Mackinlay & Co.*, the Leith whisky blenders. He

180

seems to have served them well, but in under five years he had left to set up in business on his own in London with the assistance of some capital from a friend. His timing appears to have been impeccable since he was soon getting orders, his very first customer being Dolamore Ltd, the London wine and cigar merchants. He traded at first in whisky by the barrel, but soon saw the potential for bottled whisky. He set about perfecting a blend acceptable to the English palate, which appreciated neither the pungent Highland malts nor the suspect unmatured grain or blended whiskies flooding the market. But it was not only the quality of his product which ensured success and enabled him to repay his loans within the year, it was the salesmanship of the man himself. By sheer hard work and a surfeit of self-confidence, he managed to seduce or bully some of the top London hotels and restaurants into carrying his Buchanan Blend, gradually becoming widely recognised in its black bottle and white label. His two most important customers, in terms of public prestige, were the London music halls belonging to the United Music Halls Co., and the Members' Bar at the House of Commons, for both of which he secured contracts. Always with an eye to promotion, his brand became House of Commons Whisky, then Buchanan's Special and finally Black & White, since this was how it was known to most because of the distinctive bottle. Buchanan's continue to blend and bottle for the House of Commons catering department the House of Commons Number One Scotch Whisky, a private 12 years old label.

His phenomenal success in London encouraged Buchanan to appoint agents elsewhere in Britain. He then looked abroad, with France as his first target after his Buchanan Blend had won a gold medal at the Paris Centennial Exhibition of 1889. The proselytizing he undertook himself, and he was especially successful in Germany, Canada, the United States, New Zealand and South America. This led to him setting up his own export department to replace the London agents who had hitherto handled his foreign business, and branches were opened in 1902 in Paris and New York. Offices had already been set up in several of the principal cities of the United Kingdom, and Hamburg and Buenos Aires soon followed.

James Buchanan, as one of the largest purveyors of blended Scotch, inevitably became embroiled in the great debate which raged between the pot-still malt distillers on the one hand and the grain spirit distillers and the blenders on the other. But he came out of this better than most since his blend, which he insisted should always be of well aged whiskies, was often held up as an example of the quality which could be achieved by the careful blending of mature malt and grain whiskies. Quality was, indeed, of great importance to him and he owed much in this to his association with W.P. Lowrie & Co. Ltd,* a Glasgow whisky broker who had branched into blending and bottling. Buchanan depended heavily on Lowrie for supplies of good whiskies both in bulk and bottle, and the relationship blossomed, inevitably leading to Buchanan acquiring his supplier on Lowrie's retirement from the company in 1906.

Buchanan saw the need for completeness in his operations and so built his own Highland malt distillery in 1898, Glentauchers-Glenlivet at Mulben in Speyside, in association with Lowrie and two other partners. The new distillery impressed the experts of the day and drew many favourable comments as to its design. The venture prospered as the Glentauchers-Glenlivet Distillery Co. Ltd until 1906, when the other interests were completely absorbed by James Buchanan & Co. Ltd. The latter continues as licensee today. The product is not currently available in bottle as a single malt, although James Buchanan & Co. did for a time market it as such at 5 and 12 years old. During this phase, Buchanan acquired two other distilleries: the Lowland Malt distillery of Bankier, which has long since been defunct, and Convalmore Highland malt distillery, which is still on the DCL inventory, but under licence to W.P. Lowrie & Co. Ltd.* He had already owned since 1898 the Black Swan Distillery in London, but redesigned it as a bottling plant. A further distillery venture was the purchase in 1919 of Lochruan at Campbeltown, but this was to be closed in 1925 by DCL.

Whilst few at the time would challenge the quality of Buchanan's whisky, it was the man's flair for promoting it which really ensured his continuing success. He saw the important role which advertising could play and his was amongst the first whiskies to use newspaper advertising. The symbol of the black and white terriers was his own idea, as was that of using finely groomed horses and handsomely liveried vans for the delivery of his whisky throughout London. It was only with the greatest reluctance that these were finally withdrawn in 1936.

Despite the widespread acceptance of his Black & White, Buchanan had other brands — Red Seal, Finest Old Liqueur, Rare Old Liqueur, to name but three.

The early years of the century saw great ructions in the Scotch whisky industry, with companies crashing, amalgamating or even emerging for the first time. Rumour was rife as to the possibility of a merger between the three great independent blenders — Buchanan's, Dewar's and Walker's — to challenge DCL. This led to the formation in 1915 of Scotch Whisky Brands Ltd, for which Buchanan's and Dewar's each provided three directors whilst retaining their separate identities. This rather anaemic title was dropped in 1919 in favour of Buchanan-Dewar Ltd and the partnership had by 1922 acquired or held interests in eleven distilleries. Further expansion followed, including the purchase of James Watson & Co. Ltd* in 1923, and the great amalgamation with DCL in 1925 was no more than a marriage

Dalwhinnie

postponed. James Buchanan was, of course, now on the DCL board, and although his firm's identity was preserved, it had to operate within the confines of a new — and much bigger — corporate structure.

Buchanan had throughout his career been dogged by illness, and longish absences for convalescence were a feature of his life. Yet he was about eighty-six when he died, his latter years being devoted largely to philanthropy, of which many fine examples can be quoted. Like Tommy Dewar, he combined the life of an English country gentleman and racehorse owner with public service. However, his country was slow to recognize him and he was seventy before he received his knighthood. But his peerage followed swiftly thereafter in 1922.

Today James Buchanan & Co. Ltd have an extensive blending and bottling network at Stepps near Glasgow, which came on stream in 1969. Apart from Glentauchers, Buchanan's also carry the licence for another Highland malt distillery, Dalwhinnie, Inverness-shire. It commands a good position at the entrance to Drumochter Pass and is one of the highest distilleries in Scotland at 1,174 feet above sea level.

Dalwhinnie means in Gaelic a 'meeting place', and the location was a crossroads for whisky smugglers and cattle drovers, and much illicit business no doubt took place there. The area is steeped in history, with part of General Wade's original Highland road passing through the distillery grounds; the moorland behind the distillery was the site of the encampment for Prince Charles Stuart and his army after he had raised his standard at Glenfinnan in 1745, and was

183

also the site of a great clan battle between the followers of Atholl and the Macphersons of Cluny in which the latter were badly thrashed. The distillery itself is of comparatively recent origin, George Sellar and Alex Mackenzie, both of Kingussie, combining in the venture in 1898. Bankruptcy soon visited them and A.P. Blyth & Son took over, only to sell out in 1905 to an American syndicate trading as James Munro & Son Ltd.* Ownership passed to Sir James Calder in 1921, to J. & G. Stewart Ltd* in 1926 and to Scottish Malt Distillers Ltd* in 1930. Production was interrupted in 1934 by a serious fire. However, it was soon brought back into production and has been under the James Buchanan flag for some years. Some of the 1962 production has been bottled by Gordon & MacPhail, and for a spell it was available at 8 years old from from the distillers themselves.

Brands

Black and White
Black and White Premium
Buchanan Blend
Buchanan's De Luxe
Buchanan's Reserve
Dalwhinnie 8 years old
    Highland Malt†

Glen Tauchers 5 years old
    Highland Malt†
Glen Tauchers 12 years old
    Highland Malt†
Royal Household
Strathconon Vatted 12 years
    old Malt

Markets All overseas countries for Black and White. Buchanan's De Luxe in Central and South America; Black and White Premium in the Far East, Buchanan's Reserve in all other markets.

John Buckmaster & Sons Limited

91 Jermyn Street, London SW1Y 6JZ

Blenders and merchants

Glorious 12th was launched as a De Luxe blend with much fanfare in 1980. It is very much an 'up-market' whisky to be found in the best stores, hotels and restaurants both in Britain and in certain overseas countries.

The brand name refers to the opening of the pheasant season on 12 August, and known as the 'Glorious Twelfth' in shooting circles.

Brand

Glorious 12th 12 years old De Luxe

Bucktrout & Company Limited

PO Box 27, Waterloo House, St Peter Port, Guernsey, Channel Islands

Wine and spirit, tobacco and cigar merchants

Much better known for their tobacco interests, Bucktrout's have for long had their own Gold Label blend of whisky. This has recently been joined by Thomas Bucktrout Gold Label.

The company dates back to 1830 when a Frenchman, William Cadic, began trading from the Three Tuns Inn and continued to do so successfully for thirty-five years. In 1866 he was bought out by two Englishmen, Thomas Bucktrout and John Whitehead who traded as Bucktrout & Co. Bucktrout died in 1878 but the name was retained as part of the sale agreement with the new owners. The present Chairman, Nicholas Wheadon, is the great-grandson of George Samuel Wheadon who joined the company in 1865 and was subsequently to become a director. The Wheadon involvement with Bucktrout has continued ever since.

Brands　Bucktrout's Gold Label　　Thomas Bucktrout Gold Label

Market　Guernsey.

Bulloch Lade & Company Limited

Trafalgar House, 75 Hope Street, Glasgow G2 6AW *Member of SWA*

Distillers and blenders　　　　*A subsidiary of Distillers Company PLC**

The company dates back to 1830, and enjoyed almost 100 years of independence before being absorbed by DCL in January 1927 for the consideration of over half a million pounds, having earlier gone into voluntary liquidation in 1920 and been taken over by a group of distillers and blenders led by DCL. Along with the various Bulloch Lade brands, the purchase included 1,430,000 gallons of maturing whiskies and the assets of Bulloch Lade's associated company, Wright & Greig Ltd, which was noted both for the prominence of its Roderich Dhu brand and ownership of Dallas Dhu Distillery until just after the close of the First World War.

One of DCL's three Islay distilleries, Caol Ila, is licensed to Bulloch Lade, who had owned Camlachie Lowland Malt Distillery from 1859 until it was closed in 1920. Caol Ila Distillery is found in the most sheltered bay in Islay, at Port Askaig, and boasts its own pier. The distillery's early history is obscure but it is thought to have

185

been built around 1846. Bulloch Lade & Co. Ltd were the proprietors from 1880 to 1920. Caol Ila Distillery Co. Ltd was then formed specifically to run the distillery for the parent company Robertson & Baxter Ltd.* This persisted until 1927 when DCL gained control. It is fitting that management should be back in the hands of Bulloch Lade who had previously had the longest continuous ownership.

A little of Caol Ila's production is used in a vatted malt for export, mainly to Italy, under the name of Glen Ila.

Brands

B. & L. Gold Label	King Arthur
Glen Ila Vatted Malt	Old Rarity De Luxe

(Wright & Greig Ltd)
The Aristocrat†	Roderich Dhu
Marlboro'†	Special
Premier	

Markets United States, South America (especially Venezuela), Canada, Italy, Belgium, France, Germany and New Zealand.

Caol Ila, pre 1974

Burn Stewart & Company Limited

79 Marylebone Lane, London W1M 5GA

Blenders, exporters and brokers

A wide variety of blends are marketed in bulk and in case by the Company and its associates.

Brands

Burn Stewart De Luxe	Highland Rose
Glen Blair Pure Malt (vatted)	Old Argyll
Gold Label	Old Friend
Golden Thistle	Old Royal

(Burn McKenzie & Co. Ltd)

Club Imperial	The Master
Full Sail	Premier
McKenzie De Luxe	

(Northern Blending Co. Ltd)
King's Whisky

(Petnor Blenders (London & Glasgow) Ltd)

Captain Bob	Gold Label

(Ross Bros (Blenders) Ltd)
Scottish Leader

(Tower Blending Co. Ltd)

Glen Royal	King Alfred
Highland Captain	Queen Margaret
Highland Tower	

Edward Butler Vintners Limited

289-293 Regent Street, London W1R 7PD

Wine and spirit merchants

With their purchase in 1982 of the trading assets of Foregate Vintners from Amalgamated Distilled Products PLC*, these wine and sherry shippers acquired, for the first time, their own Scotch whisky blend.

Brand Highland Prince

William Cadenhead Limited

18 Golden Square, Aberdeen

Blenders and merchants

Cadenhead's was a household name in Aberdeen for well over a century as wine and spirit merchants, but better known for their rum than their whisky. The firm reduced its activities in Aberdeen in the late seventies and now carry on most of their operations in Campbeltown. In addition to their own blended brands, the company bottles an extensive range of fine malt whiskies, up to 35 years old.

There is a retail shop in Edinburgh. The firm is associated with Eaglesome Ltd and J. & A. Mitchell & Co. Ltd* of Springbank Distillery.

Brands

(*Wm Cadenhead Ltd*)
Hielanman
Moidart
(*Eaglesome Ltd*)
Allan's
Cairnbaan
Campbeltown Loch

Putachieside 12 years old 75°
De Luxe

Eaglesome's
Eaglesome 12 years old De Luxe
Old Spencer

Markets Far East, Middle East, EEC, USA and UK.

J.W. Cameron & Company Limited

PO Box 21, Greenbank Offices, Lion Brewery, Hartlepool, Cleveland TS24 7QS

Brewers and blenders

A large regional brewer with many tied outlets, the company is now a subsidiary of Ellerman Lines Ltd, and in turn has its own subsidiaries engaged in brewing and the wine and spirit trade. The present company dates from 1872 although J.W. Cameron first started work at Lion Brewery in 1865.

Unfortunately, the company suspended producing its own blended whiskies in June 1980 and stocks must now be almost exhausted. Scotch Cream and Five Sovereigns boasted high proportions of top quality malts, 45 per cent and 55 per cent respectively, and so it is hoped that they may one day be reintroduced. The formulae for these blends pre-date the First World War. They have also recently suspended the export blend, Cameron's Finest Scotch Whisky.

Brands

(J.W. Cameron & Co. Ltd)
Club†
Cameron's Finest†
Five Sovereigns De Luxe†

Scotch Cream†
VOH 8 years old†
VOH†

(John J. Hunt Ltd)
Ebor†

(Scarborough and Whitby Breweries Ltd)
Target†

Campbell & Clark Limited

35 Robertson Street, Glasgow G2 8HF　　　　*Member of SWA*

Blenders and exporters

This firm was originally set up in 1934 as a subsidiary of the now defunct Train and McIntyre Ltd. It was reconstructed in 1970 with American interests taking up half the equity in the form of the Sazerac Co. Inc. of New Orleans. However, it is an operation of fairly modest proportions, being one of the many companies whose whiskies are exclusively for the export market. Accordingly, it purchases new whisky from a wide variety of Scottish distilleries which the company then matures in its own warehouses for periods of up to twelve years before blending. It deals with approximately 350,000 proof gallons per annum, which is equivalent to about 120,000 cases.

It has two subsidiaries which are now dormant for trading purposes but whose brands are still marketed. The firm is associated with Speyside Distillery and Bonding Co. Ltd.*

Brands

(Campbell & Clark Ltd)
Camros
Camros HL1
Clark's Reserve
David Ross De Luxe
Murdoch's Perfect Lion

Old Monarch
Pleasant Thoughts
Private Cellar
Private Stock
Tranquillity

(Colin Forbes Ross & Co. Ltd)
Bonnie Heather
Glen Bowie
Glen Hardy

King's Crest
Royal Chester
Scottish Prince

(Douglas Murdoch & Co.)
Duncan's Reserve

Murdoch's Special

Markets Exclusively export, principally United States, France and Italy.

189

David Campbell

255 High Street, Perth

Wine and spirit merchants

Family licensed grocers established in 1845, with their own house brand.

Brand   Old Grantully

P. & J. Campbell

The Glenlivet Whisky Depot, Tomintoul, Banffshire

Off-licence

Brand   Campbell's Tomintoul Special 100° Vatted Malt

Ross Campbell Limited

121 St Vincent Street, Glasgow G2

Blenders, exporters and brokers

Known until recently as Arnold Campbell Ltd, associated companies are M.G. Campbell Ltd and B. & S. Ross (Whisky) Co. Ltd.

S. Campbell & Son Limited

The House of Campbell, West Byrehill, Kilwinning, Ayrshire KA13 6NL   *Member of SWA*

Distillers and blenders   *A subsidiary of Pernod Ricard*

The House of Campbell dates back to 1879. For most of its history it has been a blending house whose whisky was widely exported. Campbell's became directly involved in distilling in 1945 through acquisition of the Aberlour-Glenlivet Distillery, and the subsequent incorporation of Aberlour-Glenlivet Distillery Co. Ltd.* At the same time they expanded into a bottling operation after the outright purchase of the Glasgow Bonding Co. Ltd. In 1979 the head office, blending and bottling operation moved to a new site at Kilwinning in Ayrshire.

In 1974 the House of Campbell was purchased by the French Pernod Ricard group, the seventh largest producers of spirits in the world and owners of such well known brands as Bisquit Dubouche Cognac, Dubonnet, Byrrh and Suze, as well as the famous brands of anisette, Pernod and Ricard. The company's principal whiskies, White Heather and Clan Campbell, are now represented respectively by Pernod and Ricard, covering distribution in France with sales in excess of 5 per cent of the French market. Capital investment by the French principals has allowed Campbell more expansion since 1976 than it had been experiencing in the past, with new markets being opened in Japan, Spain, Canada, Venezuela, Peru, Brazil, Germany, as well as Australia, Italy, USA and South Africa, which they were supplying before the merger. Sales of the company's products in the United Kingdom are at the moment confined to Scotland. In 1982 the group expanded its Scotch whisky interests by acquiring the assets of Wm Whiteley Ltd* from J.G. Turney Ltd, and thus added a second distillery to its inventory.

Brands

(Campbell's Distillery Ltd)
Aberlour 12 years old V.O.H.M.

(Duncan Fraser & Co.)
Gold Seal	Scots Lord
King's Special	Special Reserve

(James Jeffrey & Co.)
Royal Stuart   Royal Stuart 5 years old

(Moorcrest Blending Co.)
Victoria Club

(Muir Mackenzie & Co. Ltd)
Clan Campbell 5 years old   High Commissioner

(Scott Bruce & Co.)
Scott Bruce's

(White Heather Distillers Ltd)
White Heather	White Heather 8 years old
White Heather 5 years old	White Heather 15 years old

Markets Scotland and France, Australia, Italy, United States, South Africa, Japan, Spain, Canada, Venezuela, Peru, Brazil, Germany.

Caperdonich Distillery Company Limited

45 Frederick Street, Edinburgh

Distillers   *A subsidiary of The Glenlivet Distillers Ltd**

This company was established in 1965 by The Glenlivet and Glen Grant Distilleries Ltd* in order to run the Caperdonich distillery, alongside the famous Glen Grant distillery. Caperdonich had had a brief history from 1897 to 1901 as the Glen Grant No. 2 Distillery. In its present guise, it has established itself as a valued production unit in the Glenlivet group, with an output in excess of 700,000 gallons per year. This follows extensive modernisation, although the original copper pot stills from Glen Grant No. 2 have been retained in working order. Caperdonich is used almost exclusively for blending, although Gordon & MacPhail* do bottle it as part of their Connoisseur's Choice range of selected malt whiskies, as do Wm Cadenhead at 14 years old.

Capital Wines & Travers Limited

King Georges Avenue, Dover Court, Harwich, Kent

Merchants

This is a major firm of wine and spirit merchants who have for long had their own Scotch whisky brands. They also have the agency for Bruichladdich Islay Malt for England and Wales.

Brands

Glenmorden†	Red Cap†
Highland Duke	Slogan†
Kirsteen†	Vanguard†
Old Ship	

James Catto & Company Limited

17 Cornwall Terrace, London NW1 4QP   *Member of SWA*

Blenders   *A subsidiary of International Distillers and Vintners Ltd* *

James Catto began life as a whisky blender in Aberdeen in 1861 when he set up a warehouse for this purpose. He also dealt in other spirits and tea. He bottled his blended whisky under his own name and soon established a good reputation locally for it. He then turned his eye to the expanding overseas markets and in particular to countries where Scots emigrants were settling in increasing numbers. He was helped in this by two fellow Aberdonians who had been his contemporaries at Aberdeen's ancient Grammar School and who had founded the two famous shipping lines, the P & O and the White Star. The ships of these lines carried Catto's whisky to far-flung destinations and also sold it on board to emigrating Scots.

Robert Catto succeeded his father in 1900 and turned his attention to the all important English market with considerable success. But the family connection was not to last much longer. The founder died in 1908 and his heir, Robert, was killed on active service in France in 1916. The administrators of the Catto estste, which included a valuable stock of maturing whisky, approached W. & A. Gilbey Ltd (now Gilbey Vintners Ltd*). The latter purchased the stock of whisky and James Catto & Co. Ltd was temporarily closed down. It was, however, re-incorporated on 1 April 1918, with Gilbey's as a minority shareholder, the majority of the issued capital being acquired by Corney and Barrow Ltd,* the wine and spirit merchants, and their nominees. W. & A. Gilbey gradually increased its shareholding, buying out the shareholding of Corney and Barrow Ltd* in 1945 in order to acquire Catto's stocks and overseas sales. Thereafter, the history of Catto followed that of Gilbey into International Distillers and Vintners Ltd in 1962.

Sales of Catto have grown rapidly in recent years and now stand at about 400,000 cases annually.

Brands

Catto's Rare Old Scottish
    Highland
Catto's 12 years old Scottish
    Highland

Gold Label (USA only)

Markets UK and some fifty export markets, including USA, Canada, Mexico, Chile, Uruguay, Spain, Italy, France and Japan.

Central Export Agency Limited

161 Woodville Street, Glasgow G51 2RE

Exporters

Chalie, Richards & Company Limited

88-92 South Street, Dorking, Surrey RH4 2E2

Wine and spirit merchants

A very old and distinguished Welsh firm whose origins go back to 1700. The founder of the company, Chalie, had two sons Francis and Matthew. Matthew Chalie's daughter married into the Richards family in 1819, leading to the present company title. In 1900 the firm celebrated its 200th anniversary by selecting two Scotch whisky blends called Old Francis and Old Matthew. The former was withdrawn in 1943, but Old Matthew still comes from the same blending house in Glasgow; it remains substantially unchanged although the grain content was increased slightly after the Second World War, but is said to be still less than in most blended whiskies.

Chalie, Richards can claim an impressive list of Royal appointments going back to King George IV. The company was acquired in 1982 by Lawlers Ltd, the wine shippers.

Brands   Old Francis†   Old Matthew

Chennel & Armstrong Limited

Manor Lane, Shipton Road, York YO3 6TX

Wine and spirit merchants

This family business goes back more than 150 years and has since the 1930s been owned by the Adams family. Today it comprises eleven off-licence premises and three public houses as well as a flourishing wholesale business. The company's telegraphic address is 'Sobriety, York'. Its Grand Highland Blend goes back many years, winning medals at London exhibitions in 1912 and 1914.

Brand   Grand Highland Blend (G.H.B.)

Markets UK only.

Chivas Brothers Limited

111-113 Renfrew Road, Paisley and 387-391 Union Street, Aberdeen

Member of SWA

Blenders and exporters   *A subsidiary of Seagram Distillers PLC* *

The Chivas story begins in Aberdeen in 1801 when William Edward started as a wine merchant and grocer at 49 Castle Street. He moved to 13 King Street in 1838 and was joined by James Chivas. Edward died in 1841 and Chivas carried on the business in partnership with another grocer and wine merchant, Charles Stewart. In that year the firm changed its name to Stewart and Chivas and remained as such until 1857. On the dissolution of the partnership, James Chivas was joined by his brother John. However, he died in 1862 and James Chivas in 1886. By that time James's oldest son, Alexander, was in the business and he carried on as sole partner. His early death in 1893 broke the Chivas line and the business was carried on by two employees, Messrs Smith and Taylor, although the firm remained as Chivas Brothers. In 1895, Alexander Smith took control, in partnership with Charles Stewart Howard, and at this point greater emphasis was put on the whisky side of the business, since Howard
194

had gained much experience of that trade working for J. & G. Stewart Ltd* of Edinburgh. In 1920, a third partner was added in the person of William Mitchell, who had developed a nose for whisky whilst with John Bisset & Co. Ltd.* The partnership broke up in 1935 and the business became a limited liability company, its directors being already well established in the whisky trade, especially in broking. The advent of war virtually put an end to Chivas Brothers' whisky activities, which had largely been in exports, but it remained in being to serve the local population in groceries and wines and spirits.

In 1949, Chivas caught the eye of Seagrams and became a wholly owned subsidiary, the main object of the Seagram purchase being to get use of the well established Chivas Regal label, which has become, through Seagrams, one of the biggest selling De Luxe quality Scotch whiskies in the world. Apart from this, the name of Chivas lives on in Aberdeen as a highly respected firm of licensed grocers, with a popular restaurant on the same premises and extensive wholesale wine and spirit interests all over northern Scotland. Chivas Brothers Ltd boast the Royal Warrant as suppliers to Queen Victoria and King George V. A further connection was the creation of Royal Salute in 1952 to commemorate the coronation of Queen Elizabeth II. It is still marketed as a 21 years old Super De Luxe whisky in Spode china flagons.

Brands

Chivas†
Chivas Old Vat†
Chivas Regal 12 years old
Glendee†
Glen Keith (blended)
Lochan Ora Liqueur
Magna Carta†

Royal Glendee†
Royal Loch Nevis†
Royal Old Vat†
Royal Salute 21 years old
Royal Strathythan†
Scotmore†
Strathoyne†

Markets Heavily promoted on a world-wide basis, Chivas Regal 12 years old sells in 179 different countries, with United States, Canada and United Kingdom being the most important markets.

Clydesdale Scotch Whisky Company Limited

190 Clarence Gate Gardens, Baker St, London NW1 6AR

Blenders and exporters

This company exports a range of whiskies under its own labels or those of associate companies. Established only in 1973 with a commencing capital of £20,000, it has achieved remarkable progress in a short time and now has a paid up capital of £150,000 and a turnover of about £2 million per annum. A private family company, the active members of which still span three generations of the same family.

For the time being at least, Clydesdale's whiskies are exclusively for export to regular overseas clients. On six occasions during the last four years, when Clydesdale have entered their 12 years old De Luxe whiskies in international competitions, they have each time been the recipients of a Gold Award.

Brands

(*Clydesdale Scotch Whisky Co. Ltd*)

Cavalry	Curzon
Clydesdale De Luxe	Curzon 12 years old

(*Clydebank Blenders Ltd*)
Gold Label

(*Desmond & Duff Distillers Ltd*)
Desmond & Duff 12 years old De Luxe

(*Tartan Scotch Whisky Co.*)
Highland Dance

Markets Export only.

Cockburn & Campbell Limited

Cockpen House, 20-30 Buckhold Road, Wandsworth, London SW18 4AP

Wine and spirit merchants

This old and much respected establishment ha been blending whiskies for over 150 years. It is now a subsidiary of Young and Co.'s Brewery Ltd of Wandsworth, but the principles of blending and maturing which have long been practised by Cockburn & Campbell Ltd continue, although not since 1972 in the old Bonded Warehouse No. 10 in Duke St, Leith. There the vaulted cellars lay about twelve feet below street level, had an earthen floor and a regular moist temperature of 50°F. It was these unusual conditions which reputedly gave rise to an uncommon occurrence whereby the natural loss of whisky, which takes place during maturation, was found to be in the strength of the spirit rather than in the liquid content. This caused Customs and Excise officers some consternation when finding casks 'bung full' on examination, rather than reduced by several gallons as would normally be the case.

Cockburn & Campbell Ltd still produce a range of whiskies and although now principally for the home market these were once known widely abroad, especially in India. The Laird O'Cockpen's is

Old Leith cellars of Cockburn & Campbell

a 60/40 malt to grain blend bottled at 10 years old, whilst The Royal and Ancient is a 7 years old blend of 38/62 malt to grain. Both were registered in 1913.

Brands

Cockburn's No. 1† (known
   also as Pure Malt Blend;
   Red Seal; and Red Capsule)
Cockburn's No. 2†
Cockburn's No. 3† (known
   also as Black Capsule)
Laird O'Cockpen's Rare
   Old (De Luxe)

Loch Troon†
Special Malt (vatted)
The Royal and Ancient
   (formerly Cockburn's
   No. 4†)
White Capsule†

Markets Mainly UK, but some exports.

Cockburn & Company (Leith) Limited

1 Melville Street, Edinburgh EH3 7PR

Blenders and wine and spirit merchants   *A subsidiary of The Drambuie Liqueur Co. Ltd**

Founded in 1796 in Leith by the brothers Robert and John Cockburn, this highly regarded establishment has served generations of distinguished Edinburgh citizens, as well as a wider clientele,

197

including such celebrities as Sir Walter Scott, Charles Dickens and Thomas Carlyle, to say nothing of members of the Royal Family. In the book *Drinking with Dickens* is a summary of the wine cellar of the great scribe at Gad's Hill which was drawn up shortly after his death in August 1870, as part of his estate; it shows '17 dozen very fine old Highland Whiskey Cockburn & Company, Leith' (note the old spelling). Records show that on 31 December 1868, Charles Dickens paid for a cask of Cockburn's whisky at a cost of £35. 8s. Whether he then had it bottled, and what was in his cellar at the time of his death was the same whisky or a further consignment of Cockburn's own bottled whisky, is unknown, but he clearly had a high regard for it.

The Cockburns themselves were of a very well known Scottish family. Robert Cockburn left the partnership with his brother to go to Portugal where he established Cockburn's as an outstanding name in the Port trade. A third brother, Henry, Lord Cockburn, is a legendary figure in Scottish Law and in the history of the New Town of Edinburgh. Almost by right, the Cockburns established a fine reputation as Scotch whisky blenders and wine merchants which was soon to become a tradition. The company changed hands several times in its later history, and included a spell under Seagram's ownership, and in 1981 it was bought by the Drambuie Liqueur Co. Ltd.Cockburn's O.V. 8 years old at 70° has been exported for more than one hundred years.

Brands

Cockburn's O.V. 8 years old
Cockburn's Pure Highland
   Malt
Dominie

Imperial Gold Medal
Old Decanter 12 years old

Markets Cockburn's O.V. 8 years old is for export and the UK markets whilst the others are for the home market only.

Conqueror (Wine & Spirit) & Company Limited

121 St Vincent Street, Glasgow G2 5HW

Blenders   *Member of SWA*

There is an associate company, Sovereign (Wine and Spirit) Co. Ltd, which has a subsidiary, Moray Malt Whisky Co. Ltd.

Brands
Old Secret

William The Conqueror
   Premium

(Sovereign (Wine & Spirit) Co. Ltd)
Executive 12 years old De Luxe

(Moray Malt Whisky Co. Ltd)
First Class

Co-operative Wholesale Society Limited

Fairhill Road, Irlam, Manchester M30 6BD

Blenders

As well as owning its own brands for exclusive sale through co-operative retail outlets in the UK, CWS also bottles many other brands for other companies at its plant at Irlam in Manchester. Irlam has a capacity of 100,000 bottles per day and is linked to a bonded warehouse; the entire complex is operated on the open bond system.

Brands

Heatherdale	Majority
Highland Abbey	

Corney & Barrow Limited

12 Helmet Row, London EC1

Wine and spirit merchants

Although this firm's wine interests have always been to the fore, they have had in the past more than a passing interest in Scotch whisky, being for many years between the two World Wars the principal shareholder in James Catto & Co. Ltd*. They used also to be original fillers and blenders of Scotch whisky, but today their whisky activities are restricted to supplying their own blend in limited quantities to regular customers. The company was established in 1780.

Brand   Corbar

George Cowie & Sons Limited

Mortlach Distillery, Dufftown, Banffshire AB5 4AQ

Distillers   *A subsidiary of John Walker & Sons Ltd**

This hitherto little-known branch of the Distillers Company has achieved more prominence of late with the launching in 1978 on the domestic market of a new DCL brand, John Barr, in place of the world renowned Johnnie Walker Red Label which, as explained in Chapter 8, had to be withdrawn from Britain due to EEC compli-cations. However, the history of the company itself is a distinguished one and is very much tied up with that of Mortlach Distillery.

The distillery owes its name to the parish in which it is situated. Mortlach is derived from the Gaelic word for 'bowl shaped valley', and this is certainly an accurate description of the locality. Mortlach Distillery went legal in 1823, having previously been an old smuggling bothy sited next to a fast-flowing spring known as Highland John's Well. The first legal owner was James Findlater, but he was joined in 1825 by two local partners, Messrs Gordon and Mackintosh. By 1854 only Gordon remained as the sole partner and in that year George Cowie joined him, becoming himself the sole owner in 1865. Up until then, trade had been modest and restricted to the immediate vicinity of the distillery. However, the new owner was intent on expansion and sought fresh markets to the south. George Cowie & Sons, as the company had become, enjoyed modest success as an independent operator and had the distillery extensively refurbished in 1903, eventually attracting the attentions of John Walker & Sons Ltd,* which acquired the company and its entire stock in 1923.

The product, sometimes known as Mortlach-Glenlivet, is a traditional Speyside malt, but is somewhat under-peated, and much admired for this. The whisky is full-bodied, not light, and is considered by many to be amongst the top Highland malts. It is bottled at 12 years old by Gordon & MacPhail.*

| *Brands* | Mortlach 12 years old |
| John Barr | Highland Malt |

Markets Exclusively UK.

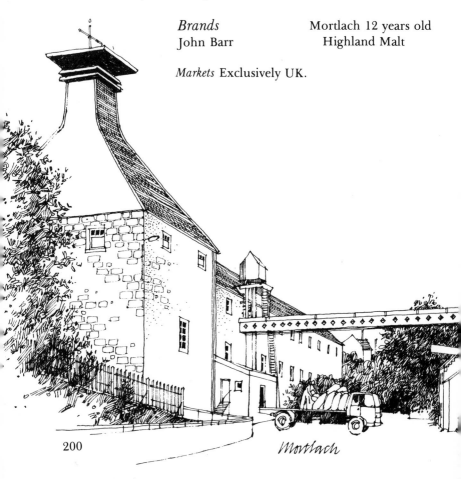

Mortlach

John Crabbie & Company Limited

108 Great Junction Street, Leith, Edinburgh EH6 5LF

Distillers and blenders　　　　*A subsidiary of Distillers Company PLC**
　　　　　　　　　　　　　　　　　　　　Member of SWA

One of the minor branches of the Distillers Company, Crabbie's take a low profile but, nevertheless, have their own following of devotees of their brands of whisky and, more importantly, of their green ginger wine for which they are a household name in Scotland. The company, which until its incorporation into DCL was a strictly family blending business, traces its origins back to 1801. However, it has for some time been the licensee for Balmenach Distillery, set in the beautiful Haughs of Cromdale in Morayshire. The distillery's founder was James McGregor who established it on the site of an old smuggler's bothy at the turn of the eighteenth century. McGregor went legal by obtaining a licence to distil in 1824 and quickly set about selling his whisky over a wide area; he could boast customers of distinction in Edinburgh and Aberdeen.

Balmenach Distillery almost came to lasting grief in the same storm which many miles away had brought down the Tay Bridge on 28 December, 1879. The distillery's chimney stack was blown through the roof of the still house and collapsed on the stills which were at work below. These were badly damaged and the hot liquid contents spread to the furnaces and, due to their alcoholic nature, caught fire. Fortunately, the stillman had the good sense to run the liquor away by opening the discharge cocks, thus averting disaster.

In 1897 ownership passed from John McGregor & Son to Balmenach-Glenlivet Distillery Ltd under the management of the founder's grandson. Considerable improvements followed, including the building of a private branch line linking the distillery directly to Cromdale Station, about a mile away. A change in ownership took place with reconstruction of the company in 1922 when the principal shareholders became Macdonald Greenlees Ltd,* Peter Dawson Ltd* and James Watson and Co. Ltd.* Shortly thereafter the entire shareholding passed to DCL. Balmenach is rarely found bottled, but Wm Cadenhead* offer it at 19 years old.

Brands

Crabbie 8 year old　　　　　　Crabbie 12 year old (De
　　　　　　　　　　　　　　　　Luxe)

Markets USA, Canada, Mexico and Europe.

Craighall Bonding Company Limited

99 Borron Street, Glasgow G4 9XF

Blenders   *A subsidiary of Distillers Company* PLC*

This is one of the smallest companies within the DCL Group and operates in association with one of DCL's main subsidiaries, White Horse Distillers Ltd.* It sells a small number of blends mainly for export, aimed at the bargain price market.

Brands

Clan Mackenzie	Inverary
Craig Castle	Mackie's

Markets Mackie's is sold almost exclusively in Scandinavia.

A. & A. Crawford Limited

93 Constitution Street, Leith, Edinburgh EH6 7AN *Member of SWA*

Distillers and blenders   *A subsidiary of Distillers Company* PLC*

The brothers Archibald and Aikman Crawford went into business in Leith in 1860. With their deaths in 1880 and 1885, David Ireland became senior partner and mentor to the founders' sons. The interruption caused by the First World War was quickly overcome and the business of spreading Crawford's whiskies far and wide was undertaken with renewed vigour. Three Star was a widely popular brand and it is interesting to note that the label introduced at the turn of the century is still in use today. By 1937 Mr W.W. Winton had become sole partner. A. & A. Crawford became a limited company in 1942 prior to its takeover by DCL in 1944.

Crawford's had been exclusively whisky blenders and merchants but the licensing to them of DCL's Benrinnes distillery now permits them to describe themselves as Scotch Whisky Distillers. The earliest known reference to Benrinnes dates from 1826, when Peter McKenzie was recorded as licensed distiller. The next known occupier was a William Smith who, on going bankrupt in 1864, sold Benrinnes to a David Edward. He, along with his son Alexander, owned and promoted many distilleries in Speyside.

The Benrinnes-Glenlivet Distillery Ltd was formed in 1897 and operated as such until it attracted the attention of one of the domestic giants, John Dewar & Sons Ltd,* who acquired control in 1922 and placed it under their name in 1926. Ownership was subsequently transferred in 1930 to Scottish Malt Distillers Ltd* and through internal company reorganisation later became licensed to

202

A. & A. Crawford Ltd. It has had a long and happy operating history, apart from a brief closure during the winter of 1932-3 and again in 1943. The distillery owes its name to the nearby Ben Rinnes mountain which provides a ready supply of pure hill water. It is one of the Connoisseur's Choice of single malts available from Gordon & MacPhail.* In April 1981, A. & A. Crawford & Associates Ltd was formed to handle the domestic sales in Scotland of ten of DCL's smaller companies, who retain their independent trading identities in export markets.

Brands

Five Star De Luxe   Three Star
Special Reserve

Markets USA for Special Reserve in bulk; France, Italy and Japan for Three and Five Star; Greece, Switzerland and Belgium for Three Star; and South Africa for Three Star and Special Reserve.

Daniel Crawford & Son Limited

93 Constitution Street, Leith, Edinburgh EH6 7AN *Member of SWA*

Blenders and exporters   *A subsidiary of Distillers Company PLC**

One of the smallest companies in the Distillers Company empire, Daniel Crawford & Son Ltd came into being in 1850 as a family firm of whisky merchants in Glasgow.

The move to Leith came in 1974, long after the firm had passed into DCL's control. For a period it was the licensee of Parkmore Highland Malt Distillery which has been inoperative for many years. Daniel Crawford's has a modest export trade under its own name and that of the Invercairn Blending Co.

Brands

(*Daniel Crawford & Son Ltd*)
Bene Vobis De Luxe   Red Star
Old Matured

(*The Invercairn Blending Co.*)
Glen Stewart

Markets
Old Matured is sold in a range of overseas countries, the principal markets being France, Greece, Corsica, Andorra, Bahrain, Dubai, New Zealand (in bulk), Mauritius, Netherlands and Austria. Bene Vobis is sold also in France and Mauritius, Red Star in Mauritius and Glen Stewart in Greece.

Cutty Sark (Scotch Whisky UK) Limited

106 West Nile Street, Glasgow G1 2QH   *Member of SWA*

Blenders and merchants

Jointly owned by Berry Bros & Rudd Ltd* and Robertson & Baxter Ltd,* this is the firm charged with marketing the famous Cutty Sark brand in Britain. Reference to the entries dealing with the two parent companies will relate the full and fascinating story behind its notable success.

Dakin & Company (No. 1 London)

333 Central Markets, London EC1A 9NB

Wine and spirit merchants

Apart from their own brand, they also stock a wide range of malt whiskies.

Brand   No. 1 London

Dambrosio, McKinlay & Lombard Limited

65 Otago Street, Glasgow G12

Blenders and merchants

Brands

Auld Curlers   Glen Farg
Auld Curlers Black Label   Glen Shian
Glen Douglas Malt (vatted)

Davenports Brewery PLC

The Brewery, Bath Row, Birmingham B15 1NB

Brewers and wine and spirit merchants

With a chain of about 130 tied houses, this brewer has ready outlets for its own whisky blend.

Brand   King Select

Peter Dawson Limited

Trafalgar House, 75 Hope Street, Glasgow G2 6AP *Member of SWA*

Blenders and exporters   *A subsidiary of Distillers Company PLC**

The Company was established in 1882 and was a family concern until its incorporation in DCL in 1925. They had briefly owned Auchnagie and built Towiemore, both Highland malt distilleries now long since extinct, and partly owned Balmenach Highland Malt Distillery at the time of the takeover. For nearly sixty years, up to 1982, the company was the licensee of Ord Distillery, in which year it reverted to John Dewar & Sons Ltd. At the same time Peter Dawson gave up marketing Ord as a single malt.

Brands

Dawson De Luxe	Peter Dawson Special
Old Curio	Rare Reserve†
Ord Malt 12 years old†	

Deanston Distilleries Limited

Doune, Perthshire

Distillers   *A subsidiary of The Invergordon Distillers Ltd**

Distilleries and mills have a common need — plenty of pure, soft water. It is, therefore, not all that surprising to find that Deanston was originally a cotton mill and one that was ideally situated on the south bank of the River Teith, about a mile away from Castle Doune.

The mill was built in 1785 and converted to a distillery in 1965 when the original mill owners decided to concentrate their textile interests elsewhere. The man who had the inspiration was Mr Brodie Hepburn, a well-known figure in the industry, whose imagination was fired by what he found at Doune. Enormous premises, beautifully situated on the River Teith with some vital equipment — a water turbine and stand-by generator — installed and in working order. He lost no time in putting his ideas to the mill owners, the prominent Glasgow firm of James Finlay and Co. Ltd. Somewhat to his surprise, the reaction was cautious enthusiasm and plans were drawn up whereby Finlay's took two-thirds of the equity in the Deanston venture and Brodie Hepburn Ltd the rest, plus responsibility for management. Conversion of the mill was a herculean task involving the removal of four very solid interior floors and the installation of two wash and two spirit stills. But production began in October 1969, only nine months after the decision had been taken to go ahead. However, the long-term plans of the owners to use Deanston's considerable potential production as the basis for building up sales of an already established brand which they might acquire were never realised. Deanston Distillers Ltd became a wholly owned subsidiary of Invergordon Distillers Ltd in 1972 by means of a share excange with James Finlay and Co. Ltd and the acquisition by Invergordon of all of the Brodie Hepburn interests.

Existing buildings provide plenty of storage space and the distillery is equipped with a capacity of 750,000 proof gallons per annum. The whisky is not only in steady demand from blenders but is also finding a growing acceptance as a single malt. Originally known as Deanston Mill, the whisky is now called simply Deanston. Not yet a long-aged whisky, but its light, fruity character makes it easy on the palate.

Brand   Deanston Highland Malt

Markets UK, mainly Scotland, and export markets.

Dew Hill Blending Company (Glasgow) Limited

45 19 Blythswood Square, Glasgow G2 4AP

Blenders

A. Dewar Rattray Limited

103 West Regent Street, Glasgow G2 2BA

Brokers and exporters

Established originally in 1817 as licensed grocers, the company is now operating on a modest scale as whisky brokers and wholesale wine and spirit merchants. Their own brands have long since been discontinued, but two of them were Glenburn and Hero.

John Dewar & Sons Limited

Dewar House, Haymarket, London SW1Y 4DF   *Member of SWA*

Distillers and blenders   *A subsidiary of Distillers Company PLC**

The Dewar story is, in many ways, the story of the evolution of modern blended Scotch whisky. The role of the Dewar brothers both in that and in the growth of DCL is touched on in the appropriate chapters of the book and this short essay is no more than an outline of the history and present circumstances of one of DCL's key member companies.

It all began in 1806 with the birth of John Dewar in a small Perthshire croft. Scarcely in his majority, Dewar took himself off to the fair city of Perth to work in the cellars of a local wine and spirit merchant, who was also a relative. He became a partner within less than ten years, in 1837, but broke away to set up his own business in 1846. He began to blend and bottle his own whisky in a modest way and sought sales beyond Perth. Indeed, one of Dewar's many claims to fame is that they were the first to sell whisky in branded bottles.

John Alexander Dewar was made a partner in the firm in 1879, a year before his father's death, and the younger son, Thomas, joined the company in 1881, becoming a partner in 1885. Both had been apprenticed to the trade in Leith and knew what they were about. They saw their future in the South and Tommy was sent to London to make an impression on that all-important outlet. Despite the fact that, of his only two contacts there, one was found to be bankrupt and the other dead, the younger Dewar set out to make a splash. He did so by resorting to bizarre — and some thought outrageous — stunts. At the Brewers' Show of 1886 he employed pipers to drown out all other sound by playing the bagpipes as loud and for as long as possible in order to draw attention to his wares. Dewar's whisky was soon in the bars of most of London's fashionable hotels and restaurants and by 1893 they had received Queen Victoria's Royal Warrant for the supply of whisky to Her Majesty's household.

Not content with merely blending and selling whisky, the Dewar brothers decided to go back to first base by taking over in 1890 the lease of Tullymet (or Auchnagie) Distillery (now defunct) at Ballinluig and then building another from scratch at Aberfeldy, near the humble birth-place of their father, and for which Dewar's still hold the licence.

The Dewar partnership was enormously successful, with the eldest brother John remaining in Perth to oversee production and administration whilst the more flamboyant younger brother set out to capture world markets. In this, Tommy Dewar achieved remarkable results. By 1891 he could boast agents as far away as Australia and South Africa. He himself embarked in 1892 on a two-year world tour in which he visited 26 countries and appointed 32 principal agents, and arranged shipment of Dewar's whisky to the major ports and cities which he had visited. This set the foundations for a world-wide sales network which Dewar's retain, with necessary changes, to this day. Tommy Dewar recorded his impressions arising from this trip in a book *Ramble Round the Globe*.

Dewar's wanted to keep themselves on the map and an example of their determination in this respect was their reaction to a situation which threatened the firm's South African operations. Their agents in Johannesburg were of German origin and with the outbreak of hostilities in 1914 became the object of anti-German demonstrations.

Their premises were attacked and burned down and the personnel had to flee to neighbouring Portuguese territory. Peter Dewar — no relation but a life-time employee who was subsequently to become Chairman — was in Sydney when news of the Johannesburg incident came through. He immediately set out for South Africa, and on his arrival a month later set about opening a branch office and bringing staff from Scotland. By the turn of the year, the office was fully operational.

John Alexander Dewar was the first of the whisky barons, becoming Baron Forteviot of Dupplin in 1917, after having been knighted in 1901. The younger brother became Baron Dewar of Homestall in Sussex in 1919, his knighthood having been bestowed in 1902. These honours came in recognition of their public services — John in Perth and Tommy in London. Both had served in Parliament, although on opposite benches. Despite John Dewar's evident seniority, it was Tommy who was the better known of the two due not only to his livelier character, but also his proximity to London society and his passionate involvement with the turf.

The two brothers died within a year of each other. On Tommy's demise in 1930, Peter Dewar became Chairman and held that position until 1946. During this period he consolidated the company's position in the North American market, after the setback of Prohibition. Following Peter's death, the family once more took over the reins with John Arthur Dewar becoming Chairman, to be succeeded in 1954 by Evelyn Dewar, the third Lord Forteviot, and grandson of the founder, who retired in 1976.

Despite the impeccable lineage of the Chairmen, Dewar's had in fact long since surrendered their independence, having entered into 'close and permanent association' with James Buchanan & Co. Ltd* as long ago as 1915. A private holding company, Scotch Whisky Brands Ltd, was set up to pool profits and draw on the resources of the two enterprises under a joint management arrangement. Whilst the two parents retained their identity, the totality of their interests was formidable and included the largest holding of maturing whisky stocks in Scotland. But this was merely the precursor to their amalgamating with DCL in 1925. Moreover, the three had previously been in partnership to acquire Yoker Grain distillery in 1918 which was allowed to fall silent in 1927. Although primarily concerned with blending, Dewar's had several other spells — often brief — of distillery ownership, including the Highland malt distilleries of Aultmore, Benrinnes, Port Ellen and Lochnagar, as well as the long since inactive Glenfoyle and Parkmore and the now silent grain distillery of Bo'ness. However, in 1982 the company took over the licence for Ord Distillery from Peter Dawson. The distillery is at Muir of Ord in Ross-shire. Although converted to a legal distillery in 1838,

Ord was the site of a local still for many years prior to this. The founder of the legal distillery was a Mr McLennan. On his death, responsibility for the business passed to his widow and, subsequently, on her remarriage, to her second husband, Alexander McKenzie of Beauly. He built up the reputation of Ord until it was acquired by James Watson & Co. Ltd* of Dundee. They made considerable improvements to it, boosting annual production from 80,000 to 240,000 gallons of proof spirit. The distillery passed to John Dewar & Sons Ltd* in 1923 for a brief period and subsequently to Peter Dawson Ltd.*

The distillery is located near the site of one of the more despicable acts in Scottish history, the burning down in 1603 by the Macdonalds of the church at Cilliechriost when it was full of worshippers from their rival clan, the Mackenzies. Although everyone perished in the church, the Mackenzies survived as a clan and there is still quite a number of them to be found in the Ord area.

Like so many Highland malts, the Ord product owes a good deal to the water which here springs from Glen Oran and is carried past the distillery by a local burn. Another factor of note is that in the malt drying process heather is mixed with the peat. The result is a highly regarded Highland Malt available at 12 years old, now marketed as Glenordie.

Dewar's outlook has long been international and over 90 per cent of Dewar's total production is exported. Their standard brand — known variously as Dewar's and White Label — is found in every market where imported whisky is permitted to be sold.

The company's 'front office' is at stately Dewar House in the Haymarket in London's West End but the Head Office is at Inveralmond, on the outskirts of Perth, where their impressive bottling and blending plant is to be found. Aberfeldy Distillery is a mixture of old and new with some of the original buildings of 1896 still in use. Production is centred on the still house, built in 1973. Like so many others, the distillery was closed down for a period in the thirties, but has recently been modernised and doubled in capacity. The whisky is used exclusively for blending.

Brands

Dewar's De Luxe Ancestor
Dewar's Ne Plus Ultra
Dewar's Pure Malt 12 years
  old (vatted)†

Dewar's Special
Dewar's White Label
Glenordie 12 years old
  Single Malt

The Distillers Agency Limited

13 Maritime Street, Edinburgh EH6 6SG   *Member of SWA*

Distillers and blenders   *A subsidiary of Distillers Company PLC**

Shortly after DCL's formation, the company set up an Export Branch with blending, bottling and warehousing facilities at South Queensferry. Its brands, King George IV, Highland Nectar and DCL Scotch Whisky, were registered as trademarks between 1880 and 1890 and sold in export markets only. When, in the early 1920s, DCL was engaged in negotiations to merge its interests with those of several major Scotch whisky blending houses, it decided to cease conducting this business under its own name, and to form a subsidiary company to take over the business of its Export Branch. The Distillers Agency Ltd was accordingly incorporated, with a capital of £1 million, on 25th January 1924.

The arrangement also included Knockdhu Distillery and the related maltings, but this has since been allocated to another DCL subsidiary, whilst the Distillers Agency Ltd now have the licence for Rosebank Lowland Malt Distillery. It is situated at Camelon near Falkirk and goes back to 1842. James Rankine was the founder and he was succeeded in 1864 by his son, R.W. Rankine. Such was the demand for Rosebank in the 1840s that Rankine was able to charge warehouse rent and was the only distiller so able to do at that time. Despite the considerable flow from Scotland's distilleries, Rosebank was in fact on allocation.

In 1894 it went public and Rosebank Distillery Ltd was formed with Rankine holding half the capital. A further issue of shares to the public in 1897 was immediately taken up. But in common with most other distilleries, Rosebank was shortly to face a period of difficulty and after several lean years became one of five companies which amalgamated in 1914 to form Scottish Malt Distillers Limited* and, thus, became part of DCL. The present licensing arrangement followed many years later. Rosebank is available bottled at 8 years old and with its dry, distinctive flavour is outstanding as a Lowland malt.

The Distillers Agency Ltd, in spite of its name, does not occupy a special position. It operates under the same terms of reference as other Scotch whisky blending companies in the DCL Group.

Brands

Highland Club	King George IV
Highland Nectar De Luxe	Rosebank 8 years old Single Malt

Distillers Company PLC

12 Torphichen Street, Edinburgh EH3 8YT

Distillers and blenders *Member of SWA*

Such are the extent and ramifications of the Distillers Company's activities in Scotch whisky, and so closely is its development entwined with the growth of the industry itself, that full scope has been given to the history of the company in the main part of the book, especially in Chapter 5.

Descriptions of the constituent member companies listed below appear under their respective entries in this chapter. The subsidiaries engaged in distilling are:

Scottish Grain Distillers Limited   Scottish Malt Distillers Limited

There is a wide range of blending and marketing companies, as follows:

Ainslie & Heilbron (Distillers) Ltd	John Haig & Co. Ltd
	J. & W. Hardie Ltd
John Begg Ltd	John & Robt. Harvey & Co. Ltd
Benmore Distilleries Ltd	John·Hopkins & Co. Ltd
John Bertram & Co. Ltd	Low, Robertson & Co. Ltd
John Bisset & Co. Ltd	W.P. Lowrie & Co. Ltd
Bulloch Lade & Co. Ltd	D. & J. McCullum Ltd
George Cowie & Sons Ltd	Macdonald Greenlees Ltd
John Crabbie & Co. Ltd	John McEwan & Co. Ltd
Craighall Bonding Co. Ltd	Macleay Duff (Distillers) Ltd
A. & A. Crawford Ltd	James Munro & Son Ltd
Daniel Crawford & Son Ltd	John Robertson & Son Ltd
Peter Dawson Ltd	Wm Sanderson & Son Ltd
John Dewar & Sons Ltd	Slater, Rodger & Co. Ltd
Distillers Agency Ltd	J. & G. Stewart Ltd
A. Ferguson & Co. Ltd	R.H. Thomson & Co. (Distillers) Ltd
Donald Fisher Ltd	John Walker & Sons Ltd
John Gillon & Co. Ltd	James Watson & Co. Ltd
Wm Greer & Co.	White Horse Distillers Ltd

Dolamore Limited

Waterloo House, 228-232 Waterloo Station Approach, London SE1 7BE

Wine and spirit merchants

One of London's most distinguished wine and spirit merchants who had traditionally had their own blends of Scotch whisky and who

211

have, in 1983, reverted to that tradition with a new 8 years old blend, Moncreiffe, the house brand of Sir Iain Moncreiffe of that Ilk, the Albany Herald, and a leading figure amongst the Scottish nobility. Dolamore are reported to have been James Buchanan's first customer for his blended whisky when he was desperately seeking outlets in London shortly after setting out in business on his own.

Brands

Bonnie Bairn†   Pride of the Highlands†
Moncreiffe

G.F. Donaldson

5 Fairlawn Close, Claygate, Surrey

Broker

M.J. Dowdeswell & Company Limited

Oldbury on Severn, Bristol BS12 1QA

Blenders and merchants

This West Country firm has two of the quaintest named brands of Scotch whisky on the market. According to the label of The Original Oldbury Sheep Dip, 'this whisky is much enjoyed by the Villagers of Oldbury on Severn'. The owner first started selling it in about 1974 in his own Free House. It is a well married vatted malt. The even odder Pig's Nose was introduced in 1977 and is a four year old blend. The label claims that 'in Gloucestershire 'tis said that our Scotch is as soft and smooth as a pig's nose!' Although no doubt originally aimed at a local clientele, these whiskies are becoming more widely available, especially in prestige outlets such as Fortnum and Mason. Both are blended and bottled in Scotland by George Morton Ltd.*

To sell Pig's Nose whisky, the purveyor is required to become a member of the Pig's Nose Club, for which a certificate is issued.

Brands

Pig's Nose 4 years old   Sheep Dip 8 years old Pure
                                       Malt (vatted)

Markets UK, USA, Canada and New Zealand.

The Drambuie Liqueur Company Limited

12 York Place, Edinburgh 1   *Member of SWA*

Scotch liqueur manufacturers

The story of Drambuie is one of commercial success mingled with legend and family tradition. If the legend is to be believed, Drambuie has a royal pedigree going back in the mists of time to the House of Stuart. Prince Charles Edward Stuart, Pretender to the throne of Great Britain, suffered a crushing defeat which put an end to his attempt to regain the crown for the Stuarts in the Jacobite Rebellion of 1745. Fleeing Government troops after his army had been put to flight, Bonnie Prince Charlie, as he was popularly known, headed for the Isle of Skye as a temporary refuge before returning to sanctuary in France. There he stayed with a Captain Mackinnon and as a token of his gratitude is alleged to have given the highlander the recipe for Drambuie, the Prince's personal liqueur. Drambuie is the contraction of the Gaelic phrase *an dram Buidheach* which means 'the drink that satisfies'. For over 150 years the Mackinnons kept the pleasure of Drambuie to themselves and a small circle of island acquaintances. Its introduction to the world at large was a slow process and began with the arrival in Edinburgh in 1906 of young Malcolm Mackinnon of the same Drambuie Mackinnons, and sole proprietor of the old established whisky firm of W. Macbeth and Son. Being in possession of the old family recipe, he decided to try it out on the public. Using jelly bags and copper pans, a week of effort produced the first dozen bottles of Drambuie. The Edwardians were conservative people in terms of new products, and despite its ancient origins, Mackinnon had sold only twelve cases in a year. But he persevered and as orders began to increase, Mackinnon undertook in 1910 the first major publicity campaign, explaining that he had remained faithful to the original recipe. Drambuie appeared in the messes of Scottish regiments during the First World War as an alternative to Cognac, and in 1916 it was ordered for the cellars of the House of Lords. The inter-war period saw great expansion for Drambuie and it became a world-wide after-dinner drink.

With the death of Malcolm Mackinnon in 1945, preparation of the secret recipe became the responsibility of his widow, Mrs Gena Mackinnon, and her brother, Mr W.A. Davidson, became Managing Director of the Company. The present Chairman and Managing Director is Norman Mackinnon, who carries on the preparation of the secret essence.

Since the Second World War, demand for Drambuie has grown enormously and after considerable expansion of the company's original premises at Leith, a new processing plant was established a few years ago at Kirkliston, a few miles outside Edinburgh. However, despite the application of modern production methods, Drambuie is still based on the ancient recipe involving the secret essence and a selection of the finest of mature whiskies.

Marketed throughout the world and exported to more than 150 countries, Drambuie is the biggest selling liqueur in the United Kingdom.

Although not strictly a whisky, Drambuie has a reputation which warrants its inclusion in this book. That apart, the company also has its own blends of Scotch whisky. Their whisky interests were given a fillip by the acquisition in 1981 of the long established Edinburgh wine and spirit merchants, Cockburn & Co. (Leith) Ltd,* and the reintroduction of John O'Groats, a De Luxe whisky, to the UK market in 1982.

There are two other subsidiary companies in the wine and spirit trade. One is Atkinson, Baldwin & Co. Ltd of London, and the other is Innes & Grieve Ltd of Edinburgh.

Brands

Drambuie Scotch Whisky
  Liqueur
Fulstrength Scots Whisky†

John O'Groats De Luxe
Macbeth†

(*Innes & Grieve Ltd*)
Dunedin
Midlothian
Piccadilly Club

Royal Prince
Scottish Nectar
Uam Var

Markets World-wide.

Duncan, Gilbey & Matheson International Limited

52 Charles Street, London W1X 8DT

Blenders and exporters
Brand Glenmark

Alfred Dunhill Limited

30 Duke Street, St James's, London SW1

Tobacco blenders and pipe manufacturers

The Dunhill name was originally associated with high quality tobacco products and pipes, then cigarette lighters and smokers requisites usually found in good class tobacconists, and finally, expensive boutique wares through their own network of nineteen shops world-wide. In 1982 the Dunhill appellation was extended to Scotch whisky with the appearance of Dunhill Finest Scotch whisky, a high priced, up-market blend put together by International Distillers & Vintners Ltd* and sold by the latter's subsidiary, Morgan Furze & Co. No age is given for the product since, at least when it first appeared, the range of ages of the component parts was considerable — from 8 (the youngest grain) to over 20 years (the oldest malt). Dunhill has two interesting features. Firstly, it is not cool-filtered and, secondly, it is sold in an attractive replica of a Victorian green bottle designed in 1845.

Brand   Dunhill Old Master 75°

Alexander Dunn & Company (Whisky Blenders) Limited

42 Walton Road, East Molesey, Surrey KT8 0DQ

At one time a subsidiary of Tomatin Distillers PLC,* Alexander Dunn now operates and is owned by Hesselberger Steeden Associates Ltd. They include amongst their products Slaintheva Scotch whisky, which involves the inscribing by hand of the recipient's name on the label of each bottle, which comes in standard size or Kingnums (1.75 litres). For advertising purposes, they also produce a mini-bottle containing 1/20 fl oz, which according to the Guinness Book of Records is the smallest sized bottle of whisky in the world.

Brand   Slaintheva 12 years old

Markets   Austria, Belgium, France, Italy, Japan, Netherlands, Switzerland, West Germany.

Eadie Cairns

12 Waterloo Street, Glasgow G2 6JX   *Member of SWA*

Distillers and blenders

Although involvement in whisky distilling is comparatively recent, Eadie Cairns has a pedigree in associated industries going back to 1859. Eadie Cairns was born of the amalgamation of two West of Scotland families who were prominent in the licensed trade in the second half of the nineteenth century. R.W. Cairns, a successful Glasgow publican, joined forces with a younger man, John Eadie, who belonged to a well-known brewing family. The partnership thrived and interests developed both in the licensed public house and in the whisky trade. Mr Cairns retired from the business just

Auchentoshan

before the First World War and complete control passed to Mr Eadie. He introduced a number of innovations in the running of the company and was active until his death in 1938. Ownership remained in the hands of Mr Eadie's children until, in 1956, his eldest daughter, Mrs Mary Mo Eadie Milne bought out the shares belonging to the rest of her family. She had, on the death of her father, become the Managing Director, and on assuming sole proprietorship in 1956 laid plans for considerable changes to the company. In 1958 her son, John Eadie Milne, became Chairman, and so the link with one of the two original partners was maintained.

After further development of the retail side, a bold step was taken by way of acquisition of Auchentoshan distillery from the brewers Bass Charrington. Badly damaged during the bombing of Glasgow in 1941, capacity at Auchentoshan, which is only ten miles from Glasgow, was a mere 175,000 proof gallons in 1969. It now stands at one million gallons annually. The distillery dates from the beginning of the last century and has had many owners. By the 1960s it was in the hands of the Scottish brewers J. & R. Tennent Ltd, who were taken over by Charringtons (later Bass Charringtons) in 1964.

216

Auchentoshan has two particular claims to distinction. It uses a triple distillation process by means of three separate stills, and it produces a Lowland malt, although the water used is drawn from the Highlands, coming as it does from Loch Cochno, just over the 'border' or 'Highland Line'. The fact that it is lightly peated and that a rather special method of mashing is employed at Auchentoshan no doubt also contribute to the whisky's distinctive nature. It was also one of the first Lowland malts to be available in bottle, as well as being used in the firm's own blended whiskies, particularly their famous Cairns. Auchentoshan is in great demand for use in the blends of other companies too. A large part of the company's whiskies is exported and the rest is sold through their own wholesale operation and locally through the company's own retail outlets. They also provide an 'own label' service to companies such as the Hediard chain of food and wine shops in Paris. Auchentoshan 12 years old is supplied to Nicolas Wines of Paris for similar 'own label' treatment.

Since 1981 Eadie Cairns has maintained an aggressive sales and marketing campaign spearheaded by Auchentoshan.

Brands

AD†	B.C.
Auchentoshan Single Malt 5 years old	Cairns
	Cairns 8 years old
Auchentoshan Pure Malt 8 years old	Glentoshan
	Highland Ben†
Auchentoshan Pure Malt 10 years old	Marie Stuart 12 years old De Luxe
Auchentoshan Single Malt 12 years old	National Choice 12 years old De Luxe
Barley Cream	One-O-One

Markets UK and 36 overseas markets, of which the most important are Spain, Italy, France, South Africa, Japan, USA, Australia, Belgium, Germany and Netherlands.

Eldridge, Pope & Company Limited

Dorchester Brewery, Weymouth Avenue, Dorchester, Dorset

Brewers and wine and spirit merchants

One of the larger regional brewers, with wine and spirit outlets and its own blend, Eldridge Pope have been filling and blending Scotch whisky since 1908. Their Old Highland Blend is one of the few whiskies which carries a statement on the label showing the single malt whiskies used in the blend, including Glen Grant, Glenrothes-

Glenlivet, Glenfarclas and Glenfiddich. The blend is said, in fact, to contain a very high proportion of malt whisky. Its quality is further assured by the use of freshly emptied sherry wood for the maturing process. This takes place in Scotland, but the final blending is done in the company's chalk cellars in Dorset.

Brand Old Highland Blend

Markets Dorset, Somerset, Hampshire and the South of England.

Ellis, Son and Vidler Limited
Wine and spirit merchants

57 Cambridge Street, London SW1V 4PS

Primarily a wine merchanting business, Ellis nevertheless have their own brand — Waverley is currently inactive — for the benefit of regular customers. Old Farm Whisky is blended and bottled for them in Scotland.

Brands   Old Farm (formerly The   Waverley†
             Pelham)

Markets London and Hastings.

El Vino Company Limited
1 Hare Place, Fleet Street, London EC4B 4TH
Merchants

These old established City wine and spirit merchants have been selling their own particular house brand of blended whisky continually since sometime between the formation of the company in 1879 and the end of the last century. They continue to do so today through the El Vino wine bars and retail off licence sales outlets. One of these wine bars is the renowned 'Old Wine Shades' in Martin Lane, which is preserved in the state of a London coffee shop of the seventeenth century. W. Brydon Ltd, a subsidiary company, also markets its own label blended whisky, but only intermittently.

Brands

(El Vino Co. Ltd)	*(W. Brydon Ltd)*
El Vino Connoisseurs Blend	Burncastle

Markets United Kingdom only.

John E. Fells & Sons Limited

56-58 Tooley Street, London SE1 2SZ

Blenders and merchants

This prominent London wine shipper and spirits merchant no longer markets its own whisky blends, but its subsidiary, Whigham Fergusson Ltd, *acquired in 1983, does.

Brands

Fells Glen†   Punchbowl†
Fifesay†   Stilmore†
Highland Cup†   Stirling†
Highland Malt (vatted)†   Unco Guid†
Kirkcudbright Punchbowl†

(Furze & Jones Ltd)
Extra Special†

A. Ferguson & Company Limited

Leconfield House, Curzon Street, London W1A 4PN

Blenders   *A subsidiary of Distillers Company PLC**

The company in its present form was established in 1977 to market a new low priced but full strength whisky, The Claymore. In the relatively short time is has been available it has enjoyed remarkable success. It sells for considerably less than Distillers' standard brands and, indeed, most other standard brands in the UK, and is mainly distributed through the off-licence trade.

Unlike many of the Distillers subsidiaries, A. Ferguson & Co. Ltd does not have any specific DCL distillery licensed to it.

Brands

Breadalbane†   Pedigree
The Claymore

Markets UK only.

The Fettercairn Distillery Company

Dalmore House, 296-8 St Vincent Street, Glasgow G2 5RG

Distillers   *A subsidiary of Whyte & Mackay Distillers Ltd**

Fettercairn was purchased jointly by Hay and MacLeod & Co.* and W. & S. Strong & Co.* in 1971. It is an interesting combination of one of the oldest Highland malt distilleries employing the most modern equipment. There is no record of the exact date of origin, but it is known that the present distillery was in production in 1824. It was operated by various private owners until 1887 when the Fettercairn Distillery Co. was formed with Sir John Gladstone, whose son was to become an outstanding Prime Minister of Great Britain, as its first Chairman. After a lengthy period of closure it became in 1939 the property of Associated Scottish Distillers Ltd on behalf of Train & McIntyre. Thereafter, Mr Tom Scott Sutherland, an Aberdeen businessman, became the owner until 1971. The distillery is situated close to the village of Fettercairn, a few miles from Stonehaven in Kincardineshire in a fertile area known as the Howe O' the Mearns. Water comes in abundance from the burns of the Grampian Mountains. The great bulk of production is used for blending, although Fettercairn has long been available in the bottle. Young, light and dry, it is no burden on the palate and has a nice, clean-cut bouquet. Capacity at the distillery is about 500,000 proof gallons.

Brands

Fettercairn 575 5 years old Highland Malt†	Old Fettercairn Single Highland Malt
Fettercairn 875 8 years old Highland Malt†	Old Fettercairn Single Highland Malt 8 years old

Markets In the United Kingdom in limited quantities, and in Italy and many export markets.

Findlater Mackie Todd & Company Limited

Windsor Avenue, Merton Abbey, London SW19 2SN

Blenders *Member of SWA*

Part of the Beecham Group Ltd since 1968, Findlater's whiskies are of long-standing reputation. The company has close links with the Invergordon Distillers Ltd,* which still act as suppliers. Findlater's Scotch whisky enjoys a pedigree going back to 1823, which is the year in which Alexander Findlater went into business as a wine and spirit merchant in Dublin. His knowledge of Scotch whisky had come via his father, an officer of the Customs and Excise for whom Robert Burns had worked.

The younger Alexander did well and entered into a variety of partnerships in different English cities. In 1850 he went to London and in 1863 Findlater Mackie Todd & Co. opened for business and were soon to become highly respected both as wine and spirit merchants and as proprietors of Findlater's Scotch whisky. Indeed, their whisky was one of the first to bear a label giving the name of the supplier. Findlater's have always attached importance to brand image, although their range of whiskies has varied over the years and has included Findlater's Old Liqueur, Findlater's Special Gold Medal, Findlater's Regency, Findlater's All Malt and Findlater's Auld Brig.

Brands

Findlater's 8 years old (De Luxe)

Findlater's 12 years old De Luxe

Findlater's 15 years old (De Luxe)

Findlater's Finest 5 years old

Findlater's Founders (De Luxe)

Findlater's 21 years old (De Luxe)

Mar Lodge 8 years old vatted malt

Markets UK and export to over eighty countries.

Fine Fare Limited

Gate House, Fretherne Road, Welwyn Garden City, Herts

Although a prominent national supermarket chain, Fine Fare Ltd is the dominant grocer in the north-east of Scotland and claims to be the largest liquor retailer in Speyside.

Brands	Fine Fare 5 years old	Strathallan
	Fine Fare 12 years old	
	Pure Malt (vatted)	

Donald Fisher Limited

11 Maritime Street, Edinburgh EH6 6SW   *Member of SWA*

Blenders and exporters   *A subsidiary of Distillers Company PLC**

The founder of the firm was a Donald Fisher, one of the pioneers of the Scotch whisky trade. Born in the Perthshire Highlands he moved to Edinburgh where he set up the business in 1836. The company was purchased outright by DCL in 1936. The handmade stone jar or flagon has been a feature of the company from its earliest days and has become the Donald Fisher 'image' throughout the world for the De Luxe blend Ye Whisky of Ye Monks.

Over the years a considerable export trade has been built up which was recognised when the company received the Queen's Award for Export Achievement in 1982.

| *Brands* | Ben Lawers † | Ye Monks |
| | Dew of Ben Lawers † | Ye Whisky of Ye Monks |

Markets Exclusively export, mainly South and Central America.

Fitzwilliam McCullagh & Company Limited

33 Fitzwilliam Square, Dublin 2

Wine and spirit merchants

Agents for Cutty Sark and Long John in Eire.

Brand   Muir MacKenzie

Fortnum and Mason Limited

181-184 Piccadilly, London W1A 1ER

Grocers and provision merchants

Perhaps the most famous food store in the world, Fortnum and Mason has served twelve reigns of British monarchs since its foundation in 1707. Always strong in wine and spirits, the company's house brand of Scotch whisky is now Choice Old. In 1977 the firm's Perfection Brand, made up of rather older whiskies, was added. Neither brand is advertised save in the Fortnum and Mason Christmas catalogue.

Brands

Choice Old   Red Seal†
Perfection (De Luxe)

L. Frumkin & Company Limited

66 Great Titchfield Street, London W1

Wine and spirit merchants

This company traditionally has its own blends, but these are not available at present.

Brands   Historian†   Vat 30†

George Gale & Company Limited

The Brewery, Horndean, Portsmouth, Hants PO8 0DA

Brewers and wine and spirit merchants

This is an independent brewer with wine and spirit interests, including its own blended whisky, which has been on the market for

222

over one hundred years. The individual whiskies, which include a high percentage of malts, making up the blend are sent by cask to London where they are blended. This whisky is broken down and bottled, and then sent to Gale's Horndean Brewery for distribution through their public houses.

The company in its present form was started in 1888. However, its origins go back over 250 years with the purchase of the Ship and Bell Public House in Horndean by the Gale family. The present Victorian-era brewery was constructed in 1869 but has been much enlarged and modernised over the years.

Brand   Gale's Blended Glenlivet

Market Central Southern England.

Gilbey Vintners Limited

Vintner House, River Way, Harlow, Essex

Distillers and blenders   *A subsidiary of International*
                                              Distillers & Vintners Ltd*

This firm traces its origins to 1857 when the two Gilbey brothers, Walter and Alfred, set up as wine merchants and then gin distillers in London. Subsequently, the firm realised the potential of Scotch whisky and entered the industry by acquiring distilleries and buying up smaller whisky companies such as James Catto & Co. Ltd.* The Gilbey companies eventually merged with United Wine Traders Ltd to form International Distillers & Vintners Ltd* in 1962. As well as a number of subsidiary companies owning their own whisky brands, Gilbeys brought to this marriage the highland malt distilleries of Glen Spey-Glenlivet at Rothes in Morayshire and Knockando and Strathmill, although the latter two are now licensed to Justerini & Brooks Ltd.* The original owner and constructor of Glen Spey was James Stuart, who saw it into production under its original name of the Mills of Rothes in 1885, only to sell it to Gilbey's two years later. The original intention of James Stuart appears to have been to mill cereals, but he may have found distilling more profitable and thus converted the plant. In 1958 IDV Ltd set up a new subsidiary, Glen Spey Ltd, to market Spey Royal, a blend which draws heavily on the Glen Spey malt. The latter is not currently available as a single malt, but could conceivably come back on the market. There is, however, a vatted malt, Strathspey, which no doubt relies heavily on the Glen Spey product. It should not be confused with the Old Strathspey Distillery which was the forerunner to Dalwhinnie. Current capacity of Glen Spey is 750,000 proof gallons.

Gilbeys have wide overseas interests having established their own

223

plants in Canada and Australia for the production of purely local whiskies. Their Australian subsidiary today produces the Australian whiskies Bond 7 and Milnes Gilt Edge. Spey Royal is exported in bulk to the US for bottling there to be sold under its own name.

Brands

(Gilbey Vintners Ltd)
Abergeldie†

(D. Cameron & Co. Ltd)
Old Fedcal   Shooting Lodge

(Glen Spey Ltd)
Spey Royal   Spey Royal 8 years old (USA only)

(Andrew Laing & Co. Ltd)
Glenrosa†   Scot Royal†
Glenside

(Morgan Furze & Co. Ltd)
Strathspey Vatted Malt

Markets There is penetration of a wide variety of overseas markets for the bottled blends.

A. Gillies & Company (Distillers) Limited

4 Newton Place, Glasgow C3

Distillers and blenders   *A subsidiary of Amalgamated Distilled Products PLC**

This is the principal whisky company in the ADP group, having been taken over by the latter in 1970. Gillies had themselves in 1955 acquired Glen Scotia Distillery, one of the only two surviving Campbeltown distilleries. The distillery was established by the Galbraiths in 1832. One of its earlier owners, a certain McCullum, drowned himself in the nearby loch on realising that he had been done out of a large sum of money by swindlers whom he met on a sea-cruise. His ghost is supposed still to haunt the distillery. Although much of the distillery's production goes for blending, what is left is bottled as a single malt at 75°. Best described as robust and peaty, some people would say that it has something of the Irish in its composition. The company's De Luxe blended whisky, Scotia Royale 12 years old, is one of the main brands of the ADP group, with prominent sales in Japan and USA.

Brands

Glen Scotia 5 years old malt	Old Governor†
Glen Scotia 8 years old malt	Old Worthy†
Old Court†	Royal Culross 8 years old
Old Court 8 years old	(vatted malt)
Old Court 12 years old	Scotia Royale 12 years old
	(De Luxe)

Markets Blends principally for export, especially the United States. Glen Scotia is available in Campbeltown and Glasgow.

William Gillies & Company Limited

243 St Vincent Street, Glasgow G2 5RF

Merchants

Brands   Glendarroch 10 years old   Sma' Still

John Gillon & Company Limited

5 Oswald Street, Glasgow G1 4QU   *Member of SWA*

Distillers, blenders and bottlers   *A subsidiary of Distillers Company PLC**

Another of the smaller DCL companies, John Gillon and Co. Ltd is now a subsidiary of Ainslie & Heilbron (Distillers) Ltd,* the two having been parts of Macdonald, Greenlees and Williams (Distillers) Ltd which was acquired by DCL in 1925.

Today John Gillon and Co. Ltd is best known as licensee of Glenury-Royal Distillery, situated on the north bank of the River Cowie a little way out of Stonehaven in what was Kincardineshire.

The name of the distillery is taken from the district of Ury and the glen which runs through it. The distillery was built by Captain Robert Barclay, a local farmer of much distinction and MP for Kincardine. He was an outstanding athlete and became famous for his marathon walks.

Interest in Glenury lapsed with Barclay's death in 1854 and shortly thereafter it became the property of the Glasgow firm William Ritchie & Co., who remained in control until it was sold in 1937 to Glenury Distillery Ltd. The following year it was resold to Associated Scottish Distilleries Ltd, a subsidiary of Train and McIntyre Ltd. The acquisition of the latter by DCL in 1953 brought under DCL control both the distillery and Associated Scottish Distilleries Ltd, and shortly thereafter the distillery was licensed to John Gillon & Co. Ltd. Mainly a blender's whisky, the firm nevertheless bottles it at 12 years,

The firm's origins go back to 1817, when it was set up by Sir John Gillon of Linlithgow.

Brands

Gillon's 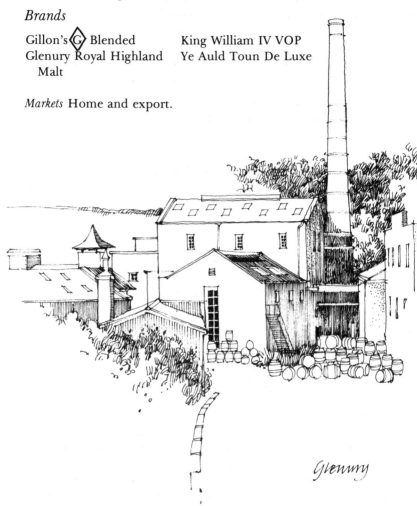 Blended   King William IV VOP
Glenury Royal Highland   Ye Auld Toun De Luxe
  Malt

Markets Home and export.

Giordano Limited

38-40 Windmill Street, London W1P 2BE

Wine and spirit merchants

This company was established in 1927.

Brand

Aberfeldie Club

Glenallachie Distillery Company Limited

Aberlour, Banffshire AB3 9LR

Distillers *A subsidiary of The Waverley Group Ltd**

Glenallachie is a comparatively recent distillery, and production began in 1968. The distillery was designed by Delmé Evans, as were those at Tullibardine and Isle of Jura. Although the product is used mainly in blending particularly in Mackinlay's Legacy and Finest Old Scotch Whisky, it has recently become available as a single malt and was put on the export market for the first time in 1982.

Brand Glenallachie Glenlivet 12 years old Highland Malt

Markets Limited supplies for export.

Glen Burn Blenders Limited

132 Golders Green Road, London NW11 8HB

Blenders, exporters and brokers

This company blends, bottles and exports a wide range of whiskies to a variety of countries. It also deals in bulk and is one of the biggest bulk exporters to France either for bottling under the Glen Burn labels or under local labels. When the company began business in 1975 it was mainly as brokers, but it has expanded considerably since then in the other fields.

Brands

Capson	Highland Baron
Congratulations	Och Aye
Contraband	Polo Club
GB	Reunion
Glen Burn	Rossmore Abbey
Gold Label	Scots Piper
Greatness (vatted malt)	

Glen Catrine Bonded Warehouse Limited

Laigh Road, Catrine, Strathclyde KA5 6SO

Blenders and bottlers

Apart from providing the usual bonded warehouse facilities, this company has its own blends

Brands	High Commissioner	Clansman
	Scots Earl	Glen Catrine

Glen Garioch Whisky Company Limited

13 Royal Crescent, Glasgow G3 7SU

Distillers   *An associate company of Stanley P. Morrison Ltd**

The Glen Garioch (pronounced Glen Geerie) Distillery is to be found in the village of Old Meldrum in Aberdeenshire, about twenty miles to the north of Aberdeen itself. It dates back to 1797 and has had a number of owners during its history, including J.F. Thomson & Co. of Leith and William Sanderson & Son Ltd,* who eventually brought it into the DCL empire. However, it was never fully expolited by them. The site was not considered satisfactory from the point of view of water supply and chronic shortages led to the distillery being closed in 1968. It was sold to Stanley P. Morrison Ltd two years later. They had better luck and uncovered a new source of water by digging a deep well in a neighbouring field. Distilling was soon under way again and in 1973 a new wash still was brought in. Apart from that, the distillery retains much of its originality, right down to doing its own malting, although this is now insufficient to meet the requirements of a much expanded output. Peat comes from the New Pitsligo Moss, about ten miles away. Production had reached 500,000 gallons by 1973, a far cry from the 140,000 gallon capacity known during the previous ownership. For the first time in its history, Glen Garioch is being bottled as a single Highland Malt, and being characteristic in taste and aroma is an ideal whisky with which to begin the single malt habit.

An interesting innovation at Glen Garioch is the erection in the grounds of glass houses for the cultivation of tomatoes and other hot-house fruit and vegetables, the heating coming from the waste heat of the distillery.

Brand   The Glen Garioch Single Malt

Markets Available in limited quantities in the United Kingdom.

Glenguid Limited

100 Wellington Street, Glasgow G2 6DJ

Blenders and exporters

This company was formed in 1961, originally as McCaffery & Son (Whisky) Ltd, on behalf of the Cinzano Group, the Italian vermouth manufacturers. The Cinzano connection gives the firm good export openings for its whiskies in Italy and elsewhere in Western Europe.

Brands   Archer's   Red Archer
           Black Archer

Glen Keith-Glenlivet Distillery Company Limited

Keith, Banffshire   *Member of SWA*

Distillers   *A subsidiary of Seagram Distillers PLC**

The distillery was built by Seagram's on the site of a meal mill which they bought from the Angus Milling Co. Ltd in 1957, on the opposite bank of the River Isla from their Strathisla-Glenlivet Distillery. It went into production at the end of 1958, after most of the original mill buildings had been demolished and rebuilt. Glen Keith-Glenlivet was the first distillery in Scotland to employ gas fired stills instead of the traditional coal fired method. It gets water from Newmill Spring and peat from Knockando. All production at Glen Keith is used for blending.

Brand   Natu Nobilis   *Markets* North America

The Glenlivet and Glen Grant Distilleries Limited

45 Frederick Street, Edinburgh

Distillers   *A subsidiary of The Glenlivet Distillers Ltd**

This firm was formed as a limited company in 1952 by the coming together of George and J.G. Smith Ltd* of Glenlivet fame and the equally illustrious J. & J. Grant,* Glen Grant Distillery. The aims of the new company were to uphold the quality and good name of their original products, whilst taking advantage of the merger to promote The Glenlivet and Glen Grant to further commercial success. This act was in essence the amalgamation of two family concerns. And so matters remained until 1970 and the formation of The Glenlivet Distillers Ltd,* bringing together in logical fashion the great malt whisky-producing traditions of the Highlands with the canny marketing expertise of the Lowlands. However, The Glenlivet and Glen Grant Distilleries Ltd continues in existence as a production company within the group.

The Glenlivet Distillers Limited

45 Frederick Street, Edinburgh   *Member of SWA*

Distillers and blenders   *A subsidiary of Seagram Distillers PLC**

Although by no means near the top in size, The Glenlivet Distillers Ltd is certainly right at the top of the league in quality, owning five Highland malt distilleries, two of which — Glenlivet and Glen Grant — are widely considered to produce amongst the best malt

229

whiskies in the land.

This high-quality whisky-producing group was formed in 1970 through the amalgamation of the Glenlivet and Glen Grant Distilleries Ltd with the blending concern of Hill, Thomson and Co. Ltd and Longmorn-Glenlivet Distilleries Ltd. The former company was itself the result of the marriage of two old distilling companies, George and J.G. Smith Ltd and J. & J. Grant, Glen Grant Ltd, in 1952. In 1970, the name The Glenlivet Distillers Ltd was adopted as the group name.

The present structure of the company, which operates through its various subsidiaries, is as follows:

Caperdonich Distillery Co. Ltd*
The Glenlivet and Glen Grant
Distilleries Ltd*
J. & J. Grant, Glen Grant Ltd* } production companies
The Longmorn Distilleries Ltd*
George and J.G. Smith Ltd*

Hill, Thomson & Co. Ltd*   marketing company for blends

The Glenlivet Whisky Co. Ltd   sales of bottled malts
Glen Grant Whisky Co. Ltd

The Glenlivet and Glen Grant   sales of new whisky and
Agencies Ltd   brokerage

Hudson's Bay Co. of Scotland
Ltd
Lawson & Smith Ltd
Moray Bonding Co. Ltd
Murrayfield Vatting Co. Ltd   } subsidiaries of Hill,
Seafield Blending Co. Ltd   Thomson & Co. Ltd
J.M. Tulloch & Co. Ltd
Turner & Nicol Ltd

Almost immediately after its formation, the group engaged in a concentrated three years of heavy investment in its five distilleries, in its bottling and blending plant at Newbridge near Edinburgh and in two by-product plants of which it owns a substantial share. This led to an increase in distilling capacity of 58 per cent.

Whilst the original family interest in the component companies was for long reflected in the management of The Glenlivet Distillers Ltd, there were two substantial outside shareholders — Courage Ltd, the brewing concern, with 27 per cent, and Suntory Ltd, the leading Japanese distilling company, with over 11 per cent. Suntory's interest no doubt reflected the sizeable quantities of bulk malt which the company was exporting to Japan. However, in 1978 The Glenlivet Distilleries was purchased by Seagram Distillers Ltd.

The Glenmorangie Distillery Company

Tain, Ross-shire

Distillers   *A branch of Macdonald & Muir Ltd**

Although the existing distillery's foundations were laid in 1843, distilling of the illegal variety at Glenmorangie goes back as far as 1738. Indeed, its site, overlooking the Dornoch Firth, is believed to have been used for brewing and distilling since the Middle Ages.

The distillery takes its name from the Morangie Burn in whose glen it lies. From the same source as used by the distillery today, a mineral-rich spring, brewers had drawn water with which to make a fine ale, whose reputation stood high in the area as far as Inverness. Thus inspired, the Matheson brothers converted the original brewery into a distillery to begin production in 1843 at an estimated annual level of 20,000 gallons. William Matheson undertook major reconstruction forty years later. In 1893 the distillery was linked to the main railway line by a private siding. Among other things, this facilitated delivery of local peat from Dunreay until supplies there were exhausted.

Glenmorangie pioneered the use of steam coils in its stills for separating the alcohol and the wash, a system followed subsequently by a number of other Highland Malt distilleries since it avoided scorching the liquid, and thus impairing the whisky's flavour. The distillery was purchased outright in 1918 by Macdonald & Muir Ltd* and soon made an important contribution to that company's subsequent rise to prominence in many world markets for Scotch whisky.

The distillery's output is now about 600,000 gallons per annum and nearly all of it is bottled at ten years maturation. It is a surprisingly light and fragrant whisky for a Highland Malt, which may have contributed to its wide-spread popularity, making it one of the best known single malts available. The product is matured in traditional distillery warehouses on the premises and is marketed by Macdonald & Muir Ltd.

Brand

Glenmorangie 10 years old Single Highland Malt

Markets Principally the UK, but also a large number of overseas countries.

The Glen Moray-Glenlivet Distillery Company

Elgin, Morayshire

Distillers　　　　　　　　*A branch of Macdonald & Muir Ltd**

Distilling got under way near the town of Elgin in 1897 on a site which had earlier accommodated the West Brewery, once owned by Henry Arnot & Co. Little is known of the early management of the distillery, which was purchased by Macdonald & Muir Ltd in 1920 after a lengthy period of closure. Considerable expansion of the premises was undertaken in 1958 and the distillery now realises an annual production of about 700,000 gallons.

Much of the production goes to blending, but an increasing amount is kept aside for bottling at 8, 10 and 12 years old. Altogether light for a Highland malt but clean and fresh on both palate and nose.

Brands

Glen Moray-Glenlivet 8
　years old Highland Malt
Glen Moray-Glenlivet 10
　years old Highland Malt

Glen Moray-Glenlivet 12
　years old Highland Malt
Glen Moray '93

Glenmoriston Estates Limited

Glenmoriston, Nr Inverness IV3 6YA

Blenders and exporters

This is an example of a company with other interests engaging in the marketing and export of a good quality blended whisky. More than 40 per cent of the blend is Spey malts over 5 years old.

Brand　　Glenmoriston Old Farm

Glenrothes-Glenlivet Limited

106 West Nile Street, Glasgow G1 2QY

Distillers　　　　　*A subsidiary of The Highland Distilleries Co. PLC**

Glenrothes-Glenlivet has been a popular malt for decades and has been bottled at a variety of strengths by various whisky merchants in Scotland. It is generally available today at 8 years old, bottled by Gordon & MacPhail, and as such was found by a distinguished tasting panel to possess 'a good fruity nose with a dryish, well rounded flavour'.

The distillery was built in 1878 by a syndicate of local businessmen and began production the following year; in 1887 it combined with the Islay Distillery Co. to emerge as the Highland Distilleries Co. Ltd. The original site was that of an old sawmill, but there are now no traces of that and, indeed, much of the original distillery edifice has disappeared as the result of extensive rebuilding. The recently completed new still-house boasts two new pairs of stills giving Glenrothes a total capacity of about 5.3 million litres of alcohol.

Brand   Glenrothes-Glenlivet 8 years old Highland Single Malt

Glen Talla Limited

Woodside Castle, Beith, KA15 2HZ

Blenders and merchants

Brands

Coachman	Tayside
Glen Stag	Tayside 12 years old
Glen Talla 5 years old Malt (vatted)	Tayside 21 years old

Glenturret Distillery Limited

Glenturret, Crieff, Perthshire PH7 4HA

Distillers   *A subsidiary of Cointreau S.A.*

Glenturret must be the nearest thing to a one-man distillery in Scotland today. Certainly that is the impression one has from a visit there, where the Managing Director and Distiller, Mr James Fairlie, is obviously involved to a hectic degree in every facet of the distillery's activities. Yet this hive of personal enterprise in no way disturbs the cool serenity of Glenturret, the beautiful valley through which the River Turret winds and on whose left bank the distillery stands. Mr Fairlie, a noted authority on distilling, is in fact assisted by a tiny staff, but the emphasis is on smallness and informality, as demonstrated by the size of the stills. However, a programme of canny expansion has seen the distillery's capacity increase gradually from about 73,000 gallons in 1964 to 175,000 gallons in 1977, with a projected capacity of 375,000 gallons following considerable extension to the still-house in 1976.

In 1981 Glenturret Distillery Ltd became a subsidiary of the French liqueur manufacturers, Cointreau, as part of the latter's diversification programme.

But Glenturret did not begin with James Fairlie, although he was,

233

in effect, responsible for its re-birth. Glenturret is in fact the second oldest distillery in Scotland. Its date of establishment is 1775, although the local parish records reveal that illicit distilling had been going on well before then on the site of the present distillery. It was a natural choice for such endeavours, for apart from enjoying an excellent supply of suitable water, it nestles between two hills which in those days provided good vantage points from which the arrival of the militia or excisemen could be observed.

Glenturret had a succession of owners during the nineteenth century, the most prominent being, perhaps, Thomas Stewart, a landowner in the Crieff area. The distillery closed in 1914 to re-open in 1919, by then under the ownership of Mitchell Brothers Ltd.* However, they decided to shut down production in 1921 and used Glenturret purely for storage purposes. But the depression years were hitting Scotch whisky perhaps even more than most industries in Britain, and so the distillery was sold in 1928, the equipment having been removed in 1923, to the adjacent landowners, the Murrays of Ochtertyre, who in turn used the premises for warehousing.

By the time Fairlie appeared on the scene as the new owner of Glenturret in 1959, no distilling had taken place there for almost forty years. Some of the existing buildings were pressed into service, but many adjustments and additions had to be made. New warehouses had to be constructed, and since 1963 six have been put up along the public road outside the distillery proper. The entire operation was planned and supervised by Mr Fairlie himself and one of the most pleasing results is that the uninitiated eye can scarcely distinguish as between new and old in the outward appearance of the buildings, which while spruce and freshly painted, nevertheless retain a certain solidness from an earlier period. The distillery welcomes visitors and has guided tours; there is a distilling shop on the premises.

As for the product of all this energy, Glenturret Highland Malt was awarded the Gold Seal in 1974 for the best bottled matured malt whisky under 12 years old in the International Wines and Spirit Competition. It is available at 8 and 12 years old. But as 89 per cent of production is sold into blending, the amount of Glenturret available in bottle can be no more than a few thousand cases per annum.

Brands

Glenturret 8 years old	Glenturret 12 years old
Highland Malt 75°	Highland Malt 80°

Markets UK, France, USA, Germany, Australia.

234

Matthew Gloag & Son Limited

Bordeaux House, 33 Kinnoull Street, Perth PH1 5EU

Member of SWA

Blenders and wine and spirit merchants   *A subsidiary of the Highland Distilleries Co. PLC*

This family firm of Perth whisky merchants, which dates from 1800, was taken over in 1970 by Highland Distilleries, who set out to promote The Famous Grouse, Gloag's long-standing blend, as a major brand, firstly throughout Scotland and then in the rest of Britain. There was already a considerable base from which to work, and so successful were the marketing tactics that Grouse became at one point the fastest growing whisky in Britain in terms of sales, and often sells at a premium over other standard brands.

At the time of Highland's take-over, sales of the Grouse were about 90,000 cases; by 1979 this had expanded to over one million and it now contests with Bells for first place in the prized Scottish market with well over 20 per cent of the total. Greater attention is also being paid to export markets.

The genesis of The Famous Grouse as a brand was the adoption in 1897 of the grouse, Scotland's most famous game bird, as the house symbol or motif for Gloag's whisky, which was known as The Grouse Brand. As its popularity grew in and around Perth it was increasingly referred to as 'The Famous Grouse' until that was eventually adopted as the registered brand name.

The Gloags had been in whisky for many years prior to this. The founder of the company, Matthew, had started business in a modest way in 1800 as a grocer and wine merchant in Perth. He soon included whisky in his wares, buying directly from the numerous Highland distilleries and building up a reputation in both whiskies and wines.

He was succeeded in 1860 by his son, William B. Gloag, who in turn was succeeded by his brother Matthew in 1896. At some point during William's stewardship the firm must have turned to blending, and by 1910, when the firm passed to Matthew 'Willie' Gloag, this was their major activity. The new owner did much to spread knowledge and appreciation of The Famous Grouse both in England and abroad, and by 1935 a bonded warehouse and bottling plant had been added to the Gloag estate.

On Willie's death in 1947, his son Matthew Frederick Gloag took over and encouraged expansion in the home and export trades. His son Matthew I. Gloag joined the company in 1967, and remains a director following Highland Distilleries' acquisition in 1970.

A recent limerick competition promoted by the company produced the following amusing result as first prize winner:

When they say that *The Times* is to end,
How the gloom and forebodings descend,
To my study I shrink,
Famous Grouse is my drink,
For the worst takes the best to amend.

Brands

Brig O'Perth†	Perth Royal†
The Famous Grouse	Rare Old Liqueur†
Gowrie House†	Torrabeg

Markets UK, plus some fifty export markets of which the most important are Australasia, USA, Italy, France, West Germany, the Middle East, Japan and Southern Africa.

Golden Mist Limited

157 Commercial Street, London E1 6BJ

Blenders

Brand   Golden Mist

Gordon & MacPhail

58-60 South Street, Elgin IV30 1JY

Blenders and whisky merchants

'Italian warehousemen' was the term once used to describe high-class grocers who tempted the palates of their customers with all manner of exotic delicacies imported from distant Europe, as well as the more traditional British comestibles. Thus, to serve the good people of Elgin and the surrounding districts, a wholesale/retail warehouse was opened in 1895 under the partnership of the two families whose names are still linked to this day as a mark of high quality and excellent service. On formation, a young man, John Urquhart, joined the business to assist one of the partners, James Gordon, in the wholesale operations and with the whisky side of the business which was gradually growing. This involved blending and bottling under the firm's own labels and dealing in mature malt whiskies. This was a natural development for an Elgin grocer, given the proximity of the town to the very heart of the finest whisky country. James Gordon had already been active as a whisky broker and it is likely that he had interests in some of the nearby distilleries.

Gordon & MacPhail's initial excursions into whisky were concerned mainly with supplying the local trade, although some of the small shops and inns continued to get their whisky by the jar directly from the distilleries of the area. There is no accurate record as to when the firm embarked upon blending and bottling, but they were advertising their Moray Brand Old Highland Liqueur Scotch Whisky in the London magazine *Today* in 1896, which was, incidentally, then edited by Jerome K. Jerome. The price quoted at that time was 45 shillings per dozen bottles delivered in London.. They had commenced to export before the outbreak of World War I, but used in-bond bottling facilities in Glasgow as the size of their trade did not justify having their own bonded warehouse. Like so many others, they looked west and the bulk of their exports went to South America.

Eventually, ownership of Gordon & MacPhail passed to the Urquharts and the firm remains a family concern under their exclusive control. The Urquharts encouraged the whisky aspects of the business, although exporting came to a halt during World War II. They recommenced after the war and for over twenty years, in association with Grant Bonding Co. Ltd, which is now dormant, exported Gordon & MacPhail's brands along with J. & G. Grant's* Glenfarclas Malt. However, with the further development of business, both companies now export direct.

Apart from the blending of their own brands and their role in promoting Grant's Glenfarclas, Gordon & MacPhail are noted as general whisky merchants specialising in fine Highland malts. Their overseas trade is extensive, but the fact that they have remained basically a small informal operation has led to their being asked on occasion to fulfil some very individual orders. By way of example, they made up special blends for two famous Scottish regiments, the King's Own Scottish Borderers and the Royal Highland Fusiliers, and provide bottled blends and vatted malts for the exclusive use of hotels and clubs under their own private labels. These 'private' whiskies have found their way to foreign parts as well, and a blend was once made up for a yacht club in Borneo. For the Queen's Silver Jubilee, they undertook the bottling and special labelling of some of Scotland's best malts of 25 years' maturity, and also made up a special blend to celebrate the bicentenary of the town of Fochabers in 1976. In keeping with this tradition, the company prepared three special vattings of Highland malt whiskies to commemorate the marriage of the Prince of Wales to Lady Diana Spencer. The whiskies chosen were Glenburgie, Glen Grant and Strathisla. Each was a vatting of whiskies distilled in 1948 and 1961, the years of birth of Prince Charles and Lady Diana.

On the retail side, Gordon & MacPhail's shop in Elgin must have one of the most extensive arrays of whiskies anywhere and they include in their stocks bottled malts laid down as early as 1936, although supplies of such rarities are now extremely limited. Here are some of their very scarce whiskies, available in bottle from probably no other source:

70° (40% vol) Glen Grant 21, 25 and 45 years old
100° (57% vol) Glen Grant 10 and 15 years old
70° (40% vol) George & J.G. Smith's Glenlivet 15 years old,
  25 years old and distilled 1938/1940
100° (57° vol) George & J.G. Smith's Glenlivet 15 years old
70° (40% vol) Strathisla 25, 30 and 35 years old
70° (40% vol) Mortlach distilled 1936 and 1938
70° (40% vol) Linkwood distilled 1938 and 1939

They also have a range of forty-eight different bottled single malts marketed under their own label, known as Connoisseur's Choice. There are a number of associated companies, including Speymalt Whisky Distributors Ltd, which also specialises in miniatures.

Brands

Ben Alder
Connoisseur's Choice
  (Single malts)
Dunkeld Atholl Brose Scotch
  Whisky Liqueur
Glen Calder
Highland Fusilier 5 years old
Highland Fusilier 8 years old
Highland Fusilier 15 years
  old
Highland Fusilier 21 years
  old Special Tercentenary
Highland Fusilier 25 years
  old
MacPhail's Pure Malt

Moray Brand Special
  Liqueur†

Old Elgin Malt (vatted malt
  distilled in Elgin and district)
Pride of Islay 12 years old
  (vatted malt)
Pride of the Lowlands 12 years
  old (vatted malt)
Pride of Orkney 12 years old
  (vatted malt)
Pride of Strathspey 12 years
  old (vatted malt)
Pride of Strathspey 25 years
  old (vatted malt)
Pride of Strathspey Distilled
  1938/40 (vatted malt)
Spey Cast De Luxe
Strathavon†

(Avonside Whisky Ltd)
Avonside (70° and 100°)

(James Gordon & Co.)
Clan Blend
Glenavon†

James Gordon's Blend 8 years
  old

Luis Gordon & Sons Limited

18 Dartmouth Street, London SW1H 9BL

Wine and spirit merchants

This is a highly regarded firm of London wine shippers whose own whisky brands are currently dormant. The company, however, has a 45 per cent stake in Ronald Morrison & Co. Ltd,* manufacturers of Glayva Scotch whisky liqueur.

Brands   Gleesdale†   Crown Special†

Grant & Levine (Scotch Whisky Merchants) Limited

9 Castleton Drive, Newton Mearns, Glasgow G77 5JU

Brokers

James Grant & Company (Highland Park Distillery) Limited

106 West Nile Street, Glasgow G1 2QY   *Member of SWA*

Distillers   *A subsidiary of the Highland Distilleries Co. PLC* *

James Grant became sole proprietor of Highland Park Distillery in 1895, it having been built as early as 1798 on the site used by a well known illicit distiller, Magnus Eunson. His position as an officer of the church provided him with good cover, but he nonetheless attracted the attention of the Excise officers and took to hiding the kegs of whisky under his pulpit. Highland Park Distillery's history during the intervening period is vague, but James Grant became managing partner in 1888 — a few years prior to taking over exclusive control — bringing with him the traditions of Glenlivet where his father had been distiller and manager of the Glenlivet Distillery. The Grants relinquished control to Highland Distilleries in 1937.

Highland Park is unique in that it is built on a hill, thus requiring its water supply to be pumped up to it.

Highland Park's location on the island of Orkney makes it the most northern of all Scotland's distilleries. It retains much that is original and traditional, including the same floor maltings as were first installed, peat cut from its own peat beds, two traditional peat-fired kilns, and water from two local springs. The local Orkney peat has a distinctive aroma which is reflected in the flavour of the whisky. This is also influenced by the heather which is burned in small

239

quantities with the peat. The result is a tangy whisky with under-currents of sweetness.

It is bottled by the distillers themselves at 12 years old and at a variety of ages and strengths by Gordon & MacPhail.*

Brands

Highland Park 12 years old   St Magnus†
Highland Single Malt

J. & G. Grant

Glenfarclas-Glenlivet Distillery, Marypark, Ballindalloch AB3 9BD

Distillers   *Member of SWA*

Dating back, as it does, to 1836 when it was built by Mr Robert Hay, Glenfarclas has had one of the longest unbroken records of legal distilling in Scotland under the careful guidance, since 1865, of five generations of the Grant family. It is today one of the few distilleries left in private ownership and goes out of its way to welcome the casual visitor. However, John Grant, who purchased the distillery from its original owner, immediately sub-let it to John Smith, a brewer at Glenlivet Distillery whose whisky, The Glenlivet, had by then established for itself an enviable reputation in the area. This association led to the Grant's distillery being renamed Glenfarclas-Glenlivet, and full direct Grant management took effect in 1870. Renovations and improvements were put in hand in 1896 which raised production to almost 300,000 proof gallons per annum. Capacity remained at this level until 1960 when far-reaching improvements were introduced, thus doubling capacity. Further improvements have put this within the million proof gallon mark.

It is worth recording the unbroken line of Grants who have owned and managed Glenfarclas for over 100 years. The original John Grant's involvement in the distillery diminished as management was put increasingly into the hands of his son George. However, the latter out-lived his father by scarcely a year and on his death in 1890, his wife assumed complete control of the business — a formidable task for a woman in those days — until their sons, John and George, were able to step into the harness, which they did in 1895. In that year they formed on an equal share basis the Glenfarclas-Glenlivet Distillery Co. Ltd with the ill-fated Leith blenders Pattison, Elder & Co. On Pattison's failure in 1898, the Grant family took over full responsibility for Glenfarclas. John Grant retired from the partner-ship with the First World War. Thereafter, George Grant remained sole proprietor until 1947 and the formation of J. & G. Grant Ltd as a private limited company. During this time George Grant had expanded his interests beyond distilling into farming and created the now celebrated Glenfarclas Distillery's Aberdeen-Angus pedigree herd. On his death in 1949, the distillery passed to his sons George Scott Grant and John P. Grant. The latter died in 1960.

Glenfarclas Distillery — which has reverted to its original name on dropping the Glenlivet from its title — makes a particularly interesting visit as the company has made a special effort to make the distillery accessible to outsiders. The setting is attractive in a fifteen acre site in Inveravon Parish and there are various displays of historical and technical interest. Moreover, Glenfarclas has the biggest pot-stills in Speyside and the overall scale of the operation makes the distilling process easier to comprehend than might be the case by visiting one of the smaller, less well laid-out distilleries.

Although 95 per cent of Glenfarclas goes for blending, it is in fact one of the better known bottled Highland Malts. Exports of Glenfarclas are handled by J. & G. Grant (Int.) Ltd. It is available at 70°, 80° and 105° proof (40%, 46% and 60%). A worthy dram at whatever age or strength; dry and mature in taste and aroma.

Brands

Glenfarclas 5 years old All Malt

Glenfarclas 8 years old All Malt

Glenfarclas 12 years old All Malt (export only)

Glenfarclas 15 years old All Malt

Markets UK for 8 and 15 years old. Italy for 5 years old. 12 and 15 years old for other export markets. Exported in bulk to Sweden.

J. & J. Grant, Glen Grant Limited

45 Frederick Street, Edinburgh   *Member of SWA*

Distillers   *A subsidiary of The Glenlivet Distillers Ltd**

In 1840 an Elgin Lawyer, James Grant, went into partnership with his younger brother John to lay the foundations of one of the most successful distilling operations in Scotland. They chose a site on the banks of the Glen Grant Burn near the village of Rothes. Expansion became the order of the day and production soon stood at 40,000 gallons per annum.

The advent of the railway, due much to the encouragement of the Grants, contributed to the prosperity of their distillery which was flourishing by the time Major James Grant succeeded his father at the helm of the business on the latter's death in 1872. He was inspired to put up another distillery adjacent to the original and in 1897 Glen Grant No. 2 came into production across the road from the first Glen Grant, the two being connected by a pipe. Thus the whiskies were mixed and the product of both stills were Glen Grant, rather than being two distinct malts. However, this venture was short-lived and No. 2 was closed down in 1901 following the Pattison crash. But James Grant's original ambitions were never entirely forgotten, and No. 2 distillery was rebuilt and renamed in 1965 under the Caperdonich Distillery Co. Ltd.* The name of the re-vamped distillery was very appropriate since the original Glen Grant had taken its water from the Caperdonich Well which, unlike many other Highland wells, has never once dried up.

All this was well after the merger in 1952 of J. & J. Grant, Glen Grant Ltd, which the company had become in 1932 shortly after Major Grant's death, with George and J.G. Smith Ltd* to form The Glenlivet and Glen Grant Distilleries Ltd,* the fortunes of which are recorded elsewhere in this book.

Glen Grant is a Speyside malt and in its five years old form is today one of the biggest selling bottled single malts. It is a pale whisky, i.e. it is not matured in sherry casks, but its traditional colour has not diminished its popularity. Glen Grant has always been widely sought after within the trade in Scotland and until recently there existed a multiplicity of Glen Grants. All were from the original distillery, but they were different strengths, age and colour. This reflected the large stock-holdings of merchants who would realise their investment by bottling their Glen Grant under their own label, and it prompted the producing company to try to standardise Glen Grant, which they did by getting the principal holders of Glen Grant to allow them to do the bottling under a common label for all Glen Grant, although there are still a number of associated bottlers who purchase Glen Grant new and bottle under a common label. One can sympathise with the desire to set standards in the retailing of Glen Grant whisky, but at the same time it is lamentable that the variety to be once found in Glen Grant has all but disappeared. The determined questor can still unearth the odd bottle of non-standard Glen Grant of different ages bottled in an earlier period by some small merchant or licensed grocer, but these gems are becoming increasingly scarce. However, the majority can take solace in the knowledge that there will be plenty of Glen Grant to go round in the future, since production increased between 1972 and 1974 by some 80 per cent. The company's bottlings of single malt are marketed by Glen Grant Whisky Co. Ltd, and are available in a variety of ages, depending on the market.

Brands

| Glen Grant 5 years old Highland Malt (export only) | Glen Grant 15 years old Highland Malt |

Glen Grant-Glenlivet

Glen Grant 8 years old
  Highland Malt
Glen Grant 10 years old
  Highland Malt (export
  only)
Glen Grant 12 years old Highland
  Malt (United Kingdom only)

Glen Grant 21 years old
  Highland Malt
Glen Grant 25 years old
  Highland Malt (bottled in
  1977 to commemorate
  Her Majesty's Silver
  Jubilee)

Markets United Kingdom and worldwide; main export market is
Italy.

William Grant & Sons Limited

206-208 West George Street, Glasgow G2 2PE   *Member of SWA*

Distillers

This is very much a family firm, although it is now one of the most
important independent distilling companies in Scotland and the
proprietor of world-famous whiskies — Glenfiddich and Grant's
Standfast. An associate company, Wm Grant & Sons (Standfast) Ltd,
is responsible for distributing the Grant whiskies in the UK. It is

243

Girvan and Ladyburn

jointly owned by Allied Breweries, Bass Charrington, Whitbreads and, of course, William Grant & Sons.

William Grant, with the aid of his seven sons, laid the foundations in 1886 by sinking his entire capital of £755 into the building of Glenfiddich distillery in the field of Glenfiddich, about half a mile from the Robbie Dubh Well at Dufftown in Banffshire. He had earlier acquired a thorough grounding in distilling through some twenty years experience at Mortlach distillery, where he eventually became manager. He was fortunate in being able to equip Glenfiddich for distilling at a cost of only £120, the sum required to purchase the existing copper stills, etc. at Cardhu Distillery where new plant was being installed. All went well at Glenfiddich with the first whisky running from the stills on Christmas Day 1887. A second distillery was constructed in 1892, not a stone's throw from Glenfiddich, at Balvenie Castle, from which the new distillery took its name, although it was known as Glen Gordon for its first few months of operation. Success in Scotland was followed by nation-wide accept-ability as a result of determined efforts by William Grant's son-in-law, Charles Gordon, to penetrate south of the border. He must have been a stayer, or so the story goes, because after making 503 calls he had sold only one case of Standfast, the name adopted for the company's principal brand after the Clan Grant war-cry 'Stand fast Craigellachie'. They had other brands too — Best Procurable, Grant's Liqueur and Hare and Hounds amongst them. But perseverence was rewarded and the home trade began to blossom. The eldest of the Grant sons then turned his attention to Canada which was to be the start of a long record of overseas achievements. In the meantime, the firm had become, in 1903, a limited liability company but still very much in family hands and with William Grant involved right up to his death in 1923.

Post-war expansion caused the company to seek a certain independence in its essential supplies, with the construction in 1963 of their grain distillery at Girvan in Ayrshire, the site having been chosen because of the ready supply of water from the Penwhapple Loch. History more or less repeated itself, for the establishment of the Girvan distillery was soon followed by Grant's building the Ladyburn Lowland Malt Distillery on the same site and using the same water. However, unlike their two Highland malts, Ladyburn is used only for blending. After the success of their blended whisky, Standfast, Grant's enjoyed phenomenal success in promoting their Glenfiddich as a single malt to the extent that in some countries the two are synonymous. Indeed, Glenfiddich was the first malt whisky to gain the accolade of the Queen's Award to Industry for Export Achievement in April 1974. The way Glenfiddich took off is gone into in some detail elsewhere in this book since it is a tale worth recording of brilliant promotion and long-term determined planning .

Glenfiddich itself is an excellent introduction to single malt whiskies, being readily available and fairly gentle on the untutored palate, since it combines both peatiness and sweetness, which negate each other in many malts. Its stable-mate, Balvenie, is becoming more widely available. With a good bouquet and a well balanced character, it too has its followers. To distinguish The Balvenie from their other products Grant's abandoned in 1982 their traditional triangular shaped bottle in favour of a tapering green glass bottle which — unusually in this day and age — employs a cork for sealing; nor is The Balvenie any longer described as an 8 years old malt since it now comprises a range of whiskies from 7 to 12 years, the entire ensemble being labelled Founder's Reserve.

Brands

The Balvenie Pure Malt	Grant's (formerly Grant's
Glenfiddich Pure Malt	Standfast)
	Grant's Royal 12 years old

(Alexander MacGregor & Co.)
Clan MacGregor

Markets 180 countries and territories world-wide for William Grant's whiskies, Clan MacGregor in the USA only.

David Green (Whisky Brokers) Limited

13-14 Golden Square, London W1R 3AG

Brokers and exporters

Dealers in bulk malt and grain whiskies.

Wm Greer & Company

Trafalgar House, 75 Hope Street, Glasgow G2 6AP

Scotch whisky merchants   *A subsidiary of Distillers Company PLC***

William Greer was a member of an Irish distillery family whose company, Kirker, Greer & Co., was prominent in Belfast in the nineteenth century. Greer moved to Glasgow in 1893 and became a leading wine and spirit merchant in that city, trying his hand, like so many others, at blending Scotch whisky for the home and overseas markets. The company was eventually bought by Mitchell Bros Ltd* and via that route eventually became a DCL subsidiary. It had a very important place in the Australian market in the 1920s but its operation is now very small. That notwithstanding, Wm Greer & Co. are to all intents and purposes distillers, holding the licence for DCL's St Magdalene Distillery at Linlithgow.

St Magdalene has, at times in the past, also been known as Linlithgow Distillery, taking this alternative name from the Royal Borough of Linlithgow, birthplace of Mary, Queen of Scots. The town once boasted five distilleries but St Magdalene is the only one to have survived. It was built in the late eighteenth century by Sebastian Henderson, but is associated with the Dawson family and it traded as A. J. Dawson for many years before becoming a limited liability company in 1895. However, the firm's history was to be short and the intense competition in the early years of this century, as between the Lowland malt distilleries, led to its liquidation and the purchase of St Magdalene Distillery by DCL, at present closed.

Rather unusually, this distillery depends on an artesian well for its water supply. St Magdalene is used in blending, but it has been bottled from time to time and is currently available at different ages from Gordon & MacPhail* and Wm Cadenhead Ltd.*

On 1 November 1979, Wm Greer's trading interests were transferred to John Hopkins & Co. Ltd.* The company still exists as a separate entity but is regarded as 'dormant'.

Brand

Greer's O.V.H.

246

Grierson-Blumenthal Limited

G.B. House, 430 High Road, Willesden, London NW10 2HA

Wine and spirit merchants

A well known firm of wine shippers whose brand of Scotch is now available on the UK market.

Brand   Grierson's No. 1 12 years old Malt (vatted)

Markets UK and export.

D. & A. Haddow Limited

164 Killearn Street, Glasgow G22 5JD

Wine and spirit merchants

Part of the Reo Stakis group.

Brand   Old Mearns

John Haig & Company Limited

7-10 Hobart Place, London SW1W 0HN   *Member of SWA*

Distillers and blenders   *A subsidiary of Distillers Company PLC**

'Don't be vague, ask for Haig' has been one of the most enduring slogans in the promotion of Scotch whisky, which is fitting for a name with one of the longest continuous associations with the product. Indeed, Haigs claim to be the oldest Scotch whisky distillers, having been active for over 300 years. Their first recorded association with distilling was in 1655, when Robert Haig was summoned to appear before the Kirk Session, having been discovered working his still on the Sabbath, a considerable misdeed in those days. He established his farm at Throsk in Stirlingshire in 1627; it is this earlier date which is taken to mark the Haig family's first entry into distilling, on the assumption that most farmers of the period indulged in the practice either for their own immediate needs or as a profitable side-line. The Haigs continued to farm, but moved to Newbigging, and later Orchard Farm, and remained there until the beginning of the nineteenth century. Their distilling interests were nourished throughout this period and received a considerable boost with the marriage in 1751 of Robert Haig's great-great grandson, John, to Margaret Stein, whose family had set up highly successful distilleries at Kilbagie and Kennetpans in Clackmannanshire earlier in the century, and who had opened up the whisky trail to London. It was to these prosperous ventures which John Haig looked to secure the future of his family, and on his own premature death his five sons underwent their training in distilling at Kilbagie. Four of them went on to establish their own distilleries. James, the eldest, went to Edinburgh where he owned distilleries at Canonmills and later at Lochrin and Sunbury. His own sons carried on with the latter two. The younger, John, was in partnership with his brother James at Lochrin and later went into business for himself by opening Leith Distillery at Bonnington Toll, also in Edinburgh. Another son, Robert, went to Ireland and bought Dodderbank Distillery near Dublin whilst the youngest, William, continued the family tradition, but in Fife at Kincaple and later, in 1810, at Seggie. The village which grew up there is now known as Guard Bridge, but distilling has long since ceased.

As fate would have it, it was in fact the youngest son who was to continue the line which was to lead to the creation of the House of Haig as a great force in the modern industry. William had two sons, John and Robert. The latter eventually took over responsibility for Seggie whilst his elder brother John had, in 1824, built his own distillery at Cameron Bridge. He was still in his early twenties, and with youth on his side he set out personally to establish his whisky's reputation. He was determined to succeed and to this end installed one of the new Stein patent stills in 1827, one year after his cousin, Robert Stein, had invented it at Kilbagie distillery. Production at Cameron Bridge was given over entirely to grain whisky and expanded enormously, and led eventually to John Haig combining with other grain whisky producers to form the Distillers Co. Ltd, of which John Haig and his son Hugh became directors, and another son, William, secretary. At this point, the blending side of the Haig business was transferred to Markinch, three miles from the distillery. In 1882 John Haig & Co. had amalgamated with David Smith & Co. of Leith and in 1894 was floated as a limited company under Hugh Haig's chairmanship. Captain Douglas Haig of the 7th Hussars also joined the board, being the youngest of the eleven children of John Haig of Cameron Bridge. A brilliant military career and sparkling social connections led to his rapid advancement to become in 1915 Commander in Chief of the British Expeditionary Force to France and the elevation to the rank of Field Marshal in 1916. For his war service he was created Earl Haig. His own career meant that he could take no more than an occasional interest in the company, but he rejoined the board in 1912 after an absence of thirteen years and eventually became its chairman.

With the contractions and rationalisations taking place in the industry following the ravages of the First World War, John Haig & Co. Ltd said farewell to the last vestiges of independence when DCL acquired the entire ordinary share capital in March 1919, which led to much rebuilding and expansion. A further move was the acquisition in 1923 by DCL and 'The Big Three' of Haig & Haig Ltd which had been set up in 1888 by John Alicius Haig, Hugh Haig's brother, to market whisky in the United States. Haig & Haig Ltd had in fact been controlled since 1906 by Robertson & Baxter Ltd,* and the transaction for the sale of extensive whisky stocks by the latter to DCL and others included Haig & Haig and their celebrated Pinch brand. In 1925 Haig & Haig became, appropriately enough, a wholly owned subsidiary of John Haig. Prosperity followed and by 1939 Haig could claim their brand to be the biggest-selling whisky in Britain, and it is today still among the national market leaders and an important export whisky.

Although John Haig & Co. Ltd rode to prosperity and fame through the rapid development of grain whisky and the unprecedented popularity of blended Scotch whisky, it has for some time enjoyed the privilege of having the licence for three of DCL's malt whisky distilleries, two Highland and one Lowland.

The Lowland distillery is Glenkinchie, by the village of Pencaitland in East Lothian. Since its inception around 1837, it has had an almost continuous record of distilling, the break coming in the early part of its history when the founder, a farmer called Rate, sold it to another farmer called Christie. Christie was not interested in distilling and used the premises partly as a combined cow-shed and sawmill. Its sale in 1880 to a group of gentlemen with brewing and wine interests quickly led to its recommissioning as a distillery, and ten years later the Glenkinchie Distillery Co. Ltd was formed. Much rebuilding and new construction took place when in July 1914 it formed a part of Scottish Malt Distillers Ltd.* Glenkinchie is one of the few distilleries still to have a farm attached to it which has won many prizes in fat stock championships. The distillery's product is essentially a blender's whisky, but a little is bottled at 13 years old by Wm Cadenhead Ltd.*

Of Haig's two Highland malt distilleries, Glenlossie is by far the more distinguished, dating back to 1876 and located at Thomshill, about two to three miles south of Elgin. John Duff, a local hotelier, set it up in partnership with two others, partial change in the partnership occurring in 1896 when The Glenlossie-Glenlivet Distillery Co. Ltd was formed. A new warehouse and a private branch line to Longmorn Station quickly followed, and the company, enjoying considerable expansion, went public in 1897. Scottish Malt Distillers Ltd gained control in 1919, and in 1930 the original company was wound up and the distillery became a unit of Scottish Malt Distillers Ltd.

The second malt distillery, Mannochmore, was constructed in 1971 alongside Glenlossie, but drawing its water from a different source. It has a capacity of one million proof gallons. There is also a by-product recovery plant which treats the effluent from a number of distilleries in the area, including Glenlossie and Mannochmore.

A little Glenlossie finds its way into bottle by courtesy of both Gordon & MacPhail* and Wm Cadenhead Ltd, but it is too soon for Mannochmore to qualify. Haig themselves have Glenleven, which is a vatting of six different malts. It is a light, dry whisky which makes a spicy impression on both nose and palate. They also have the only bottled single grain whisky, Cameron Brig.

Brands

Cameron Brig Single Grain
  Whisky
Dimple De Luxe (known as
  Pinch in some markets, and
  also available in a pewter
  decanter)
Glenleven 12 years old Vatted
  Malt

Golden Age 12 years old
  De Luxe
Haig
Haig & Haig 5 Star

Markets United Kingdom and many overseas markets. For Haig itself, the principal markets in volume terms are the UK, Belgium, France, South Africa, Australia and Japan. Pinch is sold in North and parts of Central America, and the Caribbean. In the Dimple guise it appears in Japan, Mexico, Costa Rica and a wide variety of markets where it is not sold as Pinch, with particular success in Venezuela and West Germany. Haig & Haig 5 Star is sold only in the United States and certain peripheral markets with strong American influence such as Puerto Rico, US Virgin Islands, Bahamas and Bermuda. Glenleven is available in very limited quantities and Cameron Brig is exclusively for the domestic market. Golden Age, too, is for the United Kingdom market only. Launched in July 1979, this new De Luxe brand replaced Haig Dimple De Luxe, withdrawn from the UK market in December 1977 due to EEC difficulties. However, Dimple has now reappeared in the home market as a 12 years old De Luxe whisky alongside Golden Age.

Hall & Bramley Limited

24 Fenwick Street, Liverpool L2 7NG   *Member of SWA*

Blenders and wine and spirit merchants

Established in 1860, this company has been blending and bottling Scotch whisky for well over one hundred years. Their Glen Ghoil brand bears a remarkable testimony in the form of a certificate of analysis, dated 21 October 1890, by the then analyst of the City of

Liverpool, Granville H. Sharpe. It reads as follows:

> I HEREBY CERTIFY that I have submitted to a very careful Chemical Analysis a sample of Glen Ghoil Whisky, received from Messrs Hall & Bramley Ltd, and, from the data obtained, can testify to its great purity of composition and excellent qualities.
>
> It is particularly free from Amylic Alcohol or Fusel Oil, and all other nauseous principles which characterize raw and inferior spirits, and I consider it to be a thoroughly matured Whisky possessing important dietetic properties, and well suited for ordinary and regular use.

Brands

Clan Ardroch   Glen Ghoil (De Luxe)
Glen Carren 8 years old Malt
   (vatted)

Hallgarten Wines Limited

Carkers Lane, Highgate Road, London NW5 1RR

Wine and spirit merchants and exporters

Widely known as wine importers, House of Hallgarten also have a range of export whiskies. There are a number of subsidiaries, three of which are engaged in Scotch whisky activities. Their best-known product is Glen Mist, which is a Scotch-whisky-based liqueur. In the immediate post-war period shortages of the essential ingredients (whisky, honey and sugar) led to production being temporarily transferred to the Republic of Ireland. However, Glen Mist was 'repatriated' in 1963 and followed a Peter Hallgarten formulation thereafter.

Brands

(*S.F. & O. Hallgarten*)
Ye Old Ark

(*Glen Mist Liqueur Co.*)
Glen Mist Scotch Whisky   Royal Vat 75°
   Liqueur   Savermo 75°
Old Sloop 75°

(*Savermo Ltd*)
Amber Glow Scotch Whisky   Redaleven Scotch Whisky
   Liqueur   Liqueur
Dewmiel†   Regal Butt†
Hector Macdonald†

251

J. & W. Hardie Limited

27 The Loan, South Queensferry, West Lothian EH30 9SD

Distillers and blenders   *A subsidiary of Distillers Company PLC**
Member of SWA

Established in 1861, the company is licensee of Benromach Distillery and a subsidiary of another DCL component, Wm Sanderson & Son Ltd. The Benromach Distillery Co. started operations at Forres in 1898 and went through several changes of ownership, finding its way into the DCL group in 1953 when Train and McIntyre Ltd, then the owners through their subsidiary Associated Scottish Distilleries Ltd, were taken over by DCL.

The distillery has a high reputation in the whisky industry for the excellence of its product, a Highland malt, almost all of which is used in blending. Gordon & MacPhail* and Wm Cadenhead Ltd* both bottle it in limited quantities. The distillery itself has long been considered as one of the best in the Highlands, and was extensively rebuilt in 1966 and 1974. It is at present closed.

Brand   The Antiquary De Luxe Old Scotch Whisky

Markets The principal markets are Venezuela, Paraguay, Italy, France, Spain, Portugal, Japan and Andorra. In the UK, EEC and US markets The Antiquary is sold as a 12 year old whisky.

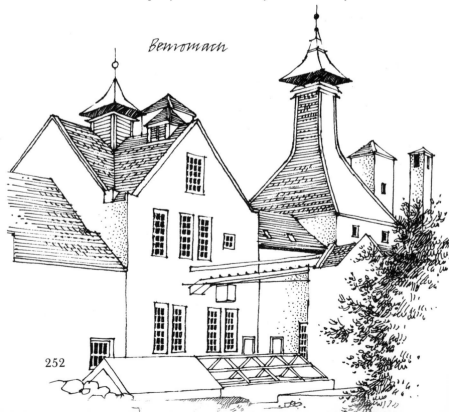

Benromach

252

Harrods Limited

Knightsbridge, London SW1 7XL

Wine and spirit merchants

The 'top people's store' has a first-rate wine and spirit department and, naturally, its own blended whiskies, some of which are produced for them by Whyte & MacKay Distillers Ltd.*

Brands

Harrods De Luxe Blend
Harrods Pure Malt Blend†

Harrods 12 years old De Luxe Blend
Harrods VOH Special Blend

Hart Brothers (Vintners) Limited

11 Forth Street, Glasgow G41 2SN

Blenders and wine and spirit merchants

There is a subsidiary company, Blairmore Blending Co. Ltd. Both are part of Hart Brothers (Holdings) Ltd.

Brands

Ailsa Craig†
Black Douglas
Harts 8 years old
Old Curlers
Old Fox
Old Glasgow
Old Keg
Sceptre†
Scots Lion
The Speaker
White Hart†

John and Robert Harvey Limited

Trafalgar House, 75 Hope Street, Glasgow G2 6AW *Member of SWA*

Distillers and blenders   *A subsidiary of Distillers Company PLC**

A very old Glasgow company dating from 1770, it was amongst the many smaller companies who felt the effects of the Pattison failure in 1898. Finding themselves in difficulty, Harvey's approached DCL with a view to amalgamation, but DCL was already tied up in negotiations with their Irish rivals, United Distillers Ltd. However, when these failed to produce results, DCL turned their attention to Harvey's, by which time their distillery at Dundashill in Glasgow had ceased production. DCL were more interested in Harvey's blending and export potential than distilling and in 1902 acquired the entire share capital, at the same time closing Dundashill permanently in view of the serious over-production in the industry at that time.

Currently, John and Robert Harvey Ltd are licensees of Aultmore Distillery, which is located about 2½ miles from Keith and 9 miles from Buckie and, as such, in the heart of what was smuggling territory. The distillery was built by Alexander Edward of Sanquhar and completed in 1896, distilling commencing the following year. In 1899 ownership passed to The Oban and Aultmore Glenlivet Distillery Co. Ltd, with Alexander Edward as Managing Director and the company owning both Aultmore and Oban Distilleries. In 1923 Aultmore was sold to John Dewar & Sons Ltd* and thence became a DCL property. Aultmore is much appreciated as a single malt; it is rich and fruity in flavour with a pleasant, fresh bouquet.

Brands

Aultmore 12 years old Highland Malt	Harvey's Special
Harvey's Gold Label De Luxe	*(The Inveravon Blending Co.)* Glen Stewart†

Haworth & Airey PLC

Walton-le-dale Winery, Preston

Wine and spirit merchants

Established in 1901.

Brands Bruce Scots Perfection
Glen Royal

Hay and MacLeod & Company

Dalmore House, 296-298 St Vincent Street, Glasgow G2 5RG

Brokers and blenders *A subsidiary of Whyte & Mackay Distillers Ltd**

This firm was prominent in whisky broking, although it also has its own blends. It was set up in 1946, but little was heard of it until the mid sixties when it joined with W. & S. Strong & Co.* to build a new Highland malt distillery at Tomintoul, and in 1971 it acquired, on the same 50/50 basis with Strong's, Fettercairn Distillery Co.* The group of four companies, i.e. the two partners and their two distilling companies, were taken over as an ensemble by Scottish and Universal Investments Ltd in 1973 and were integrated with the parent company's other whisky activities to form Whyte & Mackay Distillers Ltd* in 1975. Within this organisation, Hay and MacLeod & Co. retains responsibility for trade in bulk whisky, thus recalling its original broking function.

Brands	Craigroyal†	Hallmark†
	Cream of the Cullins†	MacLean's†
	Glen Noble†	Old Renfrew†

HD Wines (Inverness) Limited

Longman Road, Inverness

Wine and spirit merchants

This company was set up in 1961 and has twenty-nine retail and three wholesale branches.

Brand   Old Inverness

Hedges & Butler Limited

Elmbank Chambers, 289 Bath Street, Glasgow G2 4JL

Blenders and exporters   *An associate of Bass Export Ltd*

Both companies are subsidiaries of Bass Ltd, and Hedges and Butler represents this major brewer's principal Scotch whisky interests. In fact, the company is traditionally better known for its fine wines than its whiskies, but has been blending and exporting a range of Scotch whiskies since before the Second World War.

Hedges and Butler Royal Scotch whiskies are very much in the 'premium' bracket and have recently become available for the first time in the United Kingdom itself. The 12 year old Finest De Luxe has been awarded a Double Gold Medal at the twelfth International Wine and Spirit Competition held in conjunction with the Bristol Wine Fair.

For convenience, other Bass subsidiaries with Scotch whisky brands are listed here.

Brands

(Hedges & Butler Ltd)

Hedges & Butler Royal	Hedges & Butler Royal Malt
Hedges & Butler Royal Finest	(vatted)
De Luxe 12 years old	Hedges & Butler Royal Special
Hedges & Butler Royal	De Luxe 8 years old
Imperial De Luxe 21 years old	Hedges & Butler Royal Supreme
	De Luxe 15 years old

(Archibald Aikman & Co.)
Royal Marshall

(Charles Day & Co.)	*(John Wallace & Co.)*
The Duke's Own	Wallace's Standard

(*Bass Export Ltd*)
Glen Allan
JGT 8 years old
Prince Regent

Taplows
Thomson's Deerstalker 5 years
old

(*Duncan MacGregor & Co.*)
Duncan MacGregor

Golf Club Special

The Highland Distilleries Company PLC

106 West Nile Street, Glasgow G1 2QY   *Member of SWA*
Distillers

The low profile traditionally adopted by Highland Distilleries has been changed in recent years as a result of the phenomenal success of the group's leading brand, The Famous Grouse, and the attentions which that success has brought from various suitors casting covetous eyes not only on a popular brand, but also on a clutch of first-rate malt distilleries. The attempt in 1979 by Hiram Walker & Sons* to absorb Highland Distilleries came to nought when it was successfully resisted by the board of this most Scottish of companies, and its independence preserved, at least for the foreseeable future.

The formation of the company goes back as far as 1887, with the amalgamation of the Islay Distillery Co., owners of Bunnahabhain Distillery, and Glenrothes Distillery. Bunnahabhain has only recently become available in single malt bottled form. Although it possesses the traditional peatiness of the Islays, this is less pronounced in Bunnahabhain than others of the same genre, and the result is altogether more delicate than one might expect of an Islay. The distillery is located on the north-east coast of the island and commenced distilling in 1883. It is at present closed

Only one of the five distilleries in the group does not indulge in bottling a self whisky, and that is Glenglassaugh, whose product is nonetheless in great demand by blenders. The distillery is found less than two miles along the coast from the old Banffshire fishing town of Portsoy, drawing water from nearby springs. It was constructed in 1875 and bought by the present owners in 1892. Highland Distilleries completely rebuilt it in 1959 and it has an annual output of 1.2 million litres of alcohol.

The three other distilleries in the group are owned by subsidiary companies — Glenrothes by Glenrothes-Glenlivet Ltd,* Highland Park by James Grant & Co. (Highland Park Distillery) Ltd,* and Tamdhu by Tamdhu-Glenlivet Ltd.*

For many years Highland Distilleries remained very much a distillery operation, supplying its fine whiskies to meet the growing demands of the big blending houses, and marketing limited quantities of its products as single malts. Its first show of direct interest in blending came in 1948 when the company acquired shares in Robertson & Baxter Ltd,* the prominent Glasgow whisky merchants and blenders. Today Highland own 35.4 per cent of Robertson & Baxter Ltd, who in turn, through their main shareholder Edrington Holdings, has 8 per cent of the shares in Highland Distilleries. This close relationship is reflected in the extensive use of Highland's whiskies in the Robertson & Baxter blends, and the latter's role as selling agent for these malts to the Scotch whisky blending industry generally. Both companies also have their head offices in the same building in Glasgow.

Highland Distilleries' interest in blending took a new turn in 1970 when they bought Matthew Gloag & Son Ltd,* the Perth whisky merchants, which has become the jewel in the Highland Distilleries' crown.

It has long been a tradition within the industry that the chairman of the Distillers Company automatically becomes chairman of the Scotch Whisky Association. A break with that tradition came in 1983 when John Macphail, chairman of Highland Distilleries, succeeded Robin Carter on his retirement from the chairmanship of the Association and that of Distillers Company.

Brand   Bunnahabhain 12 years old Islay Single Malt

Highland Stag Whiskies

63 Falkland Road, Dorking, Surrey RH4 3AD

Blenders

A new company on the Scotch whisky scene, thanks to its acquisition of the majority shareholding of R.N. MacDonald & Company Ltd.*

Higson's Brewery Limited

127 Dale Street, Liverpool L2 2JJ

Brewers and blenders

This independent brewer dates back to 1780. It has a number of own labels belonging to its subsidiary, J. Sykes and Co. Ltd, also had its own Irish whiskies, Danny Man and O'Donnell's Old Shannon.

Brands   (*J. Sykes & Co. Ltd*)

Allanmore†	Crown Vat
Balmoral†	Highland Laddie
Black & Gold†	Jackson's†

Hill Thomson & Company Limited

45 Frederick Street, Edinburgh   *Member of SWA*

Blenders and exporters   *A subsidiary of The Glenlivet Distillers Ltd**

Like so many Scotch whisky blenders and merchants, Hill Thomson's origins were humble, in the form of William Hill's licensed grocer shop which he opened in Rose Street Lane in Edinburgh in 1793. But Hill prospered rapidly and moved in 1799 to grander premises at 45 Frederick Street, which remained the headquarters of the successor company. Following his death in 1818, two of William's sons carried on the business under the title of William and Robert Hill, and on their deaths control passed to a third son, George, who took over in 1837. Expansion of the business led to partnership in 1857 with William Thomson, and the firm then adopted its present name. Only then did the company begin seriously blending and bottling their own brands of whisky. Some twenty years later William Shaw joined the firm as export salesman, and it was he who established and promoted the company's blend of Queen Anne. His enormous success with it in a wide variety of markets ensured the company's future prosperity, and it was no surprise when he was appointed chairman. Shaw had chosen Queen Anne as the name for their whisky because she had been the last of the House of Stuart to reign, and her period on the throne had been one of great national prosperity and endeavour.

Shaw's sons joined him in 1919 and continued the tradition of promoting the company's whiskies far and wide. A third generation of Shaws subsequently occupied the key posts at 45 Frederick Street until, in 1970, what had been a purely family concern of blenders and exporters combined with important distilling interests to form The Glenlivet Distillers Ltd.* Queen Anne became the new group's principal label, and the merger ensured that this distinguished brand would have first call on the new company's five malt whiskies, including three famous ones — The Glenlivet, Glen Grant and Longmorn.

During its independent years, Hill Thomson & Co. Ltd had acquired or established a number of subsidiaries. Some of these survive today as part of the group.

Brands

(Hill, Thomson & Co. Ltd)
Queen Anne   St Leger
Something Special De Luxe

(Lawson & Smith Ltd)   *(J.M. Tulloch & Co. Ltd)*
Prince Charlie Specially Selected   Horseman

258

(*Hudson's Bay Co. of Scotland Ltd*)
1670†   Hudson's Bay Best Procurable†

Markets Queen Anne and Something Special are sold in over 100 countries, the principal individual markets being Sweden, Italy, Venezuela, Australasia and South America. St Leger is particularly successful in the Quebec province of Canada.

Joseph Holt PLC

Derby Brewery, Empire Street, Cheetham, Manchester M3 1JD
Brewers and wine and spirit merchants

A small independent Manchester brewing concern, the Derby Brewery was built on its present site in 1849. Joseph Holt Ltd have been blending their own Scotch whiskies since then, but for sale only within their own tied houses.

Brand   Fine Old Special

Markets   Manchester area.

John Hopkins & Company Limited

Trafalgar House, 75 Hope Street, Glasgow G2 6AP *Member of SWA*

Scotch whisky merchants   *A subsidiary of Distillers Company PLC**

The Company was established in 1874 by John Hopkins, who had just acquired the British agency for Otard's Brandy. With a view to developing the Scotch whisky trade, he took into partnership his brother Edward Hopkins and his cousin Edward Broughton Hopkins. The business was carried on from London by John Hopkins and his brother, and their cousin opened an office and bonded warehouse in Glasgow.

The company's Glen Garry brand of Scotch whisky was registered in April 1878 and obtained the highest award at the Chicago Exhibition in 1892. The Old Mull brand was registered in November 1880. In 1900 the company's bonded warehouse and offices at York Street, Glasgow were, with all the contents, completely destroyed by fire, but the bonded warehouse was rebuilt on the same site and opened the following year.

In 1896 the partners built the Speyburn-Glenlivet Distillery at Rothes, Speyside, and registered it as a separate company. This company had a very substantial interest in this distillery, and held the selling agency for the entire output. The distillery itself is now registered to John Robertson & Son Ltd.*

John Hopkins retired from the business in 1911, and on the death of his brother Edward in 1915 it was decided to form a private limited company, which was registered early in 1916. Edward Broughton Hopkins continued to act as a director of the company until his death in 1919.

The firm was well established in the export trade when its entire share capital was acquired by DCL in 1916, but it was not formally incorporated into DCL until 1931. Into the group it brought the Tobermory Distillery on the Isle of Mull, originally constructed in 1823 and acquired by John Hopkins in 1888. A victim of the slump, the distillery closed down in 1928, but was re-opened in 1972 by an independent company as Ledaig. It has since reverted to its original name and is now run by Tobermory Distillers Ltd.*

Today, John Hopkins owns and operates for DCL an older distillery, the Oban Distillery, located at Oban. It was founded in 1794 but only became part of the group in 1930 when Scottish Malt Distillers Ltd* acquired the entire share capital of Oban Distillery Co. Ltd, responsibility for the distillery subsequently passing to John Hopkins & Co. Ltd.

Oban Distillery is reckoned by some experts to be the oldest continuous distillery in Scotland. Since production began in the 1790s it has passed through the hands of various private owners, ending with James Walter Higgins in 1883. In 1898 it was acquired by the Oban and Aultmore Distilleries Ltd, which was set up by a combination of interests to acquire the two distilleries in question. The company was a major supplier to Pattisons Ltd of Leith and suffered considerably from the latter's failure. However, it recovered from this setback to be sold in 1923, Oban Distillery becoming the property of a partnership which formed the Oban Distillery Co. Ltd. The distillery prospered and has continued to do so following its absorption by DCL.

By taste, Oban is rather difficult to categorise, due perhaps to the mingling of a variety of geographical elements arising from its location. By classification it is a Highland Malt and, as such, is available at 12 years old. It enjoys just the merest hint of smokiness in flavour and aroma, and is one of the few single malts to have a cork closure to the bottle. The company's main brand, however, is Old Mull, and this is now being actively promoted through the Distillers Company network with the domestic market as the main target.

Brands (John Hopkins & Co. Ltd)

Glen Garry	Old Mull
Navy Supreme De Luxe†	
Oban 12 years old Highland	*(The Glenrinnes Blending Co.)*
Malt	Glen Royal

The Hungerford Wine Company

128 High Street, Hungerford, Berks

Wine and spirit merchants

Brand   Old Farm

International Distillers & Vintners Limited

17 Cornwall Terrace, London NW1 4QP   *Member of SWA*

Distillers and blenders

The ultimate holding company is Grand Metropolitan PLC who acquired International Distillers and Vintners Ltd (IDV) in 1972 as part of Watney, Mann & Co. Ltd, who had bought the group only six months previously. IDV's corporate history goes back only as far as 1962 when it was set up as a result of the merger of United Wine Traders Ltd and Gilbey's Ltd. For the group's pedigree it is, therefore, necessary to consider the origins of these two prominent 'parents' in the wine and spirit trade. Indeed, IDV's two-sided heritage is still evident today, for under IDV (Exports) Ltd, the group's whisky activities are represented by Justerini & Brooks on the one hand, and a combination of the Gilbey companies (including Glen Spey Ltd and James Catto & Co. Ltd) on the other. Records of the principal IDV companies engaged either wholly or partly in the Scotch whisky industry appear elsewhere, but it is helpful to set out here which they are:

D. Cameron & Co. Ltd
James Catto & Co. Ltd*
Peter Dominic Ltd
Dunhill Scotch Whisky Sales Ltd
Gilbey's Ltd
Gilbey Vintners Ltd*
Glen Spey Ltd
Justerini & Brooks Ltd*
Justerini & Brooks (Scotland) Ltd
Andrew Laing & Co. Ltd
Morgan Furze & Co. Ltd
Strathspey Highland Malt Whisky Co. Ltd

The activities of the group embrace practically every aspect of the production of wines, the distillation of spirits and the distribution of the end products worldwide, and it therefore has important interests in things other than Scotch whisky. The well known port firm of Croft & Co. Ltd is, for example, one of its subsidiaries. But as far as Scotch whisky is concerned, the group's operations, from distilling

Highland malt whisky at its four distilleries at Auchroisk, Knockando, Strathmill and Glen Spey, to blending and distribution, are totally integrated. The first three are licensed to Justerini & Brooks Ltd, and Glen Spey to Glen Spey Ltd.

Expanding business led IDV to break ties with its traditional blending home of Aberdeen, which was considered somewhat remote for a large-scale operation, and in 1969 extensive warehouses and other facilities were built on a thirty-one acre site at Blythswood near Renfrew. Now whisky is delivered there by road tanker for maturing and eventual blending. Bottling takes place at Dumbarton by Strathleven Bonded Warehouses Ltd. The group's total warehousing capacity at Blythswood and Auchroisk is now about thirty-five million gallons.

Within the low-level, rather stark and entirely functional complex at Blythswood is to be found the cooperage, which features a working combination of traditional tools and the latest coopering machines.

All IDV whiskies are marketed through the subsidiaries, rather than in the group name.

Inverdice Auld Alliance Scotch Whisky Company Limited

Suite 289, 93 Hope Street, Glasgow G2 6LD

Blenders

The Invergordon Distillers Limited

Ashley House, 181-195 West George Street, Glasgow G2 2NL

Distillers, blenders and exporters   *Member of SWA*

This grouping of six distilleries (one grain and five malt) belongs to Carlton Industries PLC, which in turn is part of the Hawker Siddeley Group. The company dates from 1960, with the acquisition of Invergordon Distillery, construction of which had started only the previous year. The other distilleries were either purchased or constructed later. Although Invergordon engage in all aspects of the whisky industry, the group is, above all, concerned with distilling, with a total capacity of eighteen million proof gallons. Under the control of the holding company, Invergordon Distillers (Holdings) Ltd, there are a number of subsidiaries. Those engaged in malt whisky distilling are themselves subsidiaries of the principal distilling company, The Invergordon Distillers. These are Bruichladdich

Distillery Co. Ltd,* Deanston Distillers Ltd,* Tamnavulin-Glenlivet Distillery Co. Ltd,* Tullibardine Distillery Co. Ltd.* Each of these companies operates the distillery from which it takes its name. The two other distilleries in the group, Ben Wyvis Highland Malt and Invergordon Grain, belong directly to The Invergordon Distillers Ltd.

Other subsidiary companies are as follows:

Grey Rogers and Co. Ltd, which was acquired in 1979 from the sherry shippers, Pedro Domecq. The company is responsible for blending and marketing one of the group's principal blends, Scots Grey.

Invergordon Whisky Holdings Ltd, which is responsible for the maturation of the group's stocks of whisky.

Longman Distillers Ltd, which is widely known abroad as the overseas marketing arm of Invergordon, selling whiskies both in the bottle and in bulk. It supplies many blends for use under exclusive labels in overseas markets.

Pentland Bonding Co. Ltd, which undertakes bottling for the group's proprietary brands of whisky and for other brand owners.

Andrew R. Wilson (Whisky Brokers) Ltd, which provides a broking function for the group as a whole.

As the main operating company, The Invergordon Distillers is the employer of all group personnel and responsible for all financial transactions throughout the group.

Invergordon, the site of the group's main operating unit, took its name from a local laird, Sir William Gordon, early in the eighteenth century. Invergordon soon developed into an important coastal station, first as a commercial port and later as a naval base. No doubt ready supplies of local barley and clear water helped establish Invergordon as the site for Scotland's most northerly grain whisky distillery. It was thought by the late Provost James Grigor of Inverness that more employment in the industry would be kept in the Highlands if grain whisky was distilled there as well as the traditional Highland malt. Production began in 1961 and has increased steadily. Nearby there is a vast spread of warehouses which can hold over thirty-five million proof gallons of maturing whisky.

Ben Wyvis distillery, taking its name from a local peak, stands in the shadow of Invergordon grain distillery, and is in fact located within the Invergordon complex. It opened in 1965 and its product has yet to be bottled as a single malt.

Invergordon undertake their own blending and are extremely active in the export market. Much of their export business is in blended bulk form for marketing under the importer's own label.

Brands

Markets 10 per cent UK. Main overseas markets are USA, Italy, Japan and Germany.

Inver House Distillers Limited

Moffat Distilleries, Airdrie, Lanarkshire   *Member of SWA*

Distillers and blenders   *A subsidiary of Publicker Industries Inc., Greenwich, USA*

Publicker Industries Inc. appeared rather late on the Scottish scene, establishing their subsidiary only in 1965. They were already well known in North America through their bourbons and American blended whisky, such as Old Hickory and Philadelphia, and the move to Scotland was a logical extension of their interests. However, instead of buying up existing whisky interests Publicker set up their own complex, now known as Moffat Distilleries, on the site of a disused paper mill three miles east of Airdrie. The town's central location was no doubt one of the determining factors in choosing the site.

Inver House boasts both a grain distillery and a pot-still malt whisky distillery which, together with the adjacent blending and bottling plant, combine to form the Moffat Distilleries complex. Inver House Distillers produce a grain whisky called Garnheath, but Glen Flagler, their Lowland malt whisky, has not been produced for several years. From 1973 to 1983 Inver House owned Bladnoch Distillery Ltd, when it was sold to Arthur Bell & Sons.[*]

The principal whisky brands of the company are Inver House, MacArthur's and Pinwinnie. The latter is a De Luxe brand which has a growing market in South America. MacArthur's is sold generally within the UK, principally through supermarkets. Indeed its impact in the British market, due to its lower than average price, caused a number of leading blenders to introduce secondary brands in order to compete on price. A whisky cream liqueur has recently been developed, called Heather Cream. It is the first to use Scotch malt whisky, and it will be marketed extensively in Britain and abroad.

Brands

(Inver House Distillers Ltd)

Brae Bassie†
Coldstream Guard
Dougherty's†
Glen Flagler Lowland Malt 5 years old†
Glen Flagler Lowland Malt 8 years old†
Inver House Green Plaid
Inver House Red Plaid

Killyloch Vatted Malt
Kiltarie
Kilt Castle†
Kinsey
Pinwinnie Royale De Luxe
Pinwinnie Royale 12 years old

(R. Carmichael & Sons Ltd)
Heather Cream Liqueur

(J. MacArthur Jr. & Co.)
Highland Breeze
MacArthur's

MacArthur's Red Label 8 years old

(Glen Mavis Distillers)
Glen Mavis

(Dalting Distillers)
Dalting†

(Mason & Summers Ltd)
Auld Shepp

Golden Glen

(Munray Distillers)
Munray

(Old Blairmohr Whisky Co.)
Old Blairmohr†

Markets USA and UK are the main markets, but brands are sold in practically all countries.

Isle of Jura Distillery Company Limited

Craighouse, Isle of Jura, Argyll

Distillers   *A subsidiary of The Waverley Group Ltd**

The first distillery on Jura was a small building erected in the seventeenth century on the site of the present distillery in Craighouse, although illicit distilling was certainly carried on before this in a nearby cave.

In 1810 a much larger distillery including maltings was built. The distillery buildings were owned by the Campbell family, who also owned the Jura estate, and the plant and machinery became the property of James Ferguson, who also operated the distillery on his own behalf. Production continued until 1901 when the two sides had a disagreement, and Ferguson, who had no heir, left with the plant and machinery. The roof was then removed to avoid rate-paying, and the buildings fell into disrepair. The last whisky left the island in the early 1900s.

In 1958 the present distillery was conceived, in an effort to bring life and work back to an island whose population had suffered badly from two world wars and the Depression. Two Jura landowners, Mr Riley-Smith and Mr Fletcher, approached Scottish Brewers, and with their support the construction of the new distillery went ahead under the expert design of Mr Delme Evans. It was opened in 1963, its first Isle of Jura Pure Malt 8 Years Old coming on to the market in 1974.

Isle of Jura has a distinctive flavour which is often said to be nearer that of a Highland malt than the malts of neighbouring Islay. The whisky ages in cask under the shadow of the magnificent 'Paps', the three peaks which dominate the island, and the distillery uses water from a burn rising some thousand feet up in the hills at Loch'a Bhaile-Mhargaidh. Production is used in blending, particularly in Mackinlay's Legacy and Finest Old Scotch Whisky.

Brand   Isle of Jura Pure Malt 8 years old

Markets UK and export

Robert James, Son & Company Limited

79 Aslett Street, London SW18 2BE

Wine and spirit merchants

Mr Robert M.C. James first went into business as a merchant of wines and spirits in London's famous Bloomsbury in 1829, where his premises were augmented by three acres of cellar space. The cellars had originally served as a brewery under the ownership of Alderman Combe, a former mayor of London. The company's main activity was the supply of wines and port to a select group of customers, including the Royal Family. However, like so many other distinguished London wine merchants, they saw the advantage of blended Scotch whisky and had their own blends specially made up for them.

The firm remained in the James family until the last surviving member, Stanley, sold it in 1960 to the Blumberg family who already

266

owned their own vineyards in South Africa. The accent, therefore, continues to be on wine but whisky is not forgotten.

Brands

Glen Rannoch	(*World Wines Ltd*)
Glen Tulloch†	Alexander McLeod†
Wee Drappie	

R. & H. Jefferson

Lowther Street, Whitehaven, Cumbria
Wine and spirit merchants

This old family business dates from 1785.

Brand Jefferson's

Jenks Brothers Limited

Castle House, 71-75, Desborough Road, High Wycombe, Bucks HP11 2HS
Wine and spirit merchants

Although their own whiskies are not currently available, Jenks Brothers are actively marketing in Britain and the United States the Pig's Nose and Sheep Dip brands which they jointly own with M.J. Dowdeswell & Co. Ltd.*

Brands   Royal Heather†   Royal Pheasant†

D. Johnston & Company (Laphroaig) Limited

Laphroaig Distillery, Port Ellen, Islay, Argyll   *Member of SWA*

Distillers   *A subsidiary of Long John International Ltd**

One of Scotland's most distinguished distilleries, Laphroaig was owned and managed by the Johnston family from its inception in 1815 until 1954. It was founded by two brothers, Donald and Alex Johnston, whose father, Alexander, had arrived in Islay with his two brothers to farm shortly after the 1745 rebellion. Donald Johnston became the sole owner in 1836. On his premature death in 1847, the distillery was managed by trustees until his son Dugald was able to take over in 1857 on coming of age. On his death in 1877, ownership passed to a cousin, Alex Johnston of Tallant, who had married Dugald's sister Isabella. When Alex Johnston died in 1907, the distillery passed to his side of the family and responsibility for it eventually fell to Ian Hunter, a nephew. In 1928 he became sole owner, until 1950, when he formed a private limited company, with himself as managing director. He died in 1954. D. Johnston & Co. Ltd merged with Seager Evans in 1962. A feature of Laphroaig's history has been rivalry and dispute with the owners of the nearby Lagavulin distillery, Mackie & Co. (now White Horse Distillers Ltd *) to the point of litigation.

The distillery is found in a most attractive setting, on a small bay sheltered by some rocky islands. It uses peat cut in its own peat bogs, which helps to give Laphroaig its very distinctive peaty flavour. As well as being available in its original form at 10 years old, Laphroaig is used in blending, notably in the company's own Islay Mist.

The Scotch whisky industry has by and large been a male preserve, but Laphroaig was one of the few exceptions to the general rule since for many years the company was run by Miss E.L. Williamson (later Mrs Campbell) who was in effect the only lady distiller in Scotland. She became Secretary and a director of the company in 1950, becoming Managing Director in 1954 until its acquisition in 1967 by Long John. Thereafter, she continued as Chairman and Director until her retirement in 1972.

Brands Laphroaig 10 years old Islay   Islay Mist 8 years old
        Malt 75°   De Luxe

Markets Laphroaig is available in Britain and in certain Long John export markets. Islay Mist is sold in Britain, Canada and Western Europe.

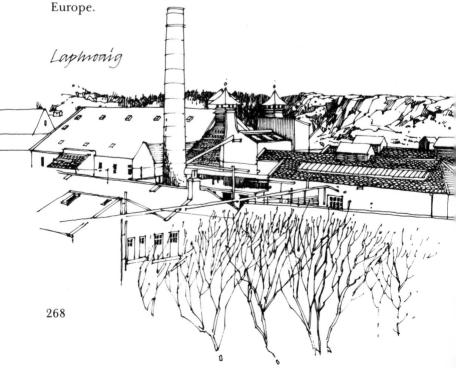

Laphroaig

Charles H. Julian Limited

52-58 Weston Street, London SE1 3QJ   *Member of SWA*

Blenders and exporters

This small, independent family firm has, somewhat against the odds, made a name for itself through the successful promotion of its Excalibur De Luxe brand. The company's history is brief, having been set up by Charles H. Julian, a former chief blender of Justerini & Brooks'* whiskies; it is now in the hands of his sons. There is a subsidiary company, Julian Bonding Co. Ltd, which handles warehousing and distribution activities, and an associate company which also markets its own brands.

Brands

(Charles H. Julian Ltd)

Camlan	Juleven
Excalibur 12 years old	Julian's
House of Julian	Monument

(Davison, Newman & Co. Ltd)

Carlton Finest	Davison 1650

Justerini & Brooks Limited

61 St James's Street, London SW1   *Member of SWA*

Wine merchants and distillers   *A subsidiary of International Distillers and Vintners Ltd**

Perhaps the doyen of all the great London wine houses, whose incursion into Scotch whisky has been the most outstandingly successful. A young Italian from Bologna called Giacamo Justerini arrived in London in 1749 in pursuit of romance and in search of fortune. He quickly found a business partner who could provide the financial backing for a joint venture, and so in that year Johnson and Justerini was established, dealing mainly in liqueurs made on the premises from recipes which Justerini had brought with him from his distiller uncle in Italy. Justerini retired to his native land in 1760, and although already rich can have had no inkling that the name he had left behind was eventually to be linked with another English surname, which together were to become very well known indeed. The Johnson side of the business held on for some time longer, but the last of the line, Augustus Johnson II, sold out to Alfred Brooks in 1830, and in that year the firm became Justerini and Brooks.

Justerini's went from strength to strength, establishing their reputation as fine wine merchants, but when Scotch whisky began to make a serious appearance in London in the 1880s they were among the first of the London merchants to buy up old bonded stocks in Scotland from which they established their own blend, Club. However, their true period of growth was to come in the 1950s and 1960s, thanks to the phenomenal success of their whisky in the United States. The credit for initiating this venture goes to Eddie Tatham who joined the firm at the end of the First World War. Accurately foreseeing the end of American Prohibition and the liberating of an enormous market, he made a probing expedition there in 1930 to assess its potential. Small quantities of Justerini's whisky had been shipped there to individuals before Prohibition, but an agent was established only in 1936. The following year an exclusive agency contract was signed with Charles Guttman of The Paddington Corporation. Modest progress was made with J & B in the New York area, but the appearance of Abe Rosenberg on the scene at the Paddington Corporation in the mid fifties led to the successful promotion of J & B throughout the United States. From this strong base J & B expanded into other overseas markets to become a truly worldwide blend. Today it is the brand leader in the US and the second biggest selling Scotch in the world, with an annual output of about four and a half million cases.

By the time that J & B whisky was beginning to make a name for itself in the American market, Justerini & Brooks Ltd had pooled their assets with those of Twiss and Browning and Hallowes in 1952 to form United Wine Traders Ltd. This was followed ten years later by amalgamation with another great name in wine and spirits, that of W. & A. Gilbey, to form International Distillers and Vintners Ltd. This merger further facilitated the promotion of J & B Rare in export markets through the use of the Gilbey overseas companies, particularly in Australia, New Zealand, Canada, South Africa and Ireland.

Although Justerini's themselves had never owned any distilleries, two of the three distilleries which Gilbey's had brought to the merger, Knockando and Strathmill, are now registered in their name, as well as IDV's own particular venture, namely Auchroisk Distillery.

Auchroisk at Mulben in Banffshire is something of a phenomenon: a brand new whisky distillery, opened in January 1974. A local farm gave its name to the distillery, which means 'the forest of the red stream'. The all-essential water for the distillery is drawn from a nearby spring called Dorie's Well and from the Mulben Burn, a tributary of the Spey. The distillery buildings are of a most pleasing design, and blend well not only with the local countryside but also with the traditions of the craft. IDV have slavishly followed the well-tried patterns of design in construction and equipment at Auchroisk, but have made concessions to modernity where these have been to obvious advantage, such as the employment of stainless steel instead of wood in the washbacks, and remote control in the mash and still houses. Auchroisk distillery represents an investment of £1 million and its eight stills have a production capacity of 1,500,000 gallons per annum. No doubt IDV are anxiously waiting to see if their product will be suitable for bottling as a single malt as well as for blending purposes.

Knockando distillery was built in 1898 by Ian Thomson. After a couple of years of operation on a modest scale it appears to have fallen into disuse until it was acquired in 1904 by Gilbey's for a mere £3,500. Its remote location requires the distillery workers to live in tied cottages on the 'estate'. Although the bulk of production goes to blending, Knockando — which means 'the little black hillock' in Gaelic — has been available for many years as a single malt of 12 years old. The rather plain label states both the date of bottling and the distillation season, a rather uncommon practice now. The distillery has a capacity of 500,000 gallons. The whisky it produces is uncommonly light for a Speyside malt, but has a clean bouquet and a pleasant hint of nuttiness in the taste.

Strathmill Distillery, known in earlier days as the Glenisla-Glenlivet Distillery, goes back to 1823 when it was built as an oatmeal mill by A.G. Johnston. It was converted to a distillery in 1891 and purchased by Gilbey's in 1895 for £9,500, and renamed. The output is used exclusively for blending, and capacity is 750,000 gallons.

Brands

J & B Rare	Justerini & Brooks 20 years old
Royal Ages De Luxe	Finest Malt (vatted)†
Club (available only in Justerini & Brooks' two shops in London and Edinburgh)	Knockando 12 years old Pure Malt

Markets J & B Rare is available in 156 different countries including USA, Italy, France, Spain, Switzerland, Greece, Caribbean, Latin America, Far East, Africa, etc.

Kilglass Wine & Spirits Limited

6 Bouverie Street, Rutherglen G73

Wine and spirit merchants

Brands

Glentarvie 5 years old	Kilmor

Killingley & Company Limited

Daybrook, Nottingham NG5 6BU

Wine and spirit merchants

The archives of Nottingham City Council show Mrs Killingley in business as a spirit dealer in Smithy Row in Nottingham in 1745. It would not be rash to assume that the origins of the business go back even further, but there are no records to prove it. Smithy Row took its name from the blacksmith's shop — or smithy — which stood opposite the 'Black Boy', a very old Nottingham inn. Mrs Killingley's spirit shop was next to the smithy. Alas, all trace of these ancient buildings has been swept away by reconstruction, but the Killingley connection with Smithy Row remains by virtue of their house whisky blend — Olde Smithy.

Killingley & Co. Ltd were purchased by Home Brewery Co. Ltd in 1926, and their whisky is distributed throughout the latter's area of operation. It is claimed that Olde Smithy is a blend of 55 per cent grain and 45 per cent malt whiskies, all of at least 6 years of age, which puts it more in the De Luxe class although it is sold as a standard blend. Approximately 3,000 cases are sold annually.

Brands   BB†   Olde Smithy

Markets Nottinghamshire and neighbouring counties.

Kinross Whisky Company Limited

PO Box 112, Suite E, The Priory, Haywards Heath, Sussex

Blenders and exporters

This company markets its blended whiskies under its own labels and those of its subsidiary, Scottish Albion Blending Co.

Brands	*(Kinross Whisky Co. Ltd)*	*(Scottish Albion Blending Co.)*
	Derby Special De Luxe	Albion's Finest Old
	Glen Baren (vatted malt)	
	Gold Blend	

Douglas Laing & Company Limited

35 Robertson Street, Glasgow G2 8HJ

Blenders and exporters

This is entirely a family firm, founded in 1950. The main thrust of its business has been in developing sales of matured Scotch whisky by being more adjustable to customers' wishes than is possible for some of the older companies with long established brands. It has experienced steady expansion. The two main brands, King of Scots and House of Peers, are available in ages ranging from 3 to 20 years old. There are back-up or secondary brands, some of which are marketed by subsidiary or associate companies.

Brands

(Douglas Laing & Co. Ltd)

Clydebank	Kentshire
DL 13	King of Scots
Eaton's Special Reserve	King of Scots De Luxe
House of Peers	

(Douglas Export Agency Ltd)
Select

(Langside Distillers)

JPS 15 years old De Luxe	Langside

(Douglas McGibbon & Co. Ltd)	*(Raleigh (Glasgow) Ltd)*
McGibbon's Special Reserve	Sir Walter Raleigh

Markets Worldwide, especially Far East, Western Europe and South America.

Lambert Brothers (Edinburgh) Limited

9-11 Frederick Street, Edinburgh EH2 2HA *Member of SWA*

Blenders and wine and spirit merchants

This firm dates from 1849 and is one of Edinburgh's most highly regarded wine and spirit merchants.

Brands	Piper	The Monarch
	Talisman	

Lang Brothers Limited

100 West Nile Street, Glasgow G1 2QX *Member of SWA*

Distillers and blenders *A subsidiary of Robertson & Baxter Ltd**

Alexander and Gavin Lang started business in 1861 as whisky merchants and blenders and their successors, also Langs, continued the independent existence of the company until its acquisition in 1965 by Robertson and Baxter Ltd.

The Lang brothers had gone into distilling quite early, with the purchase in 1876 of what was then called Burnfoot Distillery at Dumgoyne in Stirlingshire. The distillery had previously been known as Glenguin, when it was first licensed in 1833 to Archibald McLellan, and was renamed Glengoyne Distillery when Lang Bros took it over. The distillery is amongst the most attractively sited in Scotland, in a wooded glen resting at the foot of Dumgoyne Hill. The layout of the distillery makes it particularly suitable for visitors interested in viewing the distilling process in a compact space. Water comes from a fifty-foot fall at the bottom of the Campsie Fells. The merger of Lang Bros with Robertson & Baxter Ltd has led to extensive modernisation.

The product is bottled at 8 years old, as well as being used extensively in Robertson & Baxter's blends. It is classified technically as a Highland malt, although it only just qualifies as such, being located square on the Highland Line. Its features are, therefore, more of a Lowland malt, but it is nonetheless a handsome whisky, light in body and fresh on nose and palate.

The company's former bonded warehouses at 16 Oswald Street in Glasgow had an interesting history, as the building was originally the Argyll Free Church. Initially, Lang Bros occupied only the basement whilst normal church services continued above. A local newspaper commented appropriately:

> The spirits below were the spirits of Wine
> and the spirits above were the spirits Divine.

However, the building was taken over in its entirety for 'spirituous' purposes in 1893.

Brands

Aberfoyle†	Langs Supreme
Dew of Dungoyne†	L.B.W.†
Glengoyne 10 years old Pure Malt	Tam O'Shanter†
Langs Select	

William Lawson Distillers Limited

288 Main Street, Coatbridge ML5 3RH *Member of SWA*

Distillers and blenders

William Lawson hailed from Dundee. He went into business in 1849 as a whisky merchant and subsequently turned his hand to blending. However, the venture was not of significance and the company was dormant for many years. Shortly after the Second World War it was reconstituted in Liverpool to blend and export whisky, and subsequently moved to Coatbridge in 1967 where a blending and bottling complex was set up. The William Lawson brand was promoted mainly on the Continent through the extensive network of outlets of the Martini and Rossi organisation, with which it is closely associated, having become in 1980 part of the General Beverage Corporation of Luxemburg (the holding company for Martini and Rossi). The whisky had been known previously as Lawson's, but this was dropped in favour of the longer name for fear of confusion with Dawson's, owned by Peter Dawson Ltd.*

In order to have direct access to malt whisky, William Lawson Distillers purchased Macduff Distillery near Banff in 1972, constructed some ten years previously by a consortium including Block, Grey and Block Ltd and Brodie Hepburn Ltd. The new owners extended the warehouses and built a dark grains plant alongside the distillery, and Stanley P. Morrison Ltd* took an interest in it between 1966 and 1969. Capacity stands at about 750,000 proof gallons per annum. Macduff draws water for cooling purposes from the near-at-hand Deveron River and thus the bottled single malt from Macduff Distillery is called Glen Deveron. Glen Deveron is available in bottle at 12 years old. There is a subsidiary company — Clan Munro Whisky Ltd.

Brands

Glen Deveron 12 years old	(*Clan Munro Whisky Ltd*)
Highland Single Malt	Clan Munro
William Lawson's Finest Blended	King Edward I
William Lawson's 12 years old	

Markets Over forty throughout the world, but principally Western Europe, because of the Martini and Rossi connection.

The Loch Skaig Trading Company Limited

6 Chatterton Court, Kew Road, Richmond, Surrey
Merchants

A rather small enterprise of recent origins which is trying to establish a market for its brands, especially in hotels in London and Scotland. It already sells in the duty-free market, mainly on certain Channel crossings. The vatted malt consists of three malts, and the blend has a malt content of about 30 per cent.

Brands

Old Loch Skaig 6 years old 75°	Old Loch Skaig 8 years old Malt (vatted)

Lombard Scotch Whisky Limited

18 Parliament Street, Ramsey, Isle of Man

Brokers, blenders and exporters

Brands

Lombard's Gold Label
Lombard's 5 years old
  Premium
Lombard's 12 years old
  De Luxe

Lombard's 12 years old Pure
  Malt (vatted)

London Wine Exchange Limited

West Street, Horsham, Sussex

Brokers and merchants

Brands   L.T. Liqueur   P.G.H.

Long John International Limited

123-157 Bothwell Street, Glasgow G2 7AY   *Member of SWA*
Distillers and blenders   *A subsidiary of Whitbread & Co. Ltd*

Long John is a name well established in the Scotch whisky trade, but it has a two-sided history: the commercial evolution of the company itself and the more romantic story of the brand name. Let us start with the business side of the tale, which goes back to 1805 when the partnership of Seager and Evans was formed in London for the purpose of distilling gin. And gin remained the basis of their operation for well over a hundred years, until they diversified into Scotch whisky in 1927, with the establishment of the Strathclyde grain whisky distillery on the south bank of the River Clyde in Glasgow, in the name of their subsidiary, the Scottish Grain Distillery Co. Ltd. Having thus gained a considerable foothold, albeit in a particular sector of the industry, Seager Evans looked around for other ways of increasing their Scotch whisky interests. This was achieved in 1936 by acquisition of the London wine and spirit merchants W.H. Chaplin & Co. Ltd, who had bought the brand name Long John in 1911 from the successors to Long John Macdonald at the Ben Nevis Distillery. By that time the product had become a blended whisky. The title Long John Distillers Ltd was retained by Seager Evans as a subsidiary company.

The next step was the purchase of Glenugie Distillery, near Peterhead in Aberdeenshire, in 1937. This was a rather small distillery of 1875 vintage, and its capacity remained modest for some time. However, warehousing has recently been extended and there is currently a considerable modernisation programme in progress. It is the most easterly-situated distillery in Scotland, within hearing distance of the North Sea. The distillery gets its water from the Ugie burn. All of the production is used in blending.

With the purchase in 1954 of Westthorn Farm, again on the banks of the Clyde, the company was able to construct what has become one of the biggest concentrations of down-stream activities in the Scotch whisky industry, with 100 acres of storage, cooperage and blending facilities. The warehouses alone can hold twenty million proof gallons. No doubt recalling that the site for Strathclyde had been chosen partly because the water of Loch Katrine in the Trossachs could be drawn on, it was decided to build a malt distillery in the vicinity, and so in 1958 Kinclaith joined the select ranks of the handful of distilleries in Scotland producing Lowland malt. Not surprisingly, given its proximity to Strathclyde, the entire output was used for blending. However, it has been demolished recently as part of the Strathclyde rebuilding and expansion programme. All of this reflected a well-planned policy of enlargement following the purchase in 1956 of Seager Evans by Schenley Industries Inc. of the United States. Another new distillery was completed in 1959, a Highland malt distillery at Tormore, near Grantown-on-Spey, the first such entirely new distillery to be built this century. It is of unique design by the late Sir Albert Richardson, a past President of the Royal Academy.

Although the bulk of Tormore is used in blending, it is available in bottle at 10 years old, and, as a typical Spey malt, has confounded those critics who did not believe that a newly constructed distillery could produce a traditional Highland malt. Indeed, Tormore not only has all the right characteristics, but also a distinctiveness in the aftertaste which makes it stand out.

Again in 1959, the Aberdeen blenders Gordon Graham & Co. Ltd were purchased, bringing with them their Black Bottle blend. Initially this had been very much a local whisky, but footloose Aberdonians must have taken it with them to other parts of Britain and even abroad, since despite the lack of promotion Black Bottle enjoys a considerable following of devotees.

A further development was the purchase in 1962 of a shareholding in D. Johnston and Co. (Laphroaig) Ltd,* proprietors of Laphroaig distillery, which is now a fully owned component of Long John International Ltd, the name adopted by the group in 1971 to reflect the importance of its principal product. Having become an important part of the Scotch whisky industry under the tutelage of Schenley, Long John returned to British ownership when it was sold to Whitbread & Co. Ltd, the London brewing giant, in 1975. The company is currently pursuing an extensive modernisation programme and constructing additional warehousing.

The corporate history, one of vigorous expansion, is rather complicated and the dry facts need a little diluting with some reference to the more romantic angle to the Long John story. John Macdonald stood 6′ 4″ tall, which was considered an unusual height 150 years ago. It was in 1825 that Long John, as he was known, built a distillery at Fort William, the first legal distillery in the area following the Act of Parliament of 1823. For a brief description of the man, we can do no better than to recall the words of a contemporary author, Alexander Smith, who wrote of him in his book *A Summer in Skye* (published in 1864) as follows:

> When a man goes to Caprera he, as a matter of course, brings a letter of introduction to Garibaldi — when I went to Fort William I, equally as a matter of course, brought a letter of introduction to Long John. This gentleman, the distiller of the place, was the tallest man I ever beheld, and must in his youth have been of incomparable physique. I presented my letter and was received with the hospitality and courteous grace so characteristic of the old Gael. He is gone now — the happy-hearted Hercules — gone like one of his own drams!

Long John Macdonald could trace his ancestry back to John Macdonald, Lord of the Isles, and beyond him to Somerled, King of Argyll. Long John's branch of the Clan Macdonald had its origins in Alexander Macdonald, a son of the Lord of the Isles, who was the first chief of the Macdonalds of Keppoch. Long John's great-grandfather, Alexander Macdonald, fought with the Earl of Mar in the 1715 Jacobite Rebellion, fleeing to France after defeat at the Battle of Sheriffmuir, but he returned to Scotland some years later and joined with his brother Donald in rallying the Keppoch Macdonalds in the 1745 Rebellion. Sadly, both were to die a year later at the Battle of Culloden. By the time Long John was born — it is believed in 1796 at Torgolbin — the Highlands had been pacified, save for the skirmishes between the revenue men and the illicit distillers.

Long John was a farmer turned distiller, and the product of his still was known as Long John's Dew of Ben Nevis, and quickly attracted a high reputation in what were the beginnings of a very competitive local trade. His reputation was enhanced when Queen Victoria, on one of her Highland jaunts, visited Fort William and his distillery. She was partial herself to a drop of the golden liquid and, according to the *Illustrated London News* for April 1848:

> Mr Macdonald has presented a cask of whisky to Her Majesty and an order has been sent to the Treasury to permit the spirits

to be removed to the cellars of Buckingham Palace free of duty. The cask is not to be opened until His Royal Highness the Prince of Wales attains his majority, i.e. fifteen years later.

Lucky Prince of Wales!

On his death in 1856, Long John's son Donald Peter Macdonald succeeded to the Ben Nevis Distillery, which in turn passed to his son John. It was for long owned by Ben Nevis Distillery (Fort William) Ltd* but in 1981 was purchased by Long John International, which must be one of the happiest events in Scotch whisky history.

Long John International Ltd now owns a total of five distilleries — one grain and three malt, and Ben Nevis is currently silent, but was until its closure, operating both as a malt and grain distillery — as well as a number of subsidiary marketing companies which have either been acquired at different stages in the group's development or set up for trading purposes to sell secondary brands. Amongst these is Stanley Holt and Son Ltd, a once private firm which held the largest stocks of whisky in England. However, many of the brands have been allowed to lapse. Although the Group is administered from Glasgow, its registered office is located in London in a fine town house which was the birthplace of Lord Palmerston. To commemorate Trafalgar there is a room known as the Captain's cabin, which is a replica of Nelson's cabin on HMS Victory and where many Nelson relics are preserved. Another Long John activity is the management, on behalf of Whitbread & Co. Ltd, of Highland Distillers Corporation in which the brewing giant has a 55 per cent holding. Highland Distillers Corporation are successfully marketing a US bottled Scotch called Scoresby Rare, a blend which relies heavily on Long John whiskies.

Brands

(*Long John International Ltd*)
Long John De Luxe
Long John Special Reserve
Long John 12 years old

Royal Choice 21 years old
  De Luxe
Tormore 10 years old
  Highland Malt

(*Gordon, Graham & Co. Ltd*)
Black Bottle
Royal Gold

Stewart's Yellow Label

(*Stanley Holt & Son Ltd*)
Holt's Buff Label
Holt's Liqueur

Holt's Mountain Cream
Holt's Pure Scotch

(*J. & G. Oldfield Ltd*)
Oldfield's Blue Label

Oldfield's Gold Label

(*Grant, Macdonald & Co. Ltd*)   (*Ian Scott & Sons Ltd*)
Highland Chieftain   Scott's Special

Markets The principal brands are shipped worldwide to some 150 individual markets, with a strong base in the domestic market, especially in Scotland and Wales. Long John is particularly strong in France, Spain, Italy and Scandinavia. About 70 per cent of production is exported, including bulk blended whisky to the United States for bottling there under local labels.

The Longmorn Distilleries Limited

45 Frederick Street, Edinburgh

Distillers   *A subsidiary of The Glenlivet Distillers Ltd**

John Duff's first excursion into distilling was in 1876 when he built Glenlossie near the River Lossie, which is now the property of John Haig & Co. Ltd.* Fully in step with the whisky boom of the day, John Duff & Co. Ltd went on to construct two further distilleries to the south of Elgin and on adjacent sites, which came into operation in 1897. They were called Longmorn and Benriach.

Responsibility for the Longmorn distillery passed in 1898 to James R. Grant and eventually to his two sons P.J.C. Grant and R.L. Grant, who kept up continuous production as the Longmorn Distillery Co. The Longmorn Grants were in time to become associated with the Grants of Glen Grant on the formation in 1970 of The Glenlivet Distillers Ltd.*

Longmorn is believed to be derived from the Welsh word Lhangmorgund, place of the holy man, and the ancient history of the

Benriach

area suggests that the distillery warehouse occupies the site of what was once a chapel. The distillery is blessed with ample supplies of local spring water and peat from Mannoch Hill. The product is considered to be one of the best Speyside/Glenlivet malts. However, the company has itself ceased to bottle it for the time being as a single malt, but Gordon & MacPhail* do so. It is a well-bodied whisky with a fresh, nutty taste.

Although Benriach has had nothing like the continuous history of Longmorn, being closed from 1903 to 1965, it has of recent years been producing a highly regarded malt whisky which has the reputation of rapid in-cask maturation and so is much sought after for blending purposes. A little is bottled by Gordon & MacPhail.

Both distilleries have been the object of enlargement. Between 1972 and 1974 capacity at Benriach was increased by 85 per cent through the addition of two new stills to give a total annual capacity of 780,000 gallons. In the same period Longmorn's capacity grew by 67 per cent.

Brand   Longmorn 10 years old†

Low, Robertson & Company Limited

10 Links Place, Leith, Edinburgh EH6 7HA   *Member of SWA*

Distillers and blenders   *A subsidiary of Distillers Company PLC**

Founded in 1812 and subsequently incorporated in the DCL group, Low, Robertson and Co. Ltd are the registered owners of Port Ellen Distillery, situated in Islay. The distillery was built in 1825 by A.K. McKay and Co. and passed to John Ramsay in 1836. He was a leading figure of the time in the Scotch whisky industry, as well as being MP for Stirling and Chairman of the Glasgow Chamber of Commerce. He was a man of considerable foresight and it was he who pioneered the export of Scotch whisky to the United States, large shipments being made directly from the distillery to American ports. His distillery was the first to use the spirit safe which was to be generally adopted by HM Customs and Excise several years later, and he subsequently persuaded the government to allow the bonding of whisky free of duty. Part of the research work of Robert Stein and Aeneas Coffey resulting in the patent still for the manufacture of grain whisky was carried out at Port Ellen at Ramsay's invitation. After his death the business passed to his wife and, in 1906, to his son who, however, disposed of the property in 1920 to the Port Ellen Distillery Ltd. On its liquidation in 1927, ownership passed to John Dewar & Sons Ltd* and James Buchanan & Co. Ltd,* and to DCL in 1925, after which it was closed down. It was reopened in 1967 after much modernisation and is now licensed to Low, Robertson & Co. Ltd. The distillery is at present closed. Port Ellen is no longer available as a single malt, the entire production being used in blending.

Brands

Ben Cally	Grey Label
Dormy	Loretto
Fiddler	Old Guns
Green Tree	

The Lowland Whisky Company

Unit 10, Dalmarnock Trading Estate, Rutherglen, Glasgow G73 1AN

Owned by Peter Bryson Ltd, The Lowland Whisky Co. specialises in personalised own label whiskies for which there is a ready market amongst companies and individuals wishing to promote their name or image via Scotch whisky.

Brands Jubilee   Personal Choice

Convalmore

W.P. Lowrie & Company Limited

Cumbernauld Road, Stepps, Glasgow G33 6HR   *Member of SWA*

Distillers and blenders   *A subsidiary of James Buchanan & Co. Ltd**

A pioneer in the blending of Scotch whiskies, W.P. Lowrie & Co. Ltd found its way into the DCL group as a result of its acquisition in 1906 by James Buchanan & Co. Ltd, to whom they had for long been suppliers of whisky. The firm's founder is said to have been the initiator of the process of blending traditional pot still Scotch whisky and grain whisky from patent stills which revolutionised the industry, although this distinction is also claimed by Andrew Usher. Lowrie started business on his own account in 1869 as a whisky broker and agent, having gained experience as manager of Port Ellen Distillery in Islay. He expanded rapidly and his firm claimed to be the first to gain the permission of HM Customs and Excise to bottle in bond.

Lowrie, in 1904, acquired Convalmore Distillery and held a substantial part of the share capital in Glentauchers Distillery which belonged to James Buchanan. Convalmore still trades under the name of W.P. Lowrie & Co. Ltd, although Scottish Malt Distillers Ltd* are the operators. It was built in 1894 by the Convalmore-Glenlivet Distillery Co. Ltd. Much of it was destroyed by fire in 1909, but in the immediate rebuilding the opportunity was taken to add a number of considerable improvements to the plant, including a continuous still with a capacity of 500 gallons of wash per hour. It was quite an innovation for a Highland malt distillery to imitate the methods of a grain distillery, but there was a flaw in the maturing of the spirit and the experimental plant was abandoned six years later. The distillery takes its name from the Conval Hills from whence it draws its water and is located at Dufftown, Banffshire. The product is all used for blending, save for the odd butt put aside for bottling by individual merchants such as Wm Cadenhead Ltd*, who currently offer it at 16 and 18 years old.

When William Lowrie retired at the age of seventy-five, he invited James Buchanan to succeed him as chairman of the company. Buchanan inherited what was probably one of the most self-contained whisky companies in Scotland. It embraced not only distilling, blending and coopering, but also had its own case works, an extensive transport fleet and, most unusually, its own bottle works. However, it was in the field of coopering that Lowrie's were most prominent and their Glasgow cooperage was the largest of its kind in the world. In recent years the cooperage has been transferred to the ownership of Scottish Grain Distillers Ltd, whilst the remaining Lowrie operations have been combined with those of James Buchanan & Co. Ltd.

Brand Lowrie's

Lundie & Company Limited

48 West Regent Street, Glasgow G2 2QP   *Member of SWA*

Brokers and blenders

One of the best known of the traditional brokers, the present managing director's father began his career in Scotch whisky with David Sandeman in 1904. Apart from their extensive broking activities Lundie are sole UK agents for Macduff Highland malt, owned by William Lawson Distillers Ltd.* There is an associate company which trades in the firm's own blends.

Brands

(William Lundie & Co. Ltd)

Gow's   Royal Heritage
Lismore

Macallan-Glenlivet PLC

Macallan-Glenlivet Distillery, Craigellachie, Banffshire

Distillers   *Member of SWA*

After a history of more than 140 years of private ownership, Macallan-Glenlivet PLC became a public company in 1966.

The distillery lies in the ancient parish of Macallan, now incorporated in Knockando, on the bank of the Spey about a mile to the west of the village of Craigellachie. Macallan Distillery was first licensed in 1824, which is its legal date of establishment, although it is a fairly safe bet that distilling of the illegal kind had been going on there for some years previously. Its location near one of the few fords across the River Spey, which was part of one of the known cattle drove routes from the Morayshire plains to the South via the Spey valley, lends credence to the theory that distilling had been undertaken at Macallan Farm for many years previously. This would have helped establish the early reputation of the whisky further south and thus hastened the establishment of a legal distillery.

During the nineteenth century, the distillery changed hands on several occasions ending up, in 1892, as the property of Roderick Kemp who had acquired it from James Stuart. Kemp applied the experience he had gained at Talisker Distillery to improve Macallan. Output was expanded and the whisky's reputation went from strength to strength, and it was soon regarded as one of the finest on Speyside. Roderick Kemp died in 1909. A trust was set up for the benefit of his two married daughters and their offspring, and today Roderick Kemp's direct descendants, the Herberson and Schiach families, are still important shareholders in the company.

Easter Elchies Manor, by Macallan

A six year work programme of rebuilding and modernisation was launched in 1950, during which period the distillery remained in full production. Further work was carried out in 1959, and as a result of all these efforts output was tripled from what it had been in the immediate post-war period. Enhanced production meant greater storage requirements and a programme of steady expansion in this area was put under way. But demand continued to rise and construction of a second distillery alongside the original started in 1964, coming into operation in 1966. However, it is not considered to be separate from the parent distillery, as is the case in some instances where two distilleries have been built next to each other and given different names.

Macallan, although by industry standards a large distillery, producing as it does some one and a half million proof gallons per year, is much in demand and it is rated for quality as one of the top three Highland malts. Part of the success of Macallan may be due to the use of very small stills equivalent in size and shape to the originals. In addition, Macallan has two features which make it stand out from other malt whiskies: it is matured only in sherry casks — preferably dry oloroso — and caramel is never added for colouring, the Macallan colour being achieved by the right blending of whiskies from different casks. A subsidiary, Highmac Ltd, is responsible for the production and marketing of dark grains for animal feeding.

Macallan is available in bottle at a variety of ages. Limited supplies of Macallan distilled in 1938 and 1950 have recently been released on allocation, the older of the two retailing in Japan in personalised bottles at about £300 each.

Brands

The Macallan 8 years old	The Macallan 50 years old
The Macallan 10 years Old	The Macallan 1963
The Macallan 12 years old	The Royal Wedding Macallan
The Macallan 25 years old	

Markets United Kingdom, Italy, France, Germany, Belgium, Switzerland, United States, Australia, New Zealand and Japan.

D. & J. McCallum Limited

4 Picardy Place, Edinburgh EH1 3JZ   *Member of SWA*

Blenders and exporters   *A subsidiary of Distillers Company PLC**

Two Edinburgh brothers, Duncan and John McCallum, went into business together in 1807 as inn-keepers and blenders of whisky. Their whisky soon became famous and their hostelry, known colloquially as the Tattie Pit, became a favourite watering-hole for the worthies of that city.

Fame and fortune soon led to expansion and the acquisition of premises across from the original inn. There, a thriving retail trade in wines and spirits developed. Further extensions were added, but the McCallum premises were completely destroyed during the German air raid on Edinburgh in April, 1916. However, ownership of the company had long since passed into the hands of Duncan McCallum Stewart, the nephew of the two brothers, who had remained life-long bachelors. Their successor had quickly seen the export potential for high quality whisky, and through patient cultivation of overseas markets McCallum's Perfection eventually commanded a considerable following, particularly in Australia, where the company has a branch office in Sydney, and in New Zealand due, no doubt, to the consistency of the blending as originally specified by the founders.

McCallum's enjoy the distinction of describing their product as 'Scots Whisky' rather than 'Scotch'. This was how it was first labelled and continues to be so today. It is also one of the few brands of blended whisky for which a budding scribe has written poetry:

> Time was when every misty glen,
> From Cruachan to Cowal Shore,
> Saw Clans that gathered for the fray,
> Their gathering cry McCallum Mhor.
> Those days are dead and gone and now,

Be it Auckland, Sydney or Quebec,
Where Scots foregather day by day,
Their gathering cry is More McCallum.

Like many of the family blending houses, D. & J. McCallum Ltd went through many changes in organisation and management, culminating in its joining the DCL empire in 1937. This eventually led to the DCL-owned Cragganmore Distillery being licensed to McCallums. The distillery, like several others, is at Ballindalloch, near the River Spey. It dates from 1869 when it was built by John Smith who had left his former employer, Minmore Distillery, in order to strike out on his own as a farmer and later as a distiller. There is a large stone at the entrance to the distillery: the story goes that Smith removed the stone by his own physical effort from a field that was being ploughed on his farm, and in doing so uncovered some ancient treasure. He is reputed to have prospered thereafter. Gordon Smith inherited the distillery from his father, and Gordon's widow sold it in 1923 to a syndicate which formed the Cragganmore Distillery Co. Ltd. One of the partners was Peter J. Mackie of White Horse Distillers Ltd,* and eventually Cragganmore became a wholly owned subsidiary of DCL when the residual minority shareholding was acquired by them in 1965. Cragganmore is now available as a 12 years old single malt.

Brands

(*D. & J. McCallum Ltd*)

Cragganmore 12 years old
    Single Malt
McCallum's De Luxe

McCallum's Perfection Scots
    Whisky

(*Picardy Blending Co.*)

Auld Acquaintance†

Calton

Markets Australia and New Zealand and some seventy other countries.

T. & A. McClelland Limited

13 Royal Crescent, Glasgow G3 7SL

Blenders and exporters   *A subsidiary of Stanley P. Morrison Ltd* *

This firm of Glasgow blenders and exporters can trace its origins to 1818. It did not always restrict itself to those aspects of the industry, having ventured into distilling at one time as owners of the Bladnoch Distillery Ltd.* Perhaps McClelland's are best known for their association with a prominent industry personality, Jimmy Barclay, who, on his death in 1963, was Chairman and Managing Director of T. & A. McClelland Ltd. After a distinguished career with Mackie &

Co. Ltd (now White Horse Distillers Ltd*) he had gone into business on his own as a merchant and broker. To do this, he took over James and George Stodart Ltd* and in addition later became a director of Chivas Bros Ltd.* By procuring T. & A. McClelland Ltd and its various subsidiaries, Morrisons inherited a number of useful export labels.

Brands

(T. & A. McClelland Ltd)

Brae Dew	King's Pride
Clan Roy	McClelland's

(Samuel Birch & Co.)

Auld Dram†	Birch's Liqueur†
Birch's Black Bottle†	Birch's Red Seal†
Birch's Black Crest	

(W.V. Douglas & Co.)

Old Squire†	W.V.D.†

(Colin Forsyth & Co.)

Peerage	Peerage Special Reserve

(Fraser, Scott & Co.)

King's Favourite	King's Grant

(James Hogg & Co.)

Auld McDougall†

(Lang, Fulton & Co.)

Rare & Royal†	Scots Aristocrat†

(Macbeth & Young)

Old Macbeth†

(McKenzie Duff & Co.)

Bonnie Dee†	Prime Vat†
Highland Mist†	

(Moffat, Dunbar & Co.)	*(Alister Stewart & Co.)*
Glenbrae†	Brig O'Doon†

Markets Principally Western Europe

Macdonald Greenlees Limited

Palmerston House, 39 Palmerston Place, Edinburgh EH12 5BH

Distillers and blenders   *A subsidiary of Distillers Company PLC**
Member of SWA

Macdonald Greenlees Ltd traces its history back to 1840 in which year the firm of Alexander and Macdonald started selling Sandy Macdonald whisky. In 1871 the brothers Greenlees, James and Samuel, set themselves up as whisky distillers, blenders and merchants. They enjoyed considerable success in the burgeoning London market with their Old Parr brand. It was — and still is — a De Luxe whisky and was named after one Thomas Parr who is reputed to have lived for 152 years, dying in 1635. He is buried in Westminster Abbey. Because of the excellence of the whisky, Old Parr became a big seller in London. Oddly enough, this hold on the London market did not survive and Old Parr was later to become much more of an export whisky, the first consignments having been sent to Canada and Brazil in 1905.

The two original parents of the present company were brought together towards the end of the last century when both were

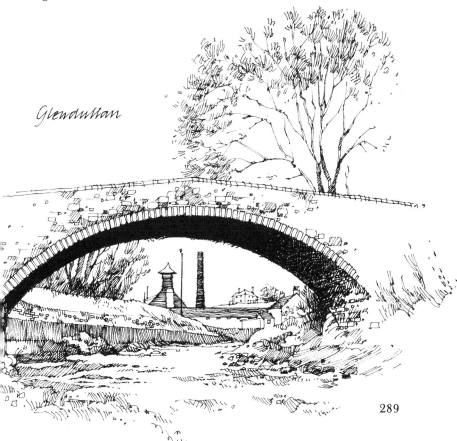

Glendullan

acquired at about the same time by Sir James Calder, a prominent Scottish businessman. They were amalgamated to become Macdonald Greenlees and Williams (Distillers) Ltd and adopted the existing title when the company was acquired by DCL in 1925. This deal entailed the passing to DCL ownership of a number of subsidiaries — James Munro & Son Ltd,* R.H. Thomson & Co. (Distillers) Ltd,* Ainslie & Heilbron Ltd,* Donald Fisher Ltd* and John Gillon & Co. Ltd* — all of which are still functioning within the DCL family. Of these, James Munro & Co. Ltd and R.H. Thomson & Co. (Distillers) Ltd remain within the Macdonald Greenlees group. This deal also gave DCL an impressive addition to their distillery estate since it included the malt whisky distilleries of Auchenblae, Argyll, Dalwhinnie, Auchtertool and Glendullan.

Glendullan remains licensed to Macdonald Greenlees Ltd; it was erected in 1897 at Dufftown where six distilleries already stood. The original owners were William Williams & Sons Ltd of Aberdeen who used most of the Glendullan production for their Strathdon and Three Stars brands of blended whisky. They merged during the First World War into Macdonald Greenlees and Williams (Distillers) Ltd. The whisky from Glendullan has for some time now been bottled as a single malt and is now available in many markets in the world. A testimony to its quality is that it was supplied in 1902 to King Edward VII and for a number of years thereafter casks bore the inscription 'By appointment to HM The King allowed by the Commissioners of Customs and Excise on 2nd December 1902.'

Brands

Glendullan 12 years old single malt	President Special Reserve De Luxe
Grand Old Parr De Luxe	Real Antique†
Lorne†	Sandy Macdonald
Old Parr 500	Sportsman†
Old Particular†	Strathdon†

Markets Exported to over 100 countries. Principal markets are Latin America, Far East and Japan.

Macdonald Martin Distilleries PLC

Queen's Dock, Leith, Edinburgh EH6 6NN

Distillers and blenders

This is the holding company for a group of family companies formed in 1949. Today the group, which is one of the few remaining independent family-controlled Scotch whisky houses marketing a range of international brands, comprises the following subsidiaries directly involved in the trade:

> The Glenmorangie Distillery Co.*
> The Glen Moray-Glenlivet Distillery Co.*
> Macdonald & Muir Ltd*
> Andrew McLaggan & Co.
> Douglas MacNiven & Co. Ltd
> James Martin & Co. Ltd*
> Chas Muirhead & Son Ltd*
> Nicol Anderson & Co. Ltd

The group's brands belong to the individual subsidiary companies and are available in 120 countries. That represents worldwide coverage, save for the Eastern Europe bloc. However, the group has strong interests in the domestic market and 20.6 per cent of sales are in Europe, including the United Kingdom, 65.2 per cent in the Americas and the rest in a wide variety of markets in Africa, Asia and Australasia. Within the group, Macdonald & Muir Ltd is responsible for production and administration whilst James Martin & Co. Ltd concentrates on the export side of the business.

Macdonald & Muir Limited

Macdonald House, 186 Commercial Street, Leith, Edinburgh
EH6 6NN   *Member of SWA*
Distillers and blenders   A subsidiary of Macdonald Martin Distilleries PLC *

This firm is still essentially a family affair, being the result of a successful partnership of two Edinburgh whisky entrepreneurs, Roderick Macdonald and Alexander Muir, who joined forces in 1893. Both were already well known in the whisky trade, having first worked together for Messrs A. & J. Alexander. However, when the A. & J. partnership split up, Alexander Muir joined Mr Alexander Alexander in a company called A. Alexander & Co. whilst Roderick Macdonald formed with the other Mr Alexander the firm of Alexander & Macdonald. But the marriage of Alexander Muir's sister to Roderick Macdonald brought the two men into partnership, leaving the firm of Alexander & Macdonald to become associated with Macdonald Greenlees Ltd.*

The business prospered and in 1901 Macdonald & Muir were able to take over more commodious premises at Queen's Dock after the crash of Pattisons Ltd. Prior to this, they had operated from a house in the Kirkgate in Leith, having their blending done at Edinburgh and Leith Warehousing Co. and using the facilities of William Sanderson and Son * for storage.

Success at home inevitably led to the search for export markets. The Company, to commemorate the association between Mary Queen of Scots and Leith Harbour where she had landed in 1561 on arrival from France, named their principal brand Highland Queen. With it, they pioneered the sale of Scotch in Egypt, Mexico, Scandinavia and parts of South America and the Far East.

The wish to expand from being mere blenders and bottlers was natural in view of the firm's prosperity, and between 1912 and 1921 seven subsidiaries were acquired, the most important of these being the Glenmorangie Distillery Co.* and the Glen Moray-Glenlivet Distillery Co.* In these two cases, Macdonald & Muir changed from being minority shareholders to outright owners of both distilleries in order to ensure continuing supplies of matured malt whisky. Other important acquisitions were to follow later in the form of James Martin & Co.* and Charles Muirhead and Son.*

Although Alexander Muir had no issue, Roderick Macdonald's two sons entered the company, and today a grandson, David Macdonald, is Chairman and Managing Director, thus maintaining the family tradition. This tradition, as expressed today in the company's literature, is 'to provide consistent quality with each blend, and to preserve distinctive character through a higher than average proportion of malt whisky, aged well above the minimum required by law.'

Brands

(*Macdonald & Muir Ltd*)
Highland Queen
Highland Queen Grand 10†
Highland Queen Grand
  Reserve 15 years old
Highland Queen Grand
  Liqueur†

Highland Queen Supreme 21
  years old
Milord's 12 years old De
  Luxe
Milord's Premium
Three Seals

(*Alistair Graham Ltd*)
MacAndrew's

White and Gold

(*Andrew MacLaggan & Co. Ltd*)
Major Gunn's

(*Murdoch McLellan Ltd*)
Clan Murdock

(*Nicol Anderson & Co. Ltd*)
Baillie Nicol Jarvie

Souter Johnnie†

(*Douglas MacNiven & Co. Ltd*)
Glen Niven
MacNiven's Finest†

MacNiven's Royal Abbey†

Markets Principally United Kingdom, United States and Europe, 108 markets in all.

Andrew Macdonald (London) Limited

Bolton House, 19-20 Bolton Street, Piccadilly, London W1Y 7PA

Blender, brokers and exporters

When it first opened its doors for business in 1946 Andrew Macdonald Ltd did so as whisky blenders and merchants. However, in the 1970s the company became involved in selling Scotch whisky to overseas investors to be stored duty free in bonded warehouses. Subsidiary companies connected with the investment service were set up in the United States, Malaysia and Singapore.

Despite its venture into the whisky investment service, Andrew Macdonald Ltd has continued to blend and export whisky both under its own name and through its associated companies.

Brands

(Andrew Macdonald (London) Ltd)

Campbell's Green Tartan†
Macdonald's Black Label 10 years old Vatted Malt
Macdonald's Cream of the Glen†
Macdonald's Finest
Macdonald's Gold Crest 5 years old
Macdonald's Gold Label†

Macdonald's Gold Label 12 years old De luxe
Maclean's Special Reserve
Pride of Islay†
Pride of Montrose†
Royal St George
Strathduie

(Black & Gold Blending Co. Ltd)
Black and Gold

(Glencree Bonding Co. Ltd)
Glencree

Markets Worldwide, but particular emphasis on United States and Far East.

R.N. MacDonald & Company Limited

Glencoe, Argyllshire

Blenders and merchants

The company's founder, Major Andrew Macdonald, is the great grandson of 'Long John' Macdonald, the famous giant of Scotch whisky distilling in the early nineteenth century whose story is told in connection with Long John International Ltd.* This particular MacDonald venture was established in 1970 and their whisky, a blend or vatting of fine Highland malt whiskies, is now available widely in the United Kingdom. In 1982, Highland Stag Whiskies acquired a majority shareholding in the company.

Brand   Glencoe 100° proof 8 years old Highland malt

Markets UK and some overseas countries, especially Germany.

Linkwood

John McEwan & Company Limited

10 Links Place, Leith, Edinburgh EH6 7HA

Distillers and blenders   *A subsidiary of Distillers Company PLC**

One of the smaller member's of the DCL group, John McEwan and Co. Ltd has nevertheless built up a fine reputation for its small range of whiskies. Established in 1863, it has for some time been the registered owner of Linkwood Distillery at Elgin. The founder, Peter Brown, built his distillery in 1821 and named it after an old mansion house that formerly stood on the site — just a mile from Elgin in a delightful wooded setting. His son rebuilt and extended the premises in 1873. From 1897 the distillery was run as a limited liability company known as Linkwood-Glenlivet Distillery Ltd. Linkwood's reputation was established largely as the result of the efforts of Mr Innes Cameron, its Managing Director from 1902 until his death in 1932. Thereafter, the company was wound up and the distillery sold to DCL, after which John McEwan and Co. Ltd became responsible for it. Another figure who has been prominent in building up the Linkwood tradition was Mr Roderick Mackenzie who was in charge of distilling for many years. To avoid even the

294

remotest chance of any change to the character of his beloved Linkwood Highland malt, he would only allow a piece of equipment in the distillery to be replaced when absolutely necessary and even forbade the removal of such integral parts of the premises as spiders' webs. Linkwood is available as a 12 years old single malt.

Brands

Abbot's Choice	Linkwood 12 years old
Arbiter†	Highland Malt
Chequers De Luxe	Magistrate†

Markets Worldwide

W.G. McFadden & Company (Blenders & Exporters) Limited

16 Atholl Drive, Gifnock, Glasgow G46 6QR

Blenders and exporters

W.G. McFadden went into business as a whisky blender in the early years of this century and the firm has remained in family hands ever since. It is presently run by the founder's grandson, Mr Ronald Sinclair.

Most blenders are very guarded about the make-up of their blends. McFadden & Co., on the other hand, make no secret of the fact that the pride of their portfolio, Queen's Liqueur, which is 10 years old, has a malt content of 50 per cent and that the only malts used are The Glenlivet and Glen Grant. The formula was devised by W.G. McFadden, and was supplied on a very limited basis and retained more in memory of the originator than for any other reason. W.G. McFadden had another blend registered to him known as S.O.S. (Special Old Scotch), but this never got to the point of being marketed.

The company's two other whiskies were introduced by the founder's son-in-law, A.W. Sinclair.

Brands

Queen's Embassy 5 years old†	Queen's Realm 3 years old†
Queen's Liqueur 10 years old	S.O.S.†
(De Luxe)	

Markets Glasgow, Germany and Italy.

Mackay and Company Limited

Le Marchant House, Le Truchot, St Peter Port, Guernsey, Channel Islands

Wine and spirit merchants

The Real Mackay has been available to Guernsey islanders for many years, having been introduced shortly after Alexander Mackay established himself on the island in 1909 as successor to a well known local wine merchant called Stickland. Mackay himself had first arrived in Guernsey from Scotland in 1903, having had to move to a balmier clime on grounds of health. The Stickland business had been devoted exclusively to wine importing, but Alexander Mackay soon changed that by adding whisky from his native Scotland to the commodities previously for sale. It gained a handsome reputation locally, and no wonder: an advertisement in 1934 claims none of the whiskies in the blend to be less than 20 years old and to include 1898 Glenlivet, 1899 Glenury, 1906 Ardbeg, 1911 Glen Grant and Caledonian grain whisky distilled in 1914, giving an average age of over 25 years. The price then was 8 shillings (40p) at Guernsey preferential prices! Today the whisky is blended for Mackay's by Long John Distillers Ltd*. Mackay & Co. Ltd soon established themselves as a high quality enterprise and expanded within the island to become eventually one of the major firms in Guernsey.

Brand   The Real Mackay

Mackenzie Brothers, Dalmore

Dalmore Distillery, Alness, Ross-shire

Distillers   *A non-trading subsidiary of Whyte & Mackay Distillers Ltd* *

Dalmore Highland Malt Distillery was founded in 1839, and was acquired by the present owners, Mackenzie Brothers, in 1867. They subsequently merged with Whyte and Mackay Ltd in 1960, although a third generation Mackenzie is on the board of the Group, providing an unbroken line. A curious episode in its history was its use during World War I for the assembling of mines. Due to the ravages of war service, Dalmore did not recommence distilling until 1922.

Despite its age, it has always been to the forefront in adopting new techniques, although one of its stills dates from 1874. Capacity today stands at 1.2 million gallons. Its setting is superb, looking over the Cromarty Firth and the Black Isle. Dalmore has the sole rights to water from the River Alness. A lot of Dalmore's output goes to make up the Whyte & Mackay blends, but some of it is bottled for selling straight at 12 years old and, as such, has all the body and taste one might demand of a northern Highland malt.

Brands

Dalmore 8 years old Highland Malt†

Dalmore 12 years old Highland Malt

Dalmore 20 years old Highland Malt†

Michael MacKenzie

112-114 Loch Leven Road, Lochore Lochgelly, Fife KY5 8DA

Wine and spirit merchants

Brand   Highland Glee

W.D. Mackenzie Limited

Dunvorist, Brae Street, Dunkeld, Perthshire

Brokers

Apart from the usual broking activities, the family firm of Mackenzies holds an extensive range of bottled single malt whiskies. They also have a number of collector's 'specials' such as Old Vatted Glenlivet of 1898 recovered from the wreck of the *Firth of Cromarty* off the Ayrshire coast, The Glenlivet at 34 years old which was bottled to celebrate the 150th anniversary of the first licensing of the distillery, and Old Gloag bottled from an old cask and reputed to be over 60 years old and Dalintober malt bottled in 1905.

Charles Mackinlay & Company Limited

9-21 Salamander Place, Leith, Edinburgh EH6 7JL *Member of SWA*

Distillers and blenders   *A subsidiary of The Waverley Group Ltd* *

Established in 1815, this company is now into its fifth generation of whisky distilling and blending. The company was acquired by Scottish & Newcastle Breweries Ltd in 1961, becoming part of Mackinlay-McPherson Ltd in 1962 which subsequently came under the control of Waverley Vintners Ltd in 1974, itself a subsidiary of Scottish & Newcastle Breweries Ltd. The current Chairman is Donald Mackinlay, great-great-grandson of the founder, Charles Mackinlay.

The business has always passed from father to son. Charles Mackinlay started in Leith as a wine merchant in 1815. His son James joined him after a brief apprenticeship in London with a firm of sherry shippers, taking over control in 1867. Between then and his death in 1926, when he was succeeded by his son Charles, proprietary brands were introduced into the whisky industry. The Mackinlay family first became agents for Macfarlane's whisky, later known as Port Dundas, before introducing their own brands, beginning with Mackinlay's Vatted Old Ben Vorlich. They became suppliers to the Houses of Parliament, and it is known that Shackleton carried Mackinlay's whisky on his North Pole expedition. On the death of Charles Mackinlay in 1934, his son Ian took over responsibility for the continuity of the Mackinlay's blend. Donald Mackinlay is his son, and in the family tradition keeps a careful 'nose' on sampling and blending, in between travelling widely in the UK and overseas on industry business.

The family's distilling interests began with the firm of Mackinlay & Birnie, and today extends to the two distillery companies within The Waverley Group — Glenallachie Distillery Co. Ltd* and Isle of Jura Distillery Co. Ltd.*

Brands

Ben Vorlich†
Cameron Highlander†
Legacy 12 years old De Luxe
Legacy (Spode Imperial Flagon)
Mackinlay's Finest Old
    Scotch Whisky

Mackinlay's Reserve
Mackinlay's 1815 (Royal
    Worcester Porcelain
    Decanter) 20 years old
Silver Peg†

Markets The company's whiskies, particularly Mackinlay's and Legacy, are sold in about a hundred overseas markets in addition to the UK. Small quantities of whisky are exported in bulk to Australia and New Zealand, where it is sold as Mackinlay's.

Macleay Duff (Distillers) Limited

75 Hope Street, Glasgow G2 6AN   *Member of SWA*
Distillers and blenders   *A subsidiary of Distillers Company PLC* *

This company dates from 1863 and, after seventy years of independence, became part of DCL in 1933. Whilst its principal activity is the marketing, almost exclusively abroad, of a range of blended whiskies, it also boasts the ownership under licence of Millburn's Distillery, on the outskirts of Inverness.

Millburn's official establishment dates from 1807 and it was one of the earliest legal distilleries. At first, it must have been hard for its owners to show a profit in the face of competition from the illicit alternatives, who paid no taxes or fees. But as the smugglers were gradually squeezed out of business by the relentless Excise, so the legal distilleries began to prosper. There is clear evidence of this in Millburn's case in a report in the *Inverness Journal* of 25th March, 1829:

> The Session Lands of DIRIEBUGHT, Inverness, were this day let on a 14 years lease to The Millburn Distillery Company for the sum of £136 per annum. The former rent on the old lease held by Mr Walsh of only £16 per annum.

Millburn became the property, in 1853, of David Rose, an Inverness corn merchant. In 1876 he had it extensively rebuilt and enlarged in time for his son, George, to succeed to it in 1881. In 1892 it was acquired by two members of the Haig distillery family, who set up as A. Haig & Co., Distillers, Millburn. In 1904 the company reverted simply to the Millburn Distillery Co.

This early period of Haig control also saw expansion and improvement, including much additional warehousing. Millburn was, therefore, an attractive proposition when it passed to Booth's Distillery Ltd, of gin-making fame, in 1921. But this change was not a good omen, since a serious fire the following year damaged most of the essential buildings and the distillery had to be completely re-designed.

Now firmly in the DCL family, Millburn was transferred to Scottish Malt Distillers Ltd* in 1943, who continued to enhance the plant, including the installation of mechanical stokers for the still furnaces. In keeping with DCL practice in their other distilleries in the area, Millburn does its own malting in Saladin boxes. Although not bottled as a single malt, the distillery's product is a major ingredient in the firm's vatted malt, The Mill Burn 12 years old.

Brands

Antique
Auld Scottie
Macleay Duff Fine Old

Macleay Duff Special Matured Cream
The Mill Burn 12 years old Pure Malt (vatted)

(Glen Lyon Blending Co.)
Glen Lyon Pure Malt (vatted)†

McMullen and Sons Limited

The Hertford Brewery, Hertford, Herts

Brewers and merchants

This old established firm of independent brewers and wine and spirit merchants has had its own brands for over fifty years. Up to about twenty years ago McMullens bought single whiskies and blended them at the brewery in Hertford. The practice was discontinued on economic and practical grounds and the whisky is blended for them, but to their specification, in Scotland by one of the major distillers. The quantity sold is modest — about 2,500 proof gallons annually.

Brands

Gairloch   Scottish Chief†

Markets In Hertfordshire through the company's tied houses and free trade outlets.

Macnab Distilleries Limited

Lochside Distillery, Montrose

Distillers and blenders

From its outward appearance, Lochside does not resemble in any way a Highland Malt distillery; and this is not surprising, as it was originally a brewery. Its date of construction in the eighteenth century, and its early owners, are unknown. At the beginning of the nineteenth century it was owned by William Ross who sold it to James Deuchar & Sons Ltd of Newcastle-upon-Tyne, which eventually became part of Scottish & Newcastle Breweries Ltd. Beer from Lochside was shipped directly by coastal barge from Montrose to Newcastle. In 1957, however, the late Joseph W. Hobbs of Ben Nevis Distillery (Fort William) Ltd* purchased Lochside and converted it into a distillery. The Ben Nevis experiment of having pot malt and grain stills on the same premises was repeated at Lochside. A controlling company, Macnab Distilleries Ltd, was set up and the blend Sandy Macnab's promoted.

In November 1973 ownership passed to Destilerias y Crianza del Whisky S.A. of Madrid, or DYC as it is popularly known in Spain. In an industry steeped in history and tradition, such a move caused something of a stir. It was one thing to have Canadians and Americans established in the trade, since they already knew something about whisky, and had not the Scots gone to North America in great numbers to settle, carrying with them the secret skills of distilling. But it was quite another thing for Continentals to buy into the industry. There was considerable apprehension as to what was going to happen at Lochside, but the sceptics must have been disappointed. No great changes were instituted, except that the grain still was closed down and now Lochside's production is entirely of Highland Malt. And so, in a way, DYC conformed with the traditional view that two entirely different kinds of whisky could not be distilled successfully at the same location. The possibility

300

Lochside

remains, however, for grain whisky production to recommence with the minimum of adaption, as the grain still is *in situ* ready for operation.

Only a small percentage of Lochside malt is shipped to Spain in bulk to use in DYC Spanish whisky. The vast majority ends up in other Scotch whisky blends, whilst some is kept for the firm's own house brand, Sandy Macnab's, and for bottling as a single malt at 8 and 12 years old.

Sandy Macnab's is another of the few brands of whisky about which someone has actually written a poem. Perhaps the fact that the minimum malt content is 35 per cent and that seventeen to eighteen different malts are used in the blend inspired this amusing piece of consumer literature.

> We are sitting to-night in the fire glow,
> Just you and I alone,
> And the flickering light falls softly
> On a beauty that's all your own,
> It gleams where your round smooth shoulder
> From a graceful neck sweeps down;
> And I would not exchange your beauty
> For the best-dressed belle in town.

I have drawn the curtain closer,
And from my easy chair
I stretch my hand towards you,
Just to feel that you are there
And your breath is laden with perfume,
As my thoughts around you twine,
And I feel my pulses beating
As your spirit is mingled with mine.

And the woes of the world have vanished
When I've pressed my lips to yours;
And to feel your life-blood flowing
To me is the best of cures.
You have given me inspiration
For many a soulful rhyme —
You're the Finest Old Scotch Whisky
I've had for a long, long time.

Sandy Macnab's is exported as bulk blend to certain markets for bottling under the registered brand name. Some Lochside malt is sold in bulk to Italy.

Lochside's distilling capacity is one million gallons per annum. There are ample storage facilities for the end product in the extensive warehouses built by Macnab Distilleries on the filled-in loch, which gave the brewery its name.

Brands

Lochside Highland Malt 8 years   Sandy Macnab's Old Blended
     old
Lochside Highland Malt 12
     years old

Markets Italy, France, Spain, Portugal, USA, Germany, Australia, Argentina.

John E. McPherson & Sons Limited

9-21 Salamander Place, Leith, Edinburgh   *Member of SWA*

Blenders   *A subsidiary of The Waverley Group Ltd**

This company was established in 1857, and today forms part of Waverley International Ltd, the export operation of The Waverley Group Ltd, having been acquired in 1952 by Scottish and Newcastle Breweries Ltd.

The company's main brand is Cluny Scotch Whisky. The Chief of Clan McPherson is traditionally called Cluny, after the place close to the clan stronghold. In 1857 the founder of the company, John E. McPherson, received permission to name his special blend of whisky Cluny, in honour of his cousin the Chief.

Brands

Clan Chattan (vatted malt)	Cluny 12 years old
Cluny	Heirloom†

Markets UK and many overseas countries. Scottish & Newcastle Importers Co. (another subsidiary of The Waverley Group Ltd) import Cluny whisky from John E. McPherson & Sons Ltd into the USA.

John Makay Limited

89 Sevington Road, London NW4 3RU

Blenders and merchants

A new company offering a De Luxe blend. Exporting is undertaken by a sister company, Levitta Ltd.

Brand Gold King De Luxe

Malpas Stallard Limited

9 Copenhagen Street, Worcester

Wine and spirit merchants

This ancient establishment has a recorded history going back to 1642, although it is believed to be even older than that.

Brand J.M. & Co. Superior Mountain Dew

E.D. & F. Man (Produce) Limited

Sugar Quay, Lower Thames Street, London EC3R 6DU

Brokers, blenders and merchants

Brand Man's Old Scotch

E. Marcus & Son

233 Mile End Road, London E1 4AA

Wine and spirit merchants

Brands

Gombene†	Red Seal†

Marston, Thompson & Evershed PLC

The Brewery, Shobnall Road, Burton-on-Trent

Brewers and wine and spirit merchants

This company from the great brewing centre of Burton-on-Trent was formed in 1905 with the amalgamation of J. Marston, Thompson & Son Ltd and Sydney Evershed Ltd. The former had itself only been created seven years earlier when J. Marston & Son Ltd (founded 1834) and John Thompson & Son Ltd (circa 1765) had joined forces. It is not clear when these companies first started blending whiskies, but a price list for 1910 shows three principal blends on offer:

Berwick Blend
Special Old Blend (Brown Label)
Special Liqueur (White Label)

Only one of these survives today, along with the whisky brand owned by W.H. Milner & Co. Ltd, a firm of wine and spirit merchants, which was acquired in 1957 as part of the take-over of Taylor's Eagle Brewery Ltd of Manchester.

Brands

Brown Label Special

(W.H. Milner & Co.)
Rare Old Black Bottle

James Martin & Company Limited

Quality House, 58 Commercial Street, Leith, Edinburgh EH6 6NF

Blenders and exporters   A subsidiary of Macdonald Martin Distilleries PLC*
Member of SWA

James Martin, or 'Sparry' Martin to use the nickname which he acquired reputedly as a result of his performance in the boxing ring, set up his own business as a whisky merchant in Edinburgh in 1878. Prior to that he had been employed as a traveller for another whisky merchant, John H. Bertram of Leith. A noted philanthropist in his home town, James Martin developed overseas markets for his whiskies. This trend was followed by Edward Macdonald, his partner, who took his younger brother, Daniel, into the business on Marin's death in 1899. The United States became especially important and Martin's has counted itself in the top ten premium brands since 1933. This is remarkable given Martin's policy on advertising, which was to have virtually none.

Martin's whiskies earned themselves a notable place in English literature when Sir Compton Mackenzie wrote in his novel *Whisky Galore* of a cargo vessel loaded with dollar-earning war-time whisky bound for America hitting rocks off the Hebrides. In the real incident, the whisky was Martin's V.V.O. and Martin's De Luxe being carried on the SS *Politician*, which met its fate on 4 February 1941. Many of the crates of whisky were washed ashore only to disappear mysteriously before the arrival of the officers of HM Customs and Excise. Their search for the missing whisky, with the aid of the Home Guard, is brilliantly recorded in one of Mackenzie's most amusing novels, where the real events and names are thinly disguised. Martin's still have some of the salvaged whisky stored in their cellars as proof of the story.

Macdonald & Muir Ltd* eventually acquired James Martin & Co. Ltd in the 1920s and a holding company, Macdonald Martin Distilleries PLC was set up in 1949.

Brands

Dalvegan Old Highland Malt 10 years old (vatted malt)	James Martin & Co.'s Old Vatted†
James Martin's De Luxe 12 years old	James Martin & Co.'s Fine Old Highland†
James Martin's Fine and Rare 20 years old	Martin's Royal Scotch†
James Martin's V.V.O. Gold Bar 8 years old	Martin's Tally Ho!†
James Martin & Co.'s Gold Crest Old Scotch Whisky†	Martin's Wee Drop†

Markets Principally United States, and twenty-nine other countries. Not available in the United Kingdom.

B.B. Mason & Company Limited

1 York Gate, Regents Park, London NW1 4PU

Wine and spirit shippers　　　　*A subsidiary of International Distillers and Vintners Ltd**

This company was originally established in the nineteenth century at Hull in Yorkshire as importers of rum. It owns a number of subsidiaries engaged in the wine and spirit trade and these were absorbed and amalgamated by the parent company at various dates up to the late 1960s. The last company to join the group was Norton and Langridge in 1972 and in that year Bilbao Wines Ltd became the group holding company controlling the interest of all subsidiaries. However, ownership of the B.B. Mason group of companies passed to IDV Ltd in 1978. Two of the subsidiaries had their own brands, but these have fallen into disuse and there is no plan to re-introduce any of them. The group's only active brand is Prince of Scots, which is marketed by James Murray (Glasgow) Ltd, independent of IDV.

305

It is a standard blended whisky available in 65.5° and 70° strengths throughout the United Kingdom, although it may soon appear in one or two European countries. It is found principally in supermarkets and off-licence premises, but is beginning to appear in restaurants and hotels.

Brands

(*B.B. Mason & Co. Ltd*)
Prince of Scots

(*Buxton, Norton & Langridge Ltd*)
Angus McBain's†   Old Jester†
Imperial Liqueur†

(*Norton & Langridge Ltd*)
Yellow Seal†   Three Crescents†

Markets United Kingdom only.

H. Mayerson & Company Limited

2-4 Russia Row, Milk Street, London EC2V 8BL
Brokers

This firm of whisky brokers also blends under their own label and those of their subsidiary. They also trade in bulk exports and supply bottled whisky under buyer's own labels. The company was formed in 1953, and is one of the most active whisky brokers in the City of London.

Brands

(*H. Mayerson & Co. Ltd*)
Glenrob   Scottish Envoy

(*Glen-Roye (Blenders) Ltd*)
Strath-Roye

Melrose Drover Limited

East Mains, Industrial Estate, Broxburn, West Lothian, EG52 5AY
Whisky blenders   *A subsidiary of Saccone & Speed Ltd.* *

This firm was founded as wine and spirit merchants, whisky blenders and gin rectifiers in 1872. It remained in private hands until 1968 when it became part of Saccone & Speed Ltd. All blending and bottling is now carried out at Saccone & Speed's new plant on the East Mains Industrial Estate, west of Edinburgh.

In addition to their own brands of Scotch whisky, Melrose Drover are East of Scotland agents for Glenfarclas Highland Malt fillings sold to blenders. They are also responsible for Club Blend, the own label brand sold by the Arthur Cooper chain of off-licences.

Brands
(Melrose Drover Ltd)

Gold Crown	Old Country†
Invergregos†	Prince Consort
Malcolm Stuart	Puritan†
MD Doctor Label†	Queen Victoria
Old Castle†	Ross's Ancient & Honourable

(W.A. Ross & Brother)
Club Blend

A. Middlemas & Son Limited

Distillery Lane, Kelso, Roxburghshire
Wine and spirit merchants

Established in 1874, this company is a member of The Merchant Vintners Co. Ltd and has two outlets.

Brand
McRobert's

Adam Millar & Company Limited

10-16 Thomas Street, Dublin 8
Wine and spirit merchants

Millar's have for long had their own blend of Scotch whisky. However, Millar's connection with Scotland is also historic since the company, which was established in Dublin in 1843, was founded by Adam Millar who went from Alloa to Ireland in the 1830s for the purpose of going into business. After a number of partnerships he set up under his own name to wholesale the products of his cousin, John Jameson, who was to become prominent in the distilling of Irish whisky. The firm also developed interests in wine and tea.

It remained essentially a family affair until 1980 when a majority stake in the company was taken by Furor Investments Ltd, which is controlled by Mr Peter Barry T.D., the Deputy Leader of one of the two principal political parties in Ireland, Fine Gael. But happily, members of the Millar family remain actively engaged in the business.

Brand Glenmillar

307

John Milroy Limited

3 Greek Street, London W1

Wine and spirit merchants

This is surely London's Mecca for the true Scotch lover, given the extensive range of single malts and De Luxe whiskies always available. The Milroy family established the firm, known also as the Soho Wine Market, in 1964 and have contributed enormously over the years towards the wider appreciation of the single malt.

Brand Milroy's 8 years old Malt whisky (vatted)†

Mitchell Brothers

Trafalgar House, 75 Hope Street, Glasgow G2 6AP

Scotch whisky merchants   *A subsidiary of Distillers Company* PLC*

On 1 November 1979 the trading interests of this company were transferred to John Hopkins & Co. Ltd,* but Mitchell Bros still exists as a company, although it is now regarded as 'dormant' for trading purposes.

Mitchell Bros has an Irish slant to its history as it was acquired by Distillers Finance Corporation, comprising eight of the principal distillers in Ireland and some of the best known blenders in Belfast

North Port

and Dublin, in 1913. However, it fell back into native hands when DFC itself was taken over by DCL in 1922.

Mitchell Bros is the licensee of the North Port Distillery, also known as the Brechin Distillery. It was constructed in 1820 by a local family called Guthrie, when it was known as the Townhead Distillery Co. However, it changed its name to Guthrie, Martin & Co, and became a limited company in 1893. In 1922 DCL and W.H. Holt and Co. Ltd acquired the entire shareholding and the distillery and its valuable stocks of whisky were put into the charge of Scottish Malt Distillers Ltd.* The plant was closed down for a period from 1926 but has been active in the post-war period under the control of Mitchell Bros, becoming silent again in 1983. The distillery's product is rarely found in bottled form, but Wm Cadenhead Ltd* have it at 15 years old.

Brands HD   Greybeard†
                Heather Dew   V.O.M.
                Glen Dew 5 years old Highland
                    Malt (vatted)

J. & A. Mitchell and Company Limited

Springbank Distillery, Campbeltown, Argyll

Distillers

This is one of the few private companies still distilling in Scotland and their Springbank Distillery is one of the only two surviving in Campbeltown, which has long been known for the distinctiveness of its whiskies.

The present owners are directly descended from the distillery's founding family, the Mitchells. The existing buildings date back to 1828 when the distillery was first licensed. Springbank can be counted amongst the handful of distilleries which still has its own traditional floor maltings. Moreover, it is one of only two distilleries — the other being Glenfiddich — which bottles its whisky at the distillery. Modifications to the distillery have enabled it to produce two distinct malt whiskies. The principal product remains Springbank and the other is known as Longrow, which recalls another Campbeltown distillery but of the last century. J. & A. Mitchell & Co. Ltd are associated with Eaglesome Ltd and Wm Cadenhead Ltd.*

Brand

Springbank 12 years old Campeltown Malt

Market World-wide, but especially in Japan.

Montrose Whisky Company Limited

16b West Central Street, London WC1A 1JJ

Blenders and exporters

Of recent origin — 1973 — this firm blends its own whiskies and exports to a wide range of overseas markets.

Brands

Glen Kindie

Great Mac

Old Montrose De Luxe

Old Montrose Pure Malt
   (vatted)

Pipe Major 5 years old

Pipe Major 12 years old

Pipe Major 21 years old

Morrison's Bowmore Distillery Limited

13 Royal Crescent, Glasgow G3 7SU

Distillers   *A subsidiary of Stanley P. Morrison Ltd**

Bowmore is the second oldest legal distillery on the Isle of Islay, dating from 1779. It has another distinction in that it was owned by those who ran it, while the other Islay distilleries were traditionally leased out to operators by the proprietors. The first owner was a Mr Simson, a local merchant, and the beginnings were extremely modest. There is no agreement as to the precise date on which it passed to the Mutters, a family of German extraction. They kept it until the 1890s, after which it was run by the Bowmore Distillery Co. Ltd, and during their ownership introduced a number of technical advances; Bowmore has been noted for its adaptability to change and new ideas ever since. James Mutter was a man of boundless energies and combined the task of distiller with that of farmer, as well as with the duties of Ottoman, Portuguese and Brazilian Vice-Consul in Glasgow! He expanded the distillery and demand for Bowmore grew. He even had a small iron steam ship built and named after him to bring in barley and coal and to deliver the whisky to Glasgow. Bowmore is on the shores of Loch Indaal, and the very walls of the distillery are lapped by the sea. Loch Indaal was the ideal site, for, in the words of a contemporary scribe, it was ' . . . a fair and spacious harbour, with a fine quay at the village of Bowmore.' Moreover, ' . . . the rearing of barley is much practised by the common tenantry . . . and no country is better supplied with fire and water,' meaning of course peat and the nearby River Laggan. Bowmore still does its own malting of the barley, but production has grown so much that it is now necessary to have malted grain brought over from the mainland in order to supplement the distillery's own production. Bowmore has two pairs of stills for wash and spirit distillation, all of which are steam heated.

Ownership of Bowmore passed to J.B. Sherriff & Co. in 1925 and from them to William Grigor & Son Ltd of Inverness in 1950; both companies are now defunct. The distillery was, like all of its kind, closed during the two World Wars. The second brought an unusual temporary tenant in the form of the Air Ministry, which used Bowmore as a base for Coastal Command flying boats engaged on anti-submarine duty. Morrison's took it over in 1963 and immediately set about expanding and renovating it. The distillery now has an annual capacity approaching one million proof gallons, but production as far back as 1880 had reached 200,000 gallons, a prodigious output for those days. Bowmore is available in bottle at 12 years old and is sold extensively abroad in domestic and duty free markets. The distillery's bicentenary was celebrated in 1979 by a special bottling. At 12 years old, Bowmore has less of the peat and the sea than most other Islays. It is a more rounded whisky and lacks the Islay bite.

Markets USA, Denmark, Germany, Netherlands, Italy, France, Australia, Japan, New Zealand and Canada and duty free outlets in Europe and Scandinavia.

Brands

Bowmore 12 years old
  Islay Malt
Bowmore Bicentenary

Bowspey

Ochtomore

311

Ronald Morrison & Company Limited

Loanhead, Edinburgh EH20 9QW

Scotch whisky liqueur manufacturers   *Member of SWA*

Famed for their Glayva Liqueur, Ronald Morrison & Co. Ltd have also had various brands of blended whiskies but they currently concentrate on Glayva.

Brands

Ben Loyal†	Highland Supreme†
Firva†	KKC†
Glayva Scotch Whisky Liqueur	Morrison's Special Reserve

Stanley P. Morrison Limited

13 Royal Crescent, Glasgow G3 7SU

Distillers, blenders and brokers

In historical terms, Stanley P. Morrison Ltd is not particularly ancient, although its two distilleries at Bowmore and Glen Garioch take its adopted pedigree back to before the legalisation of distilling.

The founder, Stanley P. Morrison, was a highly regarded whisky broker in Glasgow with a deep knowledge of every facet of the trade. In 1951 his growing interests caused him to form with James Howat a limited company. On Morrison's death in 1971, Howat succeeded him as Chairman, although the former's two sons continue in the Company as directors.

Apart from the setting up of Morrison's Bowmore Distillery Ltd* and Glen Garioch Whisky Co. Ltd* to run the two distilleries they had acquired, Morrison's also took over the Roseburn Bonding Co. in Glasgow. In 1965 the Tannochside Bonding Co. was set up to provide warehousing and blending facilities and has a capacity of over four million gallons. Two years later, the Scottish Trading Co. Ltd was bought out and with them their Rob Roy brand. This was followed by the acquisition of T. & A. McClelland Ltd,* the prominent Glasgow blenders and exporters, with their various subsidiaries, and, in 1983, of James Sword & Son Ltd.*.

Despite a record of expansion, Stanley P. Morrison Ltd remains a private company and its original broking side is still very active, although its importance in relation to the company's over all interests began to decline from about 1970. As the founder diversified into other branches of the industry, the possibility of opposition from those against whom he would be competing was clearly an important factor. He skilfully avoided any such clashes by refusing to compete in areas where those whom he served as a broker were already active. Morrison's distilling capacity is 1.5 million proof gallons.

Brands   Old Highland   *(Rob Roy Distillers Ltd)*
                               Rob Roy

George Morton Limited

Chapel Bond, Eastern Road, Montrose DD10 8HX

Blenders and exporters   A subsidiary of Amalgamated Distilled Products PLC*

The company, like many others, started as licensed grocers, but the blending, bottling and wholesaling of Scotch whisky gradually became the major part of the business, leading to the eventual exclusion of the original retail activity. It started life in 1838 as Robert Don and Co. and was changed to its present title when George Morton bought it in 1868. He died in 1890 and was succeeded by his son, James Morton. A limited liability company was formed in 1898 but on his death in 1909 the direct Morton connection was interrupted for a lengthy period during which time the company was directed by William Stewart. When he died in 1949 he was succeeded as Managing Director by James Morton's son, George, who had been a director since 1923. On the latter's death in 1953, his nephew, James Morton Elvidge, became Managing Director.

In 1973 the Bow Butt's Bonding Co. in Montrose was bought and the company's blending, bottling and storage facilities are now based at Montrose.

George Morton Ltd is also well known as a rum importer and was bought by Amalgamated Distilled Products in July, 1981.

Brands

Auld Brig	Morton's Blended
Christy & Brooks	Morton's Royal Mile 12 years
Copper Pot 8 years old	old De Luxe
Pure Malt (vatted)	Morton's Special Reserve
Dundee Cream of Scotch	

Charles Muirhead & Son Limited

186 Commercial Street, Leith, Edinburgh

Whisky merchants   A subsidiary of Macdonald Martin Distilleries PLC*

This well-known Edinburgh merchant and shipping firm dates back to 1824 when it originally dealt in wines. However, they eventually branched out to become blenders and exporters of Scotch whisky. They consolidated their position in the Edinburgh wine and spirit trade by acquisition of another city wine shipping firm in the early 1920s, but were themselves eventually to become part of Macdonald Martin Distilleries.

Muirhead's still maintain a thriving wholesale trade throughout the UK, selling principally Muirhead's Blue Seal.

Brands

Muirhead's Blue Seal	Muirhead's Rare Old Maturity
Muirhead's Gold Label	Muirhead's Silver Label

Markets Muirhead's main markets are UK, USA, South America, Spain, New Zealand, South Africa, Middle East, EEC and the rest of Europe.

James Munro & Son Limited

Palmerston House, 39 Palmerston Place, Edinburgh EH12 5BH
Distillers and blenders   *A subsidiary of Distillers Company PLC**

Part of the Macdonald Greenlees* group within Distillers Company, James Munro & Son Ltd is currently licensee of Knockdhu Distillery at Knock near Huntly. The distillery was brought into operation by DCL in 1894 and was the first malt distillery constructed by them. It was for a period (1924-30) run by the Distillers' Agency Ltd,* being transferred to Scottish Malt Distillers Ltd* in 1930. Its original purpose was to supply malt whisky for John Haig & Co. Ltd* for their then still independent blending operation at Markinch, as part of Haig's original agreement with the other grain whisky distillers at the formation of DCL, and as a move by the latter to prevent Haig building their own malt distillery. It is, therefore, an historically significant distillery, but its product has never been bottled as a single malt. It is at present closed.

The origins of James Munro & Son Ltd itself are much more obscure and the firm came into the DCL empire as part of the absorption in 1925 of Macdonald Greenlees and Williams (Distillers) Ltd. James Munro & Son Ltd were at one time operators of the Dalwhinnie Distillery (now assigned to James Buchanan & Co. Ltd*) on behalf of their then American parent company, Cook & Bernheimer, who disposed of their subsidiary in 1920 to Sir James Calder, the man behind Macdonald Greenlees.

Brands

Albion†	Peerage†
King of Kings	The King's Choice†
Munro's Square Bottle†	

James J. Murphy & Company Limited

Lady's Well Brewery, Leitrim Street, Cork, Republic of Ireland
Wine and spirit merchants

Established in 1856.

Brand Bonnie Scot†

Navy, Army and Air Forces Institutes (NAAFI)

Imperial Court, Kennington Lane, London SE11 SQX

This well known and much loved British institute, the official trading organisation of HM Forces, markets an own-label NAAFI whisky.

Brand NAAFI Special Reserve

Neal & Company (Blenders) Limited

Central House, 36 Oxford Street, London W1N 9FL
Blenders, exporters and brokers

Established in 1941, this is another of the numerous London whisky merchants engaged in blending and exporting both under their own labels and those of their subsidiary, Mozel and Brocha (Blenders) Ltd.

Brands
(Neal & Co. (Blenders) Ltd)
Neal's Royal   Royal Sceptre†
(Mozel & Brocha (Blenders) Ltd)
Mozel & Brocha

J. & W. Nicholson & Company Limited

Windsor House, 83 Kingsway, London WC2B 6SF

Blenders and exporters   *A subsidiary of Stewart & Son of Dundee Ltd**

This firm is much better known for its gin distilling than its whisky blending, although it has been purchasing single whiskies and acting as blenders for at least one hundred years. Indeed, they were doing substantial business in whisky by the late nineteenth century, but now their brands are exclusively for the export market. These are marketed under their own name, in the case of Black Swan, and through a number of subsidiary companies.

   In 1982, the company was taken over by Allied-Lyons PLC, and its

315

distilling and blending activities for whisky, gin and vodka made the responsibility of Stewart & Son of Dundee Ltd.

Brands

(*J. & W. Nicholson & Co. Ltd*)
Black Swan

(*Anderson & Co.*)
Anderson's

(J. Brown & Co.)
John Brown's Special

(*P.D. Carnegie & Sons Ltd*)
Carnegie 1860   Special Reserve

(*Reid, Wright & Holloway (Distillers) Ltd*)
Johnny Wright's

(*Sewell & Blaikie*)
Highland Command

(*W. Shepperd & Co.*)
Leabank†   Royal Highlander†

(*Simpson Shepherd & Sons Ltd*)
Fortification

(*J.S. Smith, Druce & Co.*)
Macfie   Target†

(*Tapping & Co.*)
Bridge of Allan

Markets Export only to Europe, South America, Australia and other parts of the world.

Nordren McCall Limited

15 Whitcomb Street, London WC2H 7HA

Blenders

This company is a member of the Henkes United Distillers Group of Holland. Nordren McCall Ltd are engaged in filling, blending, exporting and marketing their Black Prince range of whiskies.

Brands

Anniversary†
Black Prince Select
Black Prince 12 years old
    (De Luxe)

Black Prince 17 years old
    (De Luxe) in ceramic flagon
Dunross†
McCall's†

The North British Distillery Company Limited

Wheatfield Road, Edinburgh EH11 2PX   *Member of SWA*

Distillers

There is little doubt that the spreading tentacles and increasing power of the Distillers Co. Ltd (DCL) gave the impetus to the establishment of The North British Distillery Co. Ltd in 1885, in order to ensure an alternative and independent source of grain whisky for the booming blending industry. The fact that four of the founding participants — Andrew Usher & Co., William Sanderson & Son,* John Crabbie & Co.* and James Watson & Co.* — were all to be absorbed by DCL at later dates is confirmatory proof that fears of DCL dominance were well founded. An interesting side effect of the appearance of North British was that DCL was driven to seek new markets abroad, a move which was to have far reaching implications for that company.

The site of the distillery, in the Gorgie district of Scotland's capital, was dictated by its proximity to adequate rail facilities and abundant water supply. It was a bold concept and the original plans allowed for rapid expansion, which is just as well since the original capacity of three million proof gallons per annum was doubled within four years of distilling having commenced. Extensive rebuilding and enlargement have taken place since then and capacity currently stands at fifteen million gallons.

The First World War saw a partial and then total interruption in distilling when the works were made over for the manufacture of ammunitions, and cereals, in any case, fell into critically short supply. However, by the beginning of 1920 normal production was under way again.

The North British is not a public company and shares can be held only by recognised whisky blenders and merchants, as required by the Articles of Association. The shareholding is spread widely throughout the industry and includes DCL and some North British employees. When a shareholder ceases to qualify, whether by retirement, death or withdrawal from the trade, or any other reason, the Directors are vested with power to pre-empt the shares. Moreover, The North British avoids competing with its customers in that it holds very little stock of its own and does not have a blending business. Thus, The North British comes close to being a whisky co-operative within the industry. The present board includes representatives of the following companies:

Highland Distilleries Co. PLC*/Robertson & Baxter Ltd*
International Distillers and Vintners Ltd*
William Lawson Distillers Ltd*
Macdonald Martin Distilleries PLC*

Seagram Distillers PLC*
Wm Teacher & Sons Ltd*
The Waverley Group Ltd*

The North British is impressive in its layout and size. There are four Coffey patent stills, three of which can distil 9,000 gallons each of wash per hour and the fourth as much as 12,000 gallons per hour. The original capacity of the plant has been more than quadrupled during the life-time of the establishment which, mainly for ware-housing needs, quickly outgrew its original confines and expanded into adjacent sites, including the former Bernard's Brewery and then to a new site twenty miles westwards towards Glasgow. Storage capacity now stands at fifty million gallons. There is close co-operation with Scottish Grain Distillers'* nearby Caledonian Distillery to which carbon dioxide given off in the fermentation process is piped, with spent wash coming in the opposite direction for processing by The North British.

The company's practice is for virtually all the whisky produced to be sold new directly to customers either for immediate removal or for storage in its own warehouses.

North of Scotland Distilling Company Limited

35 Robertson Street, Glasgow G2 8HQ

Distillers

This very neat and compact distillery was set up as an entirely private venture by the Christie family on the one and a half acre site of Knox's Brewery at Cambus in 1957. At its rebirth, it was known as Strathmore Distillery when it went into production in December that year for malt whisky using patent stills. However, this curious experiment did not last very long and in January 1960 production was switched exclusively to grain whisky. Alas, none of the Strathmore Malt survives although a blend of that name was marketed by a subsidiary company. Under its present title, the distillery, which is the smallest grain whisky distillery in Scotland, helps to meet the requirements of many of the blenders which are not in the DCL group. It has a capacity of three million proof gallons, and it is associated through the Christie connection with Speyside Distillery & Bonding Co. Ltd.* The distillery is said to be haunted by a former brewer and the spectre has been sighted by both employees and excise officers. Production is temporarily suspended.

Brands   (*North of Scotland Distilling Co. Ltd*)   (*Strathmore Distillery Ltd*)
     Ben MacDhuit†   Strathmore†
     Strathairdt†

Oakfield Limited

100 Wellington Street, Glasgow G2 6DJ

Blenders

Brands

Oakfield 5 years old
Oakfield 12 years old

Oakfield 10 years old Malt
(vatted)

Old St Andrews Limited

144-148 Kirkdale, London SE26 4BD

Exporters

As a marketing enterprise Old St Andrews first appeared on the export whisky scene ten years ago, with a project in Japan to sell half-gallon bottles fitted into a hand-made miniature leather golf bag on miniature trolleys. This was highly successful with the golf-mad Japanese, and the company has gone from strength to strength, although their launch product is now sold using the standard 75cl bottle. On the same theme, the company has just introduced golf ball miniatures of whisky, each containing 50ml of Old St Andrews, which are sold in presentation packs of six.

The company is partly owned by Tomatin Distillers Ltd* whose whisky features strongly in the Old St Andrews blends. The emphasis is on age and quality and the youngest whisky used is 5 years old. The bulk of Old St Andrews is sold overseas, but it is available in certain high-class stores in Britain.

Brands

Old St Andrews 5 years old
Old St Andrews 12 years old

Old St Andrews 21 years old

Markets Ninety per cent export, principally to the Far East and Canada.

Paisley Whisky Company Limited

Wellington Chambers, 62 Fort Street, Ayr, Ayrshire

Blenders and exporters

There are a number of associate companies including Ayr Distillery Co., Brodie Crawford & Co., which deals with export, McAllister of Ayr, Cumbrae Supply Co. (Whisky) Ltd and Irving F. Garrett Ltd, which is responsible for the group's broking activities.

Brands

Brodie's Supreme	Old Barrister
Burn's Nectar	Old Troon
Ferguson's 64	Strathayr (vatted malt)
Glen Garret (vatted malt)	Three Scotches

(Brodie, Crawford & Co.)
Mac King Gay Ghost†
Stag Royal

J.C. & R.H. Palmer Limited

Old Brewery, West Bay Road, Bridport, Dorset

This small West Country brewer has its own blended whisky sold through the tied houses in Bridport and the surrounding area.

Brand Golden Cap

T. Pease, Son & Company Limited

Hill House, Gainford, Darlington DL2 3EY
Blenders and merchants

This is a family company of wine and spirit merchants which has temporarily suspended blending whiskies under their own labels. The firm was established in 1808.

Brands

BOS†	Goblin†
Gladiator†	Rocket†

James Pickup & Company

Larkhill Street, Blackburn, Lancs BB1 5BU
Blenders and merchants

A subsidiary of the Lancashire independent brewers, Daniel Thwaites PLC, they at present have only one of their brands available, Royal Huntsman is described as being of export quality and over 5 years old.

Brands

Burnhut†	Special Liqueur†
Loch Lurkie†	Thwaites†
Royal Huntsman	V.O.S.†

Praban na Linne Limited

Eilean Iarmain, An t-Eilean Sgiathanach (Isle of Skye), Scotland IV43 8QR

Blenders and merchants

If ever a Scotch whisky company tried to recapture the spirit of old Scotia in its everyday dealings, then Mr Iain Noble has come closest to achieving it by producing a blend constructed and marketed specifically for the Gaelic speaking islands of the Hebrides, and by running his operations from the Isle of Skye. Te Bheag nan Eilean is the result. The use of Gaelic (pronounced Chey Vek nan Yellan) is no gimmick since most sales are in the West Highlands and the Hebrides where the language is still widely spoken; a little is also sold in France and Nova Scotia. The brand name in English means 'the little lady of the islands', but 'Te Bheag' itself is used widely in the Hebrides as an affectionate term for a dram. The blend is mainly of 5 to 12 years old Speyside malts combined with North British grain.

This unusual blended whisky has now been joined by a 12 year old vatted malt, Poit Dhubh, or 'Black Pot' in English, which is pronounced 'potch dhu'. This is the common term used in the Highlands to refer to an illicit still, which in the old days was considered to produce the best whiskies.

Brands

Te Bheag nan Eilean   Poit Dhubh (vatted malt)

Markets Scotland, mainly the West Highlands and the Hebrides. France, mainly Paris and Brittany, and Nova Scotia.

Quellyn Roberts & Company Limited

11-23 Watergate Street, Chester CH1 2JX

Wine and spirit merchants

This firm once boasted a wide range of its own products which it had been marketing since its inception in 1863, including its own whisky blends. Production is now much narrower and is today restricted to fortified wines. Their Old Crypt Scotch whisky was a first-rate blend, being a combination of 50 per cent malt and 50 per cent grain whisky, the youngest ingredient being 7 years old. They still occasionally bottle under their own label fine single malts, a recent example being a 1969 Dalmore bottled in 1980.

Brands

Old Crypt†   V.O.L.†

Red Lion Blending Company Limited

Red Lion House, 1 The Village, North End Way, London NW3 7HA

Blenders, exporters and brokers

This company specialises in private label Scotch whisky for various groups around the world, in addition to marketing their own brand which is a 5 year old De Luxe blend available at 40° and 43°.

An associate company, Douglas Denham Ltd, produces and markets worldwide the special label whiskies sold by Diners Club Inc. It comes in four ages and one of them — 12 years old — won prizes two years in succession in the International Wine and Spirit competition in 1979 and 1980. Success has perhaps been due to the method of blending employed. This allows a lengthy marrying period of four years in cask after blending and before bottling takes place.

Brands

(Red Lion Blending Co. Ltd)
Prince Albert

(Douglas Denham Ltd)

Custodian	Diner's 12 years old
Diner's 5 years old Gold Label	Diner's 15 years old
Diner's 8 years old	vatted malt

Richmond Distillers (Scotch Blenders) Limited

Chile House, 20 Ropemaker Street, London EC2Y 9BA

Blenders and exporters

There are associated companies: Ballac Whisky Ltd, Auld Alec (West Regent St) Ltd, City Gate Whisky Blenders Ltd, Richmond Distillers (Zurich) Ltd and a subsidiary, Latelin Ltd, with a whisky-wine blend called Sandy Dandy.

Brand Lord Richmond

Robertson & Baxter Limited

106 West Nile Street, Glasgow G1 2QX   *Member of SWA*

Distillers, blenders and merchants

This famous Glasgow firm's close relationship with The Highland Distilleries Co. PLC* and Berry Bros and Rudd Ltd* is discussed elsewhere. This apart, Robertson & Baxter Ltd market a variety of brands and own one distillery, through their wholly owned subsidiaries. The principals amongst these are Hepburn & Ross Ltd and Lang Bros Ltd,* the latter controlling Glengoyne Distillery. These were acquired in, respectively, 1959 and 1965. Hepburn & Ross are particularly associated with their Red Hackle brand which recalls the plume of small red feathers worn in the head-dress of the famous Black Watch Regiment. This distinction was in honour of their valour at the Battle of Gildermalsen in 1795. The original Hepburn & Ross partners served with the regiment.

Robertson & Baxter Ltd, founded in 1857, were traditionally whisky blenders, agents and wine and spirit merchants and have acted as sole selling agents for the Highland Distillers PLC.* The company is an essential link in a much larger-scale operation and comes under the control of Edrington Holdings, which in turn is owned by the Robertson Trust, a charitable trust set up by the three Misses Robertson whose family gave the firm one of its original partners. Robertson & Baxter's important profile in the industry owes much to the late John Robertson who, in his later years, was not only Chairman of the family firm, but also of the Highland Distilleries Co. PLC and The North British Distillery Co. Ltd* making the link between pot-still malt distilling interests and those of grain distilling which only a blender could provide.

From 1 April 1983, Mr John Macphail, Managing Director of Robertson & Baxter Ltd and Chairman of Highland Distilleries PLC, was appointed chairman of The Scotch Whisky Association, and this is the first occasion the post has not been held by the chairman of Distillers Company PLC.

Brands

(Robertson & Baxter Ltd)
Strathnavar†

(Burnfoot Blending Co. Ltd)
Aberfoyle 8 years old Malt Whisky (vatted)

(Glenfyne Distillery Co. Ltd)

A1†	Glen Sannox†
Dew of the Mountains†	Grand Liqueur†
Fould's Grand Liqueur†	Loch Fyne†
Garrison†	Old Age†
Glenfyne†	

(Hepburn & Ross Ltd)

Blue Hackle†	Scottish Mist†
Bonspiel†	Silver Mist†
Red Hackle	White Hackle†
Red Hackle Reserve 12 years old	

(Kinloch Distillery Co. Ltd)
Scottish Cream

(*James McCreadie & Co. Ltd*)
Mak'Readie 12 years old Liqueur Scotch Whisky

(*Row & Co. (Distillers) Ltd*)	(*West Highland Malt Distilleries Ltd*)
Glen Graeme†	Glen Crinan†
Sandy Tamson	

John Robertson & Son Limited

10 Links Place, Leith, Edinburgh EH6 7HA   *Member of SWA*
Distillers and blenders   *A subsidiary of Distillers Company* PLC*

Originally established in 1827 in Dundee, the Company susequently became part of DCL and moved to Leith. It owned the Coleburn Distillery at Longmorn near Elgin, which was built in 1896. In 1915 it was sold for £5,000 to DCL and John Walker & Sons Ltd.* However, the company is the registered owner of Speyburn distillery at Rothes in Morayshire which was originally built in 1897 as the Speyburn-Glenlivet Distillery by the Speyside Distillery Co. Ltd, a subsidiary of John Hopkins & Co. Ltd.* The latter amalgamated with DCL in 1916, as a result of which John Robertson & Son Ltd became the licensee of Speyburn. A local builder, Robert Marshall, had the contract, and all the material for the foundations and the stones for the walls were dug from the old river or loch bed nearby, which marked an area covered in prehistoric times by a vast stretch of water from above Craigellachie to Sourdon. The Spey once flowed through the loch, but pressure of water forced it to take a new course to the sea via a narrow gorge at Sourdon. The loch drained away leaving behind the fertile plain where Rothes now stands.

1897 was an important year in Great Britain, being the Diamond Jubilee of Queen Victoria, and the proprietors wanted to get their new distillery into production so that the first fillings could bear that historic date. This was achieved by a narrow margin when production got under way in the last week of the year and only one butt was bonded bearing the date 1897.

Of modest size, the distillery's entire production is used in blending, and the ample supply of good water from the springs running down the hillside in the Glen of Rothes ensures that the product is of high quality. Speyburn was in the forefront in tackling the problem of pollution of the River Spey, having co-operated with other local distilleries at the turn of the century in constructing a large evaporating and drying plant for the pot ale. Since then a number of important improvements have been made to the premises.

Brands	BEB (Best Ever Bottled)	Piper's Dram
	JRD†	Robertson's Yellow Label

324

Peter J. Russell & Company Limited

45 Frederick Street, Edinburgh EH2 1ET   *Member of SWA*

Blenders, exporters and brokers

Leonard Russell started business in 1936 purely as a whisky broker. It was, he found, necessary to branch into other activities, principally blending and exporting. To this end the company acquired from Rigby and Evans Ltd the very old established Liverpool firm of blenders and exporters, William Maxwell (Scotch Whisky) Ltd, whose origins go back to 1796. There is another subsidiary, Ian McLeod and Co., under whose labels certain brands are traded. Two other subsidiaries, Hodder & Co. (Whisky Merchants) Ltd and Border Brands Ltd, have ceased trading. The company also sells bottled whisky under buyers' own labels.

This is essentially a family business and is now run by the founder's two sons.

Brands

Black Rooster
Black Shield
Cockburn & Murray 4 years
  old

Cockburn & Murray 8 years
  old
The Seven Stills 100% Malt 5
  years old (vatted)

(William Maxwell (Scotch Whisky) Ltd)
King Robert II
King Robert II Black Label De
  Luxe
Mason's

Maxwell
Maxwell Malt (vatted)

(Ian MacLeod & Co. Ltd)
Isle of Skye
The Queen's Seal (Black Label)

The Queen's Seal (White Label)

Markets About 60 per cent of the company's trade is in export. Principal market is Italy. Other markets are France, South America, Far East, Western Europe, New Zealand (in bulk), Hong Kong.

Saccone & Speed Limited

17 Cumberland Avenue, London NW10 7RN   *Member of SWA*

Wine and spirit merchants

Saccone & Speed Ltd is a subsidiary of Imperial Brewing and Leisure Ltd, the brewers, which, in turn, is a subsidiary of the Imperial Group. This company's close links with the forces of the Crown go back to 1839, when James Speed set up business in Gibraltar to deal with the Royal Navy and the Rock's garrison by supplying them with wines and spirits. Eleven years later Jerome Saccone also established himself there and the two firms followed the inevitable path to amalgamation at the turn of the century to form Saccone & Speed. In 1932 the company linked up with the old established West End wine and spirit merchants, Hankey Bannister & Co., whose origins stretch back into the eighteenth century. Saccone & Speed became part of the Courage Group in 1963.

Saccone & Speed Retail operates the Arthur Cooper and Roberts & Son chains of retail off-licences, and Saccone & Speed International is responsible for the company's export and duty-free trades.

At a new plant recently completed on the East Mains Industrial Estate, west of Edinburgh, the company blends and bottles a range of whiskies, the leading brand being Hankey Bannister which enjoys wide distribution on the home and export markets. In addition to marketing their own brands, Saccone & Speed are distributors in Scotland, England and Wales for Glenfarclas all malt whisky.

Some of the company's whisky interests are handled by a subsidiary, Melrose Drover Ltd.*

Brands

Blair Drummond†
Bonnie Charlie†
Glen Drummond 8 years old
   vatted malt
Hankey Bannister
Hankey Bannister 8 years old
Hankey Bannister De Luxe 12
   years old

Hankey Bannister 21 years old
Highland Milk†
Liqueur Cream 5 years old
Liqueur Cream 12 years old
Scotsmac (whisky-wine blend)
Wallace's Royal Abbey†

Markets Apart from the standard Hankey Bannister which is sold at home and abroad, the above brands are export brands only, some of the principal markets being Japan, Spain, Italy, New Zealand, Netherlands, France and South Africa.

Safeway Food Stores Limited

Beddow Way, Aylesford, Nr Maidstone, Kent ME20 7AT
Wine and spirit merchants

A leading supermarket chain with its own brand of wine and spirits.

Brand   Safeway

Sainsbury Brothers Limited

3 Edgar Buildings, George Street, Bath
Wine and spirit merchants

The firm dates from 1802.   *Brand*   Musketeer

J. Sainsbury Limited

Stamford House, Stamford Street, London SE1 9LL

Grocers and wine and spirit merchants

Perhaps the best known of the 'supermarket' whiskies, from one of the most respected grocery chains in Britain, Sainsbury whiskies, like all of their own-label products, have a defensible reputation. Most of Sainsbury's 232 supermarkets sell wine and spirits and so their own brands are becoming steadily better known. These are clearly identified as belonging to Sainsbury, which is not always the case with 'down-market' brands, and include a 12 year old Speyside malt.

In addition to its Scotch whisky brands, the company has an even more tangible link with Scotland in the form of two farms, one at Kinermony where a herd of pedigree Aberdeen Angus cattle is kept, and the other at Inverquhomery which is half arable and half fattening cattle. Sainsbury's was established in 1869.

Brands

Sainsbury's Blended	Sainsbury's Finest Old Matured
Sainsbury's Highland Malt	
12 years old	

Markets An area bounded by Leeds in the north, Exeter in the west, East Anglia and the south coast.

Wm Sanderson & Son Limited

South Queensferry, West Lothian EH30 9SD   *Member of SWA*

Distillers and blenders   *A subsidiary of Distillers Company PLC**

Few people who are familiar with the world famous VAT 69 — referred to by wags as the Pope's telephone number — know either the origins of this unusual brand name or the company to which it belongs, since the identity of the latter has been somewhat over-shadowed by its product.

William Sanderson had applied a great deal of energy and skill to the art of blending whisky and had a wide repertoire of blends. His wish, however, was to concentrate on one of these so as to have a truly excellent product. Taking a wide selection from his many recipes of blended whisky, he made up nearly a hundred of them, each one different, and had them filled in individual casks which he numbered. He then invited a group of friends and colleagues knowledgeable in whisky and the blending of it to sample each blend and between them select that which they thought was outstanding. Amazingly, there was unanimity, with all of them choosing the whisky in the cask or vat numbered sixty-nine. This was sufficient for Sanderson, who accepted it as the house blend and named it there and then as VAT 69. The name has stuck to this day as has the quaint bottle which he had made up in Leith especially for his new brand, although the bottle now used is somewhat slimmer and taller than the original design and no longer has a wax seal on the shoulder.

William Sanderson had earlier set up business in 1863, having spent ten or so years in the service of Matthew Buchan, himself a wine and spirit merchant and manufacturer of cordials in Leith. With this behind him, Sanderson undertook the making-up of whiskies and the preparation of various cordials, such as his rich green ginger wine and rhubarb wine. But it was the whisky which interested him most, and he was soon supplying special blends for particular customers, not only in Britain but also in Europe.

Sanderson's son, William Mark, joined the company in 1880 and became a partner in 1892, succeeding to the business on his father's death in 1908. Shortly thereafter, the firm's whisky activities were to overtake in importance the cordial manufacturing side, which was eventually to disappear altogether. The founder's grandson, Kenneth, joined the company soon after the end of the First World War, taking control in 1929 when his father died. In 1935 the company merged with Booths Distilleries and dropped all its other activities, including its other blends of whisky, in order to concentrate on VAT 69. The partnership was short lived, since it was absorbed two years later by DCL.

At the time of the change in ownership, Wm Sanderson & Son Ltd operated Glengarioch Distillery but gave up responsibility for it a few years later. However, Sanderson's now have licensed to them Glenesk Distillery at Montrose. It started distilling around 1897 as Highland Esk Distillery under the ownership of Septimus Parsonage

Glenesk

& Co. Ltd, but quickly passed to Heddle, a firm of distillers. The distillery was partly burned down in 1910 but was quickly rebuilt. It appears to have closed down during the First World War and reopened in 1919 as a maltings, having been acquired by then by Thomas Bernard & Co. Associated Scottish Distilleries Ltd purchased it in 1938 and converted it to grain whisky production. However, it passed into the DCL fold in 1954 and was reconverted to malt whisky distilling in 1965-6. During its relatively brief existence this distillery has endured more changes in name than most. From Highland Esk it became North Esk, and then Montrose Distillery during its grain whisky producing period. On conversion back to malt it was called Hillside and renamed Glenesk in 1980. The whisky is bottled as a 12 years old single malt as well as being used for blending.

J. & W. Hardie Ltd* is a subsidiary of Wm Sanderson & Son Ltd.

Brands

Glenesk 12 years old Single   VAT 69 Gold
    Malt   VAT 69 Reserve De Luxe
VAT 69

Markets United Kingdom and most overseas countries. VAT 69 Gold in the United States, Canada and Puerto Rico only.

The Savoy Hotel PLC

1 Savoy Hill, London WC2R 0BP

Hoteliers and merchants

One of the world's most famous hotels, which owns four other great London establishments — Claridges, The Connaught, The Berkeley and Simpson's in the Strand — and which has for long had its own house brands of Scotch whisky. Although the Savoy was founded in 1889, it was not until the ending of Prohibition in the United States that the Savoy brand was introduced. It was shipped regularly to the Waldorf Astoria in New York until the outbreak of war. Exports of Savoy Scotch whisky to the USA were resumed in 1955 but currently the only export market now exploited is France, where it is sold almost entirely through hotels and restaurants of the highest class.

Special blends were also made up for the two other great London hotels in the group for exclusive sale in these establishments.

Brands

Claridge's Old Matured†   The Berkeley Old Matured†
Savoy

Markets London and France.

Scottish Grain Distillers Limited

13 Melville Street, Edinburgh EH3 7PG   *Member of SWA*

Distillers   *A subsidiary of Distillers Company PLC**

One of the principal production companies in the Distillers Group of companies, Scottish Grain Distillers Ltd are responsible for the distilling of all Distillers' grain whisky. They then sell the grain whisky to the blending companies, either after it has been matured for the statutory three years or shortly after production, for storage and subsequent blending by their customers. Apart from their four active distilleries (a fifth, Carsebridge, having been closed down early in 1983) there are extensive adjoining warehouses and separate warehousing facilities in other parts of the country. Three of the distilleries — Cambus, Cameron Bridge and Port Dundas — have been part of DCL since its inception in 1877, whilst the Caledonian Distillery in Edinburgh was acquired a few years later. The importance of grain whisky distilling in the growth of the Scotch whisky industry and DCL's role in that, are explained elsewhere in the main body of the book.

Until its closure the oldest of the DCL grain distilleries was Carsebridge, just outside Alloa. It started life in 1799 as a malt pot-still distillery, having been built by John Bald and Co. who remained its owners until the formation of DCL. In the meantime, the switch had been made to grain distilling and by 1877 the son of the founder — also John — was running it. He was a leading power behind the great amalgamation and was known as the 'Politic Bald'. Carsebridge has enjoyed continuous production and was until 1983 the largest distillery in Scotland.

Port Dundas in Glasgow was built in 1817. Its claim to historical fame is that Aeneas Coffey is believed to have set up his first patent still in Scotland at Port Dundas. The Port Dundas still experienced some teething troubles, as did others elsewhere in Scotland, but these were soon overcome and the scene set for the advent of whisky blending on a large scale. Port Dundas was greatly helped in its prodigious expansion during the nineteenth century by its proximity to the Forth and Clyde Canal. It remained throughout this period in the hands of the Macfarlanes, and M. Macfarlane & Co. were to become founder members of DCL in 1877. By the turn of the century Port Dundas was producing two and a half million gallons of grain spirit annually. However, tragedy was just around the corner and a disastrous fire gutted much of the premises in 1903. So good had its production record been that DCL were soon determined to get it back into operation, but it was not until 1914 that an early resumption could be assured, following a total re-equipment of the distillery.

330

Cambus Distillery, at the village of that name near Alloa, began operations modestly in 1806 on the site of a disused mill. John Moubray was the initiator, and Cambus expanded at a steady pace, changing over to the patent still in the 1830s and joining DCL in 1877 under Robert Moubray's guidance. Cambus Distillery is particularly interesting since it was this whisky which featured in the 'What is Whisky?' enquiry discussed in Chapter 5. At the height of the controversy, DCL introduced in 1906 Cambus Scotch grain whisky in the bottle and under guarantee of having been stored in wood for seven years. There is little evidence of how Cambus was received by the public and the move was, of course, more of a publicity ploy than anything and a challenge to those who claimed that pot-still malt was the only true Scotch whisky. But Cambus was soon to quit the scene for a very long time, being consumed by flames in September 1914. It was not until 1937 that it was brought back on stream, since when it has made an important contribution to DCL's grain whisky programme. Cambus is highly regarded by blenders.

Cameron Bridge is perhaps the best known of the group's grain distilleries due to its associations with John Haig & Co. Ltd*, and the fact that it is the only single grain whisky now regularly available commercially in bottle, as Choice Old Cameron Brig, which Haig's sell in small quantities to loyal devotees. John Haig founded Cameron Bridge at Windygates near Buckhaven in 1824, introducing the Stein patent still in 1827 and finally the Coffey still in 1832. Cameron Bridge was, therefore, very much a test-bed for the new methods of that period.

The Caledonian Distillery is in the heart of Edinburgh and was constructed in 1855. The owners, Menzies & Co., joined DCL in 1884 having withdrawn from the earlier negotiations. Production was interrupted by a serious fire in 1911. Caledonian saw war action when some 1.2 million gallons of its whisky were lost in a fire caused by World War II incendiaries.

Distillers' grain whiskies are used extensively within the group but are also purchased by many other Scotch whisky blenders.

Scottish Malt Distillers Limited

Trinity Road, Elgin, Morayshire IV30 1UF   *Member of SWA*

Distillers   *A subsidiary of Distillers Company PLC* *

One of Distillers Company's operating subsidiaries, this company was born in August 1914 from an amalgamation of five Lowland malt distillers as part of the widespread rationalisation that was going on at this juncture throughout the industry. The distilleries were

Dailuaine

Rosebank, Glenkinchie, St Magdalene (Linlithgow), Grange and Clydesdale.

Of the original five, Grange and Clydesdale have long since been closed down and St Magdalene closed in 1983. Rosebank is licensed to The Distillers Agency Ltd,* and Glenkinchie to John Haig & Co. Ltd.*

Although the original distilleries which banded together to form SMD were all Lowland, the company soon began expanding its interests northwards by taking over Glenlossie-Glenlivet in 1919 and North Port Distillery at Brechin in 1922. DCL's amalgamation with Buchanan-Dewar and Walker in 1925 led to the new company buying out the minority shareholders in SMD, thus turning it into a wholly owned subsidiary. In 1929 it was decided that SMD should have overall responsibility for the malt whisky distilleries in the group. This was implemented in 1930. The list was impressive and demonstrated that DCL were every bit as conscious of the importance of malt whisky distilling as of grain whisky distilling and blending, the two areas on which they had originally concentrated. Further properties were added over the years and a programme of enlargement and improvement was launched. This involved the temporary shut-down of one distillery per year for major works, but without interference in the distinctive character of the 'make' of each individual distillery. Uniformity of character was to be avoided at all costs, and the original nature of the particular whisky was to be safeguarded by such means as ensuring that new stills were replicas in size and shape of the equipment being replaced.

SMD also has responsibility for the group's maltings and some of its bonded warehouses, where these exist separately from the distilleries. SMD provides technical services to other companies in the group and maintains a laboratory as well as architectural and engineering backup. It is responsible for maintaining standards in the group's malt distilleries and has a team of inspectors for this purpose.

SMD is responsible for all of Distillers Company's malt whisky distilleries. The total establishment is forty-five units, of which only thirty-four are currently operating following the closure of eleven in May, 1983. Of the Lowland malt distilleries, Rosebank and Glenkinchie are active and St Magdalene closed. Of their two Islay malt distilleries, Caol Ila and Lagavulin remain open, whilst Port Ellen is silent. However, the vast majority of their properties are Highland malt distilleries, many of them located in the rich Speyside.

The Highland malt distilleries under SMD's control are as follows:

Aberfeldy	Glen Elgin
Aultmore	Glenesk (formerly
Balmenach	Hillside)
Banff (closed)	Glenlochy (closed)
Benrinnes	Glenlossie
Benromach (closed)	Glen Mhor (closed)
Brechin (North Port)	Glentauchers
(closed)	Glenury Royal
Brora (closed)	Imperial
Cardhu	Knockdhu (closed)
Clynelish	Linkwood
Coleburn	Lochnagar
Convalmore	Millburn
Cragganmore	Mortlach
Craigellachie	Oban
Dailuaine	Ord
Dallas Dhu (closed)	Royal Brackla
Dalwhinnie	Speyburn
Glen Albyn (closed)	Talisker
Glendullan	Tenninich

The great majority of Distillers Company's malt distilleries are still licensed to the individual trading companies within the group, and details of the distilleries are given in the description of the appropriate licensee. However, SMD have Dailuaine, Talisker, Glen Albyn, Glenlochy and Glen Mhor licensed to them although only the first two of these are now operating.

Of the three silent units, Glen Albyn is the senior, having been started up in 1846 by the then Provost of Inverness, a Mr Sutherland, who used the site of an abandoned brewery on which to build it. At one stage, distilling was dropped in favour of flour milling, but Glen Albyn reverted to being a distillery in 1884 under the ownership of Gregory & Co., when it was re-sited alongside the Caledonian Canal. Scarcely one hundred yards away is Glen Mhor, also built by a Provost of Inverness, John Birnie, who did so in partnership with James Mackinlay of Charles Mackinlay & Co. Ltd.* Mackinlay and Birnie Ltd remained an independent family concern for many years, eventually controlling the two neighbouring properties which have so much in common but which produce whiskies quite distinct the one from the other. The partnership eventually attracted the attention of DCL and came into the net in July 1972 on the death of Mr William Birnie, a descendent of one of the original owners. Mackinlay and Birnie Ltd continued for a short time as a DCL subsidiary, but was eventually suppressed as a separate trading entity and now no longer exists in any shape or form.

The product of both distilleries is used by DCL for blending, although Glen Mhor is bottled at 8 years old by Gordon & MacPhail* and is much respected as one of the gentler malts with a hint of sweetness and a slightly nutty flavour.

At the other end of the Caledonian Canal is Glenlochy Distillery near Loch Lochy and Fort William. It dates from 1898 as a speculative venture by a Mr David McAndie of Nairn, who hoped to catch the great whisky boom of the day. However, its early history was marred by two lengthy periods of closure. It eventually became the property of Train & McIntyre Ltd in 1937, who ran it in the name of their subsidiary, Associated Scottish Distilleries Ltd. It came into DCL in 1953, on DCL's take-over of Train & McIntyre Ltd. Glenlochy is not bottled.

The two active distilleries were until recently both run under the management of a separate Distillers Company subsidiary, Dailuaine-Talisker Distilleries Ltd.

The company which owned the Dailuaine, Talisker and Imperial Distilleries was acquired jointly, in 1916, by Dewar,* DCL, W.P. Lowrie* and Johnnie Walker* after DCL had failed to persuade the leading Highland Malt distillers to amalgamate in the interests of greater rationalisation. It was an important step towards the big amalgamations of 1925. At the time of the takeover, Dailuaine-Talisker Distilleries Ltd also owned — but by then had shut down — Bon Accord Highland Malt Distillery in Aberdeen.

From their entry into DCL until very recently, the three distilleries had been run together as a separate company within the group.

Dailuaine lies in the shadow of Ben Rinnes and dates from 1852. It was completely rebuilt later in the nineteenth century, and became part of the Dailuaine-Talisker Distilleries Ltd in 1898 on the incorporation of the company following an amalgamation between Dailuaine-Glenlivet Distillery Ltd and Talisker Distillery Ltd. Production now goes entirely for blending. Nearby is Imperial, or Imperial-Glenlivet Distillery, built in 1897, like Dailuaine and Talisker, by Thomas Mackenzie. Despite its age, Imperial is modern in its methods following a considerable overhaul in 1955/56.

The third distillery in the trio, Talisker, is the best known because, unlike the other two, it produces a whisky which is widely available in bottled single form. Moreover, it is the only distillery on the Isle of Skye and is the oldest of the three, dating from 1833. It relies on Carbost Burn for its water and is, at least technically speaking, a Highland malt. Nonetheless, its West Coast island location has created something that is not strictly speaking Highland in character and its flavour owes something to the seaweed with which Skye abounds.

Talisker

Allt a'Bhainne

Seagram Distillers PLC

111-113 Renfrew Road, Paisley

Distillers and blenders   *Member of SWA*

This is the wholly owned British subsidiary of the Canadian giant, The Seagram Co. Ltd, the biggest producer of alcoholic beverages in the world, and which in 1976 became a $2 billion corporation in both sales and assets. This enormous concern originated from the company, Joseph Seagram & Sons, purchased in 1928 by Sam Bronfman who had emigrated to Canada from Eastern Europe, where his family had practised distilling. Bronfman survived the stormy period of American prohibition and patiently waited for the right moment to establish himself in the all-essential US market. He eventually achieved an outstanding success there for his Canadian whiskies and subsequently turned his attention to Scotland. Seagram's had in fact been distributing DCL whiskies in North America for some time, but the moment had come for them to take a direct interest. The first move was to acquire the old established Glasgow whisky house of Robert Brown Ltd, which became what is today Seagram Distillers PLC. Seagram took over Chivas Bros Ltd* in 1949 and immediately thereafter acquired the Milton Distillery at Keith, the name of which was changed and a subsidiary company, Strathisla-Glenlivet Distillery Co. Ltd,* set up to run it. William Longmore & Co. Ltd, under whose name Milton had operated for well over a hundred years, was retained by Seagrams for trading purposes. A second distillery, Glen Keith-Glenlivet Distillery Ltd,* followed in 1957. In the same year, the Keith Bond was established, to become one of the most extensive whisky storage complexes in Scotland. Seagram's set up their Scottish headquarters at Paisley by taking over an old local firm, Robert Brown Ltd, established in 1861. Paisley is their centre for bottling and case storage. Part of the establishment is a library of more than 600 types of Scotch malt and grain whiskies, and one of Seagram's three principal quality control laboratories, the others being at Montreal and New York. The head office in Paisley is the reproduction of a fine old Scottish mansion house, to the design of Sam Bronfman himself.

Further expansion was realised with the opening in 1973 of a new distillery, the Braes of Glenlivet, some nine miles from Dufftown. Capacity increased rapidly from half a million to over one million proof gallons per annum. The Braes of Glenlivet is a combination of traditional distillery architecture and the latest engineering techniques. The water supply for distilling comes from two nearby wells, the Preenie and Kate's Well. For the time being, all production is used in blending. In 1975, Allt-a-Bhainne (Gaelic for the Milk Burn) was opened not far away, some four miles from Dufftown on the slopes of Ben Rinnes, one of the outstanding physical features of Speyside. It is equipped in the most modern manner and carefully landscaped to take account of the surrounding countryside. Capacity is in the region of one million gallons and the investment involved £2.7 million. To complement expansion on the production side, further storage facilities were needed and a site at Dalmuir in Clydebank was obtained to which were transferred much of Paisley's blending and bulk warehousing operations, as well as cooperage, leaving room for expansion at Paisley for bottling and cased goods warehousing. Further storage space was acquired in 1973 at Balgray in Ayrshire, and a new vatting and blending complex opened at Keith in 1976, capable of handling three and a half million gallons of whisky per year. In February 1978, Seagram made a significant acquisition with the purchase of The Glenlivet Distillers Ltd.*

Although impressive, Seagram's Scottish operations are fairly modest when set against the group's worldwide activities in over twenty countries. They now have nine distilleries in Scotland, but a world total of twenty-nine, most of them in North America. There are a number of small subsidiaries of the Paisley company, which are retained for marketing purposes.

Brands

(*Seagram Distillers Ltd*)

Four Crown†	Old Priory†
Old Bachelor's	The Royal V.O.B.†
Old Courier	

(*Joseph E. Seagram & Sons (Scotland) Ltd*)

100 Pipers De Luxe	The Keith Classic (vatted malt)

(*Robert Brown Ltd*)
Black Watch

(*The Highland Bonding Co. Ltd*)

Balmore†	Rare Old Liqueur†
Highland Clan	Royal O.V.S.†
King's Herald†	Scots Aristocrat†

(*William Longmore & Co. Ltd*)

Passport	William Longmore De Luxe

Markets Taking Seagram's Scotch whiskies as a whole, about 50 per cent of sales are in the United States, 10 per cent in the United Kingdom and 2 per cent in Canada. Other leading markets are Italy, Venezuela, Japan, France, West Germany and South Africa. About 25 per cent of sales are in bulk form. Some of this is used for blending with local spirits to produce national whiskies in such countries as Japan, Venezuela, Brazil and Argentina for selling under the Seagram label. In Japan Seagram have a joint venture with the Kirin Brewing Company Ltd, where Scotch malt whisky is blended with a local grain spirit distilled in a jointly owned plant to make a Japanese whisky.

Walter S. Siegel Limited

5 Albemarle Street, London W1X 4EL

Blenders, brokers and merchants

The firm of Walter S. Siegel Ltd was founded in Wiesbaden in 1897 by a wine merchant of that name. Walter S. Siegel was born of a long line of vintners, so the roots of the firm go back a great deal further.

In 1937 Hans Siegel, son of the founder, established the London company in association with Ian Peebles. During the war years operations were naturally suspended, but the partners resumed trading in 1946.

The original firm had dealt mainly in German wines and to a lesser degree with French, but on restarting, and having close associations with Scotland, branched into the Scotch whisky trade.

Agencies were acquired from a number of important distillers and blenders and the company found a ready trade with the Scandinavian State Monopolies. The Directors, Messrs Siegel and Peebles, were created Knights of the distinguished Swedish Order of Vasa, bestowed upon them in recognition of the happy business relations established over the years with 'Spritcentralen', the Swedish State Monopoly, and of their work in pioneering bulk shipments of Scotch whisky to that country. With this trade and its other connections, Siegel became the largest shippers of bulk Scotch whisky in England.

Very close relations are still maintained and actively fostered with these State Monopolies today.

Brand Highland Hart

Robert Sinclair Limited

48 Waring Street, Belfast BT1 2ED

Brokers and merchants

Dealers in bulk Scotch whisky.

Slater, Rodger & Company Limited

500 Renfrew Road, Glasgow G51 4SA   *Member of SWA*

Distillers and blenders   *A subsidiary of Distillers Company PLC**

This firm of traditional Glasgow blenders and bottlers first caught the eye of John Walker & Sons Ltd* in 1898. The interest in the company deepened when Alexander Walker joined the Slater, Rodger board and John Walker & Sons eventually achieved a controlling position in 1911.

Slater, Rodger's prominence in the export field was its main attraction to Walker's. As far back as 1856, Thomas H. Slater & Co., could boast customers in Australia, India, South Africa, South America, the West Indies, Canada and the United States. By 1886 they had established a continental agency for looking after their European interests and were shipping to forty-five countries and territories. By 1888 they were in seventy different markets. The beginnings of all this go back to 1834, when Thomas H. Slater opened as a grocer and tea dealer in Glasgow, moving premises within the city in 1852 and becoming Thomas H. Slater & Co. In 1865 George Smeaton Rodger became a partner and Slater, Rodger & Co. was formed in 1873, becoming a limited liability company in 1885.

Apart from exporting a wide range of its own brands, Slater, Rodger have the licence for Banff distillery, a small unit of only two stills where no expansion has taken place this century. The original distillery followed the Distillery Act into being by becoming operational in 1824. Banff was rebuilt on a different site in 1863 only to be destroyed by fire a few years later. It was rebuilt again in 1877 but on a bigger scale. It has been dogged by ill-luck and was one of the few distilleries damaged by German bombs during the Second World War, with the loss of 16,000 proof gallons of malt whisky.

The original owners of Banff distillery were the Simpson family who were long associated with it. However, by the time DCL came to buy it in 1932, the Mile End Distillery Co. Ltd — a subsidiary of Taylor Walker & Co. Ltd — were the owners. Although not generally sold as a single malt, Wm Cadenhead Ltd* currently bottle it as a 15 year old. The distillery is at present closed.

Brands

Begbies	Lairdshall
Club	Lord Douglas
Duncraig	Napier Johnstone's N.J. Club
High Life	Rodger's Old Scots
Huntly	Rodger's Special
Huntly Blend	Scots Own
Huntly Extra Special (De Luxe)	Thistle
Kylemore	

Markets Thistle in the UK; export for all other brands.

George and J.G. Smith Limited

45 Frederick Street, Edinburgh   *Member of SWA*

Distillers   *A subsidiary of The Glenlivet Distillers Ltd* *

Here a common family name is associated with the most renowned appellation in Scotch whisky. It was in 1747 that a certain John Smith, having anglicised his name from Gow, arrived in Glenlivet to seek shelter from the persecutors of Prince Charles Edward Stuart's luckless supporters, of which he had been one. Finding his income from the farm which he worked near Tomintoul to be insufficient for his needs, he took to part-time distilling. The beautiful but remote Glenlivet provided an ideal setting for the Highlanders to distil illicitly their whisky in comparative freedom from the interference of prying government agents. Andrew Smith carried on in this vein from his father, but the family farm was moved to another site in the glen at Drumin and the distillery was rebuilt there. All of this passed to his son George in 1817, by which time Glenlivet was firmly established as the premier product of Scotland's distillers.

The fact that it was distilled illegally was no impediment to its acceptance in high circles, including King George IV who was introduced to Glenlivet on his state visit to Scotland in 1822. He quickly became an addict. The steps leading to the legalising of distilling are recorded elsewhere in this book, but suffice it to say here that George Smith, despite fierce opposition from, and open intimidation by, his neighbours, took out the first licence to distil Scotch whisky in 1824. With the aid of his landlord, the Duke of Gordon, George Smith built a proper distillery at Upper Drumin in that year, achieving an output of fifty gallons per week. By 1839 this had risen to 200 gallons. The farming side of the business expanded even more dramatically and the complementarity between these two activities was maintained.

George Smith thereafter set out to establish that only the product of Upper Drumin could properly be called Glenlivet. However, he seems to have been content that his son-in-law, Captain William Grant, should claim the same distinction for the whisky produced at his own distillery at Auchorachan. But it was not until 1880 that exclusive use of The Glenlivet was secured legally by the Smiths when John Gordon Smith succeeded in getting the court to rule that only he could use the label The Glenlivet, all others being required to use a prefix.

Captain William Grant passed away in 1850, and his distillery with him. In that year George Smith founded a second distillery on a farm near Tomintoul called Delnabo; the distillery was christened the Cairngorm distillery after the local mountains of that name. But this additional capacity was not enough to meet demand. The Smiths (George had been joined by his younger son John Gordon Smith) decided to play big. They leased further land from the Duke of Gordon at Minmore and there built a distillery with a capacity of 600 gallons per week, closing down the two smaller original units at Upper Drumin and Delnabo in 1858.

Thanks to the efforts of the firm's Edinburgh agent, Andrew Usher, Glenlivet was soon in demand for both blending and exporting, in addition to its more traditional uses, and the first Glenlivet went abroad in 1864. J.G. Smith inherited the entire Glenlivet enterprise on his father's death in 1871. He was determined that the commercial success of his whisky should in no way mar its prestige. He subsequently took legal action against other distillers who were calling their whisky Glenlivet although their distilleries were not actually located in the glen. The result was that it was decreed that only Minmore distillery could term its whisky The Glenlivet, and to this day the company in its advertising makes great play of the 'The'. Under the terms of the settlement only ten other distilleries were allowed to hyphenate their own name with Glenlivet. The Glenlivet is sold in bulk widely within the industry for blending, but since 1970 it is part of the company's conditions of sale that none of such whisky sold in bulk can on maturation be bottled and retailed as a single malt without their permission.

J.G. Smith was succeeded on his death in 1901 by his nephew George Smith Grant, son of Captain William Grant of Auchorachan. The business passed to his younger son, Captain W.H. Smith Grant, in 1921, having been managed by Mr Peter Mackenzie between 1911, on George Smith Grant's death, and 1921 when Captain Smith Grant attained his twenty-fifth year.

In 1952 George and J.G. Smith Ltd, which had become the firm's name, merged with J. & J. Grant, Glen Grant Distillery* to form a public company, The Glenlivet and Glen Grant Distilleries Ltd.* The more recent fortunes of The Glenlivet can be followed elsewhere in this book under the appropriate entries for the successor companies. However, we should say here that even today, The Glenlivet is considered to be the premier malt whisky by connoisseurs. No blender of repute can afford not to have at least a small proportion of The Glenlivet in his formula. Apart from its uninterrupted production at Minmore for well over 100 years, and the resultant aura attached to The Glenlivet, it is difficult to pin-point any other single factor that has contributed towards its wide acceptance as the finest malt whisky. It may be the local spring water which spills down the hillsides into the glen, or the rich Banffshire barley, or the seemingly inexhaustible supplies of mineral-free peat from nearby Faemussach. Most likely it is a combination of all these, plus dedication to maintaining the traditional standards associated with The Glenlivet.

Brands

(*The Glenlivet Whisky Co. Ltd*)

The Glenlivet 12 years old Highland Malt	Special Export Reserve†
The Glenlivet 25 years old Highland Malt (bottled in 1977 to commemorate Her Majesty's Silver Jubilee)	

Markets Principally United Kingdom, United States and Italy. A great part of production is sold within the domestic industry for blending.

H. Allen Smith Limited

7-11 Justice Walk, Lawrence Street, London SW3

Wine and spirit merchants

Brand Justice Walk

Laurence Smith & Son (Edinburgh) Limited

61 Pleasance, Edinburgh 8

Merchants

Established in 1883; a member of The Merchant Vintners Co. Ltd.

Brands	Glen Leog	Viking†
	John Dory	

R.B. Smith & Son

Arran Road, Perth

Blenders and merchants

This well known Perth wine and spirit merchants is part of the Cadbury Schweppes organisation, as one of the subsidiaries of Courtenay Wines (International) Ltd. R.B. Smith & Son was founded in 1820.

It has its own blended whiskies, including Moorland Pride of Perth, which enjoys a certain local popularity in Perth, although it is available in other parts of Scotland and sells particularly well in the Orkneys. R.B. Smith is also the Scottish agent for the single malts of The Invergordon Distillers Ltd.*

Brands

(*R.B. Smith & Son Ltd*)

Clanlivet†	Old Selection†
Ghillie 8 years old vatted malt	St Johnstoun†
Moorglen†	The Laird
Moorland 8 years old De Luxe	Wonmore†
Moorland Pride of Perth	

Markets Mainly Scotland. Some exports to United States, Argentina, France and Poland.

Southwood Blending Company

22 Thomson Drive, Bearsden, Glasgow G61 3NU

Blenders

Spar (UK) Limited

32-40 Headstone Drive, Harrow, Middlesex HA3 5QT

A major retail distribution chain with 2,200 licensed outlets which has recently introduced its own brand of Scotch to compete more aggressively with the standard blends and the proliferation of own label spirits.

Brand Spar   *Market* UK

Ivor Spencer

12 Little Bornes, Alleyn Park, Dulwich, London SE21

Merchant

Surely one of the smallest enterprises engaged in marketing its own

Scotch whisky brands. Mr Spencer is President of the Guild of Professional Toastmasters.

He created his own labels for Scotch — and other spirits — in about 1973. They are sold in modest quantities.

Brands

Toastmaster of England   Toastmaster of Scotland

Speyside Distillery & Bonding Company Limited

35 Robertson Street, Glasgow G2 8HG   *Member of SWA*

Distillers

The company was incorporated in 1955 as a new distilling venture by the Christie family, who are also involved in the North of Scotland Distilling Co. Ltd* and Campbell & Clark Ltd.* It is, however, a rather modest operation by normal standards in Scotland. It has a wholly owned subsidiary, Number Twelve Bond Co. Ltd.

The Speyside Distillery is located on the banks of the River Tromie, which flows into the Spey, near to the site of an abandoned nineteenth century distillery.

Brands

Old Monarch   Speyside (Single Highland
                      Malt)

Markets United Kingdom and export.

H. Stenham Limited

117 Willifield Way, London NW11 6YE

Blenders and exporters

This is strictly a family concern which was founded by Henry H. Stenham in 1953 and is still run by him personally, very much as a one man concern. Through a range of subsidiary companies he markets an incredible variety of blended whiskies, all of them exclusively for export and amounting to a total throughput of some 200,000 cases per annum. By selling directly rather than using agents, and by avoiding a costly advertising budget, Stenham claims to keep prices as low as is commercially possible, and consequently his brands are aimed at the cheaper end of the market. The company exports bulk blend for bottling overseas under the company's labels.

All of the blends are available in five ages — 3, 5, 8, 10 and 12 years old — and in a choice of bottle shapes.

344

Brands

(H. Stenham Ltd)

Black Barrel

Director's Special

King Edgar

Kingdom

Scottish Dance

(Highland Blending Co.)

Grand Scot

H.B.C.

Highland Star

Highland Vale

King Henry VIII

Mackenzie's

Old Arthur

Smith's

(Highland Shippers)

Highland Brook (vatted malt)

Highlander

Highlander Straight Malt
  (vatted malt)

King John

Nelson's

Queen Eleanor

(Metropolitan Scotch Whisky Blenders)

Golden Eagle

Highland Star

King Edmund II

Metropolitan

(Premier Scotch Whisky Co.)

Glenberry

Glenberry Straight Malt (vatted)

Glen Lily

Premier

Queen Mary I

(Salisbury Blending Co.)

Horseguards

Lord Salisbury

Salisbury's Gold Label

(Westminster Scotch Co.)

Four Seasons

Parliament

Red Lion

Westminster

Markets The group's whiskies are sold in over 100 countries, principally those of Europe, Central and South America and South East Asia.

Raphael Stern & Company Limited

206 City Road, London EC1V 2PJ

Blenders, brokers and exporters

This is another of the numerous small London firms trading in bulk whisky and exporting under their own labels. The company was founded in 1965 and also deals in other wines and spirits, as well as having its own brand of Irish whiskey, An Tur Seanda. Its associate companies are C.R. Martin & Co., Hatton Wine Co. and Miscor (London) Ltd.

Brands Lochiam Martin's White Star
Martin's Old Regent Old Milone

Stewart & Son of Dundee Limited

Stewart House, Kingsway East, Dundee DD4 7RE *Member of SWA*
Blenders and exporters

Part of the giant Allied Breweries group since 1969, Stewart and Sons
of Dundee have been remarkably successful in establishing their
leading brands despite the absence of a distillery owned by the
company itself. Stewart's would no doubt argue that by not owning a
distillery they enjoy greater flexibility in the compilation of their
blends, and avoid the restriction on economic grounds which
distillery ownership often entails for a company also engaged in
blending. However, with Wm Teacher & Sons Ltd* having joined
the Allied Group in 1976, this situation may have changed somewhat.

The original company was founded in 1831 at the Glengarry Inn
in Castle Street, Dundee, by Alexander Stewart. He soon established
a reputation for his whisky, locally at first, then futher afield in other
parts of Scotland and eventually overseas. Two smaller companies
were acquired in due course: David Sandeman Ltd, whose establishment predated that of Stewart's by ten years, engaged in a wide
variety of activities connected with the wine and spirit trade and is
now no more than a trading name for Stewart's; Duncan McLeod &
Co. Ltd has been in whisky broking since the beginning of the
century and still carries out this function on behalf of the group. In
more recent years, Stewart's has been enlarged within the Allied
Breweries Group by the addition of the Curtis Distillery Co. Ltd and
Glen Rossie Distillers Ltd. The original activity of the former, which
was founded over 200 years ago in the East End of London, was the
distillation of dry gin, and while that still continues Scotch is also sold
under the Curtis label, their original brand being Scotsman's Mead.
Glen Rossie and King's Royal are house whiskies for another Allied
Breweries subsidiary, Victoria Wine Co. More recently, in 1982,
Allied Lyons acquired the J. & W. Nicholson* group, and the
production of the various brands of whisky, gin and vodka marketed
under the Nicholson banner is now under the control of Stewart &
Son of Dundee.

(*Stewart & Son of Dundee Ltd*)
Century Hyatt Cream of   Royal Stewart 12 years old
   the Barley   De Luxe

(*Curtis Distillery Co. Ltd*)
Curtis De Luxe 5 years old   Curtis De Luxe 12 years old

(*Duncan Bros & Mackay*)
Duncan Special De Luxe

(*Glenaber Scotch Whisky Co.*)
Queen's Own   Queen's Own 8 years old

(*Glen Rossie Distillers Ltd*)
Auld Petrie   Taster's Choice
Glen Rossie (Export)

(*Duncan MacLeod & Co. Ltd*)
Clan MacLeod   Glen Finnan 8 years old
Glen Finnan   Old Crofter

(*David Sandeman & Sons Ltd*)
King's Club   King's Vat

(*Victoria Wine Co. Ltd*)
Glen Rossie (UK market)   King's Royal

Markets UK and over 75 overseas markets, of which the most important are in EEC countries, the Americas and Japan.

J. & G. Stewart Limited
13 Maritime Street, Edinburgh EH6 6SB   *Member of SWA*
Distillers and blenders   *A subsidiary of Distillers Company* PLC *

This firm incorporates Andrew Usher & Co., a name of considerable importance in the history of Scotch whisky for, as already recorded elsewhere, it is Andrew Usher, an Edinburgh whisky merchant, who is generally regarded as being the first serious blender of malt whiskies. This was first undertaken in 1853 and Usher's blended whisky was, at first, a vatting of several Highland malts. Andrew Usher enjoyed the singular advantage of having been the exclusive selling agent for The Glenlivet since 1840, and thus had ready access to the finest Highland malt with which he could experiment in his blends. However, he then went on to blending pot-still malt whisky with grain whisky, thus pioneering the blended whiskies with which the world is familiar today. His two sons joined him in business in 1860 and purchased a Lowland malt distillery, Glen Sciennes, which was renamed Edinburgh Distillery due to its proximity to the capital. This helped to deepen the firm's interest in blending and need for ready supplies of both malt and grain whiskies. Their concern over the latter led Andrew Usher II to become the driving force behind — and later first chairman of — the North British Distillery Co,* which was to be for many years the biggest grain distillery in Scotland. The Ushers went from strength to strength and were eventually to

Coleburn

become outstanding benefactors to Edinburgh and other parts of Scotland with which they were associated.

J. & G. Stewart themselves were established in 1779. They had been pioneers in the export trade, making early headway in Spain, and by the 1890s their name was renowned in a number of markets, such as Sweden. Their subsidiary company, James Gray, Sons & Co. Ltd, was by then doing good business in Canada and South Africa.

In December 1917 J. & G. Stewart passed into DCL's care, and with the company went extensive whisky stocks amounting to 8,000 butts of maturing whisky. It was one of the biggest transactions on record in the industry. DCL acquired Andrew Usher & Co. Ltd some two years later, the deal having been carried out in the name of J. & G. Stewart Ltd.

The company is the licensee of Coleburn Distillery which was built in 1896 by John Robertson & Son Ltd* of Dundee on the Coleburn Estate in Morayshire. In the early years of the century Coleburn was the site of a number of successful experiments at purifying distillery effluents, and the process perfected at Coleburn was repeated in a number of other distilleries in the area. Ownership was transferred in 1916 to Clynelish Distillery Co. Ltd and in 1930 to Scottish Malt Distillers Ltd,* and thus to DCL. The distillery boasts two stills, each of 4,000 gallons capacity. Although not generally

348

available as a single malt, Coleburn is bottled at 12 years old by Wm Cadenhead Ltd.*

J. & G. Stewart Ltd hold the Royal Warrant as suppliers of Scotch whisky to HM The Queen, and hold the Warrant as suppliers to the late King Gustaf Adolph VI of Sweden.

Brands

Clan Stuart	Stewart's Finest Old Vatted
Jamie Stuart	Scotch .
Jamie Stuart Antique†	Usher's De Luxe
King Charles	Usher's Green Stripe
	Usher's Old Vatted Scotch

Markets Mainly export in a wide variety of overseas countries.

James and George Stodart Limited

3 High Street, Dumbarton   *Member of SWA*

Distillers and blenders   *A subsidiary of Hiram Walker & Sons (Scotland) PLC* *

By obtaining a 60 per cent share in Stodart in 1930, Hiram Walker took their first bold step into Scotch whisky. Six years later they bought out the minority shareholders in the firm and acquired Glenburgie-Glenlivet Distillery in which they already had an interest. Thereafter, the distillery was licensed to J. & G. Stodart Ltd.

Glenburgie-Glenlivet is one of the oldest distilleries in the Highlands, having started production in 1810 under the ownership of William Paul. Changes in ownership occurred during the nineteenth century, and with each one the distillery's capacity was increased. By the time Alexander Fraser & Co. took it over in the 1890s the size of the wash-still had grown to 1,500 gallons, compared with the ninety gallon capacity of the original. Now there are two wash-stills, each of 4,000 gallons, and two spirit stills of 3,300 gallons each. Glenburgie-Glenlivet has always been with the times, but perhaps its biggest innovation came in 1958 when the traditional coal fires were replaced with oil fired boilers for steam heating. The additional stills were installed at the same time as the new heating, and for a period the whisky produced by them was distinguished from that emanating from the existing stills by being labelled Glencraig. However, that practice was discontinued and the total production is known as Glenburgie-Glenlivet. Capacity is 1.2 million gallons per annum. The whisky is bottled as a single malt at various times, either by J. & G. Stodart Ltd or one of the independent whisky merchants.

Stodart's other distillery, Pulteney, only came into the Hiram Walker family in 1955, since when it has been all but rebuilt and re-equipped. The distillery is at Wick and is the most northerly on mainland Scotland. It was founded in 1826, but the original owner, James Henderson, was thought to have been distilling illicitly some miles inland long before then. Wick is the old herring capital of Scotland and once had an appalling reputation for lawlessness due to the influx of transient workers from the Hebrides, intent on making a killing during the herring season. For a period Wick imposed prohibition, but this had no great effect on Pulteney.

Pulteney distillery remained under Henderson control until 1920, when it was purchased by James Watson & Co. Ltd,* and then passed to John Dewar & Sons Ltd* in 1923. Like so many others, Pulteney was closed for a lengthy period from 1926 to 1951, by which time it had become the property of Mr R. Cumming. He sold to Hiram Walker a few years later, who licensed it to J. & G. Stodart Ltd. Characteristically, this change of ownership led to extensive modernisation. The distillery's coastal location has clearly been of considerable advantage as regards distribution of the whisky and delivery of supplies. Pulteney, too, has been changed from coal to oil-fired heating. But the changes at Pulteney did not affect the tangy, earthy flavour of the whisky, which is bottled at 8 years old by Gordon & MacPhail* and known as Old Pulteney. It has been christened 'the manzanilla of the north' since it is reminiscent of a dry manzanilla sherry.

Brands

Gaelic Old	Old Smuggler 18 years old
Glenburgie-Glenlivet Highland Malt	Red Seal†
	Scots Crag†
Glencraig†	Stodart's†
Gold Band†	Stodart's Crown Special†
Old Pulteney 8 years old Pure Highland Malt	Stodart's Rare Old Highland†
	The Gaelic†
Old Smuggler	
Old Smuggler 12 years old	*Markets* Exported world-wide

John Stoddart (Berwick) Limited

100 High Street, Berwick-upon-Tweed, Northumberland
Wholesale wine and spirit merchants

Stoddart's are a small Berwick firm, established in 1834. They purchase blended whiskies on the open market, keep the casks in bond for a minimum of eight years and then bottle it as their Golden Square brand (known earlier as, simply, Fine Old Scotch Whisky).

Brand Golden Square

H. Stone & Company Limited

Lawrence House, 51-53 Grays' Inn Road, London WC1X 8PP

Merchants and blenders

This is an American company, headquartered in New Jersey and with a liaison office in London. It was established in 1955 and sells its own brands of Scotch in the United States.

Brands

Craigburn
Dunfife

Glenshire

Stowells of Chelsea Limited

Deepdene House, Dorking, Surrey RH5 4BA

Wine and spirit merchants   *A subsidiary of Whitbread & Co. PLC*

This is another example of an established wine and spirit merchant making their own blended whisky available through their outlets as a cheaper alternative to the proprietary brands. Stowells, however, have reduced the range of whiskies they offer to one brand only, Braemar, which was subsequently transferred to Long John International Ltd,* the principal whisky company in the Whitbread group.

Brands

Black Label†
Braemar
Glen Shee†
Matchless Liqueur†

Old Fellah†
Portland†
Special Glenlivet†
Wiley Black Label†

Markets North of England and Scotland.

George Strachan Limited

Station Square, Aboyne, Grampian

Wine and spirit merchants

Brands

Auld Curlers
Buckie Lugger
Falcon
Grog Blossom
Heebie Jeebies
North of Scotland Grain

Old Cobblers
Pheasant Plucker
Royal Deeside
Tinkers Dram
Uisge Beatha
Wild Oats

351

Strathisla-Glenlivet Distillery Company Limited

Strathisla Distillery, Keith, Banffshire   *Member of SWA*
Distillers   *A subsidiary of Seagram Distillers PLC**

The town of Keith's recorded association with distilling goes back to 1208 when the annals show that Malcolm, Vicar of Keith, and his fellow churchmen began to make 'heather ale'. The next specific reference comes in 1545 when George Ogilvy of Milton is recorded as receiving from the Bishop of Moray a grant of lands including the 'brasina', or warehouse, of Keith. This brasina was on the present site of the Strathisla-Glenlivet distillery which local people sometimes refer to as the Milton distillery. Strathisla, in its present form, dates from 1786 and as such is the oldest operating Highland Malt distillery. The original owner was a Mr George Taylor who obtained a charter from the Earl of Findlater and Seafield. There were subsequently a number of changes in ownership, but from about 1830 onwards it was operated by William Longmore and his various successors using his name. Indeed, it remained a private company until purchased by Seagram Distillers Ltd in 1950. It was at that moment that the name was changed from Milton to Strathisla and hyphenated with Glenlivet, although it is located some distance from the Livet itself. This recalled an earlier period during the latter part of the nineteenth century when it was also known as Strathisla.

Some of the original buildings are splendidly preserved and to some extent the distillery continues to work much as it has for nearly two centuries, using the traditional small stills. Water for cooling purposes comes from the nearby River Isla, whilst the hillside springs provide water for distilling. Strathisla is bottled by Gordon &

Strathisla - Glenlivet

352

MacPhail* in a variety of ages and strengths, although the greater part goes into the Seagram blends. It is a dry, flavoursome whisky; very robust on nose and palate.

Brand Strathisla Highland Malt

Markets Principally in the United Kingdom in limited quantities.

Strathnairn Blenders Limited

7 Ardross Street, Inverness IV3 5PL
Blenders

Brands

Fraser's Supreme
Monster's Choice
Stratherrick

Strathgarve
Strathnairn

W. & S. Strong & Company

Ravenseft House, 302-304 St Vincent Street, Glasgow G2 5SA
Brokers and blenders   *A subsidiary of Whyte & Mackay Distillers Ltd* *

Dundee's role in the Scotch whisky industry has greatly diminished, but it was once important in blending and exporting. It was the original home of W. & S. Strong Ltd, prominent brokers and blenders, who were also associated with the now defunct firm of Ross & Coulter. William and Stewart Strong went into business in 1827 and were amongst the first to ship whisky to Australia and New Zealand. They built up a wide reputation for their brand Real Mountain Dew, and success led to a limited liability company being formed in 1907. Real Mountain Dew used to have on its label a most convincing testimony by Dr Ivison MacAdam of the Surgeon's Hall, Edinburgh:

> I have made a careful and exhaustive analysis of Messrs W. & S. Strong's Real Mountain Dew Finest Scotch Whisky, and find the same to be an Old and Well-Matured Spirit, free from impurity, and possessing a fine aroma and taste. It is a clear and well-blended whisky of the best class.

W. & S. Strong Ltd subsequently moved to Glasgow and later turned to distilling when they took a half-share, with Hay and MacLeod & Co.,* in the Tomintoul-Glenlivet Distillery Ltd* and Fettercairn Distillery Co.,* all eventually to be taken over by Scottish and Universal Investments Ltd in 1973.

Brands Real Mountain Dew†   Strong's
Markets Exclusively export.

353

C.C. Stuart Limited

42 George Street, Perth PH1 5XQ

Wine and spirit merchants

Also trades as J. & T. Currie. Established in 1820.

Brands Charlie Stuart   *(J. & T. Currie)*
                                Currie's No.10†

James Sword & Son Limited

4 Melrose Street, Queen's Crescent, Glasgow G4 9BJ

Blenders and exporters   *A subsidiary of Stanley P. Morrison Ltd**

One of the smaller traditional blending houses, the company, formed in 1814, was acquired by Stanley P. Morrison in 1983. William Walker, a well known personality in the trade during the wars, directed the fortunes of the company until 1950. Primarily an exporting company, its brands were marketed mainly in the United States.

Brands

Bank Note	Red Gauntlet†
Eight Reigns 21 years old	Reel†
Gauntlet	Sword
Glasgow Cross†	Wullie's Choice

Tamdhu-Glenlivet Limited

106 West Nile Street, Glasgow G1 2QY

Distillers   *A subsidiary of the Highland Distilleries Co. PLC**

The distillery of Tamdhu was built in 1897 on the banks of the Spey under the small black hill from which it takes its name, and in the following year became the property of The Highland Distilleries Co. Ltd, although it is operated by a separate subsidiary company. Tamdhu suffered a lengthy shutdown from 1927 to 1948. However, it emerged from involuntary hibernation ready to meet the great post-war surge in demand for Scotch, and is today a major component of the Highland group.

Tamdhu boasts its own Saladin maltings, and the malt is used not only at Tamdhu but at Highland's other distilleries in the vicinity. Tamdhu is described by its owners as a typical Speyside whisky with a smooth flavour and just a hint of peat.

Brand Tamdhu-Glenlivet 10 years old Highland Single Malt

Tamnavulin-Glenlivet Distillery Company Limited

Ballindalloch, Banffshire

Distillers   *A subsidiary of The Invergordon Distillers Ltd**

Another of Invergordon's wise investments, Tamnavulin-Glenlivet Distillery was built by them in 1966 and takes its name from the nearby village. Tamnavulin in Gaelic means the mill on the hill and the ruins of an ancient carding mill are nearby. The distillery stands on the west bank of the River Livet in the foothills of the Cairngorms.

Apart from being available as a single malt, Tamnavulin-Glenlivet is closely associated with the Invergordon blends. It is light in body and bouquet with a sweeter flavour at 8 years old and 70° proof.

Brand   Tamnavulin-Glenlivet Highland Malt

Markets UK, mainly Scotland.

Taylor & Ferguson Limited

3 High Street, Dumbarton G82 1ND   *Member of SWA*

Distillers and blenders   *A subsidiary of Hiram Walker & Sons (Scotland) PLC**

This was one of the minor blending companies which Hiram Walker purchased in the 1930s as part of their strategy for establishing themselves in Scotland. They also had a useful list of brands which Hiram Walker took over and promoted, especially Ambassador.

Hiram Walker acquired in 1954, in the name of Taylor and Ferguson Ltd, the famous Scapa Distillery. Constructed in 1885 by a well known Speyside distiller, Mr J.T. Townsend, it was then one of the most advanced units of its time. It is situated two miles from Kirkwall, the principal town in the Orkney Islands, on the north shore of Scapa Flow where the German World War I fleet was scuttled. After the war, it was passed to the Scapa Distillery Co. Ltd, and then to Bloch Brothers (Distillers) Ltd who sold it to Hiram Walker.

The distillery still draws its water from the Lingro Burn, and there is much evidence of improvements made to the distillery over the years, but despite these the size of the pot-still remains at 3,200 gallons, the same size as the still installed at the end of the First World War. Not surprisingly, the distillery has close historical connections with the Royal Navy dating back to the First World War. Naval ratings were billeted there, and the distillery was saved from complete destruction by fire as a result of the efforts of the officers and men of the Grand Fleet, who came to its rescue by the boat load and fought the fire. In the mill room stands a memorial to the Royal

Navy in the form of a wooden stairway made by the naval officers quartered in the distillery during the war.

Gordon & MacPhail* bottle it at 8 years old; despite its northerly origins, Scapa recalls a Speyside; a good clean whisky of darkish colour.

Brands

A1 Liqueur†
Ambassador De Luxe
Ambassador De Luxe 8 years old
Ambassador Royal 12 years old

Ambassador Twenty Five
Gold Thimble
Heather Bell†
High Card†
Loch Mardon†
Scapa
Statesman†

Markets The Ambassador range is for export, principally to the United States. Gold Thimble is shipped in bulk for bottling in Australia. Scapa is restricted to the home market.

Duncan Taylor & Company Limited

358-364 Broad Street, Glasgow G40 2UF

Blenders and exporters

This company is mainly concerned with exporting bottled blends to the United States. In addition to its own subsidiaries, it is associated with Stuart, MacNair & Co. Ltd which in turn has a subsidiary, Wm Watt & Co.

Brands

The Aberdonian 8 years old
Duncan Taylor's V.O.L.
Duncan's A Blend
Hartley Parker V.O.L.

McColl's Gold Label
Prime Malt (vatted)
Regis Regal 12 years old

(Campbell McColl & Co.)
Glen Glamis

Three Bens

(Hartley & Parker Co.)
Hartley's Red Seal

Queen Bee

(Munro Watson & Co.)
Royal Stag

Royal Thistle

(Stuart, MacNair & Co. Ltd)
Old Barony
Stuart's Rare Light

Stuart's Rare Old
Stuart's Scottish Arms

(*Wm Watt & Co.*)
The Bracken   Scotch Broth
Glen Tosh   The Whitehall

Markets Mainly USA.

Wm Teacher & Sons Limited

St Enoch Square, Glasgow G1 4BZ   *Member of SWA*

Distillers and blenders

Until it became a subsidiary of Allied Breweries Ltd in 1976, Teacher's was the largest independent Scotch whisky company still under the control of the descendents of the founder. An earlier interest by DCL in 1921 had come to nothing since the latter had been motivated largely by the prospect of acquiring Teacher's considerable post-war stocks built up partly as a result of Teacher's applying a self-imposed rationing scheme for the customers of their whisky shops during World War I, and would have been unlikely to have continued with Teacher's either as a company or a brand.

William Teacher flourished as a wine and spirit merchant during the middle years of the nineteenth century and became the single largest licence holder in Glasgow, with a chain of eighteen shops. He moved into wholesaling, where he was especially adept at making up bulk blends of whisky to customers' individual requirements. This was prior to the serious appearance of brands and William Teacher had a considerable repertoire of blends of differing composition to his credit. However, one of these was of particular merit and it was on this that the company later concentrated its efforts, registering it as Teacher's Highland Cream in 1884. Other early brands were Extra Special, Hibernian Cream, and Australian Bonded Grand Liqueur. The latter was in fact shipped to Australia, the idea being that the long sea voyage was beneficial to the marrying and maturing of the whiskies. Low sea freight rates permitted this practice to continue into the 1920s. Some years prior to this, in 1875, the company had recorded its first export order to Messrs John Reid and Co. Ltd of New Zealand. This side of the business expanded, with successes being notched up in Scandinavia, Canada, Australia, India and South America. The first shipment to the United States was in 1903.

Although William Teacher's foray into Scotch whisky had been as a blender, his successors soon realised the importance of having direct access to supplies and with that in mind they built Ardmore Distillery at Kennethmont in Aberdeenshire in 1898. Ardmore is today one of the largest and most modern distilleries in Scotland,

357

but, despite this, still manages to retain some of its original features. The stills, for example, are fired by coal and the old steam engine, which used to be the distillery's source of power and lighting, is still there in working order although no longer used for the purposes for which it was originally bought.

Ardmore is not bottled in a single form, but the product of Teacher's other Highland Malt Distillery, Glendronach, has been for a number of years. It is sited a few miles away, near Huntly. The Glendronach Distillery Co. Ltd was acquired by Teacher's only in 1960, but the distillery itself was founded in 1826 by a group of local businessmen. Its early history was not a particularly happy one involving, as it did, financial mismanagement and, in 1837, a serious fire. Ownership then passed to a Mr Walter Scott, who had learned distilling at Teaninich. There was then only one further change in ownership until Captain Charles Grant, son of Major William Grant of Glenfiddich fame, bought it in 1920. It continued as a property of the Grants until 1960. Glendronach takes it name and its water from the Dronac burn. It still has floor maltings, coal-fired pot stills and the old fashioned wooden fermenters. Nevertheless, extensive modernisation has recently doubled production. Glendronach is highly regarded in its native Aberdeenshire. It is a bright, fresh whisky with a sharpish flavour at 8 years old but richer and mellower at 12 years old. The earlier Glendronach brands — Glendronach Liqueur, Huntly Royal, Old Vatted Glendronach and Sir Walter — were all discontinued shortly after the take-over.

Teacher's boast that their Highland Cream contains an exceptionally high proportion of expensive malt whiskies. It currently occupies second place in the UK market with a share of about 16 per cent. Wm Teacher's total sales are divided roughly 55 per cent on the home market and 45 per cent abroad.

From the original family partnership, a private limited company was set up in 1923, becoming a public company in 1949. There are subsidiaries in West Germany and Brazil, and Brazil controls local bottling of bulk exports of Teacher's Highland Cream to that country.

Brands

Teacher's Highland Cream	The Glendronach 8 years old
Teacher's Royal Highland De	Single Malt
Luxe 12 years old (75°)	The Glendronach 12 years old
	Single Malt

Markets In 150 countries and territories for Highland Cream. The Glendronach is sold mainly in the UK whilst Teacher's Royal Highland is for export only.

Tesco Stores Limited

Tesco House, Delamare Road, Cheshunt, Hants

Wine and spirit merchants

Yet another of the large supermarket chains with its own label products.

Brands

Tesco

Tesco 8 years old

Tesco Mac Whisky-wine blend†

Tesco Malt (vatted)

Tesco VAT Whisky-wine blend†

Market United Kingdom

Peter Thomson (Perth) Limited

PO Box No 22, Crieff Road, Perth PH1 2SL   *Member of SWA*

Blenders and whisky merchants

By industry standards, this is a relatively small company, yet the yellow delivery vans of Peter Thomson are a familiar sight throughout Scotland, because the company's principal activity is that of wholesale wine and spirit merchants, and its customers are spread far and wide. But the whisky side of the business is of growing prominence and it is that with which we are concerned.

Peter Thomson was originally in partnership as a grocer with his brother, but in 1908 he opened his own shop in Perth and whisky and wines predominated. Success blessed the venture and the Thomson shops became four in number. Wholesale trading developed in the late thirties and expanded quickly after the Second World War, leading eventually to the complete eclipse of the retail side and the closure of the last of the Perth shops in 1973. The founder died in 1939 and business passed to his son David Thomson, who is now Chairman of this private company. However, his absence on war service — much of it as a prisoner of war — left the business in the hands of the highly capable and almost legendary Miss Cameron. She had joined the firm as a fourteen year old girl, learned the trade thoroughly and became cashier and chief clerk. For the five years of the war she ran it virtually single-handed and was rewarded with a directorship when a limited liability company was formed in 1956.

Peter Thomson first started selling his own blend of Scotch as Peter Thomson's Whisky about 1908 as a result of his interest in blending and his detailed knowledge of the great Speyside malts. Subsequently, in 1922, the brand was to become Beneagles, a name inspired by the construction of the famous Gleneagles golfing hotel.

A good deal later, in 1951, the company turned to the export market and notched up some modest advances there, but real success was to come with their venture into ceramics. This involved the filling of ceramic miniatures of novel designs with Beneagles whisky. It started as an experiment in the form of a whisky barrel and a curling stone, but soon other subjects were added. Restrictions on the sale of miniatures in some American states and in Canada tested Thomson's ingenuity and led them to produce whisky-filled ceramics big enough in capacity to meet legal requirements. Their beautiful Golden Eagle decanter was the product of this necessity, and was the first in a series of decanters in the shape of Scottish birds of prey, which now includes the Osprey, Kestrel, Buzzard, Merlin and Peregrine Falcon. Another line enjoying much success is the Thistle and the Rose chess set in which the principal pieces are prominent characters from Scottish and English history reproduced in, respectively, black and white Wade porcelain. Pawns are available separately but, appropriately enough, are not whisky bearing! In an ever more competitive world, which is especially true when selling Scotch whisky abroad, the Thomson ceramics have broken new ground.

There is a sister company, the Dougal Cratur Whisky Co. Ltd, which holds stocks of maturing whisky.

Brands

Beneagles	Huntingtower
Beneagles De Luxe	McAndrew's†
Beneagles Scotch Whisky	Old Perth Liqueur De Luxe†
ceramics	Peter Thomson Fine Old
Cameron Reserve	Scotch†

Markets Principally Scotland, where Beneagles is in the top twelve selling brands, but also elsewhere in the United Kingdom and the Channel Islands. Also United States, Canada, New Zealand, Australia, Malta, Ireland, Bermuda, Germany, Denmark, Japan, Hong Kong, Singapore, Brunei and Malaysia.

R.H. Thomson & Company (Distillers) Limited

Palmerston House, 39 Palmerston Place, Edinburgh EH12 5BH

Member of SWA

Distillers and blenders   *A subsidiary of Distillers Company PLC**

One of the smaller trading companies still with a separate identity within the group, R.H. Thomson boasts the licence for Teaninich Distillery at Alness on the Cromarty Firth in Ross-shire. It is very old, dating from 1817 or possibly earlier, and there are still traces of the original buildings put up by Captain H. Munro. He was one of the

Teaninich Munros, a branch of the Munros of Foulis. The distillery is close to the bank of the River Averon and the entire area is steeped in history and folk-lore.

The Munros gave up distilling in the 1850s and let the premises as a going concern to successive tenants. An Elgin firm, Munro and Cameron, took over its operation in 1895 and three years later secured the entire lease from the Munro descendents. Robert Innes Cameron became the sole proprietor in 1905 and his trustees sold out to DCL in 1933.

The product is used exclusively for blending.

Brands

Holyroodt	Robbie Burns
Old Angus	Windsor Castle

Tobermory Distillers Limited

Main Street, Tobermory, Isle of Mull

Distillers

The reconstruction of this company has had the happy result of the distillery returning to its original name of Tobermory after a short period as the Ledaig Distillery. The distillery was built at the end of the eighteenth century and had a succession of owners, the most distinguished being, perhaps, John Hopkins and Co. Ltd,* who operated it from about 1890. It came under the DCL flag when Hopkins was bought out in 1916. However, distilling was halted in 1928 because of the Depression and only got going again in 1972 after the rebuilding of the distillery and complete re-equipping of the premises which had been used as an electricity power station. Liverpool shipping interests originally provided the capital, later supported by Spanish and Panamanian interests to set up the Ledaig Distillery (Tobermory) Ltd. However, with set-backs in the whisky industry in 1975, and its entire dependence on basically one major customer, the distillery temporarily closed down — having just doubled its capacity to some 800,000 gallons per year — and a receiver was appointed in 1976. In November 1979 the present proprietors, the Kirkleavington Property Co., discharged the bank's receiver, and the company resurfaced under its present name and will hopefully prosper, since Tobermory is the only distillery on the picturesque and historic island of Mull.

The majority of output for the time being goes to blending but the company is marketing its own Tobermory Blend, and Tobermory Pure Malt at 75°. The whiskies are freely available on the island and throughout the UK. Tobermory is also now available in several export markets.

Markets UK and general export.

Tomatin Distillers PLC

34 Dover Street, London W1X 4HX and Tomatin, Inverness-shire

Distillers, blenders and brokers   *Member of SWA*

Tomatin Distillery and the company which owns it were established in 1897 at a remote location some sixteen miles south-east of Inverness, on the site of a small distillery dating back to the fifteenth century. At 1,028 feet above sea level it is one of the highest distilleries in the land. Being built in the middle of the boom period for whisky, Tomatin got off to a good start and is one of the outstanding success stories in the industry. During the period up to the Second World War, progress at Tomatin could be described as steady. There was a pause in production during hostilities, but soon after resumption of distilling Tomatin was producing 120,000 proof gallons from its two pot stills. A major programme of modernisation and development was begun in 1956 and over £5 million was invested during the next twenty years. In the twenty years from resumption of distilling in 1945 production increased ten-fold, and by 1965 eleven stills were producing 2.25 million proof gallons per annum. Further expansion was undertaken to increase Tomatin's capacity in 1975 to 5 million proof gallons, using twenty-three stills. The highest level of production was in fact achieved in 1974 at 3,149,000 gallons.

An important feature at Tomatin is the high degree of automation employed. For example, the automatic malt intake handling and milling control systems are designed in such a way as to permit a single operator to control the two processes simultaneously from a panel set up next to the mill room. With the help of an illuminated mimic diagram of the entire lay-out the operator is able to see which bins are being used and which sections of the system are operating. Mixing of differing quantities of malt from the different bins is similarly controlled. For milling, the main and auxiliary machinery start up automatically as the sliding covers open in the bin. The panel counter automatically cuts off the supply to the mill when the pre-determined quantity of malt has passed the weighing machine, which is immediately below the bin, and a timing device ensures that the conveyor system is empty before it comes to rest. Another aspect of the modernisation that has gone on at Tomatin was the conversion of the conventional cast iron mash tun into a modified version of a Balfour-Schock-Gusmer Lauterin or filtering tun. This was the first use of lautering in whisky distillation in Scotland and it was undertaken in 1967 with the purpose of increasing both the mash tun output and the spirit yield.

Tomatin has other unique features: the still house is designed in such a way as to enable one man to maintain complete control of the distillation process without ever having to leave the ground-level working area during the course of his shift. Moreover, there is a visual control point from which the unattended operations in other parts of the distillery can be watched. The vast distillery employs a work force of only thirty and has a greater investment in equipment per worker than in an oil refinery.

Despite all the sophistication, Tomatin has done nothing to change the basic ingredients. Water is drawn from the local burn called Alt-na-Frithe which flows from the Monadhliath Mountains, passing the distillery on its way to the River Findhorn. The purity of the water contributes much to the resulting whisky which, whilst having many of the properties of a Glenlivet, is distinguished by its peatiness.

The bulk of production is used for blending by most of the principal blending firms in Scotland and also in the company's own blend. The distillery's product is also available as a single malt. Concentration has traditionally been on the UK market, but exports are becoming increasingly important to the company. In addition to exporting under its own labels, Tomatin Distillers Exports Ltd, a wholly owned subsidiary, markets several standard bulk blends which vary in quality and style, and which are bottled locally in the countries to which they are exported. This company will also supply blends to match those already used by its customers as well as blends to order. It also supplies bulk vatted malts.

At an extraordinary general meeting in April 1981 the directors of Tomatin approved a new share issue to a subsidiary of Heineken, the Dutch brewing giant, giving the latter 20 per cent of the enlarged issued share capital of Tomatin at a cost of £1.5 million.

Brands

Big 'T' 5 years old	Tomatin Highland Malt 5 years old
Big 'T' 12 years old De Luxe	Tomatin Highland Malt 10 years old

Markets UK 89 per cent, Europe 4 per cent, North and South America 3 per cent, Asia, Australasia and Africa 4 per cent — about thirty five countries in total.

The Tomintoul-Glenlivet Distillery Limited

Ballindalloch, Banffshire

Distillers   *A subsidiary of Whyte & Mackay Distillers Ltd* *

This distillery was a child of need, such was the shortage of malt whisky in the industry in the 1960s. Two Glasgow whisky brokers, Hay and MacLeod & Co.* and W. & S. Strong & Co.,* subsequently to merge with Whyte & Mackay Ltd, were thus compelled to come together in a joint venture to erect an entirely new Highland Malt distillery. They were drawn by a mixture of romance and logic to the Glenlivet area, the Canaan of malt whisky. The prime necessity was a reliable supply of good water and a site was chosen to give the distillery access to the Ballantruan Spring, about five miles north of Tomintoul, Scotland's highest village. Production commenced in July 1965 and subsequent improvements increased capacity to over one million proof gallons with on-site storage facilities for two and a half million gallons. Tomintoul-Glenlivet is the most modern of the Whyte & Mackay triad. It has been available as a single malt in bottle since 1974. Youthful in character, light in aroma, it is nonetheless a whisky of some potential.

Brands

Tomintoul-Glenlivet Single
    Highland Malt
Tomintoul-Glenlivet Single
    Highland Malt 8 years old

Tomintoul-Glenlivet Single
    Highland Malt 12 years old

Markets United Kingdom and duty-free international outlets.

J. Townend & Sons (Hull) Limited

Red Duster House, 101 York Street, Hull HU2 0QX

Wine and spirit merchants

This company took over in the 1930s an old established firm set up in 1840 called J.J. Rippon, marketing a whisky under the brand name of Dalmeny which had been in existence since the nineteenth century. A testimony to its quality appears in a book entitled *Industries in Yorkshire* published in 1893:

> Amongst the specialities may be mentioned a very fine brand of Highland whisky favourably known as Dalmeny. This well-known brand is steadily increasing in public favour and can with confidence be recommended.

Not surprisingly, J. Townend & Sons have continued with Dalmeny and it is still the firm's house brand. It is said to contain top class malts and North British grain, the minimum age of any of the constituents being four years. It is also available as a De Luxe whisky of which the minimum age of any whisky in the blend is eight years.

The company has another blend, Dad's Favourite, at 66° proof, and produces Highland Mac Whisky Wine, which is a British wine blended with whisky. White Rose is another brand registered in the name of the House of Townend but is not in use at present. It was acquired in order to protect the firm's own brand of White Rose Gin.

Townend's practice is to fill all the whiskies when they are new, bring them down from Scotland when 3 years old to their own bonded warehouses in Yorkshire, where they are blended once they have been matured for the required length of time. J. Townend & Sons is the only firm of whisky blenders left in Yorkshire.

Annual production of their whiskies is modest at about 2,500 cases.

Brands

Dad's Favourite	Dalmeny De Luxe
Dalmeny	White Rose†

Markets Yorkshire and Lincolnshire, and South of France.

Tullibardine Distillery Company Limited

Blackford, Perthshire   *Member of SWA*
Distillers   *A subsidiary of The Invergordon Distillers Ltd**

This is the Invergordon group's second Perthshire distillery, the other being Deanston. Tullibardine Distillery is housed on the site of one of the ancient Blackford breweries of the seventeenth century. It was created by the noted distillery designer and builder, Mr W. Delmé Evans, in 1949. The first owners were Wm S. Scott Ltd but it became the property of Brodie Hepburn Ltd in 1954, passing into Invergordon's ownership in 1972. They acquired, as part of this transaction, the disused Glenfoyle Distillery which had been silent since 1923 but used subsequently for warehousing. Capacity at Tullibardine was doubled in 1974 after much reconstruction.

The distillery takes its name from the moor of Tullibardine where stands the Gleneagles Hotel. The excellence of the waters which served the old breweries at Blackford is still an important factor today at the distillery. As Alfred Barnard said in his nineteenth century book *The Noted Breweries of Great Britain and Ireland:*

> From a very remote period, the brewery at Blackford has been noted for the excellence of its ale, which is attributed to the fine character of its wells, and the peculiar adaptation of their waters for brewing purposes.

Tullibardine is bottled as a single malt but also features in the Invergordon group's blended whiskies, especially Scots Grey and Glenfoyle Reserve. Lighter than most Highland malts, it has a pleasant sweetness in bouquet and flavour.

Brands

Murray Burn

Tullibardine 5 years old
  Highland Malt

Tullibardine 10 years old
  Highland Malt

Markets UK only.

James Turnbull (Exports) Limited

51 St Ables, The Dean, Hawick, Roxburghshire

Blenders and exporters

This firm of local wine and spirit merchants branched out to wholesale exporting in 1968 when they re-named their principal blend Teviotdale. They have a variety of other blends for both local sale and export. A particular facet of their business is producing special label blends for private customers and clubs, both at home and overseas. Until recently they also produced a fascinating range of miniatures under a variety of labels.

James Turnbull set up as a wine and spirit merchant in 1855 and soon began experimenting with different blends of whiskies, until he arrived at one which particularly pleased him, based as it was on Glenlivet Highland Malt. Teviotdale today is said to follow the original formula. Since the death in 1982 of the founder's great-grandson, James, the firm is run by James' widow, her two sons and two daughters.

Brands

Johnie Turnbull†

Southern Mist

Teviotdale

Turnbull's Celebrated Blend†

Turnbull's Club

Turnbull's Extra Special†

Turnbull's Liqueur†

Turnbull's London Blend†

G. & W. Turner Limited

12-14 Little Underbank, Stockport, Cheshire SK1 1JT

Wine and spirit merchants

Brands

Alexander McNab†

Auld Blended Cream†

366

Twelve Stone Flagons Limited

35 Robertson Street, Glasgow G2 8HJ

Blenders and exporters

This company is associated with Douglas Laing & Co. Ltd. Its one brand is sold in replica stone whisky jars.

Brand   Usquaebach

Unispirits & Company Limited

Normandy House, St Helier, Jersey, Channel Islands

Blenders and merchants

Brands

Old Label   Three Blacks 3 years old
Royal Twelve   Three Blacks 12 years old

Hiram Walker & Sons (Scotland) PLC

3 High Street, Dumbarton G82 1ND   *Member of SWA*

Distillers and blenders

Hiram Walker-Gooderham and Worts Ltd (which is part of Hiram Walker Resources Ltd) appeared on the Scottish scene in 1930. The company was the result of an amalgamation in 1927 of Hiram Walker & Sons Ltd of Walkerville, Ontario, and Gooderham and Worts Ltd, also of Canada, under the chairmanship of Harry C. Hatch. The two firms were of considerable vintage, Walker's having been established in 1858 and their new partners in 1832. Shortly after the formation of the new company, it was decided to expand both in Scotland and the United States. In the case of the former, this was done by acquiring in 1930 a 60 per cent share in the Stirling Bonding Co. Ltd and James and George Stodart Ltd* (the balance was bought up in 1936). Their American venture was encouraged by the impending repeal of Prohibition, which led to their building the largest beverage alcohol distillery in the world, at Peoria in Illinois, in 1933. A further major step forward was the acquisition in 1936 of George Ballantine & Son Ltd,* which gave them a good whisky stock, established outlets and a known brand. The following year operations were under way at their new headquarters in Dumbarton, and their grain distillery was ready for production.

The move to Dumbarton involved the building of the largest grain whisky distillery in Scotland at that time, at the disused McMillan shipyard on the banks of the River Leven. This enterprising Canadian intervention was warmly welcomed, and was widely held up by Walker's as an example of imperial partnership, and of the Walkers returning to the land of their forefathers. Moreover, the scale of the Dumbarton Grain Distillery demonstrated that they were in Scotland to stay, and today Walker's and their associated companies have an annual whisky production capacity in excess of fifteen million proof gallons. Dumbarton Grain Distillery itself started production in 1938, and is at the centre of Hiram Walker's activities, which include extensive warehousing — 350 acres acres in all — in and around Dumbarton and at Beith, Ayrshire. These hold at any one time about sixty million proof gallons of maturing whisky from all of the company's distilleries. An unusual feature at Dumbarton is the Ballantine guard of eighty white Chinese geese, which has proved to be a most effective deterrent against intruders.

In contrast to Dumbarton Grain Distillery, with its tall boiling and rectifying columns and enormous spirit receivers, stands a compact malt whisky distilling complex which in fact comprises two separate distilleries — Inverleven and Lomond — with a joint capacity of 500,000 proof gallons. Inverleven produces a Lowland Malt and was introduced shortly after Dumbarton began production. There are certain advantages in Dumbarton and Inverleven being adjacent, but only to the extent that grain and malt whisky distilleries share certain common needs. For instance, the barley required for Iverleven Malt is quite different from that used in the production of Dumbarton grain, and so the barley for Inverleven does not pass through the extensive grain stores of the former. Inverleven is reputed to be the first malt distillery to apply the use of steam-heating elements in both wash and low wines stills.

Lomond Distillery is in effect a distillery within a distillery, and is a monument to a former Hiram Walker employee, the late Mr Fred Whiting, who invented this intriguing variation of the pot-still. Lomond Distillery is in fact a straight-sided still sharing with Inverleven the same spirit receiver and low-wines and feints charger. Its shape is cylindrical, it is made of copper and is heated by steam tubes. The cylinder is topped by a dome, on top of which there is an eight foot column, at the neck of which there is a water jacket which cools the distillate. This variation on the standard still may look odd but produces a whisky distinct from that of the main distillery, and thus gives Hiram Walker two Lowland Malts.

Given the totality of the Dumbarton distilling operations, Hiram Walker have done well to eliminate practically all traces of effluent through successful processing of all waste products into animal feed.

Hiram Walker's two Lowland distilleries and grain distillery are complemented by seven others owned by subsidiary companies, six of which are Highland malt distilleries and the seventh an Islay. A

recent move to improve their hand in Highland malts by bidding for
Highland Distilleries Ltd came to nought due to government
intervention. Nevertheless, the group has a good spread in terms of
production. Blending and bottling is, on the other hand, heavily
concentrated at Kilmalid, a site of approximately 100 acres located
near Dumbarton where highly sophisticated techniques are employed.

The company combines North American efficiency with native
knowledge, and follows the DCL pattern of allowing associate
companies and subsidiaries a certain degree of independence.
However, there are many others who no longer trade but exist in
name only, in order to give parentage to some of the lesser brands in
the Walker range. Some of these have a history of their own, such as
Archibald Lauder & Co. Ltd, on whose original premises there was
kept in running order the working model of a still, for which a
distiller's licence was required and held.

There are separate entries for the following subsidiary and
associate companies to which the distilleries are licensed:

Ardbeg Distillery Ltd
Balblair Distillery Co. Ltd
George Ballantine & Son Ltd (Glencadam and Miltonduff-Glenlivet)
James and George Stodart Ltd (Glenburgie-Glenlivet and Pulteney)
Taylor & Ferguson Ltd (Scapa)

Brands

(Hiram Walker & Sons (Scotland) PLC)
Jamie O'8

(James Barclay & Co. (Scotland) Ltd)
Barclay's†   King's Reserve
Barclay's Liqueur†

(Craig, Marshall & Co.)
Marshall's Extra Special

(Archibald Lauder & Co.)
Lauder's   Royal Northern Cream†

(Mackintosh & Mackintosh Ltd)
Mackintosh†   The Bankers†

(Harvey Macnair & Co. Ltd)
Macnair's   Old Times†

(Robert Macnish & Co. Ltd)
Doctor's Special   Marshall's
Grand Macnish   Royal Crag†
Grand Macnish 12 years old   St Dennis†
Macnish V.L. Special†

(Charles Marchant Ltd)
Marchant's   Marchant's Gold Label

(Scotia Distillers Ltd)
Old Original

(R. Stevenson Taylor & Co. Ltd)

Epicure	Jamie O'Eight
Griffin	Jamie O'Six

(Stewart, Pott & Co. Ltd)
King's Choice

(Stirling Bonding Co. Ltd)

Glen Laggan	Highland Rover

(Robert Thorne & Sons (Whisky Merchants) Ltd)

Thorne's†	Thorne's 12 years old
Thorne's 10 years old	Thorne's Heritage

Markets The company sells almost entirely to the export trade, and markets are worldwide, including USA, Canada, S. America, S. Africa, Europe, the Far East and Australia.

John Walker & Sons Limited

63 St James's Street, London SW1A 1NB   *Member of SWA*

Distillers and blenders   *A subsidiary of Distillers Company PLC**

The one name most commonly associated with Scotch whisky is undoubtedly Johnnie Walker, and this is not surprising since Johnnie Walker Red Label is the largest selling Scotch in the world, with total sales exceeding seven million cases per annum. Consequently, Black Label is probably the best known De Luxe whisky and sells in greater quantities than many heavily promoted standard brands.

Advertising has played a big role in all this and the smiling, striding figure of John Walker in early nineteenth century garb is a familiar sight in nearly every country. How much he resembles the original John Walker of Kilmarnock is anyone's guess, but the projection of this jovial, business-like character has had handsome results.

It all started in 1820 when Walker, who was of Ayrshire farming stock, took over a modest grocery shop in Kilmarnock which he then turned into a wine and spirit business. But many years were to go by — thirty in all — before his whisky was to make its first appearance. Indeed, it was his son Alexander who pushed him into moving from retailing into the wholesale trade, after he joined the firm in 1856. Within six years, output of their blended whisky stood at 100,000 gallons per year. The Walkers supplied ships sailing out of

Glasgow and quickly cornered a substantial part of the English market, requiring them to open a London office in 1880. The main reason for Walker's Kilmarnock whisky going south was the number of English businessmen who became acquainted with it when visiting the town, which was an important carpet manufacturing centre. Alexander's three sons also joined the company, such was the measure of its growth, the youngest, Alec, becoming the head of it on his father's death in 1889. His brother John left the next year for Australia to open an office in Sydney and later died there. However, he had laid firm foundations for an enormous expansion in exports to Australia, which was to remain until 1939 the principal overseas market for Scotch whisky. So important was the Australian market to them that another Walker went to take the deceased John's place in order to reorganise their operations there. The Walkers went to great pains to cultivate the Australian market and their whisky took the highest awards at various exhibitions and competitions — Sydney in 1880, Melbourne in 1881, Adelaide in 1887, Dunedin in 1890 and Brisbane in 1897 — as is still proclaimed on the lower label of the Red Label bottle. Agents were also appointed in New Zealand and South Africa and later in France, Burma, Malaya, Egypt and China. The worldwide network was beginning to take shape.

The expansion which the firm had enjoyed was based on sales of Walker's Kilmarnock Whisky; the Johnnie Walker brand appeared only in 1908, together with the famous square bottle. The idea of portraying the firm's founder as its trade mark came from Sir Alexander Walker, as he was by then, but the slogan 'Johnnie Walker, born 1820 — still going strong' was penned by James Stevenson, who had joined the company in 1890 and was subsequently to have great influence over its future. A prominent commercial artist of the day, Tom Browne, was commissioned to produce a sketch of John. We are all familiar with the result and the Walker product quickly changed its name, adopting the red and black liveries so as to distinguish between the two qualities of blend produced at Kilmarnock.

Like other great blending houses, Walker's recognised the need to move up-stream and to this end acquired Cardow (or Cardhu in Gaelic) Distillery in 1893. A true Speyside operation, Cardhu had been started up in 1824 by John Cummings, although the site it occupied had had a long history of illegal distilling. The lease on the original Cardhu was thought by his successors to be shaky and so a new distillery was built nearby in 1855, the first being left to fall into disrepair. Even the second Cardhu Distillery was fairly primitive, and little was done to improve it until it passed into Walker's ownership, and major modernisation took place in 1960. Walker's have retained the licence and market the product as a 12 years old single malt. It is said to go particularly well with haggis, perhaps because of the slight sweetness in the flavour of the whisky.

But Cardhu represented no more than a token gesture in the direction of pot-still malt distilling by Walker's who, under the brilliant guidance of Stevenson, followed an ever upward curve of expansion in their blending and exporting activities. James Stevenson's organisational abilities were noted by officialdom and he was called on to supervise ammunitions production during World War I, later becoming Surveyor-General of Supply at the War Office from 1919 to 1921, from all of which he emerged with a baronetcy in 1924. But in the years before the Great War Stevenson had already succeeded in establishing J. Walker & Sons Ltd as the largest blenders and bottlers of Scotch whisky.

Walker's went public in 1923, almost as a precursor to the great amalgamation in 1925 with Buchanan-Dewar and DCL, but in no way was this latter event to lead to any watering down of the Johnnie Walker image, and today John Walker & Sons Ltd is one of the most important components in the DCL empire. The company continued to trade independently and there have been various phases of expansion, culminating in the opening of an impressive new production complex at Shieldhall on the outskirts of Glasgow.

Such is the complexity of marketing worldwide a whisky of the popularity of Red Label, that more than 1,000 different labels are printed to meet the particular requirements of each country. Red Label is said to contain over forty single and grain whiskies, including, of course, a liberal proportion of Cardhu. Black Label is the De Luxe version of Red Label and, as such, has a higher proportion of malt whiskies and a greater percentage of old malts and grains. In some countries it is sold at 12 years old. It was said to be the late Sir Winston Churchill's favourite whisky, and was a regular order by the case for delivery to his London home. It was his liking for Black Label which, perhaps, inspired him to write his famous whisky minute shortly after the end of the Second World War, warning against depriving the industry of its barley supplies and thus threatening the production of Scotch whisky which, by then, was of enormous export value.

Walker's other brands are its premium export brand (available in the UK since 1982), known as Swing or Celebrity, depending on the individual market, Old Harmony, which was introduced in 1983 exclusively for the Japanese market to fill the gap between Red and Black Label, and Cardhu Highland Malt. Over 95 per cent of production is exported, which gives the company cause to claim that one in every six bottles of Scotch whisky exported is a Johnnie Walker bottle. The United States is the biggest single market. The company's position in the domestic market suffered a severe set-back following the withdrawal of Red Label in 1977 due to EEC

Cardhu

competition rules. The position has been recovered to some extent by the introduction of a replacement standard blend, John Barr, which is sold by a subsidiary company, George Cowie & Son Ltd.*

John Walker & Sons Ltd have recently expanded their single malt interests by taking over from the Distillers Agency Ltd* responsibility for marketing Talisker 12 years old Single Malt, although production of this remains under the control of Scottish Malt Distillers Ltd.*

Brands

Cardhu 12 years old Highland
   Malt
Johnnie Walker Black Label De
   Luxe
Johnnie Walker Red Label

Old Harmony
Swing (or Celebrity)

Markets Worldwide for Black Label and Swing (or Celebrity) and Cardhu. Export only for Red Label. Old Harmony exclusively to Japan.

James Watson & Company Limited

Candle Lane, Seagate, Dundee DD1 3EN   *Member of SWA*

Blenders   *A subsidiary of Distillers Company PLC**

Founded in 1815, James Watson & Co. Ltd was acquired in 1923 by Buchanan-Dewar and Walker prior to the merger in 1925 of those companies with DCL. With Watson's came large stocks of whisky, amounting to eight million gallons, and three well established distilleries, Parkmore (defunct since 1930), Ord and Pulteney, the latter eventually being acquired by Hiram Walker* and currently operated by J. & G. Stodart Ltd.* The stock was shared out between Buchanan-Dewar and Walker whilst John Dewar & Sons Ltd took on the distilleries.

Watson's soon became a mere shadow of its earlier self, having seen sales of its brands decline after 1939, when stocks of Scotch became insufficient to allow smaller-selling brands to continue at previous levels. Watson's is now 'dormant' from a trading point of view, but its two brands are still available, albeit in very limited quantities.

Brands   Baxter's Barley Bree†   Watson's No. 10†

Robert Watson (Aberdeen) Limited

15 Shore Lane, Aberdeen

Blenders and merchants

This private company is better known locally for its rum — Aberdeen being a sea port — than its whisky, but in the case of the latter it has enjoyed a not inconsequential record abroad. Its export profile is worldwide, except the United States, but the quantities involved are small. Some vatted malt is exported in bulk form to Japan and Ghana.

The company was launched in 1947 and has traditionally filled whisky at a number of distilleries, subsequently blending them on its own premises to its own particular recipe.

Brands

Balgownie	Imperial 5 years old
Balgownie 5 years old	Royal Bruce†
Balgownie 10 years old De Luxe	Royal Stag†

Markets North of Scotland and the islands. Various export markets especially Belgium and France. Vatted malt in bulk to Japan and Ghana and bulk blend to Australia.

The Waverley Group Limited

111 Holyrood Road, Edinburgh EH8 8YS

Member of SWA

Distillers and blenders   *A subsidiary of Scottish & Newcastle Breweries PLC*

The Waverley Group Ltd is the wines and spirits division of Scottish & Newcastle Breweries PLC. Amongst its operations are included two distillery companies — Isle of Jura Distillery Co. Ltd* (72 per cent holding) and Glenallachie Distillery Co. Ltd* (100 per cent holding); Charles Mackinlay & Co. Ltd*, whisky distillers and blenders; three home-trade selling companies — Waverley Vintners Ltd, wholesale wine and spirit merchants servicing the on-licence trade, Canongate Wines Ltd, brand agents dealing with multiple grocers and specialists in the off-licence trade, and Christopher & Co. Ltd, fine wine merchants and shippers since the seventeenth century and holders of the Royal Warrant; Gough Brothers, the southern-based off-licence chain; two production and bottling plants, and a network of nine distribution branches with warehousing.

The Waverley Group's overseas spirit business is handled by Waverley International Ltd, which includes the following companies: Charles Mackinlay & Co. Ltd*, Christopher & Co. Ltd, John E. McPherson & Sons Ltd,* Ewen & Co. Ltd, Bruce & Co. Ltd, Glenallachie Distillery Co. Ltd* and Scottish & Newcastle Importers Co.

Brands

(Bruce & Co. Ltd)
Northern Scot

(Christopher & Co. Ltd)
Christopher's Finest Old
Christopher's Finest Old De
   Luxe
Christopher's Four Lions

Christopher's 8 years old Pure
   Malt
Christopher's 12 years old

Northern Scot 12 years old
   (stoneware flagon)

(Ewen & Co. Ltd)
Glen Clova
Scots Club

Markets Whisky forms a major part of the Waverley Group's business, with the production division handling almost a million cases for both UK and overseas markets (up to a hundred markets) in the year 1982-83. All those brands listed above are sold in the export market, with the exceptions of Christopher & Co. Ltd's Four Lions and their Finest Old De Luxe. Marketing activity in the UK centres on the Group's three selling companies mentioned above.

375

Wellington Whisky Blending (London) Limited

100 Wellington Street, Glasgow G2

Blenders and exporters

This is a subsidiary of the important American drinks company, Heublein Inc.

Brands

Drury's Special Reserve Ye Olde Drury
Scots Bard Light

Charles Wells Limited

The Brewery, Havelock Street, Bedford, Beds

Brewers and blenders

A small independent brewer whose own label blended whisky is available only through its regular trade outlets within an area of about forty miles round Bedford.

Red Seal is not advertised but has been sold by Charles Wells Ltd for about sixty years. It is made up of ten year old whiskies and has some faithful followers who consider it to be a very good whisky indeed.

Brand

Red Seal 10 years old

Market Bedford and surrounding area.

J.H. Wham & Sons (Largs) Limited

Viking Cellars, Largs, Strathclyde KA30 8JX

Blenders and merchants

The firm which dates from 1950 has its own range of blended whiskies.

Brands

Brisbane Rare†   Old Ben†
Clan Royal   Plus Fours†
D & D   Regal Choice†
The Gentle Dram Liqueur Regal Mist
Lochmaddy Vatted Malt†   Wham's Dram
Loudon Laird†

Whigham Fergusson Limited

56-58 Tooley Street, London SE1 2SZ

Blenders and exporters

The origins of this enterprising venture go back to a wine and whisky merchanting business founded in Ayr in 1766. There are few companies of this kind today which can boast a more ancient heritage, but what is really unusual about Whigham's is that they were from their inception immediately conscious of foreign markets, despatching their first overseas shipment to New York, in the year of their establishment. A year later Whigham's acquired their own sloop known as *Buck*, to trade with Continental Europe. According to old records, this vessel was engaged in some exciting adventures, which one can believe given the incidence of smuggling and piracy in those days.

The present company has been a subsidiary of John E. Fells Ltd* since 1981. The name of the company has been retained and Whigham Fergusson's range of whiskies is highly respected. These used to be supplemented by the former Company Chairman's own blend, which naturally bore his name.

The company had common roots with Whighams of Ayr Ltd,* of which it was a branch based in Edinburgh until 1968. There is now no connection.

Brands

(Whigham Fergusson (Export) Ltd)

Whigham's No. 1

Whigham's No. 10 8 years old

Whigham's 12 years old vatted malt

(John Noble & Co.)

John Noble†

Whighams of Ayr Limited

8 Academy Street, Ayr, KA7 1HT

Exporters and wine and spirit merchants

Possibly the oldest surviving commercial establishment in the West coast town of Ayr, Whighams dates from 1766 when it was set up by a group of local merchants and lairds under the title of Alexander Oliphant & Co. At some point in its history it became Whigham, Fergusson and Cunninghame, adopting its present name with a futher change in ownership in 1968. Whigham Fergusson Ltd* branched off at this point to become a totally separate enterprise.

The outward appearance is of a small wine shop but this is deceptive since the underground cellars, comprising three tunnels, extend to 3,000 square feet. Their West Highland brand is not blended at present but Duart Castle, available both as a blend and as a vatted malt, is widely exported. It recalls Lord Maclean's ancestral home on the island of Mull and the name is used with his consent.

Brands

Duart Castle	West Highland 6 years old†
Duart Castle Malt (vatted)	West Highland 8 years old†
West Highland†	

Whitbread Scotland

Southcroft Road, Rutherglen, Glasgow G73 3RQ

Brewers and wine and spirit merchants

Part of the large Whitbread brewing group which also owns Long John International Ltd,* Whitbread Scotland has its own blends of whiskies.

Brands

Braemar	JHT†
Campbell King's Gold Seal†	VOS†
Jamie Taylor†	

White Horse Distillers Limited

99 Borron Street, Glasgow G4 9XF *Member of SWA*

Distillers *A subsidiary of Distillers Company PLC* *

This is one of the rare examples of a company taking its name from a brand, although the present title was only adopted in 1924 with the death of Sir Peter Mackie. Mackie & Co., Distillers, Ltd then became White Horse Distillers Ltd to reflect the company's enormous success worldwide with its White Horse brand, originally known as Mackies' White Horse Cellar Scotch Whisky when introduced in the late 1880s. Mackie established his company in 1883, although it can claim a more ancient heritage since he had previously worked for his uncle, James Logan of J. Logan Mackie & Co. (Distillers) Glasgow, whose origins go back to 1801 and which had acquired Lagavulin distillery in Islay. The distillery, whose name in Gaelic means 'mill in the valley' is said to have antecedents which date back to 1742. The distillery proper was built much later, in the early nineteenth century. There was a succession of owners but it was the Grahams who entered into partnership with James Logan Mackie. Thereafter, its future became part of the Mackie story and prospered accordingly.

Lagavulin is today, at 12 years old and 75°, one of the best regarded Islay malts, full in body and rich in flavour with a generous peatiness to it.

Peter Mackie's success arose from his keen appreciation of the potential of the international market for blended whisky and his determination to meet future demand with a high quality product. Mackie had close family ties with Edinburgh where the ancestral home was located near the White Horse Inn in Canongate. Famous both as a haunt of writers and actors and as the starting point of the Edinburgh-London stage, he adopted it as the name for his particular blend. Vigorous marketing at home and abroad soon established its high reputation, whilst the company's founder went on to become a prominent public figure.

Having inherited Lagavulin, Mackie went on to build a new distillery at Craigellachie in 1890 in partnership with Mr Alexander Edward. The Craigellachie-Glenlivet Distillery Ltd was eventually taken over completely by Mackie. It stands in a commanding position above the Craigellachie Rock and the famous single-span bridge across the River Spey. Its production is used only in blending although Wm Cadenhead Ltd* have bottled a little at 16 years old.

As a subsidiary of DCL, the company today also owns and operates Glen Elgin distillery in the parish of Longmorn, probably in one of the prettiest locations of any Highland distillery. Production got under way in 1900 under the ownership of James Carle and W.

Simpson, both local bankers. Original production was between 1500 and 2000 gallons due to combined mashing and distilling. Ownership soon passed to the Glen Elgin-Glenlivet Distillery Co. Ltd and, in 1907, to J.J. Blanche of Glasgow. DCL later acquired it through Scottish Malt Distillers Ltd* and responsibility for it was subsequently passed to White Horse Distillers Ltd. Glen Elgin, like Lagavulin, is bottled at 12 years old, but is, of course, a totally different sort of dram. It is slightly sweet on the palate, which is not unusual for a Speyside. The White Horse blending and bottling facility is located alongside Port Dundas Grain Distillery in Glasgow which is owned and operated by another DCL subsidiary, Scottish Grain Distillers Ltd.*

Brands

Craig Castle
Glen Elgin 12 years old
  Highland Malt
Lagavulin 12 years old Islay
  Malt
Logan De Luxe (formerly Laird
  O'Logan)

Mackies Ancient Scotch†
White Horse
White Horse Extra Fine
White Horse Liqueur†

Markets Worldwide except Craig Castle and Mackies which are exported to Scandinavia only, and White Horse Extra Fine, introduced in 1983 exclusively for Japan.

William Whiteley & Company

Atlas House, 57a Catherine Place, London SW1E 6HA

Distillers and blenders   *A subsidiary of S. Campbell & Son Ltd**

The company was founded in 1922 by William Whiteley, a Leith whisky blender who had inherited the family firm from his grandfather, the latter having set up in business in the mid nineteenth century. A US citizen, Mr Irving Haim, bought it in 1938 and the company remained in the Haim family until 1978 when control passed to another American, Mr Delbert Coleman, a financier, who ran it under the name of J.G. Turney & Son Ltd. Four years later, the Pernod Ricard subsidiary of S. Campbell & Son Ltd* purchased the business, i.e. all the subsidiaries of J.G. Turney & Son Ltd, but J.G. Turney itself was not taken over and remains an empty shell.

The J.G. Turney subsidiaries amount to no less than eighteen, of which the principals are Wm. Whiteley and Co. and Glenforres Glenlivet Distillery Co. Ltd, the others being inactive. These together own around 100 different brands, but the only brands currently marketed are House of Lords, King's Ransom and Glenforres. The company's main claim to distinction is ownership of Scotland's smallest and certainly prettiest distillery, Edradour near Pitlochry, which dates from about 1825 when it was founded by a group of Highland farmers. There were several subsequent owners but John McIntosh & Co. owned Edradour by far the longest, until selling to William Whiteley & Co. Ltd in 1933. It stands on the estate of the Duke of Atholl and has a work force of only four. It resembles more than any other the workings of a Highland malt distillery of the last century. It is a pleasure to visit, set as it is in gentle Perthshire countryside, and the air of quiet efficiency combined with a garden atmosphere is a considerable tribute to the owners, who have spared nothing to retain as much originality as possible. If the script-writers had written a distillery into the musical 'Brigadoon' it would surely have been modelled on Edradour. Indeed, until 1947 power was by water-wheel and even today automation has no place in the operations of the distillery. But then production rarely exceeds 1,000 gallons per week. The only major concession to modern methods is the employment of steam coils for heating instead of the old-fashioned coal furnaces. Alas, none of the Edradour malt is bottled single, such are the requirements for the firm's blends, since it is in blended whiskies that most of their interest lies, but Edradour is married with one other high quality malt to produce Glenforres 12 years old vatted malt.

Production at the distillery is so limited that the whisky is, unlike other malts, not traded outside the company and so no Edradour malt will pass your lips except in one of the company's products. None of their whiskies is sold at less than 8 years old, such is the importance they attach to the quality of their blends and, in pursuit of this, it is said that they were the first whisky company to ship their products around the world in order to improve the marrying of the blend. This practice goes back to the days of sail when the idea occurred as a means of saving on warehouse space since the whisky could be carried free of charge as ballast, which vessels had to take on in any case between cargoes. The ship's movement and changes in climate en route helped blend the whiskies in a very effective way and the company still sends casks of King's Ransom around the world by sea thus allowing them to claim that every bottle contains at least a tiny drop of sea-borne world-travelled whisky.

Much of William Whiteley's business had been with the United States and in the 1930s he embarked on a programme of expansion with a view to taking a position in that market following repeal of Prohibition. To this end he took over or set up a number of whisky trading companies, amongst the more notable of which were James Black & Son Ltd, acquired at the end of 1933, and William Austin Distillery Co. Ltd which fell to Whiteley a year later. However, of late, concentration on the American market, which remains important, has been diluted somewhat by a worldwide approach to selling quality whiskies with highly pleasing results, leading to the presentation of the Queen's Award for Export Achievement in 1980.

Brands

(William Whiteley & Co.)

Anchor†

Auld George†

Black Cat†

Centaur†

Club King†

Coronet†

Cream of Scotland†

Doric Dew†

Gee Gee†

House of Commons†

House of Lords

Islay Cream†

King's Ransom

Lord Bobs†

North Star†

Old Grantown†

Queen of Clubs†

Queen's Ransom†

Round the World†

Royal Flush†

Royal Knight†

Royal Montrose†

Royal Scots†

Wee Drop†

Whiteley's†

Whiteley's Liqueur†

Whiteley's Perfection†

Whiteley's Pinch †

(former brands of J.G. Turney & Son Ltd)

Camp Fire†

Cragg Vale†

Golden Fleece†

Great Scott†

The Kilty†

King's Own†

Morning Dew†

Old Colson†

Perfection†

Royal Kilty†

Royal Seal†

Silver Fleece†

Tee Tee†

Turney's†

Twinkle†

Waverley†

(William Austin Distillery Co. Ltd)

William Austin O.V.†

(James Black & Son Ltd)

Scotland's Cheer†

Speymore Liqueur†

(Gordon Campbell & Co. Ltd)

Gay Gordons†

Real MacKay†

(Campsie Glen Distillery Co. Ltd)

Campsie Glen†

Royal Charter†

(Robert Denholm & Co. Ltd)

Argyle†

Five Stars†

Royal Crown†

(Robert Duncan & Son)

Royal Vat†

Stirrup Cup†

(*George Dunlop & Co. Ltd*)
Heather King†
Royal Scot†

Tartan Pride†

(*Dun Spey Distillery Co. Ltd*)
Tatler†

(*C.C. George & Co. Ltd*
George's Perfection†
Gillie†
King Stephen†
Lord of the Isles†

Ronald Gordon†
Royal George†
Royal Gordon†
Three Castles†

(*Glenforres Glenlivet Distillery Co.Ltd*)
Auld Atholl†
Edradour†
Glenforres 12 years old vatted
    malt

Glen Tay†
King John†
Luss†

(*Henderson & Turnbull Ltd*)
Beckmore†
Glenmore†
King Dick†
King Richard†
Planter's Club†

Royal Rossmore†
Speymore†
Stanmore†
Strathmore†

(*Graham Hill & Co. Ltd*)
Glenview†
King David†
King Harold†
Lochranza†

Old Judge†
Queen's Club†
Royal Club†

(*Donald McGregor & Co. Ltd*)
Club Special†
Craigdhu†
Director's Perfection†

King James†
McGregor's Perfection†
Mountain Dew†

(*Robertson & Cameron Ltd*)
Cameron†
Cameron Club†

Cameronian Club†

(*Robertson, Stuart & Co.*)
Robertson's Special†
Stuart's Liqueur†

Taymouth Castle†

(*Malcolm Scott & Co. Ltd*)
Diplomat's Reserve†

King's Choice†

Whyte & Mackay Distillers Limited

Dalmore House, 296-298 St Vincent Street, Glasgow G2 5RG

Distillers and blenders   *Member of SWA*

This famous partnership was started in 1882 when Charles Mackay went into business with James Whyte as bonded warehousemen and whisky merchants. However, the lineage in fact goes back much further since the Whyte and Mackay partnership was based on the firm of Allan and Poynter, which James Whyte had been managing and which had been established in 1844. The two businessmen were quick to launch a new blended whisky under their joint names and so Whyte and Mackay Special, as it is still known today, must have one of the longest unbroken runs of any proprietary brand of Scotch whisky.

The firm became a private limited company in 1919 and was reconstituted in 1926. By that time, both the original partners had died, but one of Whyte's sons had become a director and another was to join the board a few years later, thus maintaining the family connection. In July 1960 Whyte & Mackay Ltd amalgamated with Mackenzie Bros, Dalmore* under a public holding company, Dalmore, Whyte & Mackay Ltd.

The vast bulk of Whyte & Mackay's business had been export, and up to the outbreak of war in 1939 sales had grown steadily, particularly in the United States, Canada, South Africa and New Zealand. In the immediate post-war years, the company concentrated on building up stocks and from a strong base launched itself on the British market with great success. The Aylesbury based wine and spirit merchants, Jarvis Halliday & Co. Ltd, were acquired in 1963 in order to handle Whyte & Mackay's Special in England and Wales. It became very popular in Scotland itself, and in its native Glasgow it is considered to be the leading brand. This success has been due to a large extent to the company's marketing innovations. Much was made in advertising of the unique and attractive bottle cap which also serves as a measure and Whyte & Mackay pioneered in 1963 the 40 oz bottle size for use in bars, which everyone else in the trade soon adopted. It has been active in promoting sports events, particularly in connection with soccer and golf, and thus attracted added popularity. Also, their blends benefit from double-marrying at the blending stage, which fewer and fewer blenders now do because of cost. Such a prosperous and go-ahead company was bound to draw suitors and so it became part of Sir Hugh Fraser's Scottish and Universal Investments Ltd, a wholly Scottish company, in 1972, which in turn is now part of the Lonrho group. A weakness in the company, however, was that it owned only one distillery, Dalmore. Further expansion was necessary and was achieved by acquiring two brokerage firms, W. & S. Strong & Co.* and Hay and MacLeod &

Co.* These two companies had gone into equal partnership in 1965 to form the Tomintoul-Glenlivet Distillery Co.* to build and run a new Speyside distillery. They formed a similar partnership in 1971 to purchase Fettercairn Distillery Co.* Fraser's move thus brought into the group two Highland Malt distilleries and extensive brokerage and blending interests. The two sides operated separately and in friendly competition for a few years more but were integrated in 1975 under a single managing director. The actual company structure, embracing the various subsidiaries engaged in the whisky trade, is as follows:

Scottish and Universal Investments Ltd (Parent Company)
Whyte & Mackay Distillers Ltd (Holding company for whisky
    activities)
Mackenzie Bros, Dalmore (non-trading)
Hay and MacLeod & Co.*
W. & S. Strong & Co.*
The Fettercairn Distillery Co.*
The Tomintoul-Glenlivet Distillery Co. *

Brands

(*Whyte & Mackay Distillers Ltd*)
Cairnbrogie†
Double Lion Liqueur†
E.P.L.†
Glendonan
Glen Osprey
Imperial†
Jockey Club
Whyte's Scotch†
Whyté & Mackay De Luxe

Whyte & Mackay 8 years old
Whyte & Mackay 12 years old
    (now available in ceramic
    pot-still decanter)
Whyte & Mackay De Luxe 12
    years old
    Royal Wedding blend†
Whyte & Mackay's Special
Whyte & MacKay's 21 years old

(*Allan, Poynter & Co.*)
Gun Club

(*Jarvis Halliday & Co. Ltd*)
Royal Decree†

(*Donald Fraser & Co.*)
Fraser's Scotch Whisky

(*Duncan Macbeth & Co.*)
Old Ross

(*Macgregor, Ross & Co.*)
Macgregor's
Macgregor's 12 years old
Macgregor's 20 years old†

Royal Heather
Scottish Heath
Vision of the North

(*A.J. Ponte & Co.*)
Five Crowns†
Five Lords
Ponte's†

Noble Queen
Ponte's Special
River Club†

(*Watson, Middleton & Co.*)   Ballochmyle

Markets United Kingdom is the biggest single market. The company has a worldwide approach to export markets and sells in sixty countries, the main ones being Belgium, Netherlands, France, South Africa and Japan. Bulk blend is sent to Australia, New Zealand and Germany for bottling under the company's own labels. Vatted malt is sold to Japan in bulk.

D.E. Williams Limited

46 Upper Baggot Street, Dublin 4
Blenders and merchants

Odd though it may seem, there is a demand for Scotch in Ireland and it is not altogether surprising that some of the Irish distillers should have their own brands of blended Scotch whisky to meet this requirement and to benefit from the wider international market for Scotch as opposed to Irish whisky.

D.E. Williams Ltd used to distil Irish whiskey, but now concentrate on marketing their own brands of both Scotch and Irish whiskies. Their Irish brands are Private Stock and Three Stills. They have a number of subsidiaries, including Irish Mist Liqueur Ltd and Royal Irish Liqueur Co. Ltd.

Brands

Auld Caledonian†   Piper's Choice†
Glendoran   Prince's Own

James Williams (Narberth)

14 Market Square, Narberth, Dyfed SA67 7AU
Wine and spirit merchants

The firm has been blending and bottling Scotch whisky, as well as other spirits, for over 100 years.

Brand Old Glomore

George Willsher & Company Limited

64 Nethergate, Dundee DD1 4ER   *Member of SWA*
Blenders and merchants

George Willsher established himself in Dundee in 1864 as a whisky merchant, although he did also own and run the now defunct

Glencoull Highland Malt Distillery for a number of years up to his death. His other interest was breeding Aberdeen-Angus, or 'Black Cattle' to use the local term, on his estate a few miles to the north of the city. Black Bull, not surprisingly, was adopted as the firm's principal brand of whisky once they had embarked on bottling their own blend. The Black Bull shown on the label is, in fact, taken from an early drawing of one of George Willsher's prize bulls.

Willsher's death in 1912 saw the business pass to his son, also George, who rode out the storm of the recession between the Wars and kept Black Bull on the market. The firm remains today essentially a family one with a third generation George Willsher now running it.

Apart from being available in the bottle, the whisky is also sold in ceramic figures of a black bull.

Brands

Angus Doddie†	Golden Morn†
Black Bull	Pride O' the North†
Camperdown†	Three Macs†

Markets USA (at 100° proof): Germany, Italy, Spain, Portugal, Luxemburg, Australia and New Zealand.

Andrew R. Wilson (Agencies) Limited

4 Woodside Terrace, Glasgow G3 7UY

Brokers and blenders

Carrick Whisky Co. Ltd and Temple Whisky Co. Ltd are associated companies.

Brands

Silver Stag De Luxe

(Carrick Whisky Co. Ltd)
Carrick De Luxe

The Wine Society Limited

Gunnels Wood Road, Stevenage, Hertfordshire SG1 2BG

Merchants

This is the popular title by which The International Exhibition Co-operative Wine Society Ltd is best known. The Society was founded in 1874 and supplies only its own members who are shareholders in the Society.

Although obviously concerned principally with wines, the Society has from the very beginning had its own blend of Scotch whisky, currently known as The Society's Special Highland Blend, the label for which depicts Dunvegan Castle, the home of the Society's first Chairman, Macleod of Macleod. The Society is one of a decreasing band of merchants which still go to the trouble and expense of purchasing new fillings of malt and grain whiskies for ageing in wood before blending and bottling.

The present blend dates from 1910 when it was first made up for the Society in a bond in Aldgate. The blend has a 40 per cent malt content, the proportion of malt to grain established in 1928. The blending then took place in the Society's own cellars in Hills Place, below the London Palladium. The final blending or marrying was still undertaken at the Aldgate bond, where 4,550 proof gallons were lost during a German raid in September 1940. Blending now takes place in Scotland, as does the bottling of the Highland Blend.

The Society also has its own bottling of a single malt, Mortlach Glenlivet Highland Malt at 10 years old, which they undertake at their Stevenage premises.

Brands

Mortlach Glenlivet 10 years old Highland Malt

The Society's Special Highland Blend

Market UK (members only).

Wolverhampton & Dudley Breweries Limited PLC

Park Brewery, Wolverhampton, West Midlands WV1 4NY

Brewers and blenders

An independent brewer, dating from 1840, with its own blended whiskies which are sold in its tied houses and those of its associate companies.

Brands Bonnie Dundee† Fide et Fortitudine
Cream of Glenlivet Finest Liqueur†

World Spectrum Trading

Canna Casa, Fairmile Park Road, Cobham, Surrey

Merchants

Although this company began life in 1946 as T.W. Hollidge Ltd, its venture into Scotch whisky is very recent and is in complete contrast with earlier trading activities. In 1980, World Spectrum acquired the entire stock and brand name of Royal Pheasant, once owned by the Wm Teacher subsidiary, Clyde Distillers Ltd. The aim is to promote it widely abroad.

Brand

Royal Pheasant

Yates Brothers Wine Lodges Limited

54 Carnarvon Street, Manchester M31 HB

Wine and spirit merchants

This Manchester firm has a subsidiary in Preston which also has its own label.

Brands

(Yates Brothers Wine Lodges Ltd)
Blue Label   John McKay

(Addison & Co. Ltd)
Special Reserve

Young & Saunders Limited

3 Queensferry Street Lane, Edinburgh EH2 3PF

Wine and spirit merchants

Brands

Collie†   Young & Saunders Specially
Young & Saunders Very Old   Selected
  Blended†   Young & Saunders Select

Mackie's Lagavulin distillery

Index

Index

Index

Index

400

Index

Index

Index

Index

Index